WALTER MURDOCH
72
ESSAYS

WALTER L. F. MURDOCH

72 ESSAYS

A SELECTION

Essay Index Reprint Series

BOOKS FOR LIBRARIES PRESS
FREEPORT, NEW YORK

First Published 1947
Reprinted 1970

INTERNATIONAL STANDARD BOOK NUMBER:
0-8369-1813-4

LIBRARY OF CONGRESS CATALOG CARD NUMBER:
76-90665

PRINTED IN THE UNITED STATES OF AMERICA

TO
V. C. M.
"Till a' the seas gang dry, my dear."

PREFATORY AND PERSONAL

HERE are the essays I chose when my publishers invited me to pick out about half of the contents of my *Collected Essays* to be printed in a more easily portable volume. This book includes not half the contents of that unwieldy omnibus, but all that I should like to be remembered by, for a few years by a few people, when I have passed from the noise to the silence.

It was a pure coincidence that at the age of seventy-two I should choose exactly seventy-two essays. It was not deliberate. It just happened so. There was no intention of suggesting that I had written an essay every year of my life, beginning to write as soon as I was born, like the learned Lipsius mentioned in *Tristram Shandy*. On the contrary, the earliest essay in this volume was written when I was over fifty years old; whatever the faults of the book may be, they cannot be set down to youthful exuberance. (I have a theory that the essay is a form of literary art fitted by its nature for the middle-aged and elderly. When you are young, by all means write poems, novels, plays, and what you will; in the evening of your life it will be time enough to fall back on essay-writing.)

It is true that I did write hundreds of newspaper articles—not essays—at an early age; and that some of these juvenilia were collected and published in a small paper-covered volume entitled *Loose Leaves*. It was, as it deserved to be, a complete failure commercially. Only a few copies were sold, and those under false pretences, a bookseller having inadvertently advertised the book as *Loose Lives*. I cherish the thought of the disappointment inflicted on the innocents who bought my first book expecting a volume of scandalous biographies.

W. M.

PREFACE

It is vain to attempt to conceal, from the readers of these ensuing essays, the author's besetting sin. There are some sins which, by their very nature, cannot be kept dark. Of my numerous private vices I trust that I know how to respect the privacy; but the vice to which I allude is, in essence, a public vice, a vice that cries from the house-tops. I refer to the vice of preaching. You may be a secret tippler or a secret murderer, but you cannot be a secret preacher. You cannot shut yourself up in your sanctum (whatever a sanctum may be) and preach to the table and the chairs. When you have fallen into the grip of this vice, there is no concealment possible.

I have, at least, the grace to be heartily ashamed of it. I resent it in others. When Ruskin is telling me about the Falls of the Rhine at Schaffhausen, I feel that I could read him for ever; but when, on the next page, he begins to try to make me a better man, I close the book, sadly. But the vice, howsoever I may blush for it, is my master. It is a matter of one's ancestry—something didactic in one's blood. I sit down, in a calm, detached, impersonal mood, to write a harmless essay, wholly innocent of a moral purpose; but my Covenanting forefathers insist on turning the thing into a sermon. Before I know where I am, I find myself thumping the pulpit cushion and thundering, "Thirty-seventhly, brethren——"

All this is, as you justly remark, frightfully egotistical. But I think you may as well know what to expect. Forewarned is forearmed; and now that I have told you about it you can always be ready to skip the pontifical passages. And remember, please, to lay the blame for these passages, not on me, but on some ancestral theologian who used to compose sermons while he was being chased across the heather by Claverhouse's dragoons. My sympathies are with the dragoons, but the fellow was too clever for them, and he is too strong for me.

Perhaps it may help you to skip the objectionable pages if I

PREFACE

tell you, here, what all my pulpiteering is about; for it is all, really, about one thing. The suburban spirit,—that is, for me, the ever-lasting enemy. That, my breth—I mean, that, as I see it, is the peril of which the world needs to be warned, in season and out of season.

By which I do not mean, of course, that there is anything specially demoralizing in a red-tiled roof, or that a croquet lawn spells death to the higher virtues. What I do mean is that young Australians must not tamely settle down to the unadventurous, barn-yard sort of life to which modern civilization is apt to condemn us. What Nietzsche meant, I take it, by his doctrine of the Superman was just this: that when we think of the long process of evolution, of the unimaginable agonies and the immeasurable efforts of the climb from amoeba to man,—and then when we contemplate the average comfortable burgess, at his work and at his play,—well, the result hardly seems worth all the fuss, does it? The gentleman symbolized by Carlyle's "respectability with its thousand gigs," the gentleman whose epitaph was written by Stevenson in terrible and scathing lines—

> Here lies a man who never did
> Anything but what he was bid;
> Who lived his life in paltry ease,
> And died of commonplace disease;

—this gentleman, when we think of the many millions of years during which the painful earth was striving to produce him, seems, —shall we say?—something of an anticlimax.

That is all my little sermons mean. What they do not mean is that, in order to be a little more worthy of the infinite groanings and travailings of the universe, one must needs go in search of the South Pole, or hunt the hippopotamus in equatorial jungles. Marcus Aurelius said that even in a palace life could be led well; who would dream of denying that life has sometimes been led well in a suburban villa? In the very humdrum town of Königsberg a great man once lived a humdrum life, a life so regular in its routine that as he passed his neighbours' windows, on his afternoon walk, they set their clocks by him. Yet for all its apparent tameness that man's life was one long adventure. He had set sail on a voyage across uncharted seas where no man else had sailed before him. His name was Immanuel Kant, and if he had lived in our time he would have inhabited a suburban villa and been very regular with the lawn-mower; but he would have been, none

PREFACE

the less, a great adventurer, "voyaging through strange seas of thought, alone."

But for the vast majority of us, these spiritual adventures are impossible, without some external stimulus. For us, the suburban atmosphere is heavy and oppressive; if we breathe it too long, we degenerate into poor spiritless conforming creatures, making comfortable livings and losing our souls. I advise every young person to travel, and not by tourists' routes. Do not tamely acquiesce in what your elders say, and meekly imitate what your elders do, and unquestioningly adopt the life mapped out for you by the wisdom of your elders. See as much as you can of strange lands and seas, strange peoples and strange ideas. Be a vagabond, for a time at least. Escape from the suburban villa, and save your soul alive.

There is an ancient proverb—*rolling stones gather no moss*—which the base and cowardly morality of the world has wrested from its original meaning. Garden rollers used to be made of stone; they were soon encrusted with lichens and cumbered with moss if you did not use them. The proverb meant, "move about a good deal if you would keep your mind bright and clean." Wiseacres twisted the proverb round and made it mean, "don't be a vagabond, if you want to succeed in life and accumulate possessions." I suppose there is truth in this too, but not the saving truth that resides in the original meaning. A divine instinct prompts us to wander, whether in strange lands or on strange seas of thought. Heed that instinct, lest the suburban spirit master you, and you end by letting your mind grow mossy.

Well, there you are; that is the doctrine on which these essays, like a necklace, are threaded; the underlying idea which gives them a kind of unity in spite of their regrettable miscellaneousness of appearance. Whenever you see that idea begin to obtrude itself, you will take warning that I am going to preach, and—as I said before—skip a page or so.

CONTENTS

CONTENTS

TRIPE AND ONIONS

THE Australians have a reputation for hospitality; and the hospitality of their newspapers is simply extraordinary. For instance, I myself have, in the past few years, been given space in various newspapers for discourses on every kind of topic, from rabbits to the League of Nations, from the poetry of Keats to the proper way of killing fowls, from cabbages to kings. But, curiously enough, I seem to have omitted, hitherto, to write an essay on tripe and onions.

It is not, of course, easy to be sure of this. I could make certain by hunting through the files; but looking back over one's past life is an insidious habit justly condemned in the Scriptural story of Lot's wife. Apart from the danger of being turned into a pillar of salt, few experiences are more painful than reading an old newspaper article of one's own. I confess, with Macbeth,

> I am afraid to think what I have done;
> Look on't again I dare not.

Still, without looking, I feel tolerably certain that I have not communed with you, heart to heart, on the subject of tripe and onions.

The reason probably is, that the subject is too great for a mere essay. It has ever so many different aspects. For example: taking it quite literally, I could easily write a column in vigorous defence of a dish which has been shamefully underrated; making this the text of a sermon on our neglected blessings. Why should tripe—I might passionately ask—be singled out for contumely? Why should it be used as a symbol for trash—as when we say that the late Ella Wheeler Wilcox wrote tripe, or that the novels of Mr So-and-so, or the political speeches of Mr Blank (you must really fill in the name for yourself) are unmitigated tripe?

A friend of mine refuses to touch tripe because he objects to eating what he calls the "works" of any animal. (Yet he swallows oysters with gusto, complete with all their works.) His objection will not explain the general attitude towards tripe. Devilled kidneys are ranked among the aristocracy of foods. Liver is not considered quite so dashing: there is a touch of the bourgeois about liver; we are a little ashamed to be seen in its company, and we call it "lamb's fry" to veil its commonness. But tripe! Tripe is a social pariah.

When someone collects into an anthology the best English poems about eating—why has it never been done?—one omission will be conspicuous. There will be numbers of songs about the Roast Beef of Old England; but nobody has thought tripe worth making a song about. Mr Chesterton has introduced sausages and mash into one of his poems: but even this democratic singer draws the line at tripe. There is felt to be something essentially prosaic and even vulgar about it. I do not know how to account for this injustice. When you consider the varied beauty of its appearance, and the incomparable delicacy of its flavour—such delicacy that it has to be reinforced with onions, to fit for our coarse human palate what would otherwise be more suitable for angels—you can but stand amazed at the perversity of mankind.

My enthusiasm, however, is carrying me off my feet. This was not the line I meant to take. Faithful readers expect from me something more than a rhapsody about a mere dish, however delectable. They expect a serious contribution to thought; they look for a Deep Inner Meaning; and they shall not be disappointed. To unfold that meaning, I must be a little personal, and tell them how tripe and onions came into my life, so to speak.

It came with an anecdote. Lady Dorothy Nevill, that incomparably witty woman who may briefly be described as the fine flower of English society in the Victorian era, was once in the company of certain ladies when the topic of conversation was food. Each of them was naming her favourite dish; there was a considerable exhibition of what, in the language of to-day, is called swank; the talk was all of wonderful things which only a *chef* of genius can prepare, and which are to be seen only on the tables of the very rich. Lady Dorothy was silent. When at last they turned to her and asked her to name the delicacy she liked best of all, this fastidious, refined, aristocratic old lady replied—"Me? Oh, gimme a good blow-out on tripe and onions."

That reply—which I advise you to learn by heart—has comforted me in some of my darkest hours. Until I knew it, I was in the habit of using another formula, the saying of a character in Dickens—in *Great Expectations*, if I remember rightly—"Wot larks!" That, too, was a comfort; but Lady Dorothy's formula is more invariably comforting.

What I mean is this. On our way through the world we are constantly reading or hearing of things which would depress us horribly if we had to receive them in silence. The soul demands to be allowed to comment on them. Something in the nature of the human mind makes it suffer unless a satisfying comment suggests itself. (I ought to say something, here, about complexes; but I do not know the jargon.)

When I read in Walter Pater, "To burn always with this hard, gemlike flame, to maintain this ecstasy, is success in life," I reply at once, "Wot larks," and feel that the danger is past. But a more satisfying reply is, "Quite; but can you really burn with a hard, gemlike flame when you are in the middle of a blow-out on tripe and onions?"

Similarly when I read in Mr Bertrand Russell an account of the universe as modern science presents it to our view, ending with the words, "only within the scaffolding of these truths, only on the firm foundation of unyielding despair, can the soul's habitation henceforth be safely built"—the obvious comment that springs to one's lips at once, is "Wot larks!" But this, though comforting, is not wholly convincing. The right comment is, "All right; and now, let's have a blow-out on tripe and onions." The moment you have said that, you know that your soul is saved. There has been a battle between high-sounding nonsense and humble common sense, and the nonsense has been beaten.

A few years ago a well-known Japanese statesman died. He was a reactionary, an aggressive imperialist, and a militarist of the most fire-eating kind; for the sake of the world's peace, he was better dead. But, of course, it would not have been proper to say this at the time. The then Governor-General of Australia said the proper thing. He informed the Japanese Government that Australia had heard the news and been saddened by it, and that all Australians felt as if they had suffered a personal bereavement. Confronted with a statement like that, what is one to say or do? You feel at once that unless you can make some comment, find some fitting outlet for your feelings, you will explode. I don't mean that you need say anything aloud; but you must—you simply *must*—find something to say to yourself about the situation. To make an imaginary addendum to the Governor-General's message,—something like "To mark the universal grief, the Government House blow-out on tripe and onions has been postponed for a week"—relieved the tension of one's mind.

The other day I read, in a textbook of economics, that "personality is the synthesis of individuality and sociality, and as it grows the forms of society evolve, they take more specific characters, opening out into manifold associations within the community just as the organs of an evolving body are differentiated within the unity of its life." After reading this three times, I felt that God's worst curse had fallen on me; my mind was gone. Then I remembered my good old talisman, and was saved. Rewrite the sentence, beginning "Personality is the synthesis of tripe and onions," and sanity returns.

You see, then, that my formula is enormously useful; with a little ingenuity you can adapt it to meet all sorts of situations. Whenever you are distressed by high-flown verbiage, by pomposity, by grandiloquence, by humbug, by the jargon of the crank, by the smooth insincerities of the public speaker, by political platitudes, by rhetorical nonsense—and the only way to escape these things is to be wrecked on an uninhabited island—remember Lady Dorothy Nevill, and murmur "tripe and onions." One application brings relief.

In conclusion, I may let you into the secret of another formula, for use in desperate cases. In Professor Eddington's book, *The Nature of the Physical World*, we read that: "The atom is as porous as the solar system. If we eliminated all the unfilled space in a man's body and collected his protons and electrons into one mass, the man would be reduced to a speck just visible with a magnifying glass." This is, I think, one of the cheerfullest facts that modern science has laid bare. When some large, impressive politician, or some well-nourished ecclesiastic—or, in short, any of our great men—is laying down the law from a public platform, I find it alleviates the pain immediately if I reflect, "My good sir, you are doubtless a tremendous fellow; but if the empty spaces were subtracted, all that is really solid in you would have to be searched for with a magnifying glass. I could gather you up on a slip of paper and put you into my waistcoat pocket, where you would be lost. Where would your eloquence be then?" But this is too cruel for use except under extreme provocation. For common emergencies, the tripe-and-onions formula is quite effective.

THE BLOKE

I HAVE been looking up the Oxford Dictionary, and find that the word "bloke"—like most other words, if the truth were told—is of uncertain origin. But even if that high authority had told me that it was derived from the French "blauque"—or the Welsh "bwlloc"—I should have remained unconvinced. Nobody can persuade me that it came to England from outside; I am certain that the splendid monosyllable first took shape in an English brain. It is as English as Dickens. It is the most satisfying of the many English efforts to find a substitute for the inexpressive "man" or "person." We do not like saying that any one is "a curious man"; we say he is a queer chap, or a rum cove, or a quaint customer, or a weird bird, or a funny sort of feller—the list is endless. "Bloke" is the best of them all—the ugliest, the most undignified, the most disrespectful, and yet somehow the most expressive of them all. It is slang at present; but like all really good slang words, it will become standard English—the future Virgil will begin his epic with "Arms and the Bloke I sing"—and finally it will become stale and colourless; meanwhile —well, it is good enough for me!

The French, at the time of the Revolution, conceived the awe-inspiring idea of addressing one another as "Citizen." It is doubtless a good thing, the sin of incivism being one to which we are all prone, to be reminded pretty often that we are all citizens; but it is a better thing to be reminded that we are all blokes. Compared with the august and serious "citizen," it is an undignified and a slightly ridiculous word; but a man is an undignified and a slightly ridiculous animal, and that is precisely what we convey when we call him a bloke. It is a salutary reminder of our common humanity.

Prosaic as it sounds, it has already found its way into poetry. Once in T. E. Brown's dialogue between a raven and a jackdaw, entitled "The Pessimist."

> "Croak—croak—croak !
> You're a d—d little bloke !"
> "Always was," says the little Jackdaw.

Here it seems to be used by the raven in a hostile or contemptuous sense, though the jackdaw—the optimist—accepts it smilingly. But there is a much better example in the stanza in which Mr G. K. Chesterton hints at the failings of an English King:

> King Charles he fled from Worcester fight
> And hid him in the Oak;
> In convent schools no man of tact
> Would trace and praise his every act,
> Or argue that he was in fact
> A strict and sainted bloke.

The piquancy of this lies in the fact that Kings—even Kings who lived so long ago as Charles II—are rarely alluded to as blokes; there seems to be something republican in the phrase, a hint of disloyalty. Charles himself would not have been offended; for, with all his weaknesses, he had a sense of humour, and he was very human. He, however his courtiers might have been horrified at the idea, recognized that he was just a bloke, and not a strict or a sainted one. He was, perhaps, a little unprofessional in his frank recognition of the fact.

I heard the word magnificently used the other day by a lift-boy. There were four of us in the lift, besides the boy; three common, vulgar people, and a dignified citizen, attired in a frock-coat and a silk hat, who looked as if he had just attended a civic reception, or been given a knighthood; and who signified his desire to ascend to the third floor. When the lift reached the second floor, one of the vulgar persons got out, and the frock-coated citizen stalked out after him. Some lift-boys, I fear, would have felt a secret glee, and allowed him to find out his mistake for himself; but this particular boy, though undistinguished in appearance, had a considerate heart. What did he do? With great presence of mind he shifted the chewing-gum to his left cheek, said "Hi! bloke," and beckoned the errant one back with a jerk of his thumb. The citizen came back, looking a little red. Evidently he was not used to being so addressed in public. As for me, I wanted to shake the lift-boy's hand; it would have considerably astonished him if I had yielded to the impulse. He was not conscious of having said anything remarkable; he did not know that neither Shelley nor Keats had ever uttered a more perfect phrase. I suppose if he had been French, and if there had been lifts in the days of Robespierre, he would have said "Hola! citoyen!"—something like that. And how pitifully weak it would have been. For the person in the frock-coat did not need to be reminded that he was a citizen. He was only too conscious of that; it was quite plain that he knew himself for a pillar of society. What he did need to be reminded of was the fact that he and the lift-boy were two specimens of the species bloke. The boy, with his two curt monosyllables, uttered more of the essential truth than some long treatises on democracy do. For democracy does not mean representative government or manhood suffrage, or any other piece of machinery. Democracy is a mental attitude. Democracy means a belief in equality. It is based on the conviction that we are all blokes.

Speaking of Shelley and Keats, you know, of course, that sublime poem which begins with the moving line,

> Dante was a Dago bloke.

Is there any line in the *Inferno* quite so compact as that? Most of the descriptions of Dante present him as inhumanly austere, aloof, ascetic; this line reminds us that he was an active politician, a town councillor, who ate garlic like his fellows. We appreciate his poetry better when we remember this. Also we ought to remember that the greatest poet in the world did not invent the beautiful words which enabled him to work his miracles; as a certain wise critic has said, "No poem that ever was written is so wonderful an achievement as the language it is written in, and that has been made by pork butchers as well as by poets." Moreover, the poet owes to common folk something more than the words he uses; he owes them his thoughts. The great writer does not originate ideas; he is the spokesman of the age he lives in, taking the ideas that are in the air around him, finding words for them, stamping them with finality. Those ideas have been gradually growing up in the minds of a multitude of common blokes like you and me.

The doctrine of equality has had to run the gauntlet of ridicule; equality, of course, is a mathematical term, and it is an obvious fact that no two men are mathematically equal. I find it hard to be patient with persons who argue as if we who believe in equality believed that William Sykes was exactly like William Shakespeare, or that the village idiot, if he were given the opportunity, would display the organizing ability of Henry Ford, the speculative genius of Plato, the religious insight of Thomas à Kempis; that with "education"—magic word—he could write a beautiful lyric, or lead an army to victory, as well as another. The abysmal differences between human beings—intellectual, moral, physical differences—may surely be taken for granted in any discussion by sane people.

The usual explanation of the doctrine of equality is that, although men do differ immensely in a number of ways, they resemble one another in a far greater number of ways; and this is true as far as it goes. You may bow down in reverence to the genius of Dante, but if you could read a very full and scandalously intimate biography of Dante, you would find that you and he, in innumerable ways, were singularly alike; and that in some ways you were his superior. I quite agree that Bill Sykes had his little peculiarities, and that it may be expedient to hang people who display those peculiarities; but that does not blind me to the fact that, apart from those special traits, he and I are fundamentally alike.

But I do not feel satisfied with this reply to the scorner. He may object that although Bill Sykes may resemble Beethoven in their common love of bread and cheese and in countless other ways, yet the points at which they differ from one another are the all-important points; not Beethoven's love of bread and cheese, but his musical genius, is the thing that really matters. Carlyle resembles John D. Rockefeller in the matter of dyspepsia, but differs from him in much more important ways. I do not know the answer to this, and so am driven to formulate another explanation of the doctrine of equality.

Equality means, in my view, equality in capacity to suffer. Pain, suffering, sorrow, death—these are the great levellers. Men's pleasures vary as men do; but a toothache is equally repulsive to the countess and the costermonger's daughter. You reply that this is not scientifically accurate; that some people are more sensitive than others. This may be so, and it is a pleasant assumption. It is pleasant to assume that the worm which we impale on a hook, and the fish we catch with that hook, do not feel pain. I do not know anything about the nerves of worms or fishes, but I know that when it comes to human beings, that assumption is not safe; the only safe assumption to act upon—the only one which will ever lead us out of our slough of injustice and cruelty and strife and waste—is the assumption that, as Shylock says, a Jew is "hurt with the same weapons, subject to the same diseases, warmed and cooled by the same winter and summer, as a Christian is."

We have recognized this truth in our noble myth of "equality before the law"—the myth which Anatole France punctures with his usual neatness when he reminds us that "the law, in its majestic equality, forbids the rich as well as the poor to sleep under bridges, to beg in the streets, and to steal bread."

I have no space to develop the idea; to thrash it out properly would need a book (which nobody would read); but—ponder my formula, and see whether it does not cover the facts, and whether a belief in this equality—equality in the capacity for suffering—does not lie at the root alike of Christianity, and of democracy, and of justice. We invent excellent machinery to do away with industrial unrest; but industrial unrest, somehow or other, refuses to be done away with. It will not give way before machinery, but only before a finer sense of justice, which mankind will have to be taught, by the experience of many painful years yet, to acquire. I do not expect to see industrial troubles diminish in my lifetime; because the indispensable medicine, the doctrine of equality, is very bitter in the mouth, and we shall try all sorts of quack remedies before we will consent to swallow that—before we learn the lesson which King Lear learned when he found himself subject to an agony from which Kings were deemed immune, and cried out—

> Take physic, pomp;
> Expose thyself to feel what wretches feel!

That was written by a bloke named Shakespeare, about whom people marvel how he came to possess such an extraordinary knowledge of other blokes' thoughts and feelings. But the solution is really quite simple; he knew how he himself thought and felt, and he recognized that the others were very like himself.

ON SITTING STILL

No new and inspired religion has come to us from the United States for over a fortnight. This is very disquieting; if there was one thing we thought we could depend on, it was the steady, uninterrupted flow of American religions. Possessing the secret of mass-production, the great religious teachers of that country have always hitherto been able to produce an unlimited supply of cheap creeds. Have the theologians gone out on strike—"downed dogmas" would, I suppose, be the technical term—or what has happened?

For the sake of those who need a new faith every week—and the world is swarming with these advanced, enlightened spirits—I wish to remark that when America fails them, there is always the East—the brooding, mystical East, the ancient home of religion. Let them turn their attention, for example, to Okada Torojiro. who died recently, and who was famous throughout Japan as the founder of "Seizaho" (which has been translated "Method of Quiet Sitting"). Okada, like some of the world's greatest teachers, wrote nothing, but taught by word of mouth and by his daily practice, leaving his system to be expounded in print by his disciples. One of the ablest of these is Professor Kishimoto Nobuta, a Harvard graduate, and a well-known teacher of English in Japan. He, although he describes the system as "simplicity itself," has contrived to write an octavo volume of over 500 pages about it, with many photographs.

I am not going to attempt to pack the substance of this large book into a few pages; but I think it may be said that the core of "Seizaho," its first and last commandment is—"Stabilize your centre of gravity." For bodily health, and for health of soul, this is the supreme rule. And the way to stabilize your centre of gravity is clearly explained in Kishimoto's book, in such a manner that every reader (especially with the aid of the photographs) can grasp the idea. The quintessence of the thing, so far as I can make out, is to sit for a certain number of hours every day

ON SITTING STILL 17

—the longer the better, but you are advised to begin with two sittings per day of half an hour each—on the floor, with your legs bent and one of your feet upon the hollow of the other, your backbone straight, and your centre of gravity in the right place; the hands are to be placed on the knees, with—this is very important—the thumbs crossing one another; the eyes are to be closed lightly, and the mouth must be kept shut; you must breathe correctly, and your mind must be "a complete vacuum." (The particular persons for whom I am writing will probably find this last condition the easiest of the lot.)

As a mere means of achieving bodily well-being, the system is claimed to be wonderfully efficacious. Kishimoto himself bears witness that it has enabled him to do without spectacles, which he had worn for thirty years; that he never catches cold now, nor feels chilly "in the tips of his hands and feet" as he used to do; that he now feels stronger and more capable of action than ever before; and that even his physiognomy has changed for the better. As a system of hygiene, however, Seizaho seems to leave something to be desired. Okada, its founder, gave it a fair trial; for fifteen years he kept it up, sitting with thirteen "societies of sitters" per day, an hour and a half with each; so that for nineteen hours out of the twenty-four he had his centre of gravity stabilized—yet he died in his 49th year. Perhaps, as the orthodox maintain, he would have died far earlier but for the system. Perhaps it is possible to have too much of a good thing.

Anyhow, it is not on the physical but on the spiritual side of Seizaho that Kishimoto insists. "A man whose centre of gravity is not stabilized," he writes, "is always irresolute, hasty, timorous; he lacks self-confidence, power of perseverance and thinking; whereas a person whose centre of gravity is firmly fixed in the right place is full of self-confidence and resolution; his words and deeds are never hurried or frivolous. Actuated by the reserve courage within him, he can on occasion, fight the savage tiger with bare fists and face a thousand armed men singlehanded." He is also, adds our author, "capable of deep and sustained thinking, and his power of perseverance is such that he can sit in meditation for nine years."

These are large claims. That results so salutary should be produced by merely sitting about on the floor will seem incredible to the Western mind, with its ineradicable prejudice in favour of energetic rushing hither and thither. To say that, after practising the system for a few weeks, one would probably welcome with relief any incident whatsoever—even a visit from "the savage tiger with bare fists"—would be to speak in a frivolous tone which I do not wish to adopt about a new religion. It certainly does seem to exert a far-reaching influence on those who come under its sway. For instance, twenty years ago Kinoshita Naoe was a well-known journalist and a fiery socialist writer and speaker. Seizaho has cured him so completely that whenever, in second-hand book-shops, he finds copies of the socialistic books and pamphlets he wrote in bygone days, he buys them and destroys them. Some people will think that this bears out Kishimoto's rather bewildering statement that the system "strengthens the stomach, intestines, and sense of justice."

I do not know anything about my centre of gravity, and am therefore not much concerned about stabilizing it; but I do think that a religion which has led to the formation of a number of "societies of sitters" has a good deal to say for itself. We have lost the art of sitting still; we have lost the art of being at leisure. We have been presented with all sorts of beautiful and wonderful labour-saving devices, from the machine-gun to the vacuum cleaner, but they have not saved our labour; we work harder than ever. Were I endowed with the eloquence of Carlyle, I should not preach his misguided Gospel of Doing Things. I should go up and down (as long as the police allowed me) preaching a gospel of leisure. "Produce! produce!" cried Carlyle. My cry would be: "Don't produce! don't produce! Were it the pitifullest infinitesimal fraction of a product, in heaven's name think twice before producing it. The world will probably be better without it." "Let us then be up and doing!" shouts Longfellow; and our modern world is only too ready to take him at his word. A far greater American poet has bidden us "loaf and invite our souls," but to our crazy world that advice sounds immoral.

Longfellow is also responsible for this inaccurate and misleading historical statement:

> The heights by great men reached and kept
> Were not attained by sudden flight,
> But they, while their companions slept,
> Were toiling upward in the night.

That would be a grand truth, if the world's "great men" were the indefatigable climbers and the incorrigible pushers, the cotton kings and the prosperous brewers and the millionaires generally. Those who have achieved "greatness" of that sort have, no doubt, been addicted to the deplorable habit of toiling upward in the night, when all respectable people were in their beds. But what did they gain by it, and what did the world gain by them? If, as I believe, the real "great men" have been the men who have been great of soul—if by "great men" we mean the immortal servants of mankind, the men whose names live in the gratitude of the race—then you will find that, one and all of them, they were far more given to "loafing and inviting the soul" than to toiling upward in the night. Far wiser and saner than the gross commercial maxim of Longfellow is the question asked by an English poet of to-day—

> What is this life if, full of care,
> We have no time to stand and stare?

But we are deaf to such warnings. In our work and in our play we must go hurrying, scurrying, ramping, tearing, whizzing about. We make gods of speed and energy; never stopping to consider the possibility that with all our speed we may be going nowhither, and that with all our energy we may be doing nothing worth while.

That, it seems to me, is the core of truth in the new Japanese religion. The period of good resolutions is drawing nigh; let us make up our minds that in the coming year we will sit about—not necessarily on the floor—more than we have done in the past. This is not, as you might hastily conclude, a plea for laziness. Thinking is the hardest work in the world; most of us are too lazy to attempt it. We prefer what we call the Strenuous Life, which means being busy and fussy, and joining a dozen committees, and imagining that we are doing a great deal of good in the world, and blinding ourselves to the fact that we are all suffering from St Vitus's Dance—a disease which we can cure only by shaking off our laziness and acquiring the difficult art of sitting still.

ON GROWLING

In one of William De Morgan's novels there is a big-game hunter who sets out to tell a young girl about one of his adventures with tigers. "I may as well tell you beforehand," says the girl, at the outset of his story, "that I am on the side of the tiger." In the same spirit I may as well warn you—in case you think this is going to be a little sermon on the duty of cheerfulness and the sin of growling, grumbling, fault-finding, carping, being disgruntled —that it is nothing of the kind. I am on the side of the growler.

The reply constantly made to critics—"Any fool can find fault"—seems to be a fool's reply. As a statement of fact it is, of course, undeniable; certainly any fool can find fault. Any fool can find fault foolishly; but it takes a wise man to find fault wisely. To see precisely what is wrong, to point the finger unerringly at a defect, to say boldly what you dislike in anything from a pair of boots to a system of philosophy, from a gas stove to a religious creed, from a new picture to an ancient social institution—this is no work for a fool; it calls for all you have of wit and wisdom. And as we look back on history, we can see what a tremendous debt we owe to the men who in all generations have undertaken this thankless task of grumbling. Our whole civilization is the work of grumblers and growlers. Protest is the sacred spring from which its tap-root drinks. There is not a decent law, on the statute-book of any country, that was not dictated by a grumbler. Look at the history of any period of the past, find out what were the crying evils of that period, and how those evils were got rid of. You will discover that, in the presence of a gross and monstrous injustice or tyranny, it was not the fools who found fault; it was the wise and brave. The fools acquiesced.

In short, mankind may be divided into two races, those who acquiesce, and those who growl. I am on the side of the growlers, always and everywhere; because I remember what I owe to them. I remember that, if it had not been for some unpopular, disgruntled cave-dweller, I should to-day be living in a cave, gnawing the bones of strange beasts.

Note, however, that there are two kinds of grumbling which must be excepted. First, it is no good growling against the inevitable. Nothing is to be gained by protesting against the roundness of the earth; to get into the habit of scolding because the polar regions are too cold, or the tropics too warm, is bad for the soul. Earthquakes, hurricanes, droughts and old age, are evils which have to be borne, and we may as well bear them uncomplainingly; they are not, like epidemics or high tariffs, evils which wisdom can avert.

Secondly, it is no good growling about what is past; for the gods themselves cannot undo the past. "No use crying over spilt milk"—I don't know any other proverb that contains so much wise philosophy of life as that one. I have read somewhere of an Eastern potentate who was sitting at dinner with his favourite wife, when her voluminous robes somehow caught fire, and she was burnt up. The potentate rang the bell, and when the servants hurried in he said, "Sweep up the remains of your mistress, and bring in the roast pheasant." There, surely, was a model of equanimity with which we should train ourselves to regard what is done and can't be undone.

These are the two kinds of grumbling in which we must not indulge; first because it is perfectly futile, secondly because it depresses others to no purpose, and thirdly because, if it becomes a habit, it makes you the worst kind of bore. But all other kinds of grumbling I applaud and, to the measure of my strength, practise as a solemn duty.

There is a common variant to that saying about any fool being able to find fault: the equally foolish saying, that merely "destructive criticism" is no use—you must be constructive. "Destructive criticism" is merely another name, used by grandiloquent people, for fault-finding. What is the matter with destruction, anyhow? I have yet to learn that destroyers are a useless part of the British Navy. The Panama Canal would never have been made if someone had not bent his energies to the beneficent task of destroying mosquitoes in the Panama zone. When I propose to abolish something I detest—external examinations for schools, for example—my friends tell me that this is merely destructive, and that unless I have some constructive proposal, unless I can tell them what I propose to put in the place of the thing destroyed, I had much better keep silence; then do I comfort myself by picturing the face of Colonel Goethals if someone had said to him, "Here, leave those mosquitoes alone! This is mere destruction, and any fool can destroy. What are your constructive proposals? What do you mean to substitute for these mosquitoes which you are so recklessly abolishing? Can you create a new race of larger, fairer, nobler mosquitoes to take the place of those we shall lose if your destructive mania is allowed to go unchecked?" After recovering from his astonishment, he might have explained in simple words, that his business was to destroy those mosquitoes in order that the work of making the canal might go on, without so much waste of human life. We might say exactly the same about those examinations; we want to destroy them, in order that the true work of education may go on, without so much waste of human life. (This particular evil is only introduced by way of illustration. I have long since given up growling about those examinations, being hopeless.)

The tendency to acquiesce in the established fact is terribly strong in the mind of every one of us. When Bismarck went as Prussian Ambassador to St Petersburg (as it was then called), he noticed a sentry, perpetually renewed, in the middle of a quiet lawn in the Summer Garden. It struck him as an extraordinary spot for a sentry, and he began to ask for the reasons; but nobody, in all the Russian Court, could tell him the reasons; nobody remembered. Being inquisitive, Bismarck set inquiries on foot, and at last the origin of the institution was discovered. One day, a century earlier, the Empress Catherine the Great, admiring some snowdrops in the grass, had ordered a soldier to stand on guard at the spot until she should return to pluck the flowers. But the flowers passed out of her mind, and she never did return; and from that day till the day when Bismarck marvelled at the spectacle, the spot had never been without its sentry standing at arms. That story, as it happens, is a true one; if it were not true, it would be a pertinent allegory. Those sentries are standing at arms at all sorts of unexpected spots; they have been there so long that none of us can remember why they were placed there; but, just because they have been there so long, we acquiesce in their continuing to be there, and if somebody growls about them, and asks of what possible use they are, we point out to him that any fool can remove sentries; but what is he going to put in their place? . . . At this point I pause, casting about in my mind for an illustration; and I find one no farther away than my own wrist. What is the purpose of those three buttons at the end of the sleeve of a modern coat? But I should not dream of suggesting to my tailor, who has a weak heart, the abolition of these buttons, which were never ornamental and which have ceased, for two centuries or so, to be useful. I merely mention the buttons as an instance of the tremendous strength and persistency of the conservative instinct; I am not proposing that we should growl at them; for there is a third kind of growling which has to be discouraged—growling about things that do not matter. There are more momentous things than buttons.

In case you care at all for logic, let me point out that every time you bring along that old tag, "any fool can find fault," you are really using an argument which destroys itself, a suicidal argument. For you are yourself, when you utter that phrase, finding fault. You are finding fault with the fault-finder; you are criticizing the critic; you are growling at the growler. If you are so keen on acquiescence, why are you not acquiescing in my growling?

Anyhow, I hope that, after this little sermon, you will think twice before repeating that extravagant nonsense about how easy it is to criticize, about destructive and constructive, and the rest of it. Those amiable and agreeable and kindly people who applaud in the theatre whatever balderdash our theatrical managers may choose to give us, who say "Bravo" to tenth-rate playing, and murmur "Beautiful" before a tenth-rate painting or a statue for which the only remedy is dynamite, and accept without protest an economic system which dooms four-fifths of the world's population to a degrading poverty, are committing a gross dereliction of duty. The sacred duty of growling.

ON CHEWING-GUM

SAY, folks (said the stranger in the smoking-carriage), this city of yours is certainly one great little old burg; but it's got to wake up. Sound asleep, that's what's wrong with it—hit the hay way back in the dark ages, and been snoring ever since. It gets me why you don't see it's time for everybody to get up and hustle some. What you got to get wise to is the rock-ribbed fact that we're not in the dark ages any longer—we're in the Age of Whizz and Pep and Zip; and if we want this little old planet to be what it might be and what it ought to be, why, every patriotic guy's got a right to quit sleeping and come right in and boost his own country along into a healthy state of punchful prosperity.

Say, I want you to understand that where you get off is when you imitate a bunch of moth-eaten, mildewed, out-of-date old British dubs. I'll tell the world! Once you wake up and kick yourselves and look around and get keyed up to what you might call intensive living, you'll get a hunch that the real model for you, the man of to-day, doesn't live in England. If you want to help make the wheels of progress go round, you got to keep both eyes glued on the red-blooded, God-fearing, successful, two-fisted American business man. Of course, I don't want to get away with any holier-than-thou stuff, but, just the same, any guy with brains under his lid must admit that for vision and forward-looking idealism and brotherhood and financial efficiency, America has the rest of the world beat to a frazzle. And my own little old burg, I don't mind telling you gentlemen in confidence, leads America. In breakfast-foods, tar roofing, culture, office furniture, righteousness, and chewing-gum it sure wins the fire-brick necklace.

Take chewing-gum. It isn't only because I happen to be travelling in that line myself—I represent the "Jaw-Bliss" Chewing Gum Amalgamated—here's some of my cards; I'd be pleased to have you pass them round—but the way I figure it, you folks don't see the real international significance of the chewing-gum habit. I'd just like to give you an earful of facts, taken from your own newspaper; I always carry the clipping round with me, and I read it with a whale of a lot of satisfaction.

"Washington, May 23.—The Department of Commerce has reported that the United States is shipping chewing-gum to more than 80 foreign countries. It is estimated that the annual consumption of chewing-gum in the United States is 70,000,000 lb., and that the total value of the gum manufactured is close to £20,000,000. Great Britain is the greatest foreign consumer, with the Netherlands second, followed by Mexico and the Philippines. Last year Japan took 50,000 dollars' worth, and China 30,000 dollars' worth."

By heck, folks, that's one mighty comforting message to read when you've got a grouch about something. Mind you, we're only just beginning. It gets my goat to think of China, and us taking no more than 30,000 bucks a year out of it for gum. I don't remember just how many folks there are in that heathen country, but you can figure it out for yourselves that very very few of them have yet been persuaded to quit smoking their filthy opium, and come over to uplift and vision and chewing-gum. Same time, maybe that's what makes it so inspiring for us missionaries who are carrying the gospel of the higher life to the ends of the earth. Just think of all there is still to do! Even we red-blooded he-men, putting one hundred per cent pep into the job, will be busy for years and years before every man, woman and kiddy, from Greenland's icy mountains to India's whatd'you-call it strand, drives to the movies in an American automobile to see an American film, assimilating American ideals and chewing American gum. Oh, baby, I guess that's some vision!

Just think what chewing-gum means for the world's peace. It's a real link between all the countries on earth. Aside from the fact that chewing—just steady, solid, quiet, uninterrupted chewing—makes you feel kind of peaceful and harmonious and brotherly—it's a mighty strong link. Nations that look at the same pictures and chew the same brands of gum never feel like they could go to war with each other. In that respect chewing-gum is the best peacemaker in the whole caboodle; it makes the League of Nations look like two cents. I don't pretend to be a little tin archangel: same time, I do say that every time I trade a ton or two of gum I feel like I'd been whooping it up for universal brotherhood and all that.

Say, folks, I want you to have a heart-to-heart talk with yourselves, and ask yourselves, frankly and honestly, where this burg

B

of yours stands in this great international chewing stunt. Walk
along any of your streets and watch the people go into any movie
theatre and look around when the lights are up; how many pairs
of jaws will you see working steady up and down? Not fifty
per cent. Perhaps you'll say this is all a bunch of fluff—or "much
ado about nothing," as William K. Shakespeare says; but let me
tell you, it's a mighty important matter. It shows you've hardly
begun to be Americanized—civilized, I mean. Folk that don't
chew gum are liable to be the same folk that don't use vacuum
cleaners or loose-leaf ledgers or any of the other signs of culture
and civilization. Tell you what it is, a real live go-getter walking
around in Australia feels like he'd visited a school dormitory in
the middle of the night.

Speaking of schools, of course, it's education you want; real,
sound, business education. Not history and poetry and other
junk like you get now. There's a lot of ballyhooing highbrows,
calling themselves the intelligentsia and other trick names—fuzzy
university professors and boneheads of that sort—that are always
shooting off their mouths about Latin and literature and all those
folderols and doodads, and calling it education. You got to quit
listening to those slobs and get wise to the fact that education
means salesmanship, first, last, and all the time. Education for
success.

First of all you want a course in English. I don't mean
Homer and Milton and other has-beens; but Business English, so
as you can write a zippy ad. or a letter that a customer will react
to. I'm a college man myself, and I know a whole lot of Ella
Wheeler Wilcox's pieces by heart, but that's for ornament, not a
real solid basis for earnest efficient endeavour.

Then of course you need a course of Psychology, so as you
can know how to handle customers. If you don't know human
nature, how in Pete's name are you going to know just how much
a customer will stand for, in the way of ornamental statement?
I'm as by golly truthful as any other man—any other man in
business, I mean; but you got to sell the goods. Psychology of
salesmanship—the only kind of psychology worth a dime—tells
you just when you can be Truthful Willy and when you can't
afford to be. There are some folks you can persuade to believe
you're in business for *their* health, not your own, but there's others
that won't fall for this, and with them you got to use other
methods; you got to handle them so as they don't rightly know

what sort of a four-flusher you are. Psychology puts you wise to all this.

These are both parts of Salesmanship and so is the great science of advertising. Here, again, you're sound asleep in this burg. In the matter of hoardings and sky-signs and such symptoms of the higher spiritual life, you haven't begun to get wise to your opportunities. I hand it to you you've got a peach of a river here, if you only knew how to use it. All along the banks there ought to be miles and miles of hoardings big enough to be read by folks on the opposite bank. I've noticed quite a lot of beauty spots in the hills, too, where there are no hoardings to speak of, and that means neglected opportunities. Course I know there's a lot of long-haired zobs that spill a lot of punk talk about the beauty of nature, and spoiling the scenery, and that. Beauty of nature, rats! It's just when folks are trying to admire the scenery that you want to butt in and inform them in capital letters that what they really ought to admire is your motor-spirit or your soap or your chewing-gum. Beauty's all right for dreamers and back-numbers, but you got to sell the goods. Till you haven't left a single landscape within a hundred miles of the city that doesn't put across some piece of useful information, you haven't begun to understand the American spirit, the spirit that sent us toiling upward through the night towards the higher life, till now we're manufacturing chewing-gum to the value of 20,000,000 plunks a year. Where would Niagara be to-day if we'd listened to the scenery boobs instead of putting up factories and making the little old cataract work for its living?

I'm going to show you. Before another year's out there won't be a beauty spot in this State that won't be giving you some useful information, in letters as big as houses, about chewing-gum.

Well, say, I got to beat it; this is my depot. Tickled to death to have met such a bunch of sociable guys; such a flow of conversation, too. It's me for Hoover and Prohibition every time on general principles, but if you gentlemen care to join me at the bar while the train waits I'll show you how a red-blooded, virile American citizen practises the ancient art of shooting a highball. You will? Fine!

THE BURDEN OF SOLEMNITY

GREAT men—I have come to the conclusion after reading many biographies—are all right, provided you do not take them too seriously. Many dire evils spring from the failure to realize the plain fact that every man, even the most august and venerable, is a bit of a joke. The delirium of hero-worship leads, in the end, to disillusionment and cynicism. Real hero-worship, the only kind that will stand wear and tear, is the ability to love a man, and honour him, and laugh at him, all at the same moment.

Pope described mankind, with singular precision, as "the glory, jest, and riddle of the world." Silly and solemn people are ready enough to accept the first and third term, but are inclined to shy at the second. Accept all three, if you seek a sane philosophy of life. There is profound truth in Stevenson's saying: "They talk of the angels weeping; but I think they must more often be holding their sides, as they look on." People are willing to admit that there may be comic characters—a Falstaff, a Panurge, a Mrs Gamp; what they are unwilling to concede is that we are all comic characters. Falstaff is not really a ridiculous exception; he is the comic aspect of us all. If Shakespeare had liked to dwell on the comic aspect of King Lear—and what could be more fatuous than that old gentleman's conduct at the beginning of the play?—he would have made King Lear one of his great comic creations.

Perhaps you remember the famous passage in which Anatole France—who remains, for me, one of the wisest of modern men, despite the furious east wind of criticism now blowing upon his memory—calls to his aid the muses of Pity and of Irony. "The Irony I invoke," he says, "is not cruel. She never makes a mock of love or of beauty. She is gentle and kindly. Her laugh calms anger, and it is she who teaches us to smile at knaves and fools, whom, but for her, we might have been weak enough to hate." But it is not only knaves and fools who deserve to be smiled at; we must learn to laugh also at the ancient and honourable of the earth, when the occasion warrants.

I know that some people will object very strenuously to this philosophy of mine; but I would ask them to suspend judgment till I have given an illustration or two. The first that occurs to me is Shelley. Nobody who knows anything will deny that Shelley is one of the great lyric poets of the world. Nobody who studies his life will deny the purity of his aims, his disinterested benevolence, his extraordinary unselfishness; even that cynic, Byron, was constrained to say that all the other men he knew were, when compared with Shelley, beasts. In his lifetime the respectable public thought him an infamous person, a very pattern of perverse wickedness. After his death, the beauty of his character came to light; there grew up a generation which regarded him as an angel. An angel he may have been; but he was, beyond all question, a crank. I can find no excuse for those who thought him wicked, ("Shelley is so beautiful it is a pity he is so wicked," said Godwin, of all people), but I think those who laughed at him had sanity on their side. While an undergraduate of Oxford, deep in Plato's Theory of pre-existence, he met in the street a woman with a baby in her arms, and demanded that the baby should tell him something about the world from which it had lately emerged. The mother, no doubt thinking him quite mad, explained that the baby could not talk. In the end, Shelley walked away despondently, remarking to the friend who was with him, "How provokingly close are these new-born babes!" Mr Robert Lynd quotes this as one of the many anecdotes which leave Shelley looking rather absurd. I dare say that in this particular instance he was laughing in his sleeve; but there are too many stories about him which show him profoundly serious and extremely ludicrous. I see no reason why we should violently suppress our sense of the ridiculous at the sight of his antics because he was a man of genius and the author of *Adonais*. The sane course is to honour the great poet and smile at his follies.

For another example, take Victor Hugo; certainly one of the greatest men of letters of modern times. Of course his fame is not what it once was, but there are still critics, in France, who think him the finest French poet of all time; there are others who think him a monstrous humbug. Why should he not be both?—and why can we not do justice to the author of *Notre ·Dame* and a hundred beautiful lyrics, and also to the windy rhetorician, the pretentious sham-prophet, the sublime egocentric? It is impossible to read his biography without hilarity; his egoism and his vanity led him to incredible heights of· absurdity; and so some people who read him and were carried off their feet by his genius when they were young, are now rather ashamed of themselves and dismiss him with disgust; but why? His genius remains as admirable as ever, no matter what pranks his biography reveals. Let us admire, and laugh.

In my own youth I was greatly influenced by Walt Whitman—whom, by the way, I still think the greatest poet America has given us—and was greatly troubled by the fact that in the middle of one of his poems I would feel an almost irrepressible desire to laugh. I had at that time a false idea of reverence, and felt that laughter, or even the inclination to laugh, was irreverent and the mark of a shallow and frivolous mind. It was quite a mistake. I was also much impressed by what I read about the "good gray poet" and his beautiful, simple life of manly independence and dignified poverty; and, later, was much distressed when I found that the good gray poet had devoted much time to the writing of anonymous articles in praise of himself and his work, and had, in fact, been very assiduous in building up a Whitman legend. All it meant was that in the man—as in his poetry—there was a ludicrous element; as there is in everybody. To defend your hero's foibles, or to make allowances for them, to be grave and solemn and portentous about them, or even to ignore them, is no part of a sane hero-worship.

Hero-worship: surely the author of that word is an illustration pat to our purpose. It is not too much to say that during the last quarter of his lifetime Carlyle was generally regarded with veneration and awe; he was the sage of Chelsea, the seer, the prophet, the oracle; no other living Englishman was held in such reverence. Then he died, and his *Reminiscences* were published, and Froude wrote his life, and his wife's letters appeared, and the reaction was tremendous. "So this was your prophet!" people said: "this irascible dyspeptic, this petty domestic tyrant, this arrogant egoist with his ill-natured gibes at better men than himself, this denouncer of shams who was himself the greatest sham of the century!" The idol had feet of clay; it was thrown to the ground, and its temple was left without a single worshipper. Was there no one in England in those days who had the rudiments of a sense of humour? Yes, but the solemn, unsmiling hero-worship brought its penalty; the idolaters were outraged in their deepest feelings, and their indignation was dreadful. We, who were not reared in the Carlyle cult, have no excuse for not seeing him as he was, a very noble human being with human weaknesses.

The attitude of Lamb towards Wordsworth seems to me to be a perfect model. He knew the poet well, valued his friendship highly, and made no mistake about his greatness as a poet; but, somehow or other, could never meet him without wanting to pull his leg. Wordsworth, for all his greatness, had a defective sense of fun, and must often have been considerably bewildered by Lamb's merriment. "What is there in me that is ridiculous?" he must sometimes have asked himself. Yet he never resented Lamb's raillery, and retained his affection for him to the end. Lamb's laughter was not the laughter of a fool; it was the laughter of a man who loved and admired and understood the man he was laughing at. His attitude to Coleridge was the same. He had known Coleridge from boyhood; and admired him as he admired no other human being. The news of Coleridge's death was such a shock to him that, they say, he was never the same man again; and he died shortly after his friend. And yet no man recognized so clearly as he did the weaknesses of that fumbling and uncertain genius, or laughed at them with so keen an enjoyment of what was ridiculous in them.

Why give more illustrations? I could prolong the list indefinitely; for it is the common lot of men to have something more or less laughable about them. If you are inclined to deny this, please send me a list of great and famous men (including yourself) in whom you think there is nothing to laugh at. I shall be happy to correct your impression. Depend upon it, you and I are both laughed at by those who know us best. What we must hope for is that some of them may laugh with affection rather than with rancour.

If you think all this is an apology for sneering at great men, I must have expressed myself abominably; for sneering I hold to be the most ignoble habit in which a mean mind can indulge. Scores of biographies have appeared of late years—I name no names—of which the whole purpose appears to be to sneer away the greatness of their subject. Even so might monkeys sneer at men. There is nothing in common between this despicable sniggering at what we cannot understand and the kind of laughter I prescribe; open, honourable and sanative laughter which makes for a clearer understanding and which may go with admiration and even veneration.

ARE YOU STOCK-SIZE?

To explain the title, I shall have to be very personal, and touch on matters more intimate than one usually deals with in public. The other day—to put the matter shortly—I visited a tailor. Not my usual tailor, who is an excellent citizen and a conscientious artist; but I could not venture to ask him to build me a suit in three days; he has a weak heart. And on this occasion (to be quite frank about it), three days was too long to wait. For some time my existing garments had been showing signs of approaching disintegration; one grows weary, after a while, of being called a blot on the landscape by those who ought to have their minds fixed on higher things than raiment. A moment comes when one makes up one's mind to procrastinate no longer, but to act. I rushed into a—not a mere shop, but a Clothing Emporium, to which I was attracted by a number of fascinating personages in the window—strong, silent men, yet with something dashing about them too.

To a shopman, or rather an emporiumist, I explained my needs. He looked me over, and seemed at once to recognize the urgency of the case. He did, I believe, his best. Suit after suit did he produce, with hopeful mien; suit after suit did he lay aside, disappointed. One suit, labelled "dressy," made me look like a boy who was growing too fast; another ("natty") turned me into a boy who had borrowed his big brother's clothes; another ("very stylish") gave me an indescribable air of deformity; another ("gentlemanly") looked as if it would split asunder with a loud report if I moved an eyelid. But why prolong the painful tale? It was a long series of blasted hopes. At last even that indomitable salesman had to own defeat. "It's no use, sir," he sighed, and added the tremendous words, which struck on my ears like a clanging of the iron doors of doom, "You are not stock-size."

The proverb tells us that a worm will turn, which is probably not true; but even I, who am, as a matter of fact, the meekest and most worm-like of men, have moments when I refuse to be stamped on any longer. "Look here, sir," I said, "your statement may be perfectly accurate; but what about it? This arrogance of yours comes but ill from one who pursues a profession which, but for the fallen state of humanity, would be entirely superfluous. Ponder that fact, proud lord of tweeds and serges. I admit the convenience of having a stock-size body; I admit that mine is not stock-size; I admit that yours may be so—hence, no doubt, your superior airs. But, after all, it is not the size of the body, but the size of the soul, that really counts. The mind is what matters, my haughty rag-merchant; the spirit which inhabits this tenement of clay. A stock-size body is a good thing; but the lack of it is not an irremediable defect. Your wretched readymades are not the only wear. There is a rival of yours across the street, who cuts his cloth according to the wearer. With an artist's eye, a tape measure, a piece of chalk and a pair of scissors, he will, with great labour, build up around me an habiliment, nòt dressy perhaps, not natty, not gentlemanly, but decent and inconspicuous. It is true he will put me to the inconvenience of remaining, for a week or ten days, a public eyesore; but in the end he will array me in such a way that at least I shall not be a thing to frighten children. He will hide from the world the shameful secret of my physical eccentricity. But for eccentricities of mind, what can be done? You, indeed, may be the lucky owner of a stock-size body, but have you—look me bravely in the eye, complacent clothier, and tell me truly—have you a stock-size mind?"

This, or something like it, was what I said to the tailor, and to you, unthinking reader, I now address the same simple and searching question. Have you a stock-size mind? If not, I pity you. Do you remember Matthew Arnold's pathetic story about Mrs Shelley? After the poet's death, she was consulting a friend about the education of her little son. "Oh, send him somewhere where they will teach him to think for himself," said the friend; whereupon Mrs Shelley cried out, "Teach him to think for himself? Oh, my God, teach him rather to think like other people!" That touching cry came from the heart of the woman who had been married to Shelley; she had seen him fall upon the thorns of life and bleed; she knew how he had suffered, and how, with the best intentions in the world, he had made others suffer; and she had learned to realize the value of the comfortable, ordinary, average, conventional, stock-size mind. Cruel is the fate of the Shelleys of this world—the square pegs in the round hole which we call life, a pleasant enough hole if you fit it, a perfectly beastly hole if you don't.

It is true that we all pretend to admire the person who has "the courage of his opinions," but this is sheer hypocrisy. Admire him? We snub him, we scoff at him, we detest him. "Dare to be a Daniel," says the hymn—dare, that is, to be a conscientious objector—and see what a nice little den of lions we have ready for you. "Dare to stand alone"—that we may the more easily throw stones at you. No, let us not humbug ourselves; you and I should be continually thanking Heaven that we have thoroughly stock-size minds.

In case you do not yet realize the importance of this blessing, consider the meaning of a few simple words, such as "Church." A church is an institution—founded by some religious genius whose mind was anything but stock-size, and who was therefore persecuted and probably put to death by the stock-size people of his own day—for providing multitudes of people with ready-made opinions about the universe. A powerful church emphasizes the advantage of having a stock-size mind by various means, including the rack and the faggot, because it knows that if everybody tried to think out the problem for himself the world would be reduced to a moral chaos. Again, the word "party." A political party is a body of men wearing a standard suit of ready-made political opinions; and we all know the fate which awaits the politician who refuses to wear such clothes and calls himself "independent." Finally, the word "school." A school is a place where children are sent, the earlier the better, to be taught not to think for themselves. I was quite wrong when I told my tailor that nothing could be done to cure eccentricity of mind. I forgot the school.

Of course this does not prevent us from being "advanced thinkers"; the beauty of that phrase is that it implies neither advancing nor thinking. An advanced thinker is merely a person who wears the latest things in theories. Those ready-made clothes at the emporium did not fit me because my body was not stock-size; but my stock-size mind wears ready-made opinions, and they fit it beautifully. My intellectual wardrobe, during the last twenty years, has included all the fads it ought to have included. If I remember rightly, I have been an enthusiast about impressionism, esoteric Buddhism, post-impressionism, paper-bag cookery, cubism, scientific management, vorticism, the photographing of fairies, imagism, guild socialism, Dadaism, auto-suggestion, futurism, psycho-analysis, eurhythmics and heaven knows what else, taking up each one at the right moment and dropping it at the right moment. I was a Kipling enthusiast when Kipling enthusiasm was right and proper. I admired Hall Caine tremendously when that was the thing to do. I was all for Joseph Conrad till the word went round that we must drop him and take up with James Joyce. When the right moment comes, I shall drop Mr Joyce, and so will you. We do wonderful team-work, we advanced thinkers. The unanimity with which we say the right thing—the latest thing— about the painting of Cezanne, the music of Keuklin, vitamines, the failure of democracy, and relativity, is wonderful.

I suppose you think this is a clumsy satire on conventionality in thinking. Far from it. Conventionality is humanity's great bulwark against chaos; what a monstrous world of jarring atoms it would be if we all attempted to think for ourselves! I have known too many cranks to sigh for more of them. I realize that civilization rests on a broad basis of ready-made opinions. I have no desire to write a new *Sartor*. My humbler aim is to write a little sermon on common honesty—which is none too common. Be honest with yourself and recognize that your mind is dressed from top to toe in reach-me-downs. When you say, "My own opinion is ——" recognize that the opinion is only yours in the same sense as a ready-made suit is yours when you have paid for it. Don't speak about Shakespeare as if you could have discovered his greatness for yourself; you know you couldn't. I no more devised "my views" on Browning than I invented the shape of the collar I am wearing. Even Shelley was original only in about a ten-thousandth part of his mental equipment; the most original mind in the world contains, in its treasure-heaps, only a few poor pennies coined in its own mint.

Let us expunge from our vocabularies that foolish phrase, "a man of independent mind"; no mind was ever independent. For the sake of our self-respect, let us be honest; and when we are airing our very original views on, say, the fiscal question, or the date of the Fourth Gospel, let us recognize that the Spirit of the Time is speaking, and not we ourselves. In a word, my brethren, let us recognize with thankfulness that we are saved endless bother by having stock-size minds.

ON SITTING ABOUT

THE other morning I found in my letter-box a printed exhortation to "Vote for So-and-so. Your Sitting Member." I don't know how it will strike the reader, but there seemed to me to be something rather pathetic about this—a sort of wistfulness; I can scarcely resist the appeal of a candidate who practically admits that he is totally unable to think of any reason why I should vote for him except that he is sitting. And a very sound reason it is, and one which must always carry great weight with those prudent persons who conceive that it is better to bear the ills we have than fly to others that we know not of. I confess this is not my own rule; I prefer, as a general thing, to vote for the new and untried candidate, on the principle that the man I do not know cannot be worse, and may possibly be better, than the man I know. Therefore the plaintive appeal of my sitting member moved me to no enthusiasm. But that is a digression. It is not with the substance of his appeal that I am here concerned, but with its form.

What really struck me was the strange beauty of the phrase—a very common and familiar phrase, no doubt, but none the less strange and beautiful when you look at it reflectively. A great many common English phrases are strange without being beautiful: for example, the kind inquiry, "How are you keeping?"—a depressing question which makes one feel like a carcass in cold storage, or a cheese, or a jug of milk in thundery weather. But "your sitting member"—even though it may, to frivolous minds, suggest the poultry-yard—has a dignity and even a splendour of its own. The man who proudly offers that description of himself is proving himself of British stock; he is displaying a national trait too often disregarded, but everywhere revealed in our language. Our speech bewrayeth us. We pretend to be a wonderfully active and industrious people, a people that simply revels in hard work, a people that is never happy unless it can be up and doing. To a certain extent we have imposed this preposterous idea of ourselves on the rest of the world. But the most cursory examination of our language shows that the life we really and truly admire is a life spent, as far as possible, sitting about on chairs.

When I was at school we used to learn that, at such and such a date, King Richard—or Henry or Edward—was sitting on the throne of England. Thus early, we imbibed the idea that sitting was the true kingly attitude. The mighty and puissant sovereigns of England did nothing but sit on their thrones—with, of course, interesting exceptions like drowning themselves in a butt of Malmsey or gorging themselves on lampreys till they died. The throne was used as a symbol for the highest power in the land. Nor was this mere childish simplicity; as grown-up people we do not speak of devotion to the principle of monarchy or anything of that sort; we speak of loyalty to the throne—and the throne is nothing but a chair. Dr Johnson, who was English to the backbone, was never more thoroughly English than when he declared that an arm-chair in a tavern was the throne of human felicity.

After the King, Parliament. A candidate for Parliament has to undergo the pain and ignominy of standing. What does he stand for? He stands for a seat in Parliament; he stands, that is, in order that he may sit. If he succeeds, he becomes "your sitting member"; sitting is a synonym for success. And what he does individually, Parliament does as a whole. We do not, unless we are pedants, ask one another, "Is our legislature functioning at present?" or "Are our representatives engaged, for the moment, on their beneficent task?" No, we say, simply, "Is Parliament sitting?" Our language shows that, though Parliament holds high debate and passes far-reaching laws, its appeal to the popular imagination resides in the fact that it sits.

All really ambitious lawyers aim at sitting, some day, on the Bench. The highest ambition of all for a lawyer, is to sit upon the Woolsack. The University—which is called, by the way, a seat of learning—when it wants a new professor, does not invite applications for a professorship, it invites applications for a chair. A university chair is an austere piece of furniture, without cushions—it is not to be numbered among the seats of the mighty —but one likes the English sound of its name.

I need not press the point further; everybody can find a thousand examples for himself. Everybody sits on some board or committee; if he is rich and influential, he sits on a great many, and is often asked to take the chair at meetings. In-woven in the very texture of our language is the Englishman's ingrained belief that the most truly dignified and human attitude is sitting—that, strenuously as he may have to work for it, the goal of a sane man's ambition is always the same: a seat.

Browning, indeed, professed to hope for a heaven in which he might be allowed to "fight on, fare ever there as here," but I fancy he could have found few Englishmen to share his desire for an eternity so strenuous. Perhaps it was the Jewish strain in Browning that spoke; the Jews are an energetic race. And yet, I am not sure; it was a Jew, after all, who carried the sedentary ideal into the realms of Theology, and penned that memorable text: "He that sitteth in the heavens shall laugh."

All this, with which you may or may not agree—and I admit there are plausible arguments on the other side—is nothing but the preamble to a personal statement. It is a long time since I last had the honour of addressing you; and now that I am resuming a pen rusty with disuse, it would seem unnatural to take up our conversation where we left off, without any reference to the causes of the interruption. The fact is, I have been abroad. . . . Do not be alarmed; I am not going to write a travel article. I abhor travel articles, and also travel books, with the exception, of course, of books by big game hunters and books by genuine explorers. I did no real exploring—and I suppose it would be straining language to include fleas among big game? I certainly do not propose to swell the throng of those who come home from their travels to afflict their acquaintances with talk about the beauty of Westminster and the tallness of the Eiffel Tower and the marvellousness of the Roman Forum. (I heard a lady in the Forum say, "this place has seen better days"; which seemed to me to be a model description, historically accurate and perfectly concise.) The Eiffel Tower, and Raphael's Madonnas, and Shakespeare's birthplace and such things may be worth seeing; multitudes travel long distances to see them, so I suppose they must be. If you like sight-seeing, I have no quarrel with you; it is at least an innocent pastime, if an expensive one. But of all human occupations it seems to me to be the most wearying and futile.

In every gallery and museum and cathedral in Europe you see tired-looking persons wandering about, each with a guide-book in his hand, from which he sucks information; or groups of tired-looking people having information pumped into them by guides. The use of the guide-book (or a guide) is to tell you what you ought to think about this or that statue or picture, and save you from admiring the wrong thing; also to supply you with the facts you ought to know. From a guide-book you learn that the Duomo at Florence was begun by Arnolfo di Cambio in 1298. Enriched with which invaluable piece of knowledge the devoted traveller, having stared for a minute or two at the said Duomo, trots away to the next sight. Trotting about in this strange manner is supposed by some mysterious process to "broaden the mind," whatever that may mean. I do not believe a word of it. Travel is mere locomotion. Sight-seeing is mere staring.

For my part, I did not go to Europe to trot about from city to city. I went there to sit about. Rome, Florence and Venice are three entrancing cities, each of them, in its own quite distinct and individual way, a city eminently worth sitting about in.

Every traveller ought to bring back with him some useful piece of advice for others who intend to travel. Here is the ripe fruit of my experience. I have come to the conclusion that, to get much out of foreign travel, one must sternly suppress one's conscience. What is the matter with the average tourist is that he is too conscientious; he busies himself overmuch; he exhausts his body with movement and his soul with sight-seeing. Travel, on these conditions, is a mere weariness, and profiteth nothing. Looking back on a year spent in foreign parts I can say quite definitely that the hours I remember with most satisfaction, the hours I regard as least wasted, are the hours spent at various open-air cafés, sipping black coffee, keeping eyes and ears open, watching the ceaseless flow of life in the city square, and trying in a humble spirit to practise the noble, the dignified, the philosophic art of sitting about.

ON ARRIVALS

"To travel hopefully," says Stevenson at the close of a famous essay, "is a better thing than to arrive." I take leave to doubt this. On the contrary, travelling, whether hopefully or not, whether by land or by sea, seems to me an inexpressibly tedious, monotonous, disgusting occupation; while arriving is one of the purest of human pleasures. (A quite irrational pleasure, of course, but so are all pleasures.) Only you must be careful to arrive at the right place and you must be careful to time your arrival rightly.

At some cities it is best to arrive at night; at some, about twilight; at some, in the early morning; and at some, not at all.

So far as my small experience goes, the most wonderful arrival in the world is at Venice; but you should time it for after dark. Venice is so unlike anything else on earth that the first impact of it must be a marvellous experience at any hour; but after dark it is magical. You may have been reading books about Venice all your life; you may have seen—as which of us has not?—innumerable pictures of the glories of the city; but no book and no picture can prepare you for the enchantment of this arrival. To step out of the glitter and bustle of the station—rather weary and jaded with the long journey from Milan—straight on to the landing stage against which the water of the Grand Canal is lapping; to step on board a gondola—your first gondola!—and to go gliding down the dark, broad, silent highway, with dim-lit, ghostly palaces on either hand: not till memory forsakes you will you forget this experience. The strange silence, broken only by the measured dip of the oar and the soft plashing of the water against your cleaving prow, and the occasional hoarse cries of the gondoliers as you pass another of these black, funereal barges; the few and feeble lamps, giving you momentary glimpses of balconies and finely carven arches; the sudden intensification of the silence and the darkness as you abruptly leave the Grand Canal and slip along one of the narrower waterways, always with tall houses on both sides of you, and above you a clear sky of stars, stars reflected tremblingly on the black waters—thousands of tourists must have tried to describe all this, but the magic and the mystery and the beauty of it defy human speech. And the spell is heightened by the consciousness that this is Venice; at the back of your mind is all that you have read about the strange history of this city, once the richest and most brilliant and most powerful in Europe, later fallen upon evil days of decay and subjection to a foreign power, now beginning to lift her head again as one of the great seaports of Italy. That palace may be where Marino Faliero lived and plotted against the republic; this other may be where Byron wrote the last canto of *Childe Harold*; this, again, may be where Browning died. These are details; you will find out about them to-morrow, when you will also see St Mark's and the Campanile, and the Ducal Palace, and the Bridge of Sighs, and the Rialto where Shylock bargained for his pound of flesh. Enough, for to-night, to surrender yourself to the hush, the gloom, the half-guessed-at beauties of a city which seems rather to be a metropolis of dreamland, or of fairyland, than a place where ordinary people lead commonplace lives and put up umbrellas when it rains.

Well, that is what I call a good arrival, a really well-timed arrival; but you must not think to match it very often. In my own personal experience there has been only one other that can be set beside it. I remember very clearly, though it is more than twenty years since, the first time I arrived at Florence. Not the actual arrival, in a narrow, literal sense. That was unremarkable enough; to emerge from a commonplace station and drive along dark streets in a commonplace cab to a commonplace hotel,—there is nothing in that,—it might have been Turin, or Manchester, or any other of those cities at which one does not arrive at all if one can help it. The next morning was Sunday, and it happened also to be Christmas Day; and I was awakened from sleep by such a chiming of bells as I have never heard before or since; the bells, as it seemed to me, of fifty churches, near and far; the whole effect was of indescribable beauty.

> Ring out, ye crystal spheres!
> Once bless our human ears. . . .

I rose, opened my shutters, and looked out; and that was my real arrival. In front of me was a great square. To the left, in the distance, were the dusky red dome of the great cathedral and the soaring white campanile beside it; to the right was the tower of the Palazzo Vecchio—which, whether beautiful or not, has this strange quality, that once you have seen it you can never forget it. Far away, I caught a glimpse of the tender-coloured hills by which this city is surrounded. And, all the while, the bells kept on chiming, as they had chimed in the days of Michelangelo, if not of Dante.

That, also, was a well-timed arrival; but I must warn you that to arrive at Florence on Christmas Eve has its drawbacks. The proper time to visit this city is certainly not the depth of winter, but early spring. Arrive about midnight, if you can.

At Rome, on the other hand, you should arrive in broad day-light; there are things you must see, and see at once. The moment you step out of the station—unlike other European capitals, Rome has but the one great central station—your eye lights on a bit of ruined wall. It is called the wall of Servius Tullius; and whether it was really built by that king or not, it unquestionably dates from remote antiquity. Opposite you, across the piazza, are the vast ruins of the Baths of Diocletian; now Diocletian was Emperor in the third century of our era. And out of the midst of those ruins springs a sixteenth-century church, designed by Michel-angelo, as your guide-book tells you. And between you and these august reminders of vanished ages whiz innumerable taxis and electric trams. And so, in the first five minutes, if you arrive by daylight, you have learned the secret of Rome's extraordinary fas-cination. In Florence you go back to the Middle Ages; in Rome you go back to antiquity. The Rome of Julius Caesar sits cheek-by-jowl with the Rome of Mussolini; the Rome that was the ruler of the western world with the Rome that is the capital of United Italy. . . . As soon as you have seen your luggage safe in the room for which you are going to pay three times too much at your hotel, go up to the Pincian Hill, walk along to the terrace, and look forth upon the most wonderful view in the world. Far away, across the Tiber, you see the dome of St Peter's; to the left of it, on the skyline of the Janiculum, you see—if the light is good, the equestrian statue of Garibaldi, the redoubtable enemy of all that St Peter's stood for. The great days of the Republic, of the Empire, of the Papacy, the days of Rome's splendour and the days of her decay and the days of her resurgence—there is some-thing to remind you of every period. No other city gives you such an impression of the linking together of the centuries in one continuous pageant. And that impression you receive, inefface-ably, on the day of your arrival, provided you take care to arrive by daylight.

MY LAST MURDER

THERE is, as the exact student of language knows, a certain ambiguity about the word "last." Thus, for instance, one of Browning's poems begins, if I remember rightly, with the line—

That's my last duchess painted on the wall,

and you imagine that the duke, who is supposed to be speaking, proposes to remain, after several matrimonial adventures, a heartbroken widower for the rest of his days; but before the end of the poem is reached you perceive that this is not so, and that he is, as a matter of fact, about to take to himself yet another duchess; whether this one will really be his last you have no means of guessing; but you have some misgivings. In like manner a friend of mine once told me that he had brought me a copy of his last poem; I innocently supposed the phrase expressed a definite promise, and on that understanding cheerfully undertook to read the poem, only to discover a few days later that what he had really meant was his latest poem.

Even so, the pedant may remark, with the title of this article. It sounds a little premature—as if I had made a New Year resolution and really believed I could keep it. Nobody, of course, ought to refer to any particular murder as his last, because nobody knows what the future may hide in its dark recesses. Pedantically speaking, I ought to have written, "My Latest Murder." But, like Pilate, I shall abide by what I have written. Every one who writes essays knows the danger of changing a title. I suppose it is not giving away a secret of our craft if I tell you that the title is the important thing about an essay. It is easy enough to write an essay if you have once found your title; the essay is written to fit the title, not the title to fit the essay. Once you let some conscientious scruple impel you to change the title, you find further changes necessary in the essay; then the title needs altering again to fit the altered essay, and so on for ever. So I stick to my title, with the warning that the word "last" must not be taken as implying finality. I have made no rash vows.

There is nothing ambiguous, at any rate, about the word "murder." I have no sympathy with our sentimental tendency to soften words and take the sting out of plain strong phrases, as if you could escape from a harsh reality by giving it a gentle name; as well try to escape from a tiger by calling it "pussy." So, when a man is in jail we say he is in trouble, and when he is a raving lunatic we say he has had a nervous breakdown; and so, instead of plain "murder," we like to use some soft word like "homicide." My murder was not a homicide, as you will see; it was murder, nothing else; a deliberate assault upon a fellow-creature, ending as it was meant to end, in that fellow-creature's death. Neither the police, nor anybody else, need have any doubt about it.

This is not a confession wrung from me by remorse or any other mid-Victorian sentiment. It is a psychological—or perhaps sociological—study, not an ethical lesson. I feel no remorse, nor any intolerable prickings of conscience. I am not haunted by the ghost of my victim appearing in the dead of night, and urging me to give myself up to justice. There is nothing melodramatic about the affair.

My victim was an unoffensive female of rather attractive appearance. (Wainewright murdered a woman because, he said she had thick ankles; my victim's ankles were not noticeable in any way.) There was really nothing in her walk or daily conversation, to justify my attack; unless you count a certain tendency to brood, and an unpleasant voice which I have even heard described as "cackling." Her eyes had an expression of puzzled virtue; she had the look, at times, of a bewildered bishop. Looking at her short life as a whole, I cannot say that she ever did anything to be ashamed of. Her life was not insured; it is really not easy to say exactly why I murdered her. Perhaps I can best explain it by referring to Sir James Barrie's neglected early story *Better Dead*. One felt, though one could not say exactly why, that she was better dead. I thought—and there were others who thought with me—that the time had come for her to go down into the valley of the shadow. I know this is a very unsatisfactory description of my motives, but most murderers are a little vague about their precise reasons for acting as they did. One thing I must add: if the legal question of "cui bono?"—"who profited by the murder?"—is raised in this case, it will be found that others, and not I alone, benefited by her death.

As to the method employed, I am glad to think that she met her death in a somewhat literary and even classical way. I did not use any of our crude modern methods, such as shooting her with a revolver, or charging at her on a motor-bicycle. I adopted the plan indicated in Webster's *Duchess of Malfy;* and if this brief statement drives a few readers to that play, to see what the plan actually was, I shall not have written in vain. I may remark in passing that the Elizabethan drama is a rich mine of suggestions for the amateur assassin. Shakespeare alone indicates more than forty-three different ways of getting rid of the objectionable. *Hamlet* is a most suggestive manual on the subject. (Is this why we prescribe Shakespeare for study in schools?) The other Elizabethans do not lag far behind; and indeed the whole literature of the Renaissance shows an astounding richness of resource; and, especially, an astounding fertility and ingenuity in devising means for administering poison. For reasons which may presently become obvious, I did not choose to poison my victim. Webster's method was altogether the most suitable I could think of.

Though I must plead guilty to an odd murder or two, I should scorn to be a torturer, and I am glad to think it was quickly over, and with no horror of anticipation and no suffering at the end. To quote Browning again—whose "Porphyria's Lover," I notice, used Webster's and my method, with a queer little variation of his own,

> No pain felt she;
> I am quite sure she felt no pain;

at least I hope so. She was calm and dignified to the end; she made no vain struggles, she uttered no unavailing reproaches, she did not plead for delay or reprieve.

> She nothing common did or mean
> Upon that memorable scene.

She accepted her doom with meekness, and it may be said of her that nothing in her life became her like the leaving it. She reminded me, at the end, of Desdemona.

But though the manner of her taking-off—a phrase invented by Macbeth, a sentimentalist who could not bear to call his action what it was, a particularly cold-blooded murder—may have been, and I trust was, painless, I hated doing it; and here is where the psychological interest comes into the affair. Why this qualm, this slight but unmistakable feeling of repugnance? Was it some queer ancestral survival, the ghostly echo of feelings we used to cherish long ago, before the war, before we read Nietzsche, vague feelings about the sanctity of life? Was it my democratic upbringing, reminding me that my victim had as good a right as I had to life, liberty, and the pursuit of happiness? It could scarcely be that; for whatever else democracy may be, it is not mild and pacific and kindly. The democrats of the French Revolution did not number among their many virtues an extreme fastidiousness about the shedding of blood, and little as we know about Soviet Russia, I think we may safely acquit her of any sentimental devotion to the dogma of the sanctity of human life. The United States, the model democracy of the world, could not even settle the question of domestic slavery without a terrible civil war. Whether you define democracy, with Mazzini, as progress under the best and wisest, or, with Talleyrand, as an aristocracy of roughs, history does not show that democratic nations have been less aggressive or more humane than others.

And yet—it does seem that we are growing more humane—not much, perhaps, but certainly a little. The reason the Elizabethan playwrights put so many murders into their plays was that they knew what the audience liked. I hardly think a modern dramatist would expect applause for such a scene as the plucking out of Gloucester's eyes, in *King Lear*. I have read somewhere, and find it quite credible, that Queen Elizabeth herself more than once watched proceedings in the torture chamber. It is hard to imagine Queen Victoria as a spectator in a torture chamber, even if the victim had been Mr Gladstone. The audiences that could enjoy such a play as *Titus Andronicus* must have been ruthless beyond all modern standards. You may call the hero of one of Fielding's or Smollett's novels a splendid, virile Englishman or a brutal savage, according to your point of view; the fact remains that he would not to-day be received into any decent society. Our standards have changed; we are become more squeamish. It may be replied that this is mere sentimentalism, and that our cruelty is now on a larger scale; that while we shudder at the thought of torturing a criminal, we are content with an industrial system which allows thousands of men, women and children to starve on the British coal-fields. But I do not think most people are content with it.

A number of other sociological speculations are suggested by my latest murder, but they must keep. Though my victim's relatives are wearing black, there is really no cause for mourning. She had had a happy life, and had laid quite a reasonable number of eggs. In her death she provided my household with a meal, and me with a subject. Peace to her ashes!

THE GREAT STRIKE

SOME say it was in 1940; others, with equal assurance, that it was in 1941; it seems extraordinary that historians should not be able to agree about the date of this stupendous event. About its stupendousness they all agree. It was an event second in importance only to the original creation of the world; in a sense, indeed, it was itself the creation of a world, the world in which we live to-day. For it ushered in the New Renaissance (as we call it), and sounded the death-knell of the old bad world in which our great-grandparents lived and suffered and died.

Though it is—for reasons—difficult, if not impossible to say exactly when the strike was actually declared, there are one or two dates about which we can be reasonably certain. For instance, looking up the files, I find that on the Wednesday before Christmas Day in the year 1940 there were no birth-notices on the front page of my morning paper. This was not unprecedented, and in all probability nobody noticed it. But on the next day, also, there were no birth-notices; nor on the next; nor on the next; nor on any succeeding day. By Christmas Day (known to history as "Black Christmas") a few people had begun to take notice and to ask one another whether the newspapers had given up recording new arrivals. It was not, however, until well on in January, 1941, that it became known that in the other Australian States, also, birth-notices had ceased to appear; and it was rumoured that the newspapers denied all responsibility. As the days passed the surprising fact became a matter of more and more agitated general comment. By the beginning of February cable messages from London had made it known that what had happened in Australia had happened in England also; and by March it was known that in China, in Patagonia, in Greenland, in the Andaman Islands—everywhere, in short, the birth-rate had come to an abrupt end. No babies were being born anywhere in the world; and the whole world was excited, dismayed and even bewildered.

By the middle of the year everybody realized what had happened. The babies had gone on strike. They had refused to take up the burden of existence. They had declared the earth black.

It was a strike, not merely on the vastest imaginable scale, but of an entirely unprecedented kind; so that all the machinery men had devised for dealing with ordinary strikes was obviously futile. You see how strange the position was. A state of strike undoubtedly existed, but the strikers did not exist—they refused to exist. No Arbitration Court would settle a quarrel when one of the parties declined, not merely to come before the Court, but even to come into existence. The suggestion of a friendly round-table conference would not be made, for the same reason. It was impossible to find out what the grievance was, or what reforms would content the strikers. The world was at its wit's end.

Bewilderment was the note of all the comment which we can read in the newspapers of the time. In every country that enjoyed the blessings of parliamentary government, the Opposition loudly denounced the Ministry for having brought about a state of affairs so deplorable, also for its criminal incapacity to deal with the situation; but the speakers somehow neglected to mention what they would do themselves if they were in power. The Ministry replied that it had the situation well in hand, and knew how to do its duty in protecting the interests of the public—but the public did not believe it. In Australia, some people said that Federation was to blame, while others, taking a broader view, declared that the whole thing was a plot against civilization, financed from Moscow. On the other hand, M. Stalin, a personage then prominent in Russia, asserted that it was a deep-laid capitalist plot whose evident purpose was to destroy the Soviet regime. Signor Mussolini, an Italian statesman who had made a hobby of the population question, took the affair as a personal affront, and indignantly put several hundred persons in prison. But the situation remained unchanged.

The newspapers rose to the occasion gallantly, and published many wise and weighty leaders, in which they deprecated pessimism, trusted that wiser counsels would prevail, and urged the recalcitrant babies not to be misled by the extremists; all of which was vaguely comforting to all except the sceptics who doubted whether non-existent babies read leading articles. The *Economist* published a series of striking and convincing articles with elaborate calculations of the weekly earnings of the human race, and the total amount of wealth sacrificed every week of the strike. This led to acrimonious controversy among the experts, no two of whom could agree, within a hundred million pounds or so, as to the actual weekly earnings of the human race; and this led to a further and still more heated debate as to whether babies could be said at any given moment to constitute the human race, some declaring that this was an obvious absurdity, and others retorting that the whole human race must obviously begin by being babies. The general public, however, did not take much interest in the discussion, feeling sure the babies were not listening.

A prominent Theosophist created a momentary sensation by reminding the world of the doctrine of reincarnation. A number of the potential infants, he said, had been union secretaries in their last incarnation; and to this fact he attributed the evidently superb organization of the strikers. It was generally felt that this, while it might be true, was not helpful. It only deepened the prevailing gloom.

A ray of hope came when the Psychical Research Society announced its intention of getting into touch with the world of the unborn. It was even rumoured that a prominent Researcher had obtained spirit photographs of eminent babies; and, though no one could positively affirm that a strike had ever been settled by taking a photograph of the strike leaders, still it was generally felt that something was being done at last. But the Researcher denied the rumour, and the whole project came to nothing. In the end, the Society explained that while it could, and did with the greatest ease, get into touch with spirits that really existed, it could not communicate with what did not exist and refused to exist.

The solution of the apparently insoluble problem was so absurdly simple when it came, and it came from such an unlikely quarter, that the world was slow to accept it. An old wise·man, with a long white beard, who had lived for many years in a monastery in Tibet. but who in his youth had travelled in many countries and seen a great deal of life, spoke to his disciples. By the end of 1942 his words had travelled round the world, as true words will.

He said that no strike would ever be settled until people used their imaginations and looked at things from the strikers' point of view. In the long series of troubles known as "industrial unrest," this, he said, was just what people never do or rarely did. That was why so many strikes had been suppressed and so few really settled, the suppression of one trouble merely paving the way for another. So, in the present instance, the great thing, the only thing, was to look at the world through the eyes of the unborn. He himself, he said, had set his imagination at work to such purpose that he seemed to hear the voices of the baby army. Being non-existent, they could not speak, but he knew what they would say if they could. They would say something like this:—

"We do not want to strike a moment longer than is needful. The will to live is strong in us. We long to exist; and since we can only exist by coming to earth and animating a piece of human clay, we long to be human beings. We are ready to take up the burden of life, with all its joys and sorrows—do not imagine that we want to shirk the sorrows which all the sons of men must endure—but not till you have made the world fit for us. At present, we say sadly but certainly, it is not good enough.

"Years ago an American gentleman said you were going to make the world safe for democracy. We do not know what democracy is; but we wish you would set yourselves a different task; to make the world safe for babies. At present it is too risky. There was another gentleman, an Englishman, who said he was going to make England a land fit for heroes to live in; as many heroes are now selling matches in the streets of London, we must suppose that he forgot. Promise to make your country a land fit for babies to grow up in; and don't forget. At present no country is like that.

"You see, we babies cannot choose our parents or our country. If I decided to exist, I might find myself the son of an American millionaire or of an Indian coolie. I don't mean that we want to be the children of American millionaires. The rich don't seem to us to be particularly happy. Most of them go through life looking for ways of killing time—which is a sort of suicide. If killing time is the great purpose of your life, you had better not live. We don't want to be rich, but we most decidedly don't want the kind of poverty which starves and degrades the soul. As things now are, the overwhelming majority of us, if we consented to come into existence to-morrow, would be condemned to that kind of poverty.

"You must set your houses in order, and introduce a little justice into your way of distributing the world's goods. At present we can see no justice in it. Those who are condemned to do the most dangerous and the most monotonous and the most disgusting kinds of work are the most poorly paid. It isn't a question of money, though; we want to know that, when we are born into the world, we shall have a reasonable chance of living a decent human life. When you can give us that assurance we shall come to earth again; at present, no, thank you.

"Why are the pictures so enormously popular? Because people find in them a refuge from the dull realities of existence. They go to the pictures to escape from life. An easier way to escape from life is to refuse to be born. You must make life a thing interesting in itself, the jolly adventure that it ought to be on your beautiful and wonderful planet.

"You can do it, if you will. But you must give up thinking that because you belong to a small and comfortable minority, with enough money, and enough leisure, and good health, all's right with the world. You must open your eyes to the vast mass and volume of preventable suffering in the world, and drop your complacent feeling that nothing but your own happiness matters much. Not that you are really happy. You will never be happy while you remain blind to the realities of life and deaf to the world's cry.

"You will have to provide schools for us—not dreary places where tired people stuff our minds with dreary and irrelevant facts, out of all relation to our future life, not places where they remove children's brains and put in sawdust instead, lest they should think for themselves, but real schools that will help us to live. And churches, too—not churches where dull men drone out formulas that once had a meaning, but churches aflame with a living faith, the churches you will never build till you have ceased this aimless buzzing of flies and sat down to think on the real significance and purpose of life."

This, and much more, speaking through the mouth of an old Tibetan monk, the unborn world said to the existing world. A few years before, men would have dismissed it all as folly and tall talk; but the threatened extinction of the human race had made them more willing to listen, and the great era of reform, of which we are now enjoying the fruits, set in. Changes which had long been thought of as Utopian dreams proved simpler and easier than any one could have imagined. Reform in religion, reform in education, reform in all social relationships, came on a wave of universal enthusiasm. And when, into a cleaner, saner world, the first batch of babies came (in April, 1956) the whole earth went mad with joy. It was known that the strike was over, and humanity had saved itself.

BAD LANGUAGE

A FEW weeks ago, you may have noticed, an Anglican clergyman was suspended for two years on account of his addiction to bad language.

The vocabulary of the clergy is not, however, the subject of this essay—it is a subject about which I am too ignorant even to write an essay,—but I may observe, in passing, that clergymen might reasonably be expected to be, of all men, the most proficient in the use of strong language. All true profanity is connected with Theology; in all countries and in all ages men have sworn by gods, angels, devils and the sacred mysteries of religion. As it needs a sober man to get drunk, so there is a sense in which it needs a religious man to be profane. Blasphemy, as Mr Chesterton has pointed out, depends on belief. "If any one doubts this, let him sit down seriously and try to think blasphemous thought about Thor. I think his family will find him at the end of the day in a state of some exhaustion." Of course, you must not carry this to extremes, and conclude that the next loud and fluent bullock-driver you may overhear is necessarily a strict churchgoer. Still, it remains true that blasphemy depends on conscious or subconscious reverence. "Holy Moses!" is now a perfectly innocent expression of surprise; it was once regarded as a wicked blasphemy. The change is due to the fact that we no longer venerate the lawgiver as our ancestors did. I remember, as a child, being rebuked for saying something frivolous about Noah, on the ground that the names of "these sacred personages" must not be taken in vain. Why that enterprising navigator should be regarded as a sacred personage was not explained.

In the past, swearing has often become such a nuisance that it has attracted the attention of legislators. In ancient Athens, for example, there were certain prohibitions: boys, we read, were not allowed to swear by Hercules, unless they did it in the open air. (This distinction between indoor and outdoor profanity seems strange to us; but there may be something in it. If, every time you broke your back collar-stud, you had to run out into the garden before saying what you wanted to say, the probability is that you would never say it.) In classical Rome, again, custom allowed the men to swear by Hercules and the women by Castor. (It is castor oil that both men and women swear by in Rome to-day.) If any such attempt were in our time made to discriminate between the sexes in the matter of swearing, what an outcry there would be! What denunciation of man-made laws! And quite justly so, for if swearing is right for a man it is equally right for a woman; although, as a matter of fact, a woman who swears always does it amateurishly, with a certain comic self-consciousness; as the schoolboy swears to show how manly he is, a woman swears to show how advanced she is.

Speaking of Rome, I am reminded that the present Italian Government has embarked on a great campaign against blasphemy. "For the honour of your country, do not blaspheme," is a notice you may read in every tram-car and in countless public places throughout Italy. I do not know what Signor Mussolini's motive may be; perhaps he suspects that, if his people swear, it will probably be at him; anyhow, he has shown a praiseworthy courage in ordering the Italians, of all people, to stop swearing—for they possess a language which is, next to Spanish, the finest language in the world for this purpose. I hope the campaign may succeed, and I am not at all sure that the time has not come for a similar campaign in Australia. I am not sure that profanity has not become a national Australian disease, like drink, gambling and high tariffs.

Notice, however, that there is a great difference between Australian swearing and Italian or Spanish swearing. A Spaniard, when he is really irritated, will curse you for three hours by the clock without once repeating himself; he will curse you, and your remotest ancestors and your remotest posterity, with an astonishing ingenuity, volubility, and vigour. You may object to profanity on principle, but you cannot fail to admire his wonderful mastery over all the resources of his rich, expressive tongue. The Australian is not a bit like that. He shows no ingenuity. He uses vain repetitions. He is nothing if not reiterative. He is probably quite as intelligent as the Spaniard, but you would never guess it to listen to him. He reveals a singular barrenness, a most limited range. He repeats, endlessly, some half-dozen nouns, adjectives, and verbs. You feel inclined to cry out to him, "For heaven's sake, either reform your swearing, and put some intellect into it, or drop it altogether! This eternal drumming on the same few words is merely bestial."

A friend of mine, knowing—I cannot guess how he knew— that I was interested in the subject, lent me the other day a book by an American psychologist, Dr G. T. W. Patrick, on *The Psychology of Relaxation,* containing a chapter on "Profanity," which is the best scientific study of the subject I have ever read; the best answer to the questions, Why do men swear? and, When they swear, why do they use the words they do use?

Dr Patrick distinguishes two kinds of swearing, asseverative and ejaculatory. (These awe-inspiring words are enough, of themselves, to make the subject respectable.) The first kind includes, of course, the swearing which is required of us in the courts of law; compulsory profanity, so to speak. It includes, also, the profanity you use when you wish to impress upon your hearer that you are telling the truth. There is not much to be said of this variety, except that it fails of its purpose, and is therefore rather silly. When a man has to swear in order to convince you that he is not a liar, you are apt to suspect that he is telling you a particularly thumping lie. Even when the man who tries to sell me a vacuum cleaner prefaces his wildest flights with the word "honestly," I at once jump to the conclusion that his vacuum cleaner will not clean. The honest man is accustomed to being believed, and takes for granted that you will believe him. When he has to swear about it, he shows that he is accustomed to being doubted, probably with very good reason.

The commoner kind of swearing is the ejaculatory, and about the origin of this the psychologists are disagreed. Some hold that it is an outlet for pent-up emotion; and this is also the popular view. When you are trying to drive in a nail with a heavy hammer, and hit your finger instead, the short, sharp monosyllable which you employ—and which I strongly suspect that even the Archbishop of Canterbury would employ in the like painful circumstance—comes of an instinctive desire to relieve the overburdened soul. There is a sudden flame of anger, an inner excitement which calls for an outlet; profanity is the only outlet available, since you cannot fight the hammer. You are like the sailor in Byron's poem: "He knew not what to do and so he swore." Profanity is a kind of safety-valve. It is the relief of a central stress; it relieves nerve tension. It has a pacifying and purifying effect on the soul.

Dr Patrick makes short work of this theory, which is based, it seems, on false psychology. Ejaculatory swearing, according to him, dates back to a time before language had been invented,

In ages when articulate speech as yet was not, man, in common with other animals, made certain sounds when he was angry; the purpose of these sounds was to frighten the enemy. The dog shows his teeth and growls, the lion roars, the cat makes his hairs stand on end so as to look bigger than he really is, the turkey-cock ruffles out his feathers for the same reason—all to overawe the foe. In the same way prehistoric man made alarming noises, and when language came to him he used words connected with alarming ideas—such as the infernal regions, eternal torments, and gods and devils. Even when you say so mild a thing as "By Thunder" you are reminiscent of a time when thunder was one of the most terrifying phenomena in nature. The French try to make the expression more alarming still by the simple method of multiplication: they say "a thousand thunders." The Germans have carried still further this quantitative method, which has never appealed to the Anglo-Saxon temperament. Where the Englishman, annoyed by the painful accident above alluded to, utters a monosyllable so expressive that it sounds as if it had been made for such an occasion, the German will say things like "Alle Welt-kreuzmohrentausendhimmelsternundgranatensakrament," which is certainly an alarming word. In either case, you are using a word for a terrifying idea, to terrify the enemy. The old instinct is too strong for you, and you forget that the hammer is not an animate enemy and is not amenable to terror. Such is Dr Patrick's explanation of profanity, which, he says, can be explained only from the standpoint of phylogeny. As I do not know what phylogeny means, and have no dictionary at hand, I shall not presume to criticize the statement, but it sounds all right.

What I wish to point out, however, is that there is a third kind of profanity which Dr Patrick does not mention, and which, at least in Australia, is the commonest of all. This may be called decorative profanity; the profanity which Australians weave into their conversation like a sort of embroidered pattern. Of this kind of profanity I declare myself heartily sick and tired. If its original purpose was, as I suppose, decoration, it has lost its pristine beauty, and has become merely ugly, barbaric, and disgusting; it is beginning to make us a byword among decent nations. I fancy it is high time we took a leaf out of Signor Mussolini's book. We might start a "Yea Yea League," sworn to dry up this murky stream which threatens to inundate our daily speech; or, if we cannot hope to dry it up altogether, we might at least, by resolute, concerted effort, dam it.

ON PIONEERING

HAIL, ye faithful, much-enduring readers! . . . But perhaps I had better explain. I spent a vacation recently in reading nearly three hundred Odes to Western Australia; and I wonder whether anybody ever spent a vacation in this way before, since the world began. I am now convalescent, thank you; except that I find a certain difficulty in not beginning sentences with "Hail!" the symptoms of odeshock have practically disappeared.

They mostly began with "hail" or "all hail" and many of them threw in an extra "hail" whenever their feelings got the better of them or the metre seemed to call for an extra syllable. They hailed everything and everybody; they hailed the country, they hailed the centenary, they hailed our wool, our wheat, our gold, our pearling industry, our wildflowers, the men of a century ago and the generations yet unborn. One of them exhorted his readers, at intervals, to "shout a loud hooray," and the variation was so pleasing that I felt inclined to take him at his word. Another invited us all to "shout and sing, and make the welkin blithely ring," but most of them were content with something less noisy than this. They were satisfied with hailing.

Of the earnest patriotism of these poets there can be no question; they have boundless faith in their land. We are a young people—"the debutante of nations," one of our singers calls us; and another, whose grammar is his servant, not his master, says, "the youngest of all thy fair sisters art thee"—and, being young, we are apt to be shy and to have too much respect for our elders. Our poets teach us a truer faith,

> Hail, beauteous land! hail, bonzer West Australia;
> Compared with you, all others are a failure.

That is the kind of thing, and it undoubtedly warms the cockles of the heart, though some may object to the rhyme—but then Western Australia is a puzzling name to fit into rhyme; one minstrel ingeniously solves the problem by turning it round:

> Hail, Groperland! Australia West!
> Of earth's fair places thou art best.

There is no doubt about the fervour of this; and most of these poems are fervid. We are the salt of the earth; other people are its scum. We inhabit the loveliest of lands; other countries are more or less blots on the landscape. Even the size of our State comes in for its meed of praise:

> Hail to Westralia!
> Hail to its bigness!
> Hail to its motto
> "Cygnis insignis."

We have done wonderful things—especially Lord Forrest, who comes into scores of odes; this, for instance, is the country

> Where the purest water flows up-hill
> In accordance with Lord Forrest's will.

Wonderful man! wonderful country! wonderful poets! Hail, every one of you! All hail, in fact.

But what most of these bards praise most loudly and continuously is the character and achievements of the men of a century ago—the pioneers. So far as I am concerned, the net result is that I never want to hear another word about pioneers as long as I live. That being so, you may object, why write an essay about them?—but I hope this essay will turn out before it is done, not to be about the pioneers at all, but about a quite different subject. Anyhow, I am tired of them,

> Those souls of priceless rarity,
> Pioneers of our State,

who seem to have been physically almost as remarkable as they were in soul:

> Lean they were, with eyes aflame,
> These strong and sturdy men from hame.

"From hame" does not mean that they came from Scotland; it only means that the bard was bothered for a rhyme. (But what was the matter with "they came"?) When I try to discover from the odes what, exactly, these persons with flaming eyes and priceless souls did when they arrived, I get no very adequate account of their achievements. One poet does, indeed, endeavour to describe their doings with some exactness.

> They stopped at Mount Eliza,
> They camped beneath a tree,
> They said to one another,
> "This is good enough for me."

But I rather doubt the accuracy of this; the idiom has a too

C

modern sound. It is wiser, perhaps, to keep to general statements, such as—

> They founded here a mighty State,
> On January 26th, 1828.

I suppose this is substantially true, though the poet seems to have
antedated the event; and I suppose it is also true that they came
to an inhospitable land, where—

> The native with his waddy, his boomerang and spear
> Held sway o'er its vast spaces by ignorance and fear.

And they got the better of him. At all events, whatever they did
and whatever they were, it is in their honour that most of the odes
beat the big drum.

> Then give to them the honour,
> For that they well deserve,
> And do your best endeavour
> To hand on the preserve.

By all means. Give them the honour they deserve; and give
others the honour they, in their turn, deserve. The centenary cele-
brations are not to be arranged, I take it, for the glorification of
the passengers on the *Parmelia* or of Thomas Peel's syndicate, but
rather for public rejoicing that Western Australia has reached a
certain stage in her journey—that she has survived the teething
troubles (or weathered the storms, if that seems a more dignified
way of putting it) of her first century; and for public thankfulness to whatsoever powers, human or divine, have guided her
steps so far. Why anybody should pick out for special gratitude
the men and women who happened to be the first on the spot it is a
little difficult to see. We might as well go farther back and sing
paeans of praise to the Angles and Saxons and Jutes, calling them
souls of priceless rarity. Or why not sing hymns in honour of
Adam, with eyes aflame, and also Eve, his beauteous dame?
The men and women who first came to settle in Australia were
of British stock, and of an honourably adventurous strain. They
came here to better their fortunes, lured by fantastic accounts of
the country (Fraser's report dwelt on the "superiority of the soil"
—and also on its "permanent humidity," a feature not conspicuous
in my garden). Captain Stirling described it as "the land, out of
all that I have seen in various quarters of the world, that possesses the greatest natural attractions." Vast tracts of this land
were to be granted to each settler for next to nothing, and they

were to cultivate cotton, tobacco, sugar and flax, to rear horses for the East Indian trade, and to establish large herds of cattle and swine for the supply of salt junk to His Majesty's shipping. They were to make fortunes easily and quickly. The land did not come up to their expectations, and they had but a thin time of it for many years after their arrival.

I do not wish to say a word against them; only, I do not see why especial praise is due to them. They showed a spirit of adventure which is the common birthright of our race—and of other races. They showed great courage in coming out to a remote and unknown world; courage, thank Heaven, is not an uncommon virtue. Are we not all born of women who have sailed gallantly into the perilous sea of marriage and faced death to bring us into the world? Everywhere in our country to-day, not only in remote and lonely places in the backblocks, but in the heart of our cities, too, men and women are confronting their fate with a high courage worthy of all honour. Those pioneers endured many hardships without whimpering; all praise to them for that; but why not praise also the innumerable persons who in our midst to-day are enduring hardships without whimpering, and who, because they do not whimper, are unhonoured and unsung? To single out the pioneers for special glorification is to libel humanity; it is to imply that virtue has been lost. The world is as full to-day as ever it was of the shining virtues of courage in danger and fortitude in adversity. Did the war show that our nation—or any nation—had lost its ancient hardihood? It is impossible to read the newspapers intelligently without being proud to belong to the indomitable human race; but the best examples do not get into the newspapers. They are to be found in all sorts of odd places; in the lonely bush and in the crowded slum; the heroic is everywhere at home.

Of course if, misled by the glamour of the past, you like to talk nonsense about the pioneers, and represent them as souls of priceless rarity stalking about with eyes aflame, I suppose no great harm is done. They were probably decent people, of average intelligence, fairly industrious and not without grit and resourcefulness; very like the normal Australian of to-day. The mistake made by the writers of some of these odes was to suppose that, to write poetry, you must talk nonsense. It is not so. Poetry and nonsense are incompatible. And this nonsense about pioneers gets, after a time, on one's nerves; hence this protest. The world is young; and we are all pioneers.

ON A THREEPENNY BIT

THIS morning I took one of these small coins out of my pocket to pay a tram fare, and, the conductor being otherwise engaged at the moment, I examined it. It is really amazing how many times you can look at a thing without once actually seeing it. I hope I shall not be accused of plutocratic boasting if I say that, in the course of a long life, hundreds of threepenny bits have passed through my hands; but I never really saw one before to-day. And, having seen it, I am somewhat puzzled, and want enlightenment.

I know what you are thinking, of course. Ever ready to believe the worst, you think that, with low cunning, I am trying to inveigle you into listening to one of my prosy sermons. From this threepenny bit it is but one step to the meaning of money in general—bimetallism—the gold standard—inflation and deflation—the economic crisis—and finally, the duty of every earnest man, in times like these, to sit down bravely and make a list of the things his wife can do without. Nothing of the sort need be apprehended. I do not understand economics; and, anyhow, this is not one of my preaching days. I merely want, as I said before, to ask for enlightenment.

On one side of the coin, everything is clear. The kangaroo and the emu are not at all puzzling. I suppose nobody ever did, in real life, see an emu imitating one of those old-fashioned ballet-dancers; but of course these are heraldic emblems, not realistic portraits. Nor am I bewildered by the motto over which these animals are standing; though there does seem an element of whimsical pathos in our keeping on saying "Advance Australia" at the moment when the rest of the world firmly declines to advance Australia another penny.

It was what was graven on the other side of the coin that disconcerted me. And since I expect that, if the truth were known, you are just like me, and have never looked a threepenny bit fairly in the eyes, so to speak, I had better tell you what you will find there: "Georgius V. D. G. Britt. Omn. Rex. F. D. Ind.

Imp.". My bewilderment must have betrayed itself on my face, for my next neighbour, who had been watching me with the air of a psychologist visiting an idiot asylum, leant over and said, "It's Latin."

"Yes, yes, I know," I replied hastily; "I did Latin at school, almost up to the Junior standard; this is child's play to me. I quite see that George the Fifth is by the grace of God King of all the Britains, and also Emperor of India; it's the F. D. that worries me."

"That," he said kindly, "stands for two Latin words, meaning 'defender of the faith.'"

"Oh, I see; but what faith does he defend?"

"When he became King, he swore to defend the Protestant religion; it's a reference to that."

"But he has a good many millions of loyal subjects who are not Protestants; how do they get on without a defender? And, since you are so kind, will you tell me whether 'F. D.' is engraved on rupees and annas; and, if so, what our Indian fellow-subjects think of them?"

But my neighbour had gone back to his newspaper, and that is why I am still seeking enlightenment.

Of what faith is His Majesty the defender? It is really not a trivial question. This British Empire of ours has moved, or drifted, towards something very like disintegration; one Imperial Conference after another has contributed to the process of dissolution, until now it seems that the one thing holding us together is our common allegiance to the Crown. We no longer take our orders from Downing Street; the Parliament that meets at Westminster has no authority over the Parliament that meets at Canberra; the sole nexus between the Englishman and the Australian is that they are both subjects of King George. This has come about in the last few years; and it means that the Crown is a far more important political fact than it has ever been before; for never before has it been the one link without which a mighty empire would cease to be. In the circumstances, it surely behoves us to know what the King's functions really are; and if the fact that he is the Defender of the Faith is so momentous that we think it worth stamping on every threepenny bit that leaves the Mint, then defending the faith must be one of the most vital of his functions; and I feel it to be shameful that I do not know what faith he defends, nor how he defends it, nor against whom. Shameful, but true.

Of course we may dismiss at once the fancy portrait, painted by my friend in the tram, of the King as the champion of Protestantism. The King is the champion of the law of the land; he is every whit as straitly bound to defend Catholicism against unlawful aggression by Protestants as he is to defend Protestantism against unlawful aggression by Catholics. Toleration on both sides is what he is constitutionally bound to maintain. In England (and Australia) the King is in theory the defender of everybody's right to his own religion—with the exception of those religions which involve cannibalism, a practice at which even British tolerance, I understand, draws the line.

It is obvious, then, that the King is not the defender of any sect; but the letters on our threepenny bits seem to indicate that there is some large faith in common which the King is expected to defend, and most people would say, offhand, that that faith is Christianity, and that, whatever quibblers may say, we are a Christian nation.

Does any one really believe this? Can any one who reads history delude himself for one mad moment into the belief that England is a Christian nation, or that a Christian nation exists, or has ever existed, on this planet?

When the Great War came, people asked one another the silly and irrelevant question, "Is Christianity a failure?" How could it be a failure, when it had never been tried?—tried, I mean, as a national religion. As an individual shows his Christianity by his relations with his fellow-men, so a nation must show its Christianity by its relations with other nations. So far as my reading of history goes, I can find not a scrap of evidence that any nation has ever allowed its foreign policy to be dictated by the principles of Christianity, as opposed to self-interest.

Of course you may reply that if any nation tried to be Christian it would at once go to the wall; that if Christianity were tried, it would certainly be a failure. With this argument I am not, for the moment, concerned. I am not discussing the question whether, if it were tried, Christianity would succeed or fail; all I am saying is that it has never been tried.

I am speaking of nations, not of individuals. I cannot subscribe to the saying of Nietzsche, that there has only been one Christian, and He died on the cross. That is surely false. I think St Francis of Assisi was a Christian; so was Shelley; so was John Woolman the Quaker; and so, for all his tragic failures, was Tolstóy. And if conspicuous examples like these are rare, that is because it is very hard for a conspicuous person to be a Christian. It is among obscure and unregarded persons that the peculiar Christian virtues are mostly to be found; and I think any elderly person has been unfortunate in his experience who has not known at least one genuine Christian. . . . I am not denying then, that there are individual Christians; I am only denying that there are any Christian nations.

"The profoundest of all the great Christian dogmas" is what a recent writer has called the doctrine of "the immeasurable and equal value of every living human soul." How do we, as a nation, look upon that difficult but fundamental Christian doctrine? We not only do not accept it; we expressly, at our most solemn moments, deny it. For instance: On Anzac Day we hold a memorial service, at which we sing a fine hymn by our great pagan poet Kipling, whose hatred of Christianity has inspired some of his most vigorous prose and verse. He tells us—and we sing his words with great fervour—that we must not talk too loudly about our own greatness—

> Such boastings as the Gentiles use,
> Or lesser breeds without the Law.

Who are these Gentiles, these inferior breeds, and what is the law outside which they dwell? Unquestionably, we mean those persons who are unfortunate enough not to be of British birth, and who somehow contrive to exist without being members of the British Empire. This is racial arrogance at its most blatant, and the express antithesis of Christianity. And later, in the same solemn service, we lift up our voices in praise of the land of hope and glory, and utter a prayer:

> Wider yet and wider
> May thy bounds be set!

Do we reflect, as we sing, that we cannot set our bounds wider without setting somebody else's bounds narrower, and that what we are really praying for is that the British Empire may be permitted to annex some more territory? And people make speeches, and tell us that our dead have fallen in the war to end war; and we sing hymns like these, finely expressive of the very spirit which makes another war inevitable, and permanent peace impossible.

If we are not a Christian nation in our attitude towards the foreigner, is it because of our relations to one another that we call ourselves a Christian nation? If so, we deceive ourselves, and the truth is not in us. Here again, I am not discussing the question whether Christianity as a scheme of life could be applied to our social and industrial relations; there are, I am well aware, plenty of people who argue powerfully that such an idea is entirely impracticable; and I am not trying, at present, to answer them. All I am saying is that we have never, as a people, made experiments to see whether the idea is practicable or not. If you can look steadily at the present relations of employer and employed in this country, and still call us a Christian nation—I should like to know your definition of Christianity.

And so I end as I began, still puzzled to know what national faith the King is expected to defend. I think we ought to examine the matter with patience and care; and if in the end we decide that as a nation we are without a faith, then in the interests of honesty we should delete those now meaningless letters from our coins.

Your conclusion may be that if the contemplation of a three-penny bit leads to such bitter reflections as these, it is better to have empty pockets. But I deny that the reflections are bitter. On the contrary, they are extremely optimistic. For the upshot of them is, that the poor old world is not yet at the end of its resources; there is one prescription which our sick humanity has never yet tried. And until it has been tried we can never pronounce the patient incurable.

A VERY SAD CASE

THE public memory is deplorably short. Only a few years ago the world was ringing with the fame of J. Pawkins; to-day, as far as I can make out, his very name is practically forgotten. The tale, though a sad one, is so charged with moral lessons that it must not be allowed to slip into oblivion.

For many years Pawkins was just a politician—first a promising politician, then a rising politician, then a successful politician. Politicians, of all three kinds, are not, in Australia, so uncommon as to cause remark. It was not till he achieved cabinet rank—he held the portfolio of Railways in the second Worple Ministry—that people noticed something peculiar about his hair.

To understand exactly what happened you must know that Pawkins was a singularly good and wise man. I have the very highest authority for this statement; in my newspaper-cutting book are the reports of scores of his speeches. I learn from frequent passages in these speeches that the public welfare was all he cared for, and that he scorned to swerve from the path of duty for any selfish consideration. There was nothing furtive or surreptitious about Pawkins; he made no secret of his rare gifts. He believed that a politician ought to set an example to the public, and that you could not set an example effectively unless you explained to the public what sort of an example you were setting. He was not an eloquent speaker; he was fond of remarking that, though he had nothing to say against fluent oratory, he for his part was content with honesty. His speeches contained many references to his passionate patriotism; and those who were privileged to know him personally were aware that he was a patriot of the most endearing kind; he always put the interests of his Australia before those of the Empire, the interests of his State before those of Australia, the interests of his party before those of his State, the interests of his constituency before those of his party, and the interests of the man he happened to be talking to at the moment before those of the rest of the world. Naturally, he became extremely popular. As a Minister he was the soul of affability, and always promised to do all that a deputation asked him to do.

We know, on the same high authority, that he was a very wise man. He specialized in wisdom. He was never known to make a mistake; I find no allusion, in my collection of his speeches, to any mistake, except, of course, those of his opponents. (His opponents, by some singular freak of fate, appear to have been uniformly half-witted.) "If I were to blunder," he used to say, "I should be the first to admit it." The fact that his speeches contain no such admission is a proof that he never blundered. Such men are all too rare.

To return to our tale. One day Pawkins was having his hair cut; opposite him was a large mirror, in which he was dreamily regarding the operation, when his attention was caught by the strange behaviour of the barber, who every few seconds was making a vicious slash with his scissors at some invisible object about an inch from Pawkins's head. "Mosquitoes?" asked Pawkins at last; whereto the barber, looking foolish, made the totally irrelevant reply that he was blowed if he didn't turn teetotaller from that moment.

The same day, at dinner, Pawkins noticed his wife giving queer little, uneasy, furtive glances at his hair. At last he demanded, with some irritation, if there was anything wrong with his appearance. Mrs Pawkins made a soothing reply. At breakfast next morning she announced that she was going into town to see an oculist.

A few days later, Pawkins laid before Cabinet his scheme for the new tramway from A to B. (I must not awaken unpleasant memories by giving the real names.) The route was marked red on the map. It was a very circuitous route, and the other Ministers, who were low-minded, suspicious fellows, wanted to know why. So little were they capable of understanding the sterling character of their colleague, that they actually suspected him of trying to take the tramway by a roundabout route so that it might pass through some property of his own. Pawkins protested eagerly that the roundabout route would benefit a greater number of residents; but he argued in vain. The Premier, whose manners were deplorable, said "No, you don't"—and, taking a pencil, drew a heavy straight line from A to B. "That's the way it's got to go," said he. "Do you insist?" asked Pawkins. "You bet I do," said the Premier, and Pawkins, almost weeping, gave way.

So the tramway was laid, in a straight line from A to B; and then it came out that the new line ran through a number of blocks recently acquired by Pawkins. At first there was some murmuring, but when Pawkins demonstrated that he had actually tried hard to take the tramway far away from his own land, but that the Premier had not allowed him, the general verdict was that Pawkins had been a miracle of unselfishness and honesty. He called a public meeting, made a full and candid statement, and was loudly cheered at the close. His carefully-earned reputation had now reached its zenith. Everybody—except perhaps his fellow-ministers—agreed that he was a good and wise man.

Coming home late at night from the meeting, and letting himself in with a latch-key, he was puzzled to notice that though he had not switched on the electric light, the hall was not in total darkness. Looking round for the cause, he caught sight of his own reflection in the hatstand mirror. Round his head was a ring of pale luminosity. . . . Doubting the evidence of his senses, he rushed upstairs to awaken his wife. As soon as she saw him she uttered a piercing shriek, and then, in awestruck tones, made a statement such as has not been heard on this earth for many centuries. She said, "Good heavens, Josiah, you've got a halo!"

Not a wink of sleep did either of them get that night, for talking about the miracle.

From the very first Mrs Pawkins was immensely pleased. She pictured her friends' faces, when she should say to them, in an offhand manner, "You know my Josiah? He's got a halo." Several ladies, who had hitherto been inclined to be uppish, would now be less than the dust beneath her motor's wheels. At all social functions she would henceforth be the unquestioned leader; of course the wife of a man with a halo must take precedence of the mere wife of a man with a knighthood. But— "My dear, we must not give way to petty personal vanities," said Pawkins. "Naturally, I am gratified; but not for my own sake,"—here the halo glowed rather more brightly—"not for any poor, paltry, selfish reason. I am glad to think that public morality will be stimulated by the sight of this signal mark of approval bestowed on honesty and integrity. No man," he added, humbly, "is more conscious of his defects than I am. But I can sincerely say that this great honour has come to me unsought; and I have won it by no disgraceful surrender of principle, no paltering with the truth, no selfish pursuit of distinction. I am gratified, Mr Speaker," he went on, forgetting his whereabouts in the fervour of his manly emotion, "that I should have been thought worthy to be the humble means of bringing this unique honour to my beloved country, the country to which I have consistently sacrificed every personal interest during a lifetime spent in its service." By the end of this noble speech, the halo was shining with its full radiance.

The next few weeks were the most exciting period in the lives of Mr and Mrs Pawkins. Large head-lines in the local press, illustrated interviews (the thing didn't photograph well, however), cables from all over the world, cabled inquiries from Sir Arthur Conan Doyle and others, cabled offers from theatrical entrepreneurs, caricatures in the comic papers, a popular music hall song (in which something was said about "Keeping politicians' pay low" for the obvious purpose of rhyming with "halo"), articles in scientific reviews, sermons in all the churches —all this made life a dizzying business for the couple.

But it is surprising how quickly one gets accustomed to things. At the end of the first week, Mrs Pawkins constructed a cardboard shade which enabled the halo to be used as a reading-lamp. The emoluments of a Cabinet Minister are not large, and they both rejoiced in this saving of current; but once you have begun to put a halo to practical use, there is an end of awe and wonder and mystery.

At the end of a fortnight, Pawkins began to feel weary of raising his hat in the street for friends who wanted to see the halo, and of hearing men say "Lorlummy!" and women "Rather weird," or "How frightfully intriguing!" Above all, he grew tired of being greeted with a playful "Hullo, old man! how's the halo to-day?" That did not strike him as brilliant the first time he heard it, and when he heard it for the thousandth time, he felt that it would drive him mad.

But the really sad part of this story is to come. In politics, where a halo, you might think, ought to be a magnificent asset, Pawkins found it the reverse. To begin with, his fellow-ministers disliked it; they had none of their own, and they resented "old Pawkins and his blinkin' 'alo," as one of them put it. The newspapers which had been kind to him for years said the same thing less brutally: "While we should be the last to speak with irreverence of the halo in its proper place. we venture to suggest that its proper place is a stained-glass window of the Middle

Ages rather than a twentieth-century legislature." Pawkins read this, admitted its truth, and made up his mind that, as a general election was approaching, he had better get rid of the thing.

At first he fancied it would be an easy matter. He simply called in the local plumber and told him to prise the halo off. The plumber, baffled, advised him to try a hairdresser; the hairdresser, having done his best, sent him to a doctor. His family doctor told him to see a specialist, but was unable to supply the name of one. (In the Middle Ages there may have been professional halo removers for politicians; in our time, for obvious reasons, the race is extinct.) He tried physicists, psycho-analysts, theosophists, spiritualists, Rosicrucians, and dentists, but all to no purpose. He found that his halo was an integral part of himself. And as a halo is incompatible with the modern political career, there was nothing for it but to retire. Mrs Pawkins was permanently embittered by the discovery that a halo gives out no heat and cannot be used as a substitute for a gasring. Hence bickering in the Pawkins home until his death, which occurred a year after his retirement.

Unfortunately, I have no space left for elucidating the valuable moral which, as I told you at the beginning, is contained in this sad tale. But I dare say it is plain enough, without any elucidation.

ON TAIL-CHASING

WHEN very old gentlemen (contemporaries of mine) shake their heads (as they all too frequently do) and assert that civilization is going to the dogs, the only reply I can think of is that I am very fond of dogs; and then, being naturally exasperated, they tell me not to put on dog. There seems to be a certain inconsistency about their phrases. How comes it that the same animal is used, first as a symbol of ruin and degradation and decay, and in the next breath as a symbol of insufferable superiority?

That, however, is not the subject of the present essay. I merely point out, in passing, that both of these two slang expressions are libels on the noblest of man's fellow-wayfarers through life. The poets have done him something more like justice. From Homer's Argos—old Argos, that knew his master Odysseus through all disguise, after ten years' absence, and died in the very uttering of his joy—to the Laureate's Crafty,—

> Poor old Crafty wagged his tail
> The day I first came home from jail,
> When all my folk, so primly clad,
> Glowered back and thought me mad—

poetry is full of praises of the dog. "Go to the ant," said the ancient Preacher; I never could discover why, for there is nothing virtuous about the ant, unless a certain fussy industry be accounted a virtue. He would have given much sounder advice if he had said "Go to the dogs." Go to the dogs, and learn from them invaluable lessons, of fidelity and courage, of cheerfulness and hardihood and tenacity of purpose, of a loyalty that never wavers and a love that suffers all things and endures unto death. Civilization would find examples of all the virtues most needful to society if, in a humble spirit, it went to the dogs.

But I have to-day made the acquaintance of an Irish terrier whom I should hesitate to hold up as an exemplar. Last night the silence of the quiet hotel where I am staying was rent asunder by an appalling outburst of noise—a hideous blend of howling and growling and yelping and snarling and barking. (It was very annoying to be wakened up out of one's peaceful slumbers only to realize that the night was dark and that one was missing an absolutely first-class dog-fight.) Quite suddenly, without any of the usual low diminuendo of growls, the noise stopped; and I lay awake wondering what had happened to bring so promising a battle to a conclusion so abrupt.

This morning I saw my landlady patting a mild-eyed intelligent-looking terrier; and I said I presumed this was not one of the dogs that were fighting last night. "Indeed he was; in fact, he was both of them," was the somewhat cryptic reply. She solved the mystery by stooping down and touching the dog's tail; whereupon, without a moment's notice, the deafening racket of last night began again, as the dog circled round and round in furious pursuit of his elusive tail. If ever voice expressed implacable hatred, ruthless ferocity, and an insatiable lust for revenge, that terrier's voice did. You would have thought his tail had done him some inexpiable wrong and that he had sworn to have its blood or perish in the attempt; but he could not quite reach it, and so he went on rotating, and singing his savage Hymn of Hate—till his mistress uttered some magic word and he became in a moment as mild and blameless and docile a little dog as you could wish to see. The transformation was incredibly sudden. He was actually wagging his tail.

Later in the day I saw him lying in the yard, and was tempted to start the battle again; but I reflected in time that I had not caught the magic word that would stop him, and that his mistress might be out, and that if so he might go on vociferously gyrating till he dropped dead of exhaustion, which would be an irreparable loss to science, for I believe him to be unique. Other dogs, of course, chase their tails occasionally; but in a playful way; not with his deadly earnestness, not with this concentrated ferocity of attack, not with this ear-shattering display of bad passions.

Nothing but the magic word would have stopped him. It would have been no use to argue with him. I might (if I had known the Irish language) have asked him why he was so foolish as to pursue an end that must for ever elude him. I might have pointed out that the pursuing jaws and the escaping tail were both parts of one body, members one of another; and that if by a supercanine effort, he did succeed in catching his tail, it was he, and not merely his tail, that would feel the pain.

A dog divided against himself, I might have argued, could not hope to prosper. I might have asked him if there were no cats and no rats, no burglars, no buried bones, no duties or purposes in life, that he should thus stoop to become a futile whirligig. All these excellent arguments, without the magic word, would, I felt sure, have been unavailing; so I left him in peace, and came away to write about him.

At this point I ought to stop, leaving the intelligent reader to draw the moral. For though that dog actually exists, and behaves in the manner described, yet is he also a parable, the significance of which I am sure that every reader has already seen. But I want, while my fountain-pen still has some ink in it, to tell another story, which is true also.

Once upon a time—a good many years ago—I stepped ashore at Fremantle after a sojourn in foreign lands; and as I wandered along the wharves, feeling very happy and yet hardly daring to realize that I was actually back in Australia, a man strolled up and said—it was nearly twenty years ago, yet I remember his exact words—"Got a match, mate?" Any one who has been away from Australia, and returned, will understand with what enthusiasm I handed out my match-box; if I had belonged to a more demonstrative race, I should probably have fallen on his neck—which would have considerably surprised him. There was no doubt, now, about my being really home again; Australia herself had spoken, in a voice unlike any other voice. If I had been a visiting bigwig, and the Mayor and all his banded councillors had given me what they call a "civic reception" and made speeches at me for an hour on end, they would have said nothing; in four short words that man said everything. He expressed that casual, free-and-easy, good-humoured mateship which was then Australia's ideal; and I still think that, though it had nothing pompous or high-sounding about it, it was a very fine ideal.

The very word "ideal" has, I am told, a savour of sentimentalism. A friend assures me that what we need to concern ourselves about is not ideals but realities. (As if ideals were not the most real things in the world!) Another—a high authority—tells me that Australia has two exceedingly clear and well-defined ideals; the ideal of the employing class being to get the maximum of work done for the minimum of wages; of the employed class, to get the maximum of wages for the minimum of work. So far as industrial relations are concerned, this seems to be somewhere near the truth; we live in a house of sand, whose builder and maker is greed. So long as this is so—so long as we try to make appetites do the duty of ideals—so long will Australia provoke the laughter of devils and the tears of angels with the spectacle of a young and athletic nation strenuously chasing its own tail.

And the futile pursuit goes on, with a din to shatter the welkin; and even our wisest do not know the magic word that shall give, for wild confusion, peace; the word that shall bring us sharply to our senses, make us see in a flash how silly we have been, and free us from our obsession of acquisitiveness and let us get on with our appointed work in the world.

We have enough organizations already—clubs and leagues, and societies, and committees for doing this, that, and the other good work. Heaven forbid that any one should propose to add to their number. But what I want to point out is, that while we have plenty of organizations for doing things, we seem to have no organization for thinking things out. I am persuaded that there is no easy way, no short cut to peace. That magic word which is to put an end to the frantic pursuit of the tail by the head, to the senseless strife of one part of the body politic with another, will be revealed only to patient study and inquiry and reflection. Those great realities which we call ideals, by which alone a nation lives and becomes great, are the creations of human thought and of nothing else. Resolutely to seek for the facts, carefully to estimate the meaning of the facts, justly to weigh conflicting claims—to seek for light rather than heat, to put wisdom above all earthly goods—this is the stern task which we are called upon to perform if we would find a way out of our present discontents.

Therefore—this is the point of the present essay—I want to see some kind of training for politics made available to young men and women fitted, by character and intelligence, to receive it. I do not mean that they should be taught how to canvass for votes, how to tell the public what the public wishes to hear, how to escape from one's promises, how to circumvent the other party by superior cunning, and all the rest of it—the kind of training by which an "old parliamentary hand" can teach a beginner the tricks of the trade. That training was, in its time, very interesting and fascinating, and perhaps it was all necessary; but for our present needs it is not enough. It will not give us the leaders we require. For leadership, in our difficult time, we need another training, a sterner discipline. And I, for one, should feel more hopeful of the future if I saw some young spirits banded together in the disinterested study of the first principles of politics, which may also be called the first principles of ethics; or, in other words, the laws governing human life; by forgetting or ignoring which we have fallen into our present troubles. That there are such laws, all history attests; "laws that in the highest empyrean had their birth, of which heaven is the father alone, neither did the race of mortal men beget them, nor shall oblivion ever put them to sleep. The power of God is mighty in them, and groweth not old."

ON RABBITS, MORALITY, ETC.

I HOPE the compositor will be especially careful over the title of this essay, and that the linotype will play no unseemly tricks. To guard against any accident, I must ask you to take notice that the word "rabbits" is, or ought to be, followed by a comma, not an apostrophe. It would be most distressing if any innocent person were cheated into reading the article in the hope of learning something about rabbits' morality—a subject on which my ignorance is profound. . . . When you come to think of it, it would not be a bad subject. The rabbit might be taken as a fine example of what we call race patriotism. His supreme ethical motive is the expansion of the race. He dreams of the day when the rabbit family shall inherit the earth from pole to pole. If we could imagine a rabbit singing, we may suppose his song would be something like "Rule, Britannia," or "Deutschland ueber Alles." He is careless of the single life; the individual is nothing to him, the race is all. "Do what you will with me," he says; "trap me, poison me, skin me, chill me in your refrigerators, pack me tight in tins, make my fur into a hat and my carcass into a pie—what does it all matter so long as my race endures and spreads and burrows its way across kingdoms until all the earth is one huge rabbit-warren?" He is the perfect Imperialist.—That, however, is not my subject to-day; nor any other day. It deserves to be treated, not in my halting prose, but in Homeric verse. It is a matter for an epic. Mine is a humbler theme.

A little while ago you may have noticed on the cable page of your morning paper the following item: "The death is reported from London of Mr John R. Collison, of Maidstone, Kent, who claimed to be the first person to introduce rabbits into Australia. He was 85 years of age." A few days later the cables informed us that Mr Collison's claim to this distinction was disputed. "Mr C. J. Thatcher contends that his father was responsible for having introduced rabbits into Australia."

Now, to begin with, this conflict of claims is surely a somewhat curious and diverting spectacle. The idea of two men each "claiming" to have been the first to introduce a deadly pest into a country hitherto free from it, has the charm of novelty. Mr C. J. Thatcher, ready to die in the last ditch defending his father's claim to have done more harm to Australia than anybody else, presents a singular example of filial devotion. It is as if a man went about boasting that one of his ancestors had the honour of bringing malaria into Europe. It is as if a man gave himself airs because his Uncle Henry, and nobody else, had started the recent bush-fires in Victoria. It is as if a statesman were to write a large book to prove that he, and he alone, had had the honour of starting the Great War.

As to the historic fact, I have no doubt that Mr C. J. Thatcher is in the right. In 1863, or thereabout, some Victorian sportsmen, sighing, like Alexander, for more worlds to conquer, bethought them that the coursing of hares and rabbits was a luxury no civilized country ought to be without. So they applied to the Acclimatization Society; and the Society, thinking it rather a bright idea, wrote to its travelling agent in Great Britain, Mr Manning Thatcher, who soon got together a sufficient herd of rabbits and started for Australia in the sailing-ship *Relief*. Ship life seems to have disagreed with the rabbits; when Mr Thatcher reached Australia, not a single one of his rabbits was alive. But he, indomitable man, went straight back to England to get some more rabbits. His next attempt was again unsuccessful; and his next. Three times he started for Australia with a cargo of rabbits; three times he failed to bring a rabbit alive to port. Three times the gods strove to save Australia; but against determination like Mr Thatcher's the very gods do battle in vain. On his third journey he had kept a close watch on his charges and found out the cause of their extraordinary death-rate; he provided a remedy, and his fourth voyage was entirely successful. It was as if the gods had given up the struggle in disgust; Mr Thatcher landed without the loss of a rabbit.

Meanwhile, owing to the long delay, the aforesaid sportsmen seem to have lost interest. Mr Thatcher found that nobody wanted his rabbits. With a companion, he went about the country offering baskets of live rabbits for sale, but he did not sell enough to pay expenses. His stock of rabbits increased faster than he could sell them. One hot summer afternoon the two men decided that they had had enough of the tedious and unprofitable business; so they took all their rabbits out into the bush —and opened the baskets.

I happen to have in my possession an old newspaper containing a portrait of Mr Thatcher—and a thoroughly benevolent old gentleman he looks—also a picture of the medal presented by the Acclimatization Society to Mr Thatcher in recognition of his splendid achievement in the matter of the rabbits. I presume Mr C. J. Thatcher still possesses the original medal; probably it hangs in a conspicuous place in his drawing-room. It is a perfect example of the irony of history.

Why have I kept that old newspaper? Well, primarily, I suppose, because I am interested in ethics, as we all are whether we know it or not. Every one of us, every day, is passing moral judgments, though not in the technical terms of the moralist. We do not, in our daily conversation, talk much about virtue, or the *summum bonum*, or the moral sense, or the categorical imperative, or the hedonistic calculus, or our ethical ideals; at least, we do talk about them continually, but not under those names. We don't say of a man that he is a highly virtuous character; we say he's a pretty decent sort of chap. We don't say that certain conduct is ethically indefensible; we say it's a bit over the fence. We mean just the same. We are passing moral judgments.

And our underlying assumption is that it is quite easy to tell a good action from a bad one, right conduct from wrong conduct. And this common assumption is favoured by popular preachers and writers, who tell us that we ought not to split straws about a plain question, and that it is a simple thing to obey conscience, that divinely-given faculty which tells us, infallibly, what we ought to do and what we ought not to do. They speak as if this conscience were a kind of moral sense of smell, by which we can tell a good action from a bad one just as certainly as we can, in the dark, tell a violet from a polecat. Well, I want to ask those who hold such a comfortable doctrine a question which puzzles me. Was Mr Thatcher's action, in introducing the rabbit into Australia, a good action or a bad one?

Mere common sense will not give us the answer. It would be hard to persuade common sense that an action which ruined thousands of innocent people and made desolate vast tracts of country, which struck a terrific blow at the agricultural and pastoral industries of a continent, can be described as a good action. Neither will common sense blame Mr Thatcher for obeying orders. He is unquestionably to be praised for his zeal, his enthusiasm, his unconquerable persistence in what he thought to be an admirable project. We have only to look at his portrait to see that he was a man of high character, a man actuated by the best intentions. If intentions, as common sense tells us, are what really distinguish right conduct from wrong, Mr Thatcher beyond doubt acted rightly. What then?—will common sense admit that a man may act rightly in doing a bad action? It sounds like a paradox. It is certainly a puzzle; and if you never, in the course of your practical life, feel that you are puzzled by it, that can only be because you never think.

We make a mistake, of course, when we talk of "an action" as if it were a simple separate whole. Merely to open a basket, as Mr Thatcher did, is a thing neither right nor wrong in itself; all depends on what is inside the basket—depends, that is, on the *consequence* of the basket's being opened. The immediate consequence, in this instance, was that the rabbits jumped out, happy in their freedom; so far, the act had added to the sum of happiness in the sentient world; so far, it was a good action. Ten years later, it began to be of a darker colour, for its consequences had begun to develop.

Surely there never was a more fallacious saying than Tennyson's:

> And, because right is right, to follow right
> Were wisdom in the scorn of consequence.

Half the disasters endured by the long-suffering human race have been produced by good men who acted in the scorn of consequence. To do a thing without considering what the result of your action will be is mere imbecility. The truth is with that other poet who tells us that

> Of waves
> Our life is, and our deeds are pregnant graves
> Blown rolling from the sunset to the dawn.

An action must be considered with its consequences; with the sum-total of its consequences. And as no human being will live long enough to see the sum-total of the consequences of any of his actions—for the ultimate consequence cannot be known until time comes to an end—we can never say that a given action is absolutely good or absolutely bad.

How then are we to choose between right and wrong conduct? Choose we must, somehow; "life's business," as Browning says, "being just the terrible choice." Some years ago, certain persons wished to introduce into Western Australia a certain kind of deer. It was pointed out, however, that this very species had been introduced into South Africa, had eaten farmers out of house and home, and had in fact been a greater plague than.ever the rabbit was in Australia. The persons who were preparing to do this thing without inquiry into the consequence of similar procedure in other countries would have been guilty, had they had their way, not merely of a bad action, but of a wrong action. It would be of no use to plead that their intentions were good—we know what road is paved with good intentions. It would be of no use to tell us that their consciences had commended the act; it is a common and deadly fallacy, that a mysterious faculty called the conscience absolves us from the duty of finding out, to the best of our ability, the probable consequences of our action. . . . Consideration of Mr Thatcher and his baskets of rabbits thus brings us round to the conclusion reached so many centuries ago by Socrates. Virtue is knowledge.

POSTHUMOUS RESPECTABILITY

I READ the other day in some American magazine or other, a little poem with the above title. The verses themselves were not, I think, very good; at least, they were not of the kind to stick to one's memory—not worthy of that alluring title, which I have taken the liberty of stealing. They were about an epitaph, and our kindly tombstone mendacity which turns the most hopeless scallywag into a decent and estimable citizen; a subject on which enough, and more than enough, has been written. But—"posthumous respectability!" The phrase packs into two words a whole philosophy of history and a treatise on human nature and a satire on civilization. It is an epigram on life. It is a summary of our social relations. It exhausts the subject; there is really no more to say on the matter; I feel that I ought to lay down my pen at this point. It seems an insult to the reader's intelligence to say another word. The inner significance needs no unfolding.

Since, however, there are persons who find considerable difficulty in thinking for themselves, and like to buy their reflections ready-made, I shall add a few paragraphs. The rest of this essay will consist of certain quite obvious truisms, set down for the benefit of such persons. Readers of the more adventurous sort, who like to form their own opinions unaided, are advised to skip all that follows.

Stevenson, in one of his earlier letters, speaks of "those two bestial goddesses, comfort and respectability." There is an exceedingly youthful ring in that expression; as we grow older, we learn to speak with more deference of comfort,—we like our toast to be of precisely the right shade of crispness, we value the warm fireside and the soft bed, let youth be as scornful as it will. And in like manner we come to see that there may be something to be said for respectability,—"respectability with its thousand gigs," in the phrase of which Carlyle never seemed to grow tired; and that the conventions, the much-abused conventions, are really humanity's bulwarks against anarchy and chaos.

There is, after all, a case for the stodgy, conventional, respectable citizen, with his umbrella; he cannot, of course, inspire enthusiasm, but there is a case for him.

My only reason for quoting Stevenson's youthful outburst is that it does serve to remind us of the two fundamental mistakes we are all in the habit of making. We have mistaken comfort for civilization, and respectability for morality. With the former of these two blunders I am not here concerned; my besetting sin is digression, and if I once began to talk on that fruitful topic I might never get back to the main theme. What is respectability? Literally, I suppose, the respectable person is a person worthy of respect; and here comes in the paradox. Looking back over history, we perceive that the persons who really command our respect are the persons who were not considered respectable while they lived, but who became respectable after—sometimes many years after—they had died. It seems to me that the only respectability that a man may honourably try to achieve is posthumous respectability.

Tennyson was a very great poet who occasionally said very silly things; and surely one of the silliest lines in Tennyson's collected works is the line which assures us that "we needs must love the highest when we see it." Must we indeed? We do not often get the chance; but once, in the course of history, the great opportunity and the supreme test came to us; once we saw the highest, and what was our response? We cried out vehemently, with one voice, "Not this man, but Barabbas!" (Now Barabbas was a robber.)

And we should do the same again. I have no belief in not facing the facts, especially the facts about ourselves. It is mere self-delusion not to recognize that if we respectable people, with umbrellas, had lived nineteen centuries ago, we should have been respectable people—without umbrellas—and should have taken sides with the orthodox respectability of the time, against the highest. On that day when the sky was darkened, and the veil of the temple was rent in twain, we should have shouted with the shouting crowd. Fruits fail, and love dies, and time ranges, but that bestial goddess, respectability, is eternal, and eternally hostile to all who refuse to accept her conventions.

And it seems to me to be a very puzzling and a very saddening fact, that so many church-going people should be so deplorably respectable, and that the leaders of the churches should be

respectability incarnate.   The Christian churches seem almost to
have forgotten that their founder,

> Whose glory still they wear,
> And print of whose design,

was despised and rejected, and feared and hated, and killed,
by the serried respectabilities of his day.   They have forgotten
that he was the sworn foe to orthodoxy, and have set up narrow
little orthodoxies of their own.   They have forgotten their own
early days, when all that was most respectable in the Roman
Empire was against them, when every good citizen regarded them
as a gang of despicable cranks, or of criminal lunatics, or of
malignant sedition-mongers.   In the Christian church, if anywhere, considering its origin and its early history, you would
expect to find a hearty hospitality for new ideas and a deep dis-
trust of the conventional, the established, the orthodox.   It is,
I repeat, one of the puzzles, one of the tragedies, of history,
that the Church should have taken sides with respectability.

Of course I don't mean that the conflict belongs to the Christian era; I am not forgetting the very noblest piece of literature that the Greeks have bequeathed to us—the *Apology* of
Socrates, in which one of the best and wisest of men states,
with noble confidence in the purity of his purpose, the nature of
his quarrel with the respectable of his day.   Respectability won;
Socrates drank the cup of hemlock and died—and took his place
with the immortal servants of mankind.   And I have no doubt
that, ages before Socrates, the same warfare was being waged,
and human progress was being secured by men who defied respectability, thought for themselves, and paid for their audacity
with their lives.

I was in London at the time of the Milton tercentenary cele-
brations.   There was never a completer case of posthumous respectability.   All the most eminent and dignified persons in England seemed to think it necessary to make speeches about Milton.
But when Milton was writing the great epic which called forth
all this eloquence, he was a discredited sectary, a regicide, a man
who had quarrelled with three churches in turn, an altogether
disreputable person.   There were no speeches made when he died.

The more recent Shelley centenary is perhaps a still better
example.   A surprising number of critics have spoken of something angelic in Shelley's nature; but when he was alive no respectable person called him an angel; many called him a devil.

A few contemporaries were conscious of his transcendent qualities of mind and heart. Byron said, "I never knew a man who was not a beast compared with him"; but then Byron was very far from being respectable. The highly respectable Poet Laureate, on the other hand, hailed him as the leader of "the Satanic School"; he was called an atheist, a revolutionary, and a madman; and the authorities decreed that he was unfit to have the upbringing of his own children. A century has passed, and he is the most respectable of men. The great university that drove him out has published ever so many books about him; and we set our children to learn his poems by heart.

Another glaring example is Burns, whom respectability, after patronizing him for a brief while, dropped with great enthusiasm; whom we now regard as the greatest poet of his country; and in whose honour statues have been set up in every great city of the British Empire. Another is Shakespeare, who was an actor at a time when every actor was considered disreputable—actors as a class being described in a legal document as "very superfluous fellows"—and who is now, of all Englishmen that have ever lived, the most widely honoured. Another is Spinoza . . . but the list grows tedious.

And the moral? There is no moral. I don't wish to suggest that there are no cranks, and no criminals; that the person we hastily call a crank ought to be venerated because some persons, called cranks by their contemporaries, have turned out to be wiser than their generation; that we ought to welcome with open arms the burglar or the forger because they may be merely persons with new and salutary ideas on the distribution of property; or that we ought to admire the drunkard, because Burns drank. But I do think the study of history ought to make us a little more tolerant, and a little more sceptical of our own capacity to judge others, seeing that contemporary judgments of great reformers and great thinkers have almost invariably been wrong. We might think twice before we call a man a crank, a fanatic, a disloyalist, a traitor, a sedition-monger, a bolshevik, or a fool, when we remember that those names, or their equivalents, have been hurled (by persons just like us) at men whom the world has subsequently learned to honour.

Another moral, if you must insist on a moral, might be this. It is no use saying that the respectable man is the man worthy of respect. The respectable man, as we really use the term, is the man who wins respect from conventional people. He is virtuous, but his virtues are the conventional virtues. He may also be as vicious as he pleases, so long as he practises only the conventional vices. His opinions are not his own, they are the conventional opinions. The aim of education is to defy respectability, in this sense. The only education out of which good can come is the education which teaches you to think for yourself instead of swallowing whatever the fashion of the moment may prescribe. This is the education that makes men; any other kind makes mere simulacra.

But, as I said, there is really no moral. I merely wished to draw your attention to a curious fact in history. Respectability pays a subtle compliment to the universe; it purrs with satisfaction over things as they are, and is annoyed with any one who tries to change things. It snubs him, scoffs at him, suppresses him, and in some cases puts him to death. But his ideas live on, and make their way, because they are true ideas and cannot be permanently suppressed. Are the respectable people beaten? Not at all. Having avenged themselves on the man of genius by putting him to death, they now take a second, more subtle and more complete vengeance—by making him one of themselves. They erect statues of him, make speeches about him, say how much they have always admired him, and, in short, drape him with the sumptuous robes of posthumous respectability.

ON TROUSERS

EVER since I came back from a brief holiday in Ceylon, people I meet have been saying to me, in tones of manly resignation, "Well, I suppose you are going to write an article about your travels." Why should they suppose any such thing? It is a preposterous idea . . . .

But the power of suggestion, as the psychologists tell us, is tremendous. Suggest to a man that he do a certain thing, suggest it again, keep on suggesting it, day in, day out, and in the end he will do that thing, no matter how preposterous or how nefarious it may be. Suggestion is responsible for many crimes. It is responsible for the fact that I am sitting down, quite absurdly and unreasonably, to write that article on Ceylon.

It is customary to begin with an allusion to spicy breezes; but I prefer to stick to what I observed for myself. There were very few breezes of any kind while I was ·in Ceylon, and what there were were not a bit spicy. It may have been different in the days when Heber coined that famous phrase; but at the present time, Ceylon, in the matter of spicy breezes, will not compare with (say) Footscray.

Coming, then, to what I saw with my own eyes, I must begin by saying that Ceylon has a great many inhabitants—any encyclopaedia will tell you how many, if you have a passion for exactitude, which I have not—and that a few thousand of these are white people, and a few millions dark-skinned. Of the dark-skinned inhabitants the vast majority do not wear trousers. The Sinhalese men wear skirts, very much like what women wear in Australia, only longer, more dignified, and more graceful.

If one were writing about India instead of about Ceylon, one would have to be very guarded on this subject, because it has there become rather a burning question. On the racecourse at Calcutta there is, or lately was. a large placard bearing the words, "Gentlemen not admitted to the grandstand without trousers." This is not. as the globe-trotter might hastily assume, an example of brutal British coercion. It is the enlightened Indians themselves who are trying to insist that their fellow-

Indians shall wear the garb distinctive of Western civilization. It is, perhaps, the ugliest garment ever devised; how ugly it is you can see by the determined efforts of portrait-painters and of sculptors to shun the subject. They realize that, though art performs many miracles, it cannot lend loveliness to a pair of trousers. But the Indians who are seeking political independence for India seem to think that there is some mystical property in clothes. They ask why they should be treated as less fit for self-government than we are, when they are obviously our intellectual equals. "Our brains are just like yours," they say; and they think it would be an advantage to be able to add, "and so are our trousers." In India, therefore, the native who appears in public in native garb is beginning to be considered not quite the thing. But in Ceylon the determination to imitate Western ways has not, I think, spread so wide. The great majority still seem content to abide by the immemorial customs of their race.

Now here is the curious point. I noticed that, for my part, the dusky gentlemen who wore skirts impressed one as being well-dressed, while those who wore trousers always struck one as having something indefinably absurd about them—something grotesque and unnatural. In the presence of the skirted ones, I felt no touch of racial superiority; it did not occur to me that I was their better, either in brains or in character; they seemed an attractive people. Whereas the trousered ones did, somehow, strike me as an inferior and—I could not help it—a rather absurd people. Why should a small detail in the matter of raiment make the difference between attracting and repelling? The answer is obvious. The men who wore skirts were wearing their national garb, as I was wearing mine. The others, in adopting European wear, had shed more than the petticoats of their ancestors; they had shed the traditions of their race. They had ceased to be Orientals and had become sham Europeans. They were denationalized, at least in appearance. That was what was wrong with them. I believe in the insignia of nationality; because I believe in nationality.

It is sometimes unjustly assumed that all who believe in the League of Nations and its ideals must be in favour of substituting internationalism for nationalism. Nationalism being the chief cause of war, we who wish to abolish war must wish, it is supposed, to abolish nationalism. Well, I can speak only for myself. I believe in the League of Nations; I believe in it with a faith that has grown firmer and deeper with every year of the League's existence. I believe that those who are disappointed with the League's achievements are the over-sanguine people who expected it to achieve the impossible. I believe that those who scoff at it, and those who are apathetic about it, are people who have never fairly faced the realities of world-politics nor considered what are the inevitable alternatives to the League's success. I believe the hope of the world lies in the ideal for which the League is working—the ideal of peaceful co-operation between the nations. What I do not believe is that, in order to co-operate, the nations must discard their national characters. I do not believe in a pallid cosmopolitanism as a substitute for patriotism.

Patriotism is not a thing one likes to talk about in public. The other day I was courteously invited to address a public meeting on the important subject of Motherhood. It was rather humiliating, but I was forced to reply that I had nothing whatever to say on the important subject of Motherhood. I had pleasant memories of an old music-hall song with the refrain—

> Whether she's well, or whether she's sick,
> Never, oh! never hit your mother with a brick!

—but this, though an excellent maxim, would hardly furnish forth an address on the subject; and I could think of nothing more that could well be said from a public platform. Now patriotism is like that; it is a fundamental thing, an instinct as indestructible as the love of one's mother; a thing one does not care to talk about. Even Walt Whitman, who talked about most things with such a disconcerting candour, is reticent on this matter, saying merely—

> America, I do not boast my love for you:
> I have what I have.

So I do not wish to dilate on the duty of patriotism, but merely to remark that when Ruskin calls patriotism "an absurd prejudice founded on an extended selfishness" he is but throwing dust against the wind, for the wind to blow back in his face. If the League of Nations is to succeed, it will be through the support of patriotic men and women. It will only succeed if it is a league of nations which believe in themselves. Dr McDougall, in his latest book, states what seems to me to be the truth, in a passage which is worth quoting in spite of its abominable jargon.   "Civilization as a whole requires, if it is to progress, the variety of social and political experiment, the varied specializations of collective function and effort, which can be provided only by the rivalry of a number of nations, each developing, under its own peculiar conditions and in accordance with its peculiar racial genius, its own unique historical process."

We who believe in the League of Nations have certainly no time for jingoism—for that miscalled nationalism which consists chiefly of arrogance and rancour and jealousy and greed. But on true nationalism we depend. As Dean Inge pertinently asks, "He who loves not his home and country which he has seen, how shall he love humanity in general, which he has not seen?"

And so, believing that nations are necessary institutions, we are inclined to feel sorry whenever we see indications of a failing national spirit. Even in Italy, one is disappointed to find all men dressed in sac suits and felt hats exactly as if they were so many Englishmen or Australians. It is not merely that something picturesque has disappeared from the world, leaving it the dingier for the loss. Clothes are, as Carlyle saw, the most significant of symbols. To discard the dress which is the symbol of your national life, of your pride in the traditions of your race, is to sap your national strength. If we feel this in Italy, how much more intensely do we feel it in the East! To find in Ceylon, in India, in Japan, and even in the islands of Polynesia, trousers, trousers everywhere, and the national costume everywhere disappearing, is depressing. All honour to our dark-skinned friends who have sufficient national self-respect, sufficient pride in the past of their race and sufficient faith in its future, to be frankly themselves and not to masquerade as members of another race. Those who look forward to a uniform and peaceful world, in which the Hottentot will wear a silk hat, seem to me to be pessimists.

I must admit that, as an account of Ceylon, this essay leaves something to be desired. Still, I hope it conveys a lesson. It is meant, anyhow, as a protest against the common assumption that we who believe in working for permanent peace must also work for a colourless cosmopolitanism. Not at all. Let us sail under our own flag, whether it be the Union Jack or the Stars and Stripes or the Tricolour or whatever it may be. Let us beware of those who would have us haul down this symbol of nationality, and who would like to see, fluttering gaily at the masthead, some denationalized ensign—a pair of trousers, for example.

MY BUSH-FIRE

THE other evening I was sitting on the veranda of a little cottage in the hills to which I sometimes retire for the purpose of peaceful meditation—or, as my family prefers to believe, of peaceful sleep; anyhow, I will swear that I was not sleeping on this occasion, but meditating. (Possibly my eyes were closed; but who can really do any serious and sustained thinking without closing his eyes and shutting out the distractions of the visible world?) I was meditating on the essential difference between characters in real life and characters in fiction, even the most realistic fiction. Of course with some characters—like Micawber or Uriah Heep, for instance,—the difference is perfectly obvious. You do not meet, in real life, a man who cannot open his mouth without expressing the hope that something will turn up, or without mentioning that he is 'umble. But even with realistically portrayed characters, like Becky Sharp or Mrs Proudie, or Madame Bovary or Anna Karenina, or one of Hardy's men, or one of Balzac's, the difference remains, and it is vital. We say we have met people just like these in real life, but that is not true; there is an enormous difference. We say, in praise of Thackeray, that we know Becky Sharp almost as well as we know our living friends; but that is quite the opposite of the truth; we really know Becky Sharp far better than we know any of our living friends. We know real people by what they say and do; we can only guess at what they are thinking and feeling. Whereas Thackeray can tell us with certainty what Becky is thinking and feeling; he is her creator, and he knows all about her, and can admit us to her innermost secrets. We know our most intimate friends from the outside only; we know a character in a novel from within; we can see the central workings of her soul. We know exactly what Père Goriot feels about his daughters' conduct; we know, because Balzac told us; and Balzac knew, because he was Père Goriot's creator, and knew all there was to be known about him.

So far it was all quite obvious, but very far from satisfactory; because it did not explain why we call some characters true

D

to life, and others false or fantastic. If their creator has a perfectly free hand—if we must believe that his characters think and feel exactly as he says they think and feel—by what standard do we judge the truth or falsehood of a portrait? Plainly their creator has not a perfectly free hand; but by what is he limited? By the facts of human nature? How do we know the facts of human nature? We only know the facts of our own particular nature; and when you condemn a character in a novel as untrue to life, all you can mean is that that character does not think and feel as you, the reader, think and feel; but that proves nothing. Who are you? You are not the only pebble on the beach; your individual soul does not exhaust the possibilities. And yet, though I must not ask the novelist to make all his characters resemble me—and as a matter of fact I do not feel myself to be a bit like Becky Sharp—I know that he has not a perfectly free hand, but is limited by—what? This was leading me on to a large meditation on the Limits of Imaginative Art; and I dare say I would have found a complete solution of the problem if I had not been interrupted—by a bush-fire. Such are the vexations by which the philosopher is beset in this ridiculous world.

"Description," said Byron, "is my forte." It is not mine. Neither have I the slightest turn for narrative art, being, I fancy, about the only scribbler in Australia who has not a manuscript novel up his sleeve. I shall therefore refrain from the vain attempt to tell you, in a piece of rapid and vivid prose, the exciting tale of that interruption. If you have ever been through the experience you know all about it; if not, you may take it from me that when one is fighting a healthy bush-fire, with a stiffish wind blowing, at the end of a dry summer, one has no time to think about the Limits of Imaginative Art. If you have not seen a bush-fire I suppose you have read an account of one in some Australian novel or other; there must be many such accounts, if our novelists have done their duty by their country—though at this moment I can remember none. When I have finished this I shall hunt through the works of Mr Vance Palmer, the best teller of tales in Australia to-day; if any one could describe the thing adequately he could. My present impression is that nobody could; that, to one who has not seen it, no language could convey an idea of the wonder and terror and beauty of the spectacle by night, when the valley below you and the hillsides around you are all one red, roaring hell of furious destruction. (I am trying my hand at description after all; and, lo! I have got every single word wrong.) Well, putting all high-flown phrases aside, we euchred the fire; my little bush humpy still stands; and in a month or two, when the rains have come, the black landscape will begin to be green again, and the fallen trees will be our only reminders of that strenuous night.

I say "we"—and here comes the point to which all this while I have been leading up. There were only two of us—myself and one other, who strolled up out of nowhere at the moment when the fire was becoming menacing. He took command of the situation at once; it was immediately obvious to me that he was the professional, I the ignorant amateur; and it was not long before I felt pretty much as the Romans must have felt at Lake Regillus when the great twin brethren appeared in the van of their army.

> The gods who live for ever
> Are on our side to-day.

Not that there was anything god-like in his appearance, or in his manners. I can write about him in this personal way because I am morally certain that he will not read these pages, and that he would not recognize himself if he did. He was lean and long-legged, and, though I have not seen him by daylight, I think he had a cynically humorous face. He was a consummate tactician; knew at a glance where the danger-spots would be; and though he never seemed to hurry, never dashed about, was not in the least fussy, and never had his pipe out of his mouth, he was always on the spot when the danger came. . . . The sight of his black figure against the fierce scarlet background was extraordinarily tranquillizing. Amid all that turmoil of blazing bush and flying flame, the growling and crackling and blustering, the loose-barked trees on fire from top to toe, and scattering with every gust of wind a shower of burning leaves and bark, burning branches whizzing down, the crashing, at intervals, of a falling giant, he never for a moment lost his presence of mind, but stuck to his job, which was to guide the whirlwind and direct the storm. "The poet extolled the firmness of that mind which, in the midst of confusion, uproar, and slaughter, examined and disposed everything with the serene wisdom of a higher intelligence." . . . Towards morning, when the fire had swept away to the westward, and my cottage (also four others, whose owners, being city-dwellers, did not happen to be there that night) needed no further defence, he remarked that he thought it was about time to turn in. When I spoke of payment for the great service he had rendered me he replied that it was all in the day's work and that any bloke would do that for another bloke. I used good arguments; but against certain deep-rooted instincts Immanuel Kant himself would argue in vain. To this man, and to men of his type, it is a kind of religion that, if you would keep your self-respect, there are certain transactions into which money must not be allowed to intrude.

To show that he had not taken offence he consented to fill his pipe from my pouch and sauntered away. He was Australian in everything he said and did. If there is an Australian type he is the type. Long, lean, quiet, humorous, inarticulate, sagacious, easygoing, loyal to his own ethical code, standing on his own feet and facing the world with a good-humoured imperturbability, careless about economics—he does not grow rich. He can never afford a trip to England, and so England never sees him, and judges Australia by another type altogether—a "better-educated" type. I see that Miss Rebecca West has a remark in her latest book about "the Australian crawl"—an unpleasant phrase, but there is no use in resenting it; it will be more useful to inquire what she means, and whether the tourists who represent us in England have contrived to convey the impression that snobbishness is an Australian trait. If so—and I believe from my own experience that it is so—I wish Mr Wells and Mr Galsworthy and a few other men of genius who have the ear of the British public could be induced to visit Australia—not our cities, which are mere plagiarisms from the old world, but the real Australia, and meet the real Australian. I should be happy to introduce Miss West to my friend of the bush-fire; she might not find him the fine flower of civilization; but "crawl" would be the very last word she would think of applying to him. If I had been a duke or a king or an emperor he would have spoken to me in exactly the same way, as one bloke to another bloke; if I had been a multi-millionaire he would have treated me just the same, with the same helpfulness and the same kindly scorn for my incompetence. (He, and men of his type, were the salt of the Australian Imperial Force, and faced death with the same kind of cool nonchalance.)   Failing such an introduction, let our novelists and poets carry his portrait to the other side of the world, and show that Australia can produce something better than snobs. Is he a disappearing type? I hope not. I hope he has come to stay, and that ten centuries hence it will be seen that his ideal—the ideal of mateship—has been Australia's great contribution to civilization.

ON BEING SOLD

SOMEBODY wrote to me last week suggesting that I should devote one of these rigmaroles—only he put it more politely than that—to the subject of sailing-ships. His letter seemed to me to be less a request than a challenge; he was daring me to fill up a column on a subject of which, he felt sure, I was absolutely ignorant. His letter touched me on the raw; because, as a matter of fact —and as he ought to have known—I did, a few years ago, write an essay on sailing-ships, and a highly practical essay it was. I advised the Government to build a life-size model of one of those queer little vessels in which the intrepid Dutch navigators visited these shores long before any Englishman had set foot in Australia; to moor it in a convenient place, and to charge sixpence for admission. If the Government had taken my advice, the ship would be there now, a source of steady revenue, which, by all accounts, is badly needed. Now, of course, it is too late; there is no money for such enterprises. This kind of thing almost makes one tired of giving the Government good advice. . . .

Still, I am always anxious to oblige, and I made up my mind at once that my correspondent should have his essay on sailing-ships. And, as I never like to write an essay without thorough preparation, I rang up my bookseller and asked him to send me a treatise on sailing-ships—some clear, concise book, not too costly, that would enable me to master the whole subject in about half an hour. He replied—the telephone was a little out of order, but I understood him to reply,—that he had just the thing for me, a quite new book, very popular in style; and that he would post it straight away. The parcel arrived next morning, and I put it aside till the time should come for me to write my masterly essay on sailing-ships.

This evening I opened the parcel and began to read the book; but I had not read many pages before I realized that a most awkward mistake had been made. When I said "sailing-ships" my bookseller must have thought I said "salesmanship"—the telephone, I must remind you, was not at its best,—and the book he has sent me is called *Twelve Tips to Travelling Salesmen,* by Herbert N. Casson; a most fascinating book, but hardly the thing for a man who wants to know the difference between a barque and a brigantine. Well, it is too late now to put the matter right; it is Sunday evening, and Sunday evening is the only possible time for writing essays. I must ask my correspondent to accept my assurance that I would have willingly written an essay on sailing-ships but for this unfortunate accident, which compels me to write on salesmanship instead.

It is true that salesmanship is not a subject on which I can feel that I have a message for the age. Still, it is a more useful topic than sailing-ships would have been. For sailing-ships are now a thing of the past; the tall East Indiaman has sailed away into oblivion, and the beautiful wool clippers will plough the deep no more; all the shipping companies have gone into steam. But salesmanship is with us to-day as never before; the subject is actual, vital, urgent; it throbs with life; it comes home to the business and bosom of every man. We are all either selling or being sold. No subject could be more up-to-date.

After reading Mr Casson's bright, practical, common-sense book—you can read it in about an hour,—the first idea that occurs to me is that I should like to invent a new science, to be called Preventive Economics; I hope nobody else has got in ahead of me with that sounding title. Just as preventive medicine helps you to ward off disease—which is better than being cured of diseases which you need never have contracted—so preventive economics helps you to ward off the salesman, which is ever so much better than being saddled with the duty of paying for things you never needed but were persuaded to buy.

Mr Casson's book is intended as a textbook for salesmen; I prefer to regard it as a textbook of preventive economics, and I should like to hear of its being read by everybody. Mr Casson imparts to the salesman a large number of very useful hints for getting the better of the reluctant buyer; but such hints can be kept in mind by others besides salesmen. They are useful to all of us; they tell us just how we are likely to be attacked and to what blandishments we are likely to succumb; and forewarned is forearmed.

For instance, when a salesman approaches a customer—or a "prospect," which seems to be the technical name for a prospective customer—he must not begin by talking business, he must approach his victim tactfully. He must be very personal. "You must ask yourself—what is he thinking about? What are his fears—his hopes—his troubles? You must fit into his present line of thought." A travelling salesman should have a card index of his customers, on which the "fads, beliefs, sports" of the customers are set down. "On one card, for instance, he may write —'Fond of fishing. Owns a Scotch collie. Goes to the Derby.' On another card he may write—'Keeps a Jersey cow and White Leghorn hens. Has won prizes for hens.'" I am sure this is quite sound advice; but the usefulness of most of Mr Casson's shrewd advice depends on his book being read by salesmen only, and never by the buyer. Having read this particular hint, I am on my guard; when I find a man sympathizing with my hopes— my fears—my troubles—I shall know that in a few minutes, if I am not careful, he will be selling me a vacuum cleaner. When a man asks me, in a genial, breezy way, what my principal hobby is, I shall curtly reply, "cutting throats," and so bring the interview to a close. Only the other day a man asked me how my canaries were; and I now know that he had been reading Mr Casson's book, but had got his cards mixed up.

Again, Mr Casson warns salesmen to "classify their time," and use the best hours of the day for their most difficult work. "The hour between 2 and 3 is the one best hour to sell goods"; you should, therefore, approach your most ticklish customer at that hour. One reason is that "he has had his lunch and that means that his brain has slowed down." I like the perfect candour of this admission that salesmanship is an art most successfully practised on people whose brains have slowed down. But, once more, notice that this fact, if it is a fact, is useful only as long as the knowledge of it is confined to the salesman; if the customer knows it, too, where are you? Soon, if the fact becomes generally known, there will be notices on all doors: "No salesman admitted between 2 and 3." If we know that that is our specially vulnerable hour, we shall shut ourselves up during that hour and see nobody. And so shall we save money.

One more example. A salesman, as soon as the customer shows the slightest interest in his goods, should take it for granted that the goods are sold. "You should then stop pointing out quality. You should as quick as lightning change the conversation to the details of delivery." You should say, "Would you prefer to have them sent by motor, instead of by rail?"—or something of that sort. The keen salesman is on the watch for his chance to take the sale for granted. "As soon as he has a nibble, he will jerk." I have no doubt that this is perfectly sound advice —to a salesman; but if he is so unlucky as to meet a customer who has read Mr Casson's book, the plan will fail; the customer will not nibble. He will know that the salesman is getting ready to jerk.

Mr Casson shows on every other page an unholy knowledge of human nature—of the little weaknesses, the little kinks in the brain, which are not spoken of in textbooks of psychology. And I feel sure that any salesman who reads this book—or another of the same kind, for I am told there are thousands of such books on the market,—and lays it to heart and practises its precepts, will be a devil of a fellow. He will never take "No" for an answer, —"The whole object of Salesmanship is to change Negatives into Affirmatives,"—he will be a master of the art of "getting the customer into a mood of desire,"—and in the end he will go anywhere and sell anything. He will persuade Eskimos to buy ice-cream freezers, and do a lively trade in Ceylon with fur-lined overcoats. He will sell pictures to the blind and gramophones to the deaf; he will fill every house in the country with things the household does not want, and would be better without. Such is the power of the sublime modern art of salesmanship—an art which Mr Casson does not hesitate to rank with the highest arts. "Is it not a fact of human nature that not one of us ever appreciates anything, not even the gift of life itself, until some writer or orator or salesman compels us to do so?" That is very finely put. Almost he persuades us to forsake all humbler callings and embrace this noble profession, to sally forth among our fellows with the splendid slogan on our lips: "Let us then be up and doing somebody."

But—as I have said already—the whole thing will collapse if too many people read books like Mr Casson's, and begin to learn the ingenious tricks by which we are wheedled, cajoled, or bluffed into buying things we do not want, or rather into wanting things we do not need and cannot afford. I rather think that everybody who wants to avoid bankruptcy should study salesmanship. It is, as I told my correspondent at the beginning, a much more useful subject than sailing-ships. More exciting; more adventurous.

A LOST PLEASURE

To satisfy your curiosity at once—the pleasure I allude to is the pleasure of being shocked; a delight in which the Victorian era appears to have indulged without restraint. I happened the other day to be glancing over the first series of *Poems and Ballads* and reflecting on the tremendous uproar that shook the welkin when this classic made its original appearance. I doubt whether any other single volume ever brought upon its author an opprobrium so heavy and so immediate. All the respectability of the most respectable era in history became, in a moment, shrill and vituperative. Swinburne awoke one morning to find himself infamous. This abominable young man was held to have overleaped all the fences and torn down all the veils. In politics he was a red republican (the word "bolshevik" had not yet been invented), in religion he was an atheist and a blasphemer, in morals he was lower than the beasts. The publisher of the book shrank appalled before the fury of an outraged public, and withdrew his name; a new title-page had to be inserted in the volume, bearing the name of another, more courageous but far less reputable publisher. On the other hand, to insurgent youth the voice of the new poet was as the voice of a trumpet. He was the flaming soul of all revolt. This was in the sixties of last century. I cannot claim to write about the hubbub from personal recollection—as a matter of fact I was not alive at the time—but when I was a boy at school the tradition lingered; Swinburne was still thought of as a youthful rebel against whatsoever things are of good report. and we read him surreptitiously, feeling very daring and advanced. And to-day! To-day this fiery leader of revolt is looked upon by the young people as merely one of the dear old mid-Victorians, a highly respectable and slightly ridiculous old uncle with quaint side whiskers and prim old-fashioned views.

What an exciting time, one reflects, our elders must have had of it, in that era now so strange and distant! How delightfully full of thrills and shudders their lives must have been! They were so easily shocked in those days, so delicately sensitive to the slightest deviation from the conventional and the respectable in thought or speech. Thackeray, in the preface to *Pendennis*, complained rather bitterly of the limitations laid upon his art by the prudery of the public, and certainly it must have been a difficult time for the writer who was determined to shock nobody. On the other hand, the writer who took a perverse pleasure in shocking must have had an absurdly easy task. Charlotte Brontë shocked the public; George Eliot shocked it; Rossetti shocked it; Darwin shocked it profoundly; Colenso shocked it; even good old Anthony Trollope somehow contrived to shock it. Meredith's *Richard Feverel* was banned by the circulating libraries, and Miss Rhoda Broughton—who seems to us the nursery governess incarnate—was denounced from the pulpit as a corrupter of morals.

Contrast all this with the present time; consider the Herculean labour that would be involved in an effort to shock the public to-day. I think any one who set out to make us shudder—us who have been fed on James Joyce and Aldous Huxley and D. H. Lawrence—would soon sink back exhausted by the vain attempt. We do not know how to be shocked. We have lost the trick of it. We are shock-proof. Anglican clergymen publish articles in the *Hibbert Journal* which would have made our grandfathers' hair stand on end. The staid *Spectator* praises a book by Bernard Shaw which would have set the *Spectator* of Queen Victoria's time clamouring for a prosecution. Our young people read, and discuss freely and openly, books which no decent father of a family in those days would have suffered to pollute his innocent home. There is no need to press the contrast further; the facts are known to everybody.

We are now at the beginning of a reaction in favour of the despised mid-Victorians. In London to-day you will see great prices paid for crystal candelabras, horsehair furniture, antimacassars, wax flowers in glass cases, and other relics of that bygone age. This, of course, is a mere fad, an amusement for people who have more money than is good for them; but I fancy it is a symptom of something deeper. I see, in the literature of to-day, manifest signs that we have come to an end of that silly contempt for the Victorians which, a few years ago, was held for a hall-mark of intelligence. The best of our younger writers are beginning to realize that the Victorian era was a very great era, great in almost every field of human activity, and that we have much to learn from it. Does this mean that we are going to regain the capacity for being shocked?

I think not, and I hope not. I have written much in defence of the Victorians, and in opposition to what seemed to me an altogether foolish underrating of the genious of that time, but I shall never write a page in defence of what in the Victorians is indefensible—their weakness for humbug. They overdid their suppressions and reticences, and modesties. They were entirely too fond of throwing a veil—in the name of the dingy goddess Respectability—over the realities of life. The young people of today, whatever their faults may be, seem to me to be superior, by the possession of certain virtues, to the young people of the Victorian time—the inestimable virtues of candour, sincerity, and intellectual courage. To laugh at humbug wherever it may raise its solemn old head, to be ready to follow an argument whithersoever it may lead, to face the facts of life without fear and without disguise, to desire the truth no matter how unpalatable it may be, to be honest and frank in speech and thought— these are among the root-virtues, and the best of our young people seem to me to possess them in a high degree. I am told that they have lost another inestimable virtue—the virtue of modesty; but what, exactly, does this mean? Do they overstep the modesty of Nature—in which case Nature herself will punish them—or only the modesty of convention, a very different and a much less important thing?

When I plead for a more respectful attitude towards the Victorian era, therefore, I do not at all mean that we should return to the drawing-room manners of *Cranford* or to the limitations deplored by Thackeray. In those respects, I think we ought to be happy to have escaped from so stuffy an atmosphere into the freer air of to-day. It is for quite other reasons that I find the Victorians admirable and worthy of respectful study; reasons which I find it exceedingly difficult to compress into a few words.

A study of the Victorian writers reveals the fact that the era was, beyond all others, the era of hope. It inherited, from the days of the French Revolution, the rapture of the forward view. It hoped for the cessation of wars among civilized nations, for a spread of internationalism. It hoped for a general increase of wealth, and a more just distribution of wealth, and the gradual disappearance of poverty. It hoped for a steady improvement of public health through the activities of preventive medicine. It hoped for a steady improvement in morals and religion. It hoped for the conquest of ignorance by universal education. It was immensely hopeful. And this era of hopefulness led the way, through a series of bitter disappointments, to the crowning disappointment of all, the catastrophe of 1914. "So this is what all your hoping comes to," men said. Every single expectation of betterment cherished by the preceding century had proved illusory.

So it was small wonder that, when the war was over, we found ourselves living through an age of disenchantment, of disillusionment. The world had supped its full of horrors; the bottom had been knocked out of all Utopian dreams; let us never again be tricked by vain hopes—let us eat and drink, for to-morrow we die. That was the mood of the moment; it is not a mood that can last, but while it does last it is bitter.

If I read aright the signs of the times, we are already beginning to emerge from that black cloud. After all, the world must go on, and it cannot go on without some notion of the path it wants to tread and the goal it wants to reach. We must live; and we cannot live without hope. There was much that was absurd in the Victorian attitude to life; Mr Lytton Strachey and his numerous disciples may be counted on to prevent us from forgetting it. (What preposterous figures of fun we, in our turn, shall be to the Lytton Stracheys of fifty years hence!) The reason why, despite what was ridiculous in them, we are in for a reaction in favour of the Victorians, is that their hopes were hopes that we can still cherish, despite the savage interruption of the war; that their ideals were, after all, sound and sane ideals for which we can still live and work.

A NEW CHARITY

THE other day a man stopped me in the street and told me that my last article had done him good. Making a desperate effort to remember what my last article had been about, and not succeeding, I could only murmur that he must surely be mistaken; it was somebody else's article he was thinking of. But no, he said, it was mine, and it had done him good. There was, of course, only one honourable thing to do, and I did it: I offered him my profuse apologies, assured him that it had been quite unintentional, and promised to be more careful in the future. He accepted my statement—with some bewilderment, I thought—and the incident passed off without any personal fracas.

I think he deserved great credit for his self-restraint; for we are all driven to thoughts of dark deeds when we meet somebody whom we suspect of deliberately trying to do us good. Miss Maude Royden, in one of her sermons, remarks that it is a very evil thing to try to set a good example; she says that if you are conscious that somebody is doing something on purpose to set you a good example, "it gives a certain chill to your feelings about that person." A chill!—I should rather think it did. But it is anything but a chill, it is a burning fury of resentment, that we are apt to feel when we are conscious that somebody is doing something, or saying something, with no other design than to do us good.

A few years ago, in a tramcar in Melbourne, a man took a revolver from his pocket, without warning, and fired at another man who had just boarded the car. (Luckily his hand was very unsteady at the time, and the bullet buried itself in the woodwork.) When he was arrested, and questioned as to the motive of his attack, all he could say was that the fellow "looked like one of them social reformers." I hope it is not necessary to say that I have no sympathy whatever with that man. He was sent to jail, and he richly deserved it. He had judged by appearances, a thing we ought never to do. He might have killed a perfectly innocent person. The doctors tell me there is an obscure disease of the liver, which, when it becomes chronic, will make any one look like a social reformer. He ought to have made sure of his ground before allowing his passions to get the better of him.

That, however, is by the way. What I was going to say was that this resentment, though perfectly natural to our fallen humanity, can be, and must be, overcome; otherwise what will become of the various organizations which we see springing up on all sides of us, organizations whose sole purpose is to do some good to somebody? How can they do good unless somebody will consent to be done good to?

An American reformer—or have I dreamed this?—who admires the work of the Little Sisters of the Poor, has established a new order which is called The Little Brothers of the Rich. Its object is to encourage generosity and liberality and unselfishness on the part of the wealthy. Each member is sworn to share and mollify the trials of abounding wealth. He quails at no sacrifice for the sake of the rich; he gives their horses exercise, he sails as ballast on their yachts; he even uses his own inside to keep their wines and victuals warm. He devotes his life to the succouring of the rich. There is a grandeur about this idea, but it does not go far enough.

What I want to see established is a Society For Being Done Good To. I feel certain that unless this is set up, and that at no distant date, a number of excellent and amiable societies, leagues, clubs, associations, fellowships, guilds and brotherhoods will have to close their doors, for lack of raw material.

You think the danger is negligible? Well, listen to this. There is a world-wide organization—I must not give its real name, but, since it had its birth in America, that land of idealists, let us call it the Uplifters. I was privileged to be present, a little while ago, at a meeting of a branch which had just been established in an Australian city. Now the purpose of this great organization is to Do Some Good; and each branch is supposed to determine, in view of the local conditions, what particular good it shall do. At the meeting I attended, various projects were mooted. One member proposed the distribution of books among taxi-drivers, to occupy their leisure; but this, we were informed, was already being done by the P.W.C.L. Another proposed a soup-kitchen for the hairpin-makers, who have been thrown out of work by the prevalent fashion of shingling. But this, it seemed, the Z.S.K.C. were dealing with. Courses in voice-production for newsboys were suggested, but too late—the A.Y.M.L. had it in hand already. Manicure sets for retired washerwomen—no; the White Life League had that in hand.

Sunday picnics in the country for decayed university professors
—no; the Ethical Reformers had met that crying need. My
memory is not very good, and I am not sure that these were precisely the schemes suggested; anyhow, I know that one suggestion after another had to be turned down; and it was when the
ninth, or perhaps it was the tenth, was rejected that I saw the
urgent necessity for a Society For Being Done Good To.

Cain has been held up to obloquy because he asked, "Am I
my brother's keeper?" Surely there is a good deal to be said for
the practical sense of the question. Obviously, we cannot all be
one another's keepers. Obviously, if my brother will not consent
to be kept, I cannot, without a flagrant violation of his rights, constitute myself his keeper. We preach the ideal of self-sacrifice,
but if we are to sacrifice ourselves for others, it seems clear that
others must allow us to sacrifice ourselves for them. "If it wasn't
for us blokes," said the criminal to the warder, "there would be
no billets for you blokes." If it were not for the selfish people,
there would be nothing for the unselfish people to expend their
unselfishness upon. You see that, don't you? Very well then. We
—the Society—will be a body of persons prepared to be frankly
selfish; you shall expend upon us the treasures of your unselfishness. By means of us, you shall keep bright your generous impulses, which might otherwise grow rusty. You shall indulge,
through us, your passion for self-sacrifice. Day after day, we
shall provide you with the comfortable consciousness that you are
doing good. (It will be objected, of course, that in thus hurling
ourselves into the breach we are displaying the noblest kind of
unselfishness, and are thus defeating our own ends. I brush these
sophistries aside.)

The subscription will be ten guineas per annum for a full
member. Some philanthropic body will, of course, pay the fees
for us. We shall certainly need a good deal of money. Think of
the enormous dinners we must eat, that the dietetic reformers
may preach to us and do us good! Think of our monstrous consumption of cigars, if the Anti-Tobacco League is to get its full
measure of fun out of reforming us!

I foresee that we shall be a happy, carefree company. We
shall have no business worries. Many of the philanthropic bodies
I have in mind are apt to be called busy-bodies, and are often told
rudely to mind their own business. That is where we shall come
in. We shall not tell them to mind their own business; we shall
invite them to mind ours. Let them wreak on us their passion
for interference. Let them take full control of our affairs; we

are here for that purpose. We hand over to them all our responsibilities. . . .

When Taine, the illustrious French critic and historian, was visiting England, a lady leant across the dinner-table one evening and asked him, "And pray, M. Taine, what is your plan for saving the world?" "Madam, I have no plan for saving the world," said the astonished Frenchman; and the lady looked disappointed. That night, before going to bed, Taine made a memorandum in his notebook, to the effect that in England everybody is expected to have a plan for saving the world, and that no Englishman is capable of understanding the French attitude of serene detachment. The observation was scarcely just to either nation. The Englishman may have a passion for saving the world, but he refuses to be saved himself; there is a prickly individualism about him which resents interference, even though it be obviously for his own good. "Mind your own business" is a thoroughly English maxim. The recalcitrant Englishman declining to be saved is one of the sights of history. On the other hand, serene detachment is hardly a French trait. Revolutionary France had a passion for saving the world, if ever a people had; she preached her new doctrines to all the nations and sent her armies forth in all directions in a fierce fury of doing good; but the other nations—and especially England—sullenly refused to be done good to. Most Germans, when the war began, believed that they were going to do good to all the world by imposing on it the splendid German ideals. For these ideals they were prepared to fight till all was blue—but it must be Prussian blue. The rest of the world fought to defend its right to choose its own colours. It is a very deep-rooted instinct—not English, not French, but human—this instinct for home rule, this stubborn reluctance to be done good to.

And so, coming back full-circle to our starting-point, you see why I was distressed and dismayed by the mild reproach of that man in the street. And since this is by way of being a valedictory address—since the patient readers of this book are about to be given a well-deserved rest—I think I may be allowed to end on a personal note. If I have abused my privilege, if I have ever used my desk as a pulpit, if I have lapsed at any time into the pompous pontifical manner—I apologize. If I have preached, I am sorry; to err is human, and it is dreadfully easy to slip into the all but universal heresy of believing that you know, better than your neighbour does, what is good for your neighbour. In brief, if any of these essays has done anybody any good, I can but express my regret for the unfortunate accident.

SATURDAY MORNINGS

ON SHEEP AND GOATS

MR ALDOUS HUXLEY's division of the human race into "the drunks and the sobers" strikes me as useful. Let us drop that worn-out distinction between classicism and romanticism; this is a much more fruitful method of distinguishng. Let us no longer say that Ben Jonson upheld the classical ideal in a romantic age; let us say, simply, that he was a sober among the drunks. Shakespeare has a way of kicking to pieces any category you try to confine him in, but among his contemporaries the distinction holds: Marlowe was a drunk, Webster was a drunk, Ford was a drunk, —Ben Jonson was for sobriety all the time. So, too, with other periods and other nations. Voltaire was a sober, Rousseau was a drunk. Stendhal was a sober, Victor Hugo and Alfred de Musset were drunks. Dr Johnson was a sober, in a society of sobers: Gibbon, Goldsmith, Richardson, Fielding,—it was a sober age. Jane Austen was a sober, Charlotte Brontë was a drunk. Scott was a sober who at times pretended to be a drunk. Thackeray was a sober, Dickens a drunk. Peacock was a sober; his friend Shelley was a drunk; that is what makes their letters to one another so piquant. Peacock's disciple, Mr Huxley himself, is a sober; so was Anatole France; so is Mr Lytton Strachey. Against these I could set the names of several eminent living drunks; but, frankly, I am afraid to. If I wrote that "Mr So-and-so is a drunk," and he took action against me for libel, he would win his case, because no jury of good men and true could ever be got to understand that the word was used in a strictly Huxleyan sense. (As a matter of fact, of course, some of the most eminent drunks have been strict teetotallers.)

Well, I prefer the drunks myself; and I suppose it is the same with you. I would not exchange one Shelley or one Blake for all the Addisons and Popes and Johnsons that have been since the world began. The cool, rational, well-balanced minds, the dispassionate spectators of life, the men of orderly thought and tranquil temper,—let us thank Heaven for them; they have given us great gifts—but not the greatest. Not theirs the lips to be touched with fire; not theirs the winged word. In the highest genius there is ever a somewhat of wildness, of extravagance, of disorderliness. The sobers are well worth listening to, with their sane, sage, shrewd, sagacious commentary on life; but they must not expect us to listen to them when there is a drunk in the room. We have ears for none but him.

This habit of labelling, classifying, putting tidily away in pigeon-holes, is one that grows on me with advancing years. I must strive against it. I once tried to prove that all literature could be divided into four classes—exactly four, no more and no less; whereupon various correspondents promptly took me to task, asserting that my four classes overlapped, or that Shakespeare or Mr Edgar Wallace or somebody would not fit into any of my pigeon-holes, or that in some other way the classification was imperfect. (Imperfect!—I should rather think it was!) To-day the bad habit is strong upon me once more. I have been proving, to my own satisfaction, that all human minds may be divided into two classes; and that the division becomes conspicuous in times like these—times of confusion and disaster. In such times all men are either Neutrals or Interventionists.

I find a perfect example of this division in the seventeenth century. Milton as a young man dedicated the whole of himself to the high task of becoming a great poet. As a preliminary training he buried himself in books and made himself one of the greatest scholars of his time—not for the sake of scholarship, but because he believed that scholarship was part of the essential armour of the poet. And so, with noble self-restraint, he held himself aloof from the writing of poetry until he should have fitted himself for the writing of the greatest kind of poetry; if he had died young we should remember him by a mere handful of verses—perfect verses in their way, but their way was far from what he himself regarded as the great way. Then, when he was travelling in Italy, educating himself and exchanging compliments with the best Italian poets, and thinking hard about the subject of the great poem he meant to write, something happened that changed the whole course of his life. He heard that the Puritan revolution had broken out; and he thought it shameful that he should be abroad, cultivating his mind, while his countrymen were fighting for their liberties. He had not the neutral mind; he was a born interventionist. He hastened home and plunged into the fray; he laid his singing robes aside for twenty years, and dedicated all the fierce ardour of his mind to the defence with his pen of the cause of Puritanism. The many volumes of his prose works stand on our shelves—unread for the most part—as the record of his intervention in the practical affairs of his time. It was only when the war was over, the cause he loved defeated, and intervention no longer practicable that he allowed himself to return to the dream of his youth. That the beaten, blind, and scarred old warrior was able after all that fighting to sit down and write the three immortal poems that place him among the world's greatest poets is one of the miracles of history. If Puritanism had kept the flag flying for a dozen years longer we should have had no *Paradise Lost* and no *Samson Agonistes*, because Milton could not have written poetry while there was any fighting to be done. He would have died in harness. He was an interventionist to the backbone.

For the other, the neutral type of mind, look at Milton's great contemporary, Sir Thomas Browne. (I have just been reading him in the new and beautiful edition which Mr Geoffrey Keynes has edited for us in a perfectly satisfying manner.) It is impossible to imagine any books more free from marks of the furious storms of the years in which they were written. The *Religio Medici*, with its serene beauty, its meditative tranquillity, was printed in 1642; I have a wretched memory for dates, but I think I learned at school that that was the year of the battle of Edgehill, and if so it must have been about the most exciting year in English history. The Civil War went raging on; Marston Moor was fought, and Naseby; but Browne, apparently, heeded nothing of all that—he was too busy reading the proofs of his *Pseudodoxia Epidemica*, or *Vulgar Errors*, all about ancient superstitions in the matter of griffins, basilisks, and mandrakes. The King's head fell on the scaffold: Browne took no notice—he was just on the point of publishing his *Urn-Burial*, the most perfect piece of music in English prose, woven round ancient modes of sepulture. When everybody else in England was taking sides with the utmost violence, Browne was writing *The Garden of Cyrus*, discussing the plans of ancient gardens, and the mystical properties of the number five. There is no finer example in literature of a mind absolutely detached from public affairs. On a sinking ship Browne would have been shaping beautiful sentences and weighing the advantages of a semi-colon and a comma.

Come nearer to our own times and look at the remarkable figure of John Ruskin: a man meant by nature, you would say to write books like *Modern Painters* and *Stones of Venice,* to discourse eloquently on painting and sculpture and architecture and literature, to open men's eyes to the beauty of art and the beauty of nature. A high-priest of beauty, you would have said as you read his early books; a man whose function it is to stand apart and aloof from the rush and roar of material existence. But it was not to be. Ruskin was an interventionist; he could not help himself; he was forced, by the inner compulsion of his soul, to stop writing art criticism and to write, instead, *Unto This Last* and other furious assaults on the economists of his day. A famous passage from *Fors Clavigera* is illuminating. "For my own part, I will put up with this state of things, passively, not an hour longer. I am not an unselfish person, nor an evangelical one; I have no particular pleasure in doing good; neither do I dislike doing it so much as to expect to be rewarded for it in another world. But I simply cannot paint, nor read, nor look at minerals, nor do anything else that I like, and the very light of the morning sky, when there is any—which is seldom, nowadays, near London—has become hateful to me, because of the misery that I know of, and see signs of, where I know it not, which no imagination can interpret too bitterly." Have you read that astonishing contribution to chaos, the book from which these sentences are taken? It is a book unique in its beauty and horror; the portrait, self-painted, of a noble mind distraught; an interventionist mind, not trained for effective intervention, and driven mad by the consciousness of his ineffectiveness. (Perhaps Ruskin's madness was the finest of all his sermons; the fact that our world is a world in which men like Ruskin and Swift go mad with indignation should provide a text for thousands of sermons.) Swift was another interventionist; while Shakespeare was a neutral—there is nothing in all his plays to indicate that, as he looked forth on the dark and troubled spectacle of life, he was ever for a moment tempted to be anything else but an impartial spectator; there are plenty of passages to show that he was fully conscious of the cruelty and injustice around him; but he sits above the dust and clang of life, aloof, detached, neutral. . . . Shelley was an interventionist—Keats was a neutral. Thomas Hardy was a neutral; Mr Shaw is an incorrigible interventionist. But why should I give more names? You can go on, separating the sheep from the goats, as long as the subject interests you; the game is an easy one.

My own trouble is that I am not sure which are the sheep and which are the goats. Was Milton the more admirable for being an interventionist, or would it have been better if he had devoted those twenty years of storm and fire to the writing of immortal verse? Would Browne have served humanity better if he had put aside, for a time at least, the writing of beautiful prose and joined the Royalist army, either with sword or pen? Do you wish that Shakespeare had taken sides?—or that Shelley had left good and evil to fight it out while he devoted himself to the weaving of lovely verse? Did Ruskin—to put it bluntly—do any good by withdrawing his mind from the contemplation of beauty in art and nature, and shattering himself in a vain attempt to remould the world? Finally, to bring it home to ourselves, should we, at this moment of chaos and confusion, confronted with the spectacle of a world of misery, throw aside all music and pictures and books, except books about economics, the one subject into which we ought to be hurling ourselves with a fierce determination to know and understand, that we may presently take a hand in the bettering of the world?

I don't know the answers to these painful questions. I have a feeling that it all depends on the kind of mind that Heaven has given you; and that if you have a neutral mind you have to be content with neutrality, even though it may look callous. This one thing I do know—that our civilization would be infinitely poorer to-day if there had not been, in the past, minds of both types; if all men had persisted in trying to reform the world; and if nobody had been content to sit aloof, writing poems or plays or stories, painting pictures, carving statues, composing music, keeping the flame of the spirit alight when all the winds of the world were conspiring to put it out.

MY ROMAN ADVENTURE

A VALUED member of my family was not feeling very well, and it had become my morning duty to go to a place—about two miles away—where I could buy a bottle of homogenized milk, which, as all the world knows, is the thing to drink when you are not feeling very well. My way led past the vast church of Santa Maria Maggiore, past the little church of Saint Praxed's (where Browning's bishop ordered his tomb), and past a little bookshop where I used to buy my penny dreadfuls. On the morning I am telling you about I bought one of these little books—in two volumes at threepence each, with pictures on the cover so lurid that the bookseller looked at me with kindly scorn when I selected it—called *L'Isola del Tesoro*, by Roberto Luigi Stevenson. (It is all about pirates and buried treasures—just the kind of thing I like. The villain of the yarn is a formidable cook with one leg, named Giovanni Silver, who was once quartermaster with the celebrated Capitano Flint. These pirates are the real thing; they sing, when not engaged in the practice of their profession, a rousing chorus—

> *Quindici uomini sul cassero dell' Uomo Morto,*
> *Ho-ho-ho, e una bottiglia di rhum!*

Where have I read something like this before?)

(In Italy, I may mention in passing, the traveller often comes across things like this,—things that awaken faint echoes of something seen or heard in a former existence. In the book-shops, for instance, one sees books bearing the name of Giorgio Bernardo Shaw, or of Giuseppe Conrad, or even of G. Shakespeare. It is the same with the picture-theatres; one day I noticed a poster announcing the imminent arrival of *La Lettera Rossa*, by "il grande romanziero americano, Nat Harriel Haw Horn." . . . Who is this Mr Horn, anyhow?) Having secured this admirable work, I trudged on and bought my bottle of homogenized milk. Then I walked down to the Via Nazionale, because I wanted a warm bath.

Some people think too much time has been spent on teaching children Latin, and also that there has been too much talk about the grandeur that was Rome. Well, I am not an historian nor an antiquarian; all I want to say is that in the matter of warm baths Rome seems to me to lead the world.

Why did I want a warm bath in the middle of the morning? The question is perhaps a trifle intimate; still, it is natural enough, and I shall not resent it. The fact is, that in Italian hotels—at least, in the inexpensive ones, the only ones I know anything about—it is not altogether convenient to have a bath. It is quite possible, of course, but it involves too much ceremonial. When you mention, in the evening, that you would like a bath in the morning, the announcement seems to throw the whole establishment into commotion. Various members of the staff have to be told, it seems, that the Signore desires a bath. They shout the news to one another along corridors. Three times during the evening someone comes and asks you at what hour you want to have your bath. After you are in bed, there is a knock at your door, and a voice assures you that your bath will be ready at the desired hour. In the morning you awake early to hear the chambermaid telling the boots about it. There is a great scurrying to and fro till the hour of fate strikes. When it does, there is an agitated knocking at your door; your bath, you are told, is absolutely ready. You proceed to the bathroom, followed by a procession bearing soap and towels. Once you have locked yourself in, your attendants rush away to tell the rest of the hotel that the Signore is now having his bath. You have an idea that your fellow-lodgers have been wakened early to hear the great news. When you go into the dining-room for early lunch, you quickly perceive that the waiters have heard. They look at you and at one another, as who should say, "There is the Signore who has had a bath." As a matter of fact your bath has been quite a success, but you quail, rather, at the thought of going through all this again. It would be too exciting for the proprietor, the boots, the chambermaid, the cook, the lift-boy, the head-waiter, and the other waiters. Have I sufficiently explained why I went to the Via Nazionale to get a warm bath?

So I went in, planked down my two lire—approximately sixpence—deposited my hat, coat, and bottle of homogenized milk in a waiting-room, and was shown by a silent and bulky lady, carrying an enormous towel and a tiny piece of soap, into a spacious room containing a marble bath obviously designed for the use of a hippopotamus. She turned on a tap, and the whole water-supply of Rome would soon be exhausted, one felt, if two such taps were turned on at once. When the lake was half full of steaming water, she turned off the tap and retired without uttering a syllable—a pleasant contrast to the garrulity of the hotel staff.

Then I had my bath. I am often accused of being too personal; I shall therefore pass abruptly to the moment when, in the midst of my wallowing, I realized that it was half-past ten, and that I had only half an hour in which to dress, go out and buy a black tie, and cross half Rome to get to the Vatican, where I had an appointment with the Pope at eleven.

You think that sounds rather magnificent. I meant it to. But as a matter of cold fact, to be granted an audience by the Pope does not imply that one is at all an important person. Travellers come back to Australia and speak about their audience with the Pope, meaning you to believe that they had a heart-to-heart talk with his Holiness. What it really means is that they managed to get a ticket for a certain ceremonial at the Vatican in which the Pope takes part. Such tickets are not to be bought for money, but any friend connected with the Church can, I understand, get one for you without much trouble. You see the Pope, and that is all. It will be a more troublesome matter, I fancy, if you wish to converse with him. I had no desire to converse with him; I was not conscious of having any valuable piece of information to impart to him; neither was I consumed with missionary zeal like a fellow-countrywoman of mine, who was surely the most enterprising heroine of modern times; for she went to Rome with the express purpose of converting the Pope to Presbyterianism. I have often wondered what would have happened if she had succeeded, and the Pope, being infallible, had become a Presbyterian, and announced to an astonished Church that its true head was in Edinburgh. The lady, however, was not successful; on the contrary, the Pope spoke to her with such tolerance, generosity, and humility, that she conceived an enthusiastic admiration for him and ultimately joined the Church of Rome. (You will probably not believe this story.)

Well, to go back to my bath. The acquaintance by whose good graces I had obtained my ticket had informed me that if you were granted an audience by the Pope you must, of course, wear evening dress. Now, for some occult reason, I have a strong repugnance to going about a city, buying homogenized milk, in evening dress. You may not sympathize, and I admit the feeling is inexplicable; but there it is. There are only, so far as I can remember, three classes of people who wear evening dress in the

daytime. First, German hangmen (but only when they are acting in the way of business); secondly, university students going up
for an examination, also in Germany; thirdly, waiters, all the
world over. It was not at all likely that, in Rome, I should be
mistaken for a German hangman. I was not even likely to be
mistaken for a German university student. Therefore the
altogether ignoble feeling at the bottom of my consciousness must
have been the fear of being mistaken for a waiter. Why any one
should not wish to be mistaken for a waiter passes my comprehension. They also serve who only stand and wait. Is there any
more honourable work in the world than feeding the hungry?—
that is what waiters do. No one who has travelled but must feel
respect and affection for the good-humoured, polite, friendly and
helpful waiter, who tries so hard to make the exile feel at home.
An admirable class of men, on the whole. Why should anybody
fear to be mistaken for one of them? And yet—well, there you
are. There is no explaining the mysteries of the human heart
and its absurdities. I decided to risk a sac suit, but felt that a black
tie was the least I could do. So I went out, found the right kind
of shop not far away, bought a black tie, hailed a taxi, and said,
"The Vatican, and will you kindly step on the gas?" which he
did, and brought me to my destination in plenty of time. And
the first person I saw, when I got past the Swiss Guards and into
the reception hall, was an American in a chocolate-coloured suit
with a bright blue tie.

I left my bottle of homogenized milk with a door-keeper,
feeling that to enter the Vatican with, under my arm, something
that looked suspiciously like a bomb wrapped in an old newspaper was hardly respectful. The ceremony lasted for more than
an hour; and when I came out, what I had seen had chased the
thought of homogenized milk out of my mind; I forgot to re-
trieve it from the door-keeper; and it was only when I got
home that the loss was discovered.

What would you have done about it? That is the question
to which I have been, all this time, leading up. Would you have
gone back to the Vatican, and made a fuss, and possibly set a lot
of Cardinals hunting round for a bottle of homogenized milk,
price fourpence? For me, I decided that the door-keeper would
probably think I had left it intentionally as a present for the
Pope; and I let it go at that. Fourpence, after all, even with
the addition of cab-fare and the price of an unnecessary black tie,
was a small price to pay for a memorable experience.

A LAPSE AT LOUVAIN

YESTERDAY forenoon, in the presence, and under the eyes of a king, a queen, three cardinals, nine bishops, a Papal legate, and a number of distinguished scholars of various nationalities, I fell asleep. But to explain how the disaster happened I shall have to begin at the beginning. . . . Know, then, that I am writing this at Louvain, a Belgian city of which you will doubtless remember having heard many things, all of them tragic, in the early days of the war. Unless your memory is shorter than it has any right to be, you have not forgotten that this was one of the martyred cities of Belgium, one of those places which the invader picked out for special ferocity, in order to terrorize the whole country by a memorable exhibition of what he could do if he liked. And afterwards, if the occupied country became at all restive, he would hold up a threatening finger and say, in effect, "Beware! Remember Louvain!" Now that the war is over and we are all for peace and concord and international amity, some people may think it unfortunate that the Belgians—and not the Belgians only—find a difficulty in dropping the habit of remembering Louvain; but I am not of that opinion. For the sake of the world's peace, I say, let us forgive but not forget; rather let the whole world remember what happened here, in this place of terrible memories; when we forget these things we shall have forgotten what war is really like, and be the more ready to slide into another conflict. . . . That, however, is a digression. Louvain was famous, before the war, for its old and great university, one of the greatest in the world. That noble seat of learning the Germans sought to destroy; they wrecked its buildings and burned to the ground its magnificent library. Happily, a university is not one of the things that any material power can destroy, because a university is a spiritual and not a material entity. You may wreck the buildings in which it is housed—nothing easier than to blow them all sky-high—but its inner self, the soul of it, being indestructible, lives on and bides its time. Yesterday the Royal University of Louvain, "re-risen from storm and fire, immortal and unmarred," celebrated the 500th anniversary of its foundation; and delegates came to join in the festivities from the ends of the earth. As a Belgian newspaper remarks this morning, there was even a delegate from Australia!

There was none from Germany. No German university was invited to send a representative. An American said to me yesterday that he thought it was time the Belgians buried the hatchet, and that in his opinion invitations ought to have been sent to Germany. I ventured to reply that the Belgians had done a much kinder thing in not sending invitations to Germany. Suppose invitations had been sent and accepted, what would have been the feelings of the German delegates when allusions were made to the sacking of Louvain?—and if, by a miracle of self-restraint, no such allusions had been made—if, when we were being shown round the new library, nobody had said a word about why a new library had been needed—would not this marked reticence have been more embarrassing still to the representatives of the nation that did the damage? No; the friendliest thing was to let the Germans stay quietly at home on this joyful occasion.

Most of us foreigners went out by a special train from Brussels in the morning—it is only half an hour's run—walked to the new university buildings, and were directed to a "vestiaire," where we donned the garb suitable to the occasion; then we took our places, according to the antiquity of the universities we represented, for a solemn procession round the town. The whole population seemed to have turned out to see us; our whole route was lined with curious and (I hope) admiring crowds. Certainly they can rarely have seen such an extraordinary mixture of colours. The reporter on one of the Brussels papers this morning grows quite excited on this point; he says our garments formed a delightful contrast to the "banal uniformity of the epoch," and compliments us on our "medieval magnificence." I felt considerably uplifted when I read these enthusiastic remarks; but I was let down with a bump when the writer continued:—"Les vieillards vénérables passent; ils ont d'amples manteaux rouges, verts, jaunes, mauves." I have no objection to being called a "vieillard," but "vénérable!" Have I come to that? On second thoughts, however, I see that I am not one of the old gentlemen alluded to, for my ample mantle was neither red, green, yellow, nor mauve. I have lowly tastes; a simple purple contents me. . . . Anyhow, we were a motley crew, and we provided each other with a variegated spectacle when the procession ended in a vast

lecture theatre, with King Albert and Queen Elizabeth sitting
on a dais, surrounded by the heads of the university and by princes
of the Church.   And then, when we had taken our places, the
speeches began.   Then, also, my troubles began.

It was not that the speeches were dull.   True, nobody tried
to be humorous—perhaps it was hardly the time or place for face-
tiousness—and perhaps they even went a little too far in the opposite direction.   But I think I never in all my life heard a speech
that ended so eloquently or so effectively as that of M. Bédier,
the philologist, who brought the greetings of the French Academy
to the University of Louvain.   He had spoken for about twenty
minutes on the past glories of the institution without making a
single reference to the war or to King Albert; he concluded with
a sentence which ran something like this:—"All the universities
of Belgium have not had the honour of nourishing such great men
as those I have mentioned, but all of them have, with Louvain,
contributed to the formation of those spiritual forces which, at
the moment of unjust aggression, ranked themselves at the call
of your King like a splendid knighthood around him, and worthy
of him."   The effect of this sudden conclusion, spoken by an
elderly Frenchman with amazing fire and energy, was quite indescribable.   The right word had been spoken; France had brought
to Belgium, and to her hero, an adequate tribute; nothing could
have more exactly fitted the occasion.   The King jumped up and
grasped the orator's hand as he was retiring to his place; the
Queen followed suit; the whole audience seemed to go off its
head with enthusiasm, and shouted itself hoarse.   It sounds
rather ludicrous, perhaps, but as a matter of fact it was most
moving.

I am a long time coming to the painful incident alluded to at
the beginning of this article.   You will, of course, understand
one's reluctance to approach the shameful subject.   Well, then—
to get the thing over—somebody, whose name I forget, made a
long and, as it seemed to me, rather tedious speech in French, in
which he told the story of Louvain during the Middle Ages.   Then,
having spoken for twenty minutes, he paused, and—began to say
it all over again in Flemish!   As every one in Belgium understands French, this seemed superfluous; but I suppose he wanted
to pay a compliment to the Flemings present.   Now Flemish, in
print, seems a very easy language for English-speaking people
to master.   A place where trams stop is called a "tramstilstand,"
which seems to require no great linguistic powers to decipher.

But spoken Flemish is another matter; and of this long speech I did not understand a single word. Have you ever sat through a long speech in a language of which you did not understand a single word? If so, you know how soporific the experience is. If I were a millionaire and suffered from insomnia I think I should hire a man to talk to me in some foreign tongue—preferably Flemish—till I dropped off. Well, this orator talked on and on, and I—suddenly found myself waking with a guilty feeling and looking furtively round to discover, from the faces of my neighbours, whether I had been snoring. "Is it perhaps that you have heard anything?" I whispered to a French priest who sat next me. As he only looked at me uncomprehendingly, and did not smile, I am tempted to hope that my lapse was not conspicuous, or, at any rate, that it was not observed by the King, for whom I have an unbounded respect.

THE BALFOUR-CONRAD QUESTION

A FRIEND—I suppose I must still call him so, though it was by no means a friendly act—has sent me a new book on the Bacon-Shakespeare question, and invites me to comment on it. Heaven forbid that I should introduce into these pages even a whiff of that long-dead controversy, a controversy which has, to quote Sha —I mean, to quote the author of *The Tempest*—an ancient and fish-like smell. In France there was once a noisy little group of persons who sought to prove that Molière wrote none of the plays attributed to him; in Spain there was a group, of similar mentality, sworn to show that Cervantes did not write *Don Quixote*. But neither in France nor in Spain do they pay much heed to such freaks; and both controversies are forgotten save as historical curiosities. The Englishman is not behind either Frenchman or Spaniard in humour, and the Bacon-Shakespeare question would promptly have died of not being taken seriously, had it not been taken up with enthusiasm in America, that hospitable country where all the new religions find asylum, and all the cranks their spiritual home. . . .

No, I am not going to venture, with my feeble argumentative equipment, into the haunts of wild Baconians. I would more hopefully try to persuade a cable-car to run backward than set out to convert a Baconian. But any alienist will tell you that you can sometimes do the patient good, not by arguing with him, but by diverting his thoughts into another channel; if he fancies himself the Emperor of China, it is no use solemnly assuring him that he spells his name differently, or that China is a republic, or that he lacks a pigtail; these arguments, sound as they may be, only make him worse; what you must do is to try to get him interested in stamp-collecting, or politics, or golf, or conchology. So I would say to the fierce Baconian, as gently as possible, "Yes, yes, my dear sir—Bacon, of course it was—careless of me not to have noticed it for myself—and now, suppose we have a little talk about the novels of Joseph Conrad." . . . But—horrible thought

—I have chosen a most unfortunate subject, for the Baconian, if
he takes my advice and turns his attention to these novels, will at
once prove to his entire satisfaction that they were not written by
the person whose name appears on their title pages, but by someone else—probably Lord Balfour. And, after his feats in the
Bacon-Shakespeare affair, he will find this a ridiculously easy task.
For, I say quite seriously, if the authorship of *Hamlet* presents a
problem, the authorship of *Victory* presents a problem ten times
more difficult.

Consider the incredible story we are asked to believe. Teodor
Korzeniowski was born in the Ukraine, in Southern Poland, in
1851. His father, for the part he played in a Polish rebellion, was
banished to Siberia, whither his wife and young Teodor followed
him into exile. At the age of eight the boy was sent back to
Poland, where, under an uncle's care, he spent his boyhood. He
began very early to show a strange longing for the life of a sailor
(though he had never seen the sea). Stranger still, his ambition
was to sail under the British flag (though he knew no English).
In spite of the angry opposition of his relatives, he made his
way to Marseilles, and went to sea—not, until several years had
passed, under the Red Ensign. In 1878 he landed at Lowestoft,
not knowing one word of English. In 1884 he became a natura-
lized Englishman, and a captain in the English Merchant Service.
In 1894 he left the sea, after twenty years of wandering on the
face of the waters, and handed to an English publisher the manuscript of a novel, *Almayer's Folly*, giving his name as "Joseph
Conrad." Three years later W. E. Henley, then editor of the
New Review, accepted for that magazine another novel, *The
Nigger of the Narcissus*, and the name of Conrad was made known
to all who were watching the firmament for new stars. He went
on to write a long succession of books, and in time came to be
regarded as, with the exception of Hardy, the greatest living
novelist writing in English. Such is the strange, wild tale; and
what a tissue of improbabilities—even of downright absurdities—
it is!

All the Shakespeare-Bacon difficulties are here, even the difficulty about the name. The Baconians make a great point of the
various spellings of the Stratford person's name—Shaxper, and so
on—but what is that compared with the difference between
"Teodor Korzeniowski" and "Joseph Conrad"? "Something decidedly fishy about this," our imaginary patient will say. (Being

a good Baconian, he will omit to mention that the boy was christened Teodor Jozef Konrad Korzeniowski.) But that is a mere preliminary. We are asked to believe that half-a-dozen novels of sea-going life, and also that marvellous prose-poem, *The Mirror of the Sea*—a book unique in our literature, sea-folk as we are—were written by a man whose youth was spent, of all places in the world, in Poland, a country without a seaboard; and, to make this miracle seem less miraculous, we are treated to a monstrous story of the Polish lad (who had never seen the sea) yearning for a life on the ocean wave! In *Lord Jim*, and some of the other novels as well, we are given a wonderful reading of the soul, not merely of the sailor-man in general, but of the British sailor-man in particular. It is the British ideal that is always celebrated in these books; and we are asked to believe that they were written by a Slav, who—though he had never met an Englishman—felt mysterious yearnings for the English service! Incredible as this is, worse remains behind. These books, from *Almayer* to *The Rescue*, show masterly power, the power that comes, as all the world knows, only as the result of life-long devotion to the art of writing; and we are asked to believe they were written by a man who never wrote a word for print till he was thirty-six years old! Finally, these books are plainly the work of a consummate master of our noble English speech; and we are asked to believe they were written by a man who knew no English till he was full-grown, and who is described by Mr Lewis Hind, who knew him only after he had become a famous writer, as saying, "I will learn zee English good, well!" In the whole history of literature, can you think of a parallel to this! It is impossible, say the Baconians, that the unlettered Stratford boy should have grown up to write *Hamlet*. It may be so, but—if there are degrees in impossibility—it is a hundred times more impossible that the Cracow schoolboy, who knew no English, should have grown up to write *Nostromo*. And yet, you know, he did; all the impossible and incredible things in the above story are actual facts; it was not Lord Balfour who wrote *Nostromo*. Which seems to show that, after all, marvellous things do happen; and the Stratford boy, in spite of appearances, may have—eh? You see the point, of course.

"Oh, but," you may say, "the cases are not at all alike. There is no mystery about Conrad. He lived and moved among us; his doings were reported by the press; he has been written about by a score of men who knew him well. Henry James lived near him, at Rye, and saw him continually; Mr John Galsworthy gave him encouragement when he was beginning; Mr H. G. Wells was his intimate friend; Mr Ford Madox Hueffer collaborated with him in a couple of novels, and has given us many pages of gossip about him; a full biography, written by one who knew him intimately, has appeared; no one out of Bedlam can doubt that he wrote his own books." Well, had Shakespeare no friends? Did Ben Jonson not know him? Shakespeare was a more genial, sociable sort of man than Conrad and had a far larger circle of acquaintances. True, they did not write about the kind of clothes he wore, because it was not the fashion in Elizabethan times to write personal gossip about the eminent; but they did write enough about him to show that they loved and honoured him, and not one of them breathed a doubt of his being the author of his own plays. Either these poets and playwrights were idiots—which seems unlikely—or they were all in a conspiracy to trick posterity. Apply that idea to the case of Conrad, and imagine some bright spirit, two centuries hence, arguing that Henry James and Mr Galsworthy and Mr Wells and the rest of them were engaged in a dark and secret plot to hoodwink future ages and to conceal the fact that Lord Balfour was a novelist. Preposterous, you say; believe me, not a whit more preposterous than the notion that Ben Jonson wrote his great lines, about his dead friend Shakespeare, with his tongue in his cheek, in order to save my lord Verulam from the suspicion of being a playwright. And, in conclusion, if you say that my choice of Lord Balfour as a possible author of these novels is evidently a joke, and rather a clumsy one, I will lay my hand upon my heart and declare that, having read most of Lord Balfour's writings, and knowing the main facts of his career, I find it decidedly easier to believe that he wrote *Typhoon* than to believe that Bacon wrote *Much Ado*.

I see I have been betrayed into an argument with the Baconians after all. It will not convert any of them, of course; but it may annoy some of them—a gratifying thought—and it may help to prevent some poor innocent young person from joining their silly sect; in which case these words have not been written in vain.

A QUESTION SETTLED

WHO could have dreamed that the great Bacon-Shakespeare controversy was to be settled—settled decisively, settled for ever—by the discovery of some musty old papers in a dusty old cabinet in (of all places in the world) Madrid? Which do you think the more astonishing find—the tomb of King Tutankhamen of Egypt, or these Gondomar papers, of which even the most hardened anti-Baconian, even Sir Sidney Lee himself, has not dared to deny the authenticity? It has long been known that Diego Sarmiento de Acuna, Marquis de Gondomar, Spanish Ambassador in England from 1613 to 1621, was on friendly terms with Francis Bacon, Baron Verulam and Viscount St Albans; what had not hitherto been known or even suspected was that the Englishman and the Spaniard were sharers of one another's most intimate secrets. Who, in his wildest dreams, has ever imagined that a twentieth-century Spanish historical student, rummaging among State papers in search of something which should throw light on the conquest of Peru, would stumble unawares on the key to the greatest enigma in literary history? An explicit statement by Bacon that he, and no other, is the author of the plays—and of the sonnets and the poems as well—has the most imaginative Baconian ever fancied for a moment such an absolutely irrefutable proof of the truth of his theory? I should like to attend, this year, the annual dinner of the Baconian Association. It will be, one may imagine, a somewhat uproarious function, though the hearts of the diners will be saddened by the reflection that it will probably be the last occasion of the kind, there being no further need of a Baconian Association. The stream of white-faced Shakespearians visiting the British Museum to inspect the fatal manuscripts, and going away silent and haggard, is a more painful subject of contemplation. But the critics who will now come forward in shoals, declaring that they have been convinced Baconians from their earliest years, will offer a diverting spectacle.

Of course I cannot here copy out, from these extraordinary

letters, all the passages which bear on the great question. Those
interested—and who can be uninterested?—must read for themselves *The Bacon-Gondomar Correspondence,* edited in a scholarly
manner by Sir Maxwell Clifton, the well-known Baconian. (It
is to be hoped that the publishers will before long see their way
to bring out a less expensive edition; a book of such transcendent importance ought to be made accessible to the poorest reader.)
But a few excerpts will suffice to convince the most hardened
sceptic. Let me say, in passing, that even had these letters contained no allusion to the great secret, they would still be valuable
as a picture of the mind of the great philosopher in a new light.
We think of Bacon as a dry, grave, pompous, sententious personage; but here he unbends delightfully, and writes real letters;
" 'tis a true *Letter,*" says he, "wherein a man expresseth his own
Minde, as if he were discoursing with the Party to whom he
writes in succinct and easy termes." And though he preserves a
sixteenth-century formalism of phrase, and signs himself "your
thrice humble and ready servitor, Fr. Bacon," or else "your Lordship's infinitely obliged friend and servant, Fr. St. Alban, Canc.,"
still you can feel that he is writing to a friend, and writing, for
the most part, as he would have spoken; and that when he says,
"I have made your Friendship so necessary unto me for the con-
tentment of my life that Happiness itself would be a kind of in-
felicity without it," he means what he says. And though he
writes much about the relations between England and Spain,
and about high political matters in general, he is not above humbler
considerations. "I thanke you a thousand times for the *Cepha-
lonia Muscadine* and *Botargo* you sent me." "I send you here-
with a couple of red deere pies, the one *Sir Arthur Ingram* gave
me, the other His Grace of *Buckingham* his cook! I pray you
let me know which is the better season'd." "If you please to
send me a barrel or two of *Oisters,* which we lack here in the
countrie, I promise you they shall be well eaten with a cup of the
best canary," and so forth. There is also a good deal of sheer
gossip. So much by way of introduction.

The first letter that really concerns us is a letter of introduction,
brought to Gondomar by William Howell, an elder brother of
that famous James Howell who wrote one of the most companionable of books, the *Epistolae Ho-Elianae.* "Beseech you, entertain him kindly for my sake; for he hath been a rarely valued
friend of mine this many year, and was, indeed, the only begetter

of those unworthy sonnets that your Lordship was pleased to approve so far beyond their deserving." So there is the vexed question of "Mr W. H." settled at last! And the famous "dark lady" of the sonnets was not Mary Fitton, as some have guessed, but a certain Dorothy Mainwaring, with whom Bacon fell deeply in love, and who behaved badly to him. Writing to Gondomar long after the event, he could take a calm view of the incident. "She was in sooth a most dainty and honey-sweet lady, albeit she could not love me, nor no man else, for long together. For her winning comportment she was fit to be the *Queene of Hearts,* and for beautie I have seene none since that would compare with her, only she did lack *Constancie.* Losing her, I saw the Worlde as it were thro' a darken'd glasse, and writ much and shrewishly concerning all Women, for her sake. And for her sake my Hamlet did roundly be-rate his mother and speak Daggers to the innocent maide Ophelia. At the last I did lively pourtraie her in the person of the Queene Cleopatra, and so having rid my bosom of that vennom I was quickly heal'd again. Howbeit forget her I may not."

The most important letter in the whole collection is the one written just after his sudden fall from place and power; and it is strange to find him concerned not so much with his disgrace as with the dark secret which is known only to himself, to Gondomar, to "Mr B. Iohnson," and to Shakespeare—the secret of his play-writing. "For my late Publick Misfortune, 'tis naught. I was the justest Judge was in *England* this fifty year, and howsoever one that hath a Tooth against me doth prevail for the time, I doubt not but the Coming Age shall do me right. That I took *Bribes,* it concerns me not to deny; 'twas a wise saying of *King Solomon* that '*the fairest diamond hath a flaw in it. . . .*' That which troubles me is the fear lest my ill behaviour in writing of playes and pasquils and other the like fopperies be discovered to the world, and the general conceit of my wisdom suffer thereby. I would fain go down to future ages as one who laboured for the glory of God, the raising of this realm, and the relief of men's estate; and how shall that be, if I be named among the ruffling gentrie of the Playhouse? *Mountaigny* saith wittily, '*that a wise man will not playe the foole before fooles.*' Between friends, these toys and tricks are very well; but in the publick eye, I would fain tread a stately Spanish *pavin* to the end, and not make myself a *Maygame* to the many-headed." He goes on to remind Gondomar how he had chosen "W. Shaxper" to be his dummy, and how this Shaxper had long been accepted as the true author of the plays. "'Twas a pleasant-conceited knave, very merry Companie withal; but shallow-pated; a right *jig-maker*; so as all who knew him marvelled that he should have writ so well." Ben Jonson had guessed the truth, but had been bribed to secrecy; others, however, had suspected something amiss. "At the last, that vile jade, Rumour, did openly proclaim that the *Tempest* was writ by the *Lord Keeper,* whereupon I bade farewell to these apish Fopperies, and dismissed the rogue *Shaxper* (with a full purse) to Stratford, where his home was; and he dying not long after, I procured *Mr Iohnson* to set his name to a paper of verses wherein he praised this *Shaxper,* saying, among other fooleries, that *'he was not of an Age, but for all Time'*; at the which he and I did laugh heartily." He goes on to express a hope that the secret may be kept for fifty years; after that, there will be no danger. "By that time, my Hamlet and my Falstaffe will be clene forgot, and my Name treasured only for the mighty Worke wherein I laboured to show men a new Way to Knowledge. Wherefore, I beseech you, breathe no word to any Soule of these my youthful follies. And I pray you to accept two Barrels of *Colchester oisters,* which were provided for my Lord of *Colchester* himself, therefore I presume they are good and all green finned."

So there you are. Behold the great question settled, once for all—at least, it would be settled, if Bacon had really written these passages. Unfortunately, he did not write them; as you have doubtless already guessed, the Bacon-Gondomar correspondence is a myth, Sir Maxwell Clifton a dream, William Howell and Dorothy Mainwaring creatures of phantasy, and even the Colchester oysters an invention. But my point is—supposing this were all genuine, and the Baconians were thus proved to be right, and Shakespeare finally deposed—after all, what then? What difference would it really make? Think it over, and you will see that it would not matter in the least, and that, in fact, this whole question, over which such oceans of ink have been spilt, is a question about which no wise man should waste a moment's thought. In fact, I have written this frivolous paper as a comment on a very just passage in Benedetto Croce's book, *Ariosto, Shakepeare, and Corneille.* "Even if we grant the unlikely contention that in the not very great brain of the philosopher Bacon there lodged the brain of a very great poet, from which proceeded the Shakespearian drama, nothing would thereby have been discovered or proved. . . . The artistic problem would remain untouched, because that drama remains always the same; Lear laments and imprecates in the same manner, Othello struggles furiously, Hamlet meditates and wavers before the problem of humanity, and the action that he is called upon to take; and in the same manner, all are enwrapped in the veil of Eternity." Do not these words contain the sum and conclusion of the whole matter?

ON DOORS

I HAVE long had it in mind to write something on the subject of doors. And since no new poet has arisen in Australia this week, and no new religion has arrived from America—a momentary lull having occurred, as it were—it may be as well to seize the chance of unbosoming oneself on this momentous topic. Do not, I beseech you, set this down at once as a piece of foppery; don't say, "Here is a pretentious fellow who fancies that he can pass himself off as a genuine essayist by proving that he can write about anything under the sun—even about doors!" Because, you know, that particular accusation—of setting up to be an essayist —would touch me on the raw; for I am one who believes that the essay, if not the highest form of literature, is the most difficult of all; that a good essay is harder to write than a good novel; that the great essayists are rarer than the great poets; that we are like to see another Shakespeare sooner than another Montaigne. I would as soon pretend to be a popular tenor or a successful company-promoter, or a heaven-sent statesman or a billiard champion, as expose myself to the derision of gods and little fishes by trying to pass myself off as a real essayist. Glance through the five volumes of *Modern English Essays* which Mr Ernest Rhys has recently edited for the "Everyman" series, and believe and tremble. Mr Rhys seems to have no clear idea of what an essay really is, and he has included a formidable quantity of rubbish— as he was bound to do if he was to fill five volumes; still, his collection contains enough specimens of the genuine article to show any discerning reader what a rare and exquisite and delightful thing is the art of the essayist. Set up to be an essayist, indeed! *Ah, no more of that, Hal, an thou lovest me!*

I admit there may be some truth in what you say about the test of the genuine essayist being that he can write about anything whatever; but you have chosen the worst possible example. "Even about doors," quotha! As if doors were a very recondite and wellnigh an impossible subject. Why, everybody who has written at all has written about doors. The whole of literature resounds with the slamming of doors. Man has sought out many inventions, but none more significant, none more expressive, none that lends itself more readily to the purposes of poetry and romance and symbol, than this ancient invention of the door. The window is a comparative upstart, a modern device; but the door is coeval with the house itself. The door is the mouth of the house, windows are its eyes; it is possible to live—and even to enjoy life—without eyes, but a mouth is indispensable. So, for uncounted centuries, men contrived to do without windows in their dwellings; but a house without a door is inconceivable. Even a rock, rolled to the opening at night and rolled away in the morning, is in essentials a door: and, though doubtless somewhat cumbrous, it was effective enough, as Odysseus found (if you remember your Homer) during his compulsory sojourn with the Cyclops. And just as the mouth is more expressive than the eyes, in a human face, so is the door more expressive than the window. This aspect of the door—its expressiveness—makes of it a universal symbol. "Then" (if you remember your Bible) "those that were ready went in with him to the marriage, and the door was shut." The door was shut; that phrase could not be bettered by any conceivable elaboration; no other words in the language could express, so simply and tremendously, the sense of finality. The symbolism of the door is in all literature; and the painters, too, have made abundant use of it.

Of course you know De Quincey's famous essay, "On the Knocking at the Door in *Macbeth*." I fancy De Quincey gets considerably more significance out of the incident than Shakespeare ever thought of; still, it is certainly one of the great moments of the play, and probably the second-best knocking at the door in all literature. (The best is in the New Testament; you had better buy a copy and find the passage for yourself.) The best shutting of the door is, I think, the end of Ibsen's *Doll's House*, where the stage direction runs: "From below is heard the reverberation of a heavy door closing." You can spoil the whole play by making the wrong kind of noise at this point; it must not be a bang, as if Nora Helmer were going away in a vulgar tantrum, and would probably think better of it and come back to Mr Helmer to-morrow; it must be a sound of doom, solemn, weighty, unanswerable, final. The act of shutting a door is surely one of the most primitive of all expressions of human emotion. None of Henry James's men or women, I imagine, ever bang a door;

they close it, softly, delicately, with varying degrees of silken subtlety, expressing thereby the finest nuances; it is wonderfully skilful, but we sometimes long as we read him for a plain, honest, crude person like that hero of Hood's,

> Who shut the door with such a slam
> It sounded like a wooden "Damn!"

The romantic possibilities of the door have been understood from very early times. The story of Bluebeard, for instance, is a story of doors; and there is one tale in the *Arabian Nights* which is a perfect riot of doors: it contains a hundred of them. Dumas —I hope you know your Dumas—is full of doors. The three immortal musketeers are for ever hammering at some door or other; for them, a door meant the permanent possibility of adventure. A door is, to the romantic eye, a thing of wonder and mystery; behind it lies who knows what of terrible or joyous, of gallant or sinister. There are two capital doors in Stevenson. Who that has once read of it can forget the Sire de Maletroit's door, left unlatched, which, when the desperate fugitive flung himself against it, swung back on oiled and noiseless hinges, but which, when he was once within, "whipped itself out of his fingers and clanked to, with a formidable rumble"? The other is the door in that rather inferior melodrama *Deacon Brodie*, perhaps, on the whole, the poorest of Stevenson's works (possibly because it was Stevenson's and Henley's); but it has its thrilling moment when the Deacon, having killed a man, goes home and climbs in through his bedroom window, takes up a candle to look at the locked door, which is to prove his alibi, and finds that it has been broken open in his absence. "Open, open, open! Judgment of God, the door is open!"

When is a door not a door? ran the old conundrum. In these degenerate days men have been known to put panes of glass in their front doors; but a glass door is not a door—it is a contradiction in terms. For a door is something more than a means of ingress and egress; a hole in the wall would serve for that. The essence of a door is that, when closed, it gives a sense of privacy and a sense of security. A door that you can see through, a door that you can shatter with a tack-hammer, does not fulfil the primary purposes of a door. It is not necessary (though it may be desirable) that your door should be of massive oak, studded with iron; but it ought to be a real door, not a sham. There are no glass doors in literature.

Do you see what I am doing?   I am suggesting a sort of game, to be played by any number of players; you can play it by yourself, in bed, when you are suffering from insomnia.   See how many great doors you can remember from your reading of prose and poetry.   The number will astonish you.   I have mentioned a few, but I have only to sit back in my chair and close my eyes, and examples come in shoals: the door with the terrible superscription in the *Inferno,* the door of Doubting Castle to which Christian at last found the key, the door which Pompilia opened at midnight and admitted her murderers, the "doors where my heart was used to beat so quickly," whereof Tennyson sings—down to that last

> Slow door.
> Which, opening, letting in, lets out no more.

Make your own list, and you will see how wonderfully fruitful is this neglected field of research.   You will no longer think of a door as a mere lifeless piece of joinery; but rather as, what I have called it, the universal symbol.   No other work of man's hands is so expressive, so significant; our imagination endows it with human attributes, and we speak of the housemaid "answering the door," as if it were a conversationalist; and there is one immortal door in literature which will indeed answer the housemaid, if she speaks the right word, which is "Sesame." . . . Yes, certainly, if I were an essayist, I should write an essay on doors.

AN ADVENTURER

"UNDISTURBED by the chatter and movement of the crowd on the terrace of the Monte Rosa Hotel at Zermatt, a young man was sitting immersed in a book. . . . He was picturesque and untidy, in loose, grey flannels, with a bright handkerchief round his neck." This sounds like the opening of a novel; as a matter of fact it is the opening of a biography; and so, or in some such wise, every biography ought, in my opinion, to open, plunging boldly *in medias res,* and cutting out all the dreary twaddle about parents and grandparents, and infancy, and teething and measles, and so forth. The book in question is the biography of George Leigh Mallory, the young mountaineer who died—no one knows exactly how—in the assault on Mount Everest a few years ago. It is written by Mr David Pye and published by the Oxford University Press. It is a small book, and it does not contain a dull page. (Almost all the standard biographies would be small books if you cut out all the dull pages.) Speaking for myself, I may say that only two classes of men appeal to me as subjects of biography. First, men of letters; and here the world seems to agree, for Boswell's *Johnson* and Lockhart's *Scott* are probably the most popular "lives" in the English language. Secondly, open-air men, explorers, mountaineers, mighty hunters before the Lord, men who have led precarious and adventurous lives, and looked often in "the bright face of danger." I fancy this taste, too, is shared by most people; and naturally, for most of us lead tame, sheltered, monotonous, suburban lives; and we like to escape in imagination—having given up all our boyish hopes of escaping in reality—out of our cages into the wonderful and various world. Reading the story of Mallory's life and death, I feel heartily ashamed of the lack of incident in my own career; and I trust that many readers will feel the same way. I have never climbed Mount Everest, nor even Mont Blanc; I have never faced a band of brigands in a pass of the Apennines; I never—let me whisper the humiliating confession—I never yet harpooned a whale! . . . It strikes me, in passing, that those words would make an excellent refrain for a ballade. Wait a moment while I hammer out the first stanza . . .

> Alas! of joys I never knew
>   A lengthy list I could compile:
> I've never been to Timbuctoo,
>   Nor stalked the hungry crocodile
>   Along the reaches of the Nile;
> I've never spent a year in gaol
>   And won my freedom with a file—
> I never yet harpooned a whale.

I was walking in Exeter Cathedral this morning, reading many quaint and curious epitaphs, one of which struck me with peculiar force. It was of a certain eighteenth-century bishop, who joined "a winning conversation to a condescending deportment" (can't you see him?) and who was a "successful exposer of Pretence and Enthusiasm." There, I think, is the eighteenth century in a nutshell. Pretence and enthusiasm—two vices, of about equal malignancy! I wonder what else but enthusiasm built Exeter Cathedral. Also I wonder whether the good bishop would have kept up his condescending deportment if he had been confronted with such a person as George Leigh Mallory, whose life was one flame of enthusiasm from beginning to end. A youth of singular comeliness, and of extraordinary personal charm, he made friends wherever he went; and he took endless trouble to serve his friends; he had an enthusiasm for friendship. (Readers of the late A. C. Benson's *Letters* will remember how that veteran, lying under a black cloud of melancholy, took comfort from the visits of a young undergraduate named Mallory. This was the man.) He had an enthusiasm for literature, too; his book on Boswell broke new ground and was full of promise. But his chief enthusiasm was for mountains. Even as an undergraduate he won a name for himself as an intrepid and skilful Alpine climber; and when the vacation (or his purse) was too short for a visit to Switzerland, he contented himself with the peaks and precipices of Wales. Mr Pye accompanied him and his young wife on one of these minor expeditions, and paints a pleasant picture of Mrs Mallory being taught the elements of mountaineering. The elements!—how few of us get so far! The description of what Mallory considered elementary fills one with shame. Prose fails me; I must contrive a second stanza . . .

Ten thousand things I meant to do
In days of dreaming infantile—
I've never ruled a pirate crew
Nor captured slaves by force or guile.
This sedentary life is vile,
Unprofitable, flat, and stale;
And, most of all, this stirs my bile—
I never yet harpooned a whale.

He was for a good many years a teacher in one of the great English public schools. His biographer hints a doubt whether he was a good teacher. What is certain is that he carried into the task of teaching the fire which lit up every cranny of his life, and that he made many adoring friends among his pupils. School-teaching is a most soul-deadening business unless you can manage to keep your enthusiasm alive by making experiments and giving play to your originality; and experiments and originality are apt to be frowned on by the authorities. Mallory's methods got him into hot water more than once; and in the end, when the first Everest expedition gave him a way of escape, I think he was glad to get out of a profession about which he had come to harbour grave misgivings. His remarks on the ideals of education, and on how, in his opinion, an English public school falls short of those ideals, deserve consideration, but I shall not consider them here, since not school-teaching, but mountaineering, is the topic of this article. He was a born mountaineer. In a sense he was a poet—though not in the sense in which his Cambridge friend, Rupert Brooke, was a poet. He expressed himself, not in words, but in the scaling of mountains. Anyone who thinks this an absurd paradox should read Mallory's own excellent essay on "The Mountaineer as Artist," of which his biographer wisely quotes long extracts. Reading that confession of faith, you see that mountaineering was not, for him, a mere matter of perfect nerve and perfect muscle, of bodily skill and nimbleness and poise. It demanded certain spiritual qualities; it was a moral exercise: it was, in fact, a kind of religion. Mallory served with distinction in the war; but he did not go to Flanders with anything like the enthusiasm with which he went to Tibet. He looked at the war with a philosophic eye; he must do his duty and serve his country, of course, but he seems to have had doubts about the kind of England that would emerge from a victorious war. But about the value of scaling a hitherto unscaled mountain-peak he had no doubts whatever. This was to him an impelling spiritual neces-sity. Men who feel like this about mountains are probably very rare; but a keen awareness that the common money-chasing life is not fit for the immortal spirit of man is, surely, not so rare as it appears. To few of us, however, does the chance come. My third stanza is now clamouring to get itself constructed.

> My life is trickling slowly through;
> I fain would leave the town a while
> On some adventure brave and new;
> On me, in far-off South Sea isle,
> No dusky queen did ever smile;
> I never donned a coat of mail;
> I've lived, so far, in cloistered style—
> I never yet harpooned a whale.

Amid snow and ice, on impossibly slippery and precipitous places on the upper slopes of Mount Everest, eight hundred feet below the very summit, this rare spirit, by what mistake or mischance no man knows, disappears from view; and it is impossible not to ask, was the end worth the sacrifice of such a life? What adequate gain to the world, what new piece of scientific knowledge, was to be hoped for from the conquest of that peak? This was a question which Mallory would never have allowed. I do not think he would have approved of that phrase of Stevenson's I quoted above, "the bright face of danger." He did not court danger for its own sake; he thought any one who took risks, where risk was not necessary to the task in hand, was a fool, and had no business to try mountaineering. But he was one who believed the value of the thing achieved was as nothing compared with the value of achieving it. He set himself to scale Everest because scaling Everest was a definite task, to the fulfilment of which he must bend every energy of mind and body. To the Philistine foolishness, to him it was a sacred crusade; you can read that in every line of the letters he wrote in the last few weeks of his life. He died an enviable death, because he was a born mountaineer. . . . No ballade is complete without its "envoy"; I have to find two more rhymes in "ile" and "ale." Well, let us do our best . . .

> The landscape stretches mile on mile,
> With many an Everest to scale;
> My hair is growing grey; meanwhile
> I never yet harpooned a whale!

THE TWO LAUGHTERS

Has it ever struck you that there are two kinds of laughter?—
I mean, there are people who laugh with, and there are people
who laugh at, the majority. This may be, to you, a truth too
obvious to need assertion; yet I cannot remember that Bergson
or Meredith, or any one else who has written wisely and learnedly
about comedy, has directed attention to this fundamental distinction—at least, to me it seems fundamental. There is the laughter
which sides with the big battalions, and a formidable guffaw it is.
And there is the laughter of the man with his back to the wall,
so to speak. There is no third kind, as far as I know. All
humorists may be placed in one or other of these two categories.
. . . I am moved to make these observations by the remark of a
recent critic, that "laughter was intended to be the consolation of
minorities." It may have been so intended, but in practice
it is far more frequently used as an assertion of the self-com-
placency of majorities. I need scarcely say which I think to be
the more honourable kind of laughter.

Take *Punch*, for example—that wonderful budget of joculari-
ties that London sends forth, week by week, to the remotest corners of the British Empire. I am not going to give myself
superior airs and say, like Queen Victoria on a memorable occasion, that we are not amused. Of course *Punch* is amusing; unless you are a foreigner, and therefore not responsive to this
strain of humour, you must laugh—not at everything, but at
something in every issue. But when people tell me that *Punch*
is a peculiarly and essentially English institution—that its humour
is English humour to the core, and that that is why foreigners
do not appreciate it—then I must either retort, "So much the
worse for England," or else point out, politely but firmly, that
they are making a mistake, and that it has never been the English
way to scoff at people because they have the misfortune to be
members of a minority. Any one who is eccentric, any one who
is unconventional, any one who in dress, speech, or manners does

not come up to the accepted standard or conform to the accepted code, is considered fair game for this kind of fun. *Punch* seems to be written by persons who have been at a public school, and then at Oxford, and there to have learned what is, and what is not, good form; to sin against good form is to make oneself ridiculous in the sight of gods and men. It is really a schoolboy humour; more urbane, more polished, neater and more ingenious, but not in essence less inhuman than the humour of schoolboys making fun of a boy who displays any sort of eccentricity—the humour that made school a hell for Shelley, for instance. It is essentially, for all its superficial elegance, a crude, uncivilized kind of humour, like that which finds something exquisitely diverting in the attempts of a foreigner to speak a language he has not mastered. It was in *Punch* that we all read, and laughed at, Anstey's series of skits called *A Bayard from Bengal*, some years ago. They were irresistibly funny, yet one laughed with a shamefaced feeling that this holding up of our Indian fellow-subjects to ridicule, because they were not like English public schoolboys, was rather a cheap and ignoble form of satire. . . . Or, again, take the famous Gilbert and Sullivan operas; forget the beautiful and haunting music of Sullivan, and study Gilbert as literature; what do you find there? Within the immensely ingenious extravagance of topsy-turvy drollery there is always a hard core of self-complacent Philistinism, laughing at whatsoever things are eccentric, unconventional, original: at any sort of aberration from the accepted code, the standard fashion. Take *Patience*, and look at it impartially; it is the laughter of the ordinary, well-fed, self-satisfied Philistine at the artist whose ideas he cannot understand. This is what I mean by laughing with, instead of at, the majority.

The laughter of Voltaire is an example of the other and nobler kind; he was against the big battalions, indomitably and implacably defiant of them. This instance shows me that I have been using the wrong word in speaking of majority and minority, as if it were a mere question of numbers. Voltaire was certainly the champion of a numerical majority, but it was an inarticulate majority, a majority dumb, driven, and powerless. He attacked a minority, but a minority that, for the time being, held all the trumps. "We cannot fight these people," he said in effect, "these people so strong and so stupid; but we can at least make fun of them. They can bruise us, and beat us, and tread us down, but they cannot prevent us from seeing how absurd they are, in all their panoply." It took great courage to laugh as Voltaire laughed; but a few years after his death the boot was on the other foot, and the brave man was he who dared to make fun of Marat or Robespierre, of the follies of the sovereign people.

The best example I can think of in our own time is Mr G. K. Chesterton, a poet and satirist whose greatness is not yet, for all his notoriety, fully appreciated. With a less biting and acrid wit than Voltaire's, with a more genial and whimsical humour, he, too, is on the side of the numerical majority; for he is on the side of the common man, and common men are certainly the more plentiful. But he is against the big battalions, against the entrenched power and the tyrannous force; he is the spokesman of those who cannot speak for themselves. Take, for instance, his famous Ode to Lord Birkenhead, a personage who, I prophesy, will be remembered in history, if he is remembered at all, as the man to whom Mr Chesterton addressed that blasting rebuke; just as Addison, if he had not written anything himself, would still be remembered as the man whom Pope transfixed with the shaft of an immortal satire. Or take that rollicking series of *Songs of Education*, and see with what genuine glee—quite different from anything in Voltaire or in Swift—a man can war with principalities and powers and folly in high places. . . . I suppose Mr Shaw is another case of the right kind of laughter; I am not quite so sure of him, though there is no doubt that he does— or did in his militant days—use his great gift of laughter on the side of the minority; sometimes a very small minority, and even, on occasions, a minority consisting of Mr Shaw. I am not sure of him because I have a lurking suspicion that, though he may be on the side of a minority here and now, we can conceive of circumstances in which he would use all his powers of ridicule on the other side. If he could persuade England to turn Communist I fancy he would be bitterly scornful of any one who dared to be a heretic. Mr Chesterton's "common man" is to Mr Shaw a poor, stupid creature who needs to be superseded by a Superman, or, failing the arrival of that splendid being, to be firmly governed, ordered about, restrained, repressed, and generally kept in his place. His fierce intellectual scorn of ordinary humanity afflicts me with misgivings—of which I ought to be ashamed, for, be his cause right or wrong, he has fought gallantly for what he believes in, and has repeatedly used the weapon of ridicule, as it ought to be used, against the accepted folly or vice.

I come back, then, to that quotation about laughter being the consolation of minorities. It is sometimes the only consolation they have. It is then that we feel it to be a divine gift—as when Socrates, for example, with a sort of secret smile on his ugly face, points out to the judges who have condemned him to death how absurd they are, and how in after ages it is they, and not he, who will look ridiculous; or when Dr Stockmann, in Ibsen's play, after his fight with the infuriated rabble, quaintly observes that "one ought never to put on one's best trousers when one goes out to fight for liberty and truth." All the same, it will not do to make a rigid rule on the subject. Minorities are often ridiculous. No sane person will maintain that there is anything immoral about laughing at a crank, a faddist, a crotcheteer. A little ridicule may be the very medicine he needs: it may even cure him. Both kinds of humour no doubt have their place in the scheme of things. English literature is full of both. But I still maintain that the laughter of Swift, of Byron, of Peacock, of Chesterton is the better kind; and that the other kind—which is of course immeasurably the commoner—is terribly apt to degenerate into a mere ignoble schoolboy snigger at whatsoever things are beyond our comprehension; the herd instinct to deride any departure from the herd's immemorial ways. . . . This theory of laughter is not my life's work; in fact, I have only just thought of it; and I have not yet had time to go round it and put putty in all the little cracks and crevices. For instance, if any one objects, "But how are you going to fit Shakespeare in?"—the only reply I can think of is, "I leave that to you. It's your turn to do a little thinking."

MOREOVER

ON HAVING ENEMIES

THE most objectionable thing I know about my enemies is that there are not enough of them. . . .

To this you obligingly reply, "Do not distress yourself; there are more of us than you suppose, but you can hardly expect us all to take the trouble to write and tell you how much we detest you."

Thank you very much; the consolation is kindly meant; but I am unable to accept it, because a mere feeling of personal detestation is not at all what I had in mind. The enmity I refer to is something far above such petty aversions. Mere dislike does not enter into the matter at all. My worst enemy is a man whom I would rather dine with than with many of my friends. We get on with one another very well, on the perfectly frank and clear understanding that he wants my blood, and that his head served up on a charger would be a sweeter sight to me than bowls of primroses. In fact—I suppose everybody must have felt this— one of the embarrassing facts about one's enemies is that many of them are such likeable fellows. But I am straying from the point.

It is pleasant to know that you have troops of friends; but you can hardly feel at ease in your conscience unless you also know that you have regiments of enemies. The more the merrier. Nothing is more repulsive than to hear well-meaning but muddle-headed people say, when a man is just dead, "He had no enemies." They might, one feels inclined to say to them, refrain from speaking evil of him until after the funeral at least. To say that a man had had no enemies is as much as to say that he has consistently shirked his duty. It is to accuse him of all sorts of cowardly compromises and mean capitulations. The planet on which we live is not a place where a man can do the right thing without making enemies. Perhaps it would be a duller planet if it were; at all events, it would be a different one. Some day, it may be, all the problems will be solved and all the quarrels settled—but not in our time, thank God. At the present stage of affairs, life has to be thought of in terms of battle; and to say that a man, in the course of his earthly pilgrimage, has had no enemies is to say that he has never played the man, but has always slunk from the field, deaf to the summoning drums of duty and a traitor to all that lends a glory to human life. It is to include him in that caitiff crew mentioned by Dante, *a Dio spiacenti ed ai nemici sui*, hateful to God and to the enemies of God; of whom Dante adds, in his terrible way, that they were never alive.

I can think of only one man in all history of whom it could be said, in an entirely honourable sense, that when he died he left no enemies behind him. When Marshal Narvaez' was on his death-bed, his father-confessor asked him whether he had forgiven his enemies. "I have no enemies," the old soldier answered, with equal piety and simplicity; "I have killed them all."

You may object that this was the reply of a pagan, or that at least it falls a little short of the Christian spirit; but are you quite sure? Christianity does by no means command us to have no enemies; quite the contrary; for it bids us love our enemies, and how can we love our enemies if we have none to love? Critics of the Christian religion, such as Nietzsche, have made a terrible blunder when they have dwelt on its meekness and submissiveness and forgotten its unquenchable pugnacity. It sends men out upon crusades. It bids you fight to the death for the cause you believe in. Fight, it says, and give no quarter; only beware, when you are fighting, lest you defile your good cause with personal ill-will. Beware of staining your sword with hatred; for hatred is of the Devil, and your sword is of God, lent you for use in His wars: that, I take it, is the high Christian doctrine, and I dare say none of us can live up to it, but I suppose we can try. That is, if we agree with it—for it is a doctrine with which it is very possible to disagree.

But I have strayed from the point again. The point is that enemies, whether you love them or hate them, are a necessary part of a man's life if he is to keep his self-respect. "It is our business," says Burke, "to cultivate friendships and to incur enmities"; and nobly did he practise what he preached, not neglecting either half of life's business. Beware of the world when it wears a smiling face; and faithfully ask yourself whether its smiles are not the result of your ignoble truckling to the world. Mistrust popularity, the rock on which many a good man has wrecked his soul. Every night, before falling asleep, count your enemies, and make sure that the number is sufficient to earn for you a night's repose.

Whose biographies do you care to read? Not, assuredly, those
of the placid, peaceful, placable people; but always of the fighters.
The lives of the others may or may not have been worth living;
but they are not worth reading about. I am not speaking of men
of action only, but of all men whom we call great; your Michel-
angelos, your Beethovens, your Tolstoys, were men of war, every
man of them—and every woman too: Saint Joan bore arms, and
Florence Nightingale has been described by her latest biographer
as a battering-ram.

When you express the hope that you will die in harness, you
mean—I hope you mean—not the harness of a yoked beast, but
harness in the ancient and honourable sense, the harness in which
Horatius threw himself into the Tiber.

But there is another side to the medal. The words I quoted
from Burke are not all; he adds that it is our business "to have
both strong, and both selected." You must select your enemies;
you must choose them wisely, and even with a certain fastidiousness. It does not matter much—this is what you really ought to
have said to me by way of consolation at the outset—if your
enemies are few, so long as they are well chosen. To have an
indiscriminate multitude of foes may mean a fatal dilution of your
energy. Select, and then concentrate: that is the true strategy. Do
not try to fight upon too many fronts.

It is terribly easy to scatter one's forces, and so to become an
ineffective fighter. "In Hell," said the Scottish preacher, "there
are mair deevils than we can ask or think." On earth at the present
day there are devils enough and to spare; it is no use taking one's
bow and spear and going out to do battle with the lot. There is
so much evil in the world that you can easily dash yourself in
pieces against its serried mass without anybody's being a penny
the worse for all your indomitable and misguided courage. Even
in our own Australia, believe me, you cannot hope to fight effectively, single-handed, against all that you see to be thoroughly
detestable. We have to organize the forces of decency, and insist
that each man stick to his allotted job. If I, for instance, were to
sally out to assail all that I hold abominable, how much damage
would I do to any one. If I hurled my puny body against the
armament firms that are doing their best to wreck the hope of
peace, and the high finance that is keeping the world in misery,
and the economists who are using their brains to support high
finance, and the people who believe the world can be saved by
tariffs, and the people who are making money out of fostering the

gambling spirit in the community, and the dull and stodgy people who are sterilizing education, and the people who bawl "Communist" at you if you want to change anything, and the politicians who are introducing graft into our public life, and the people who debauch the public mind with despicable films, and the people who make horrible cacophonies and call them music, and the humbugs and the limelighters and the puritans and the rogues—good heavens! the list will never end—what good would I do? Not the smallest shadow of a particle.

Yes, it is plain, a man can have too many enemies. But that is better, a thousand times better, than having none. It is better than to sink into the condition of the man who thinks public affairs must go their own way without his intervention, and to whom, in the end, the defeat of the English cricketers comes to be of more moment than the defeat of an evil economic system. When this happens to you, you may know that you have ceased to be a man. I am not quite sure what you have become.

Am I preaching? If so, it is to myself. The writer of essays is always talking to himself. The readers are eavesdroppers, overhearing a private conversation between the essayist and his troublesome conscience. I have been asking myself two intimate questions: have I enough enemies for my self-respect?—and do I, in my enmities, rise above paltry personal considerations? That second question sounds priggish and absurd in prose; I can only express it by breaking, for once, into verse.

DILIGITE INIMICOS VESTROS

I hated him when we began . . .
  At the first clash of steel, we knew
'Twas die who must and live who can:
  Too small the world to hold us two.

His life or mine—the prize was life
  For which with thirsting blades we fought;
Yet in my heart, amid the strife,
  There flamed a strange and secret thought.

I knew him for a splendid foe
  That fronted death with eyes serene:
He was my enemy; but oh,
  How brave a friend he might have been!

Within the secret soul of man
  What depths unplumbed, what runes unread!
I hated him when we began:
  I loved him as I struck him dead.

THE BOOK AND THE ISLAND

You are sick—but not sicker than I am—of that ancient question which has so often turned out to be an invitation to hypocrisy: suppose you were shipwrecked on a desert island, and suppose one book, and no more, were washed ashore from the wreck—which book, out of the whole range of literature, would you ask the fates to allot you? I need scarcely point out that the question lies a little beyond the frontiers of the practical; because it is fantastically improbable that, even on the most delightful of desert islands, you would find in a convenient cave the very book you wanted most of all the books of the world. The book you would really find would be—such is the natural perversity of things—a book for which a person on an uninhabited island could find no use whatever; *A Manual of Etiquette,* perhaps, or *The Stockbroker's Vademecum,* or a Calcutta University Calendar. It may also be noted that the most useful book for a prolonged sojourn on a desert island need not necessarily be of high literary merit; a book of simple vegetarian recipes might be more desirable than the collected works of Aldous Huxley.

Anyhow, it is a silly old question; and my only excuse for allowing it to raise its head once more is that, as the following narrative will show, I have lately had occasion to view it, not as a remote and fantastic hypothesis, but as a sternly practical problem; and I have seen an answer given to it which was based, not on theory, but on actual experience. And if the pragmatists are right, and the truth is to be defined as what works, then the answer in this instance seems to have been the true answer, for it has undoubtedly worked well.

Narrative, especially nautical narrative, is not in my line; therefore I shall give no description of a recent holiday cruise in a small trading schooner—on which I was the only passenger—among the South Sea Islands. Be satisfied to know that one day—a lovely day it was, with a light south-westerly breeze—we were bowling along somewhere about midway between the Marquesas and the Marshalls when we came in sight of a palm-fringed island,

and the captain announced his intention of putting in for a few hours, chiefly for fresh water, though there was also the possibility of a little trade, "You may as well go ashore and mooch around for a bit," said that ancient mariner to his passenger. "You'll be interested in the people. They're a rum crowd; take 'em all round, about as rum a crowd as ever I see. Cannibals? Lord love you, sir, they're the mildest, kindliest, cheeriest folk on the face of the earth. Not niggers, no; they're as white as you and me, and they speak English pretty near as good as you and me does. Some chaps I've spoke to reckon they're the descendants of some chaps what was wrecked here away back in old Queen Victoria's time. I dunno the truth of that, but anyway they're Christians, and they've got a book they think a terrible lot of; they won't have any other books, not even the best kind—not even Edgar Wallace, if you'll believe me; won't have 'em at any price. But in spite of their shocking ignorance, I must admit they do seem as if they knew how to behave to one another and to other people. They're so blessed innocent I feel kind of ashamed to take 'em down in a deal. The chief'll be aboard as soon as we get into the lagoon. Have a yarn with him and get him to tell you all about it."

. . . I found the chief, when the captain introduced us, a most attractive person. His way of speaking was perhaps a trifle old-fashioned and stilted; but his manners were perfect, without a touch of affectation, the manners of a perfect host. "If you will do me the honour," he said, "of being my personal guest while you are here, I shall do my best to make your visit agreeable. You must, however, excuse me for a moment while I assure myself that there is no contraband among the goods which I see that our worthy friend the captain is proposing to deposit on our shores. An excellent fellow, your captain; but, if I may say so without offence, he needs watching; he once showed a tendency"—and here his face flushed, the only sign of temper he displayed during the whole of my visit—"to attempt the poisoning of the minds of my people. Probably he does not understand what it would mean; but *I* understand, and I shall not tolerate it. No, sir; the trader may bring whatever else he pleases; but books he shall *not* bring." After he had satisfied himself that there was no literature among the stores that were being loaded on the ship's dinghy, he came back to me with unruffled brow, and we went ashore together in his canoe . . .

Of his interesting conversation I shall set down only what is strictly relevant to the question with which I have prefaced this narrative. The people of the island, he told me, were the des-

cendants of some score of men and women who had been shipwrecked there in the early fifties of last century; mainly English,
with a sprinkling of Scotch and Irish. "It was a terrible gale," he
said, "and many perished. The survivors, although naturally
saddened by the loss of their companions, found many things to
be thankful for besides their own escape from a watery grave.
Providence had chosen for their new home a beautiful and fertile
island, with a, climate more delightful than any they had ever
known. As the storm subsided, there were washed ashore many
of the necessities and even some of the luxuries of civilized life.
But what we regard as the crowning mercy, for which we ever-
lastingly give thanks to Heaven, is that in a watertight case there
came ashore—by what looked like the merest chance, but we know
that something other than chance directed its movements—the
Book." (He spoke, whenever he mentioned it, with a reverence
which I can indicate only by using a capital letter.) "Yes, sir, it
was not at first realized what an inestimable treasure Providence
had bestowed on the poor shipwrecked band. As the years passed,
and children came, and grew up and married and had children of
their own—as the small original band developed into a large community, and the lives of individuals were shaped and the govern-
ance of the whole society was moulded by the teachings of the
Book, we realized what it had meant to us to have such an infallible guide to the conduct of life. The case in which it was
found had belonged to my father; and until his death, which
occurred last year, he was held in special reverance on that account.
That is why I, as his eldest son, have the high honour and the
heavy responsibility of presiding over this people to-day."

"But, since you have gained so much from that one book," I
ventured, "I should have thought you would have wanted more
books, and more, and more; whereas, just now, you———"

"Why should we want any other book?" asked the chief. "What
does any of them contain of value that is not to be found in the
Book—the Book of Books? Perhaps I ought to explain that I am
not the untravelled South Sea Islander you might suppose me to
be. A year or two ago, preparing for my responsibilities as ruler,
I travelled abroad and saw many lands and many peoples. I went
up and down your Australia, and in your great cities I saw shops
and libraries full of books on all conceivable subjects. I read at
first greedily, but it was not long before I became convinced that
I was learning nothing that would be of value to this island." (He
always spoke of "this island" with a certain solemnity, as if his
tiny atoll had been a continent.) "Yes, sir, I found questions in

plenty, doubts in plenty, futile and irrelevant facts in overflowing plenty; but of clear teaching on the great issues of life, I found nothing that was not more plainly set forth in the Book. And I made up my mind that, if I could help it, the intellects of my people should not be bewildered nor their morals debased by the introduction of any other book, no matter how specious its appearance nor how famous its author."

"But surely," I objected, rather fatuously, "life is too complex for all departments of it to be adequately dealt with by one book, however great a book it may be?"

"Perhaps we are not complex on this island," he replied. "Perhaps we have the misfortune to be a simple people. All I know is that we are a happy people, and that we are kind to one another, and helpful, and honest in all our dealings with one another. How would it profit us to grow complex, and to possess what you call your civilization, with its vices, its crimes, its horrors, its miseries? For the life we lead and wish our children to lead, all the guidance we require is in the Book. What department—your own word—is ignored in its pages?"

"Well, for instance, economics . . . ."

"Oh, my dear sir! You surely forget that I have been in your land. I have seen your economics in action. If the state of things I saw is the result of your learning economics from your thousands of books, I must say, with all respect, that I prefer what we have learned from the Book. For it all comes back, in the end, to right and wrong; and that clear-cut distinction is on every page of the Book. Think of the multitude of characters, good and bad, that move across those pages; is there any bewilderment, any doubt which are the good characters and which the bad, which the noble and which the base? Its ethical teachings are as clear as crystal; and when we leave this veranda and take a walk round the island, I shall show you a society which has taken those plain teachings to heart, and you shall say whether it is not a happy society, happy in its industry, happy in its leisure, happy in all its human relationships. You shall tell me in what respect it is not a model for that complex society of yours to imitate if it only could. Until you can show me some point at which we are your inferiors, I shall continue to believe that there is no really important lesson of life that cannot be learned from the story of David."

"David!" I said, somewhat startled. "Am I to understand that David is your national hero?"

For the first time, a shade of severity appeared on his mild countenance. "And why not?" he asked. "David is only one of many models of upright behaviour; but if we choose him as our particular favourite, what objection can you suggest?"

"Well, I don't know," I said, with a certain hesitancy; "but it is generally thought that his conduct towards Uriah was a trifle —well—ungentlemanly, so to speak . . ."

"Uriah!" exclaimed the chief. "My dear sir, you astound me. I can only suppose that you are not so well acquainted with the story as, if I may say so, you ought to be. Uriah! He was a man who deserved all he got, and a good deal over. No, no; David's conduct, on that occasion, was without a flaw. You must read the story again; you really must." I felt inclined to agree with him.

"Portions of the Book," he went on, "in manuscript, of course, are in every home throughout the island. It is the rule that a chapter is read to the assembled household every morning, and another every evening. Certain portions are regarded as less profitable than others; but the Book as a whole is very thoroughly studied, and I venture to think that the mistake you have just made would hardly be made by a child on this island. . . . But come, I must show you what I can of our life here, and then you shall see the Book itself of which that life is the fruit—not a manuscript copy, but the very Book, the Book that was washed ashore for our guidance."

And afterwards, when I had strolled about with him for an hour and been greeted everywhere with friendly looks and cheerful words, see it I did. It lay on a kind of lectern in the middle of a temple especially built to enshrine it. It was worn—doubtless with much handling in the early years, before copies had been made—but it was now hardly ever touched; and it was with extreme care that the chief turned back the front cover to show me the title-page, which I stared at with curiosity—

THE PERSONAL HISTORY

OF

DAVID COPPERFIELD

By CHARLES DICKENS

LONDON:
BRADBURY & EVANS
1850

ON BEING AUSTRALIAN

I HAVE a good deal of (possibly misplaced) sympathy with the author of a volume of essays recently published in Australia, and reviewed, not unkindly, by some critics in England. The author is told by these reviewers that his efforts are not exactly bad, but not Australian. A writer in the *Times Literary Supplement*, for instance, gently but sadly remarks that "those who look for some attachment to the Australian environment will look nearly in vain." A writer in the *New Statesman* strikes exactly the same kind, regretful note—"The book has few native qualities." Having read the book in question with some care, I have to say, first of all, that this criticism strikes me as entirely just. The book is not Australian in subject; it is not Australian in manner; and if its author feels any "attachment to the Australian environment," he certainly does not talk about it. These English critics plainly expect from an Australian book something which they did not find in this particular book, and they were perfectly justified in expressing their disappointment. But were they justified in expecting what they did expect?—and what was it, exactly, that they expected? These are not trivial questions; they are matters of serious concern, not only to the writer of this book —who may, for aught I know, be meditating another volume of essays—but to all of us in Australia who are trying to learn to be writers. They set us questioning our consciences to make sure whether we are writing what is genuinely, honestly, and unmistakably Australian, or a mere pinchbeck imitation of English goods. When the real Australian essayist arrives, if he ever does arrive, by what sign shall we know him? On what subjects will he write? And in what language?

Take the question of language first. English critics evidently expect an Australian writer to write Australian, and they are therefore disappointed when they find him using ordinary English, just the speech they get from their own writers by the thousand. But is there an Australian language for us to use? There is, of course, an Australian slang—more than half of it, I suspect, imported—but the English critic can hardly be so unfair as to expect Australian essayists to write in slang when he does not require his own essayists to do anything of the kind. There is also, of course, an Australian accent; but unless we use phonetic spelling, which can scarcely be demanded of us, how are we to convey to English readers the delicate differences of our pronunciation? Apart from slang and accent, is there an Australian style of speech, an Australian choice of words? We might, of course, bestrew our pages with the great Australian adjective; but then, the English have stolen our adjective, and they use it more frequently than we do ourselves. . . . No, it is no use; we cannot cultivate a distinctively Australian style; there is no distinctively Australian style for us to cultivate. In the course of centuries a characteristic Australian way of using words may develop; for the present we have to content ourselves with choosing between a good style and a bad style, and I hope it may become our national habit to choose a good style—a style, I mean, simple, plain, unpretentious, and expressive of our own individual selves. A good style is the style a man uses when he has learned to say exactly what he thinks, without any affectations or questing after originality.

Coming, then, to subject-matter. What is the Australian essayist to write about, if he wishes not to disappoint an English reader? If there is no distinctively and recognizably Australian style, there must surely be distinctively Australian things to write about? There are; I wish someone would sit down and write out an authoritative list of them. The Australian bushranger is, or was, different from other highwaymen; the Australian squatter is different from the English squire or the American planter; the Australian rabbit is different—in quantity if not in quality—from the rabbit of less favoured lands. The kangaroo and the emu are our very own; so, I suppose we can still say, are our gum-trees. The Australian country town has, I think, characteristics which mark it out from any other country town; though, being a patriot, I should be disinclined to dwell on them. If I were ordered, on pain of death, to write a volume of essays on Australian subjects, I think I could get at least as far as compiling a satisfactory table of contents, one that would satisfy the most exacting English critic. The convict days, the droving days, our explorers, the gold rushes, the kangaroo, the jackeroo, the emu, the lyre-bird, blackfellows, boomerangs, billabongs, billy-tea, bushrangers, rabbit-trappers, gum-trees, dingoes, damper—with meditation and perspiration one might add a dozen more. The critic, I say, would be satisfied with the table of contents; but he could hardly be satisfied with any other page in the book, which would be the dullest book ever written, for the simple reason that in none of these momentous themes do I take a particle of interest, and it is said to be impossible to interest others in what does not interest oneself; which obvious truth may be called the golden rule of literature.

That is the real point; what is the Australian writer to be allowed to be interested in, without being held to have forfeited his right to consider himself an Australian? I rather think the Englishman's idea of the Australian is still coloured by what he has read in popular novels. The late E. W. Hornung, after a very short experience on a Riverina sheep-run, went back to England and published *A Bride from the Bush*, a story whose heroine, if I remember rightly, coo-ees to a friend across Piccadilly, and cracks a stock-whip energetically in Hyde Park. Perhaps it would be all to the good if Australian girls in London did behave in these unconventional and independent ways; but as a matter of fact, you know, they don't. The Australian who is part of other novelists' stock-in-trade is one of two things—either an incorrigible blackguard, or an enormously rich uncle with hairy face and uncouth manners. The blackguard may be a picturesque figure, and the rich uncle may be golden-hearted as well as hairy-faced, but they do not, between them, exhaust Australian possibilities. The popular novelist disregards the ordinary Australian, who would not be worth portraying, because he is exceedingly like the ordinary Englishman. Possibly the Englishman who figures in Australian prose and verse, the Englishman conspicuous by his spats and his eyeglass, who says, "Haw!" on all possible occasions, is every bit as mythical a monster as the other; but that is irrelevant to the present argument. What I want to suggest is that the ordinary Australian is interested, so far as concerns nine-tenths of his life, in precisely the same things as an ordinary Englishman is interested in. Why should it be expected of him that he will write only about the remaining one-tenth? I think it is time we issued a Declaration of Independence, the gist of which will be that we intend to write about what we jolly well please.

For instance, the author of the book in question—its title does not matter, since I am using it only as an illustration—is evidently a bookish sort of person; he is fond of literary allusions, and there is hardly a page without a quotation. What then? Is he the less Australian because he happens to be more interested in books than in boomerangs? "No," replies the English critic, if I understand him aright, "but you see we have thousands of bookish persons in England, and scores of essayists who write about books; when we open a book that comes to us all the way from Australia we expect something different,—something with an Australian flavour." And at the back of his mind is a strong suspicion that, on the subject of books, an Australian is not at all likely to say anything worth hearing. What he has learned to expect from Australia is, in Mr J. C. Squire's curt phrase, "Philistinism and frozen meat." Whether there are more Philistines in Australia, in proportion to the total population, than in England is a question which I forbear to ask—partly because I do not know the answer, partly because it is impolite, and partly because it is quite irrelevant. Let us stick to the point. If an Australian happens to be interested in, let us say, Shakespeare —and if, furthermore, he has come to some conclusions of his own about Shakespeare—is there any compelling reason why he should not state those conclusions? If what he has to say on Shakespeare is valueless—as most people's remarks on Shakespeare are—let the critics tell him so; but what right have they to tell him that, being an Australian, he ought not to have written about Shakespeare at all, or that if he did write about Shakespeare his observations ought to have had an Australian flavour? Would there be any special point in dragging in bushrangers or emus into an essay on *Hamlet*? I have an immense admiration for the stories of Henry Lawson, which are Australian to the backbone, and for the novels of Thomas Hardy, which smell of English earth; but surely we in Australia have the same right as Englishmen have to be interested in things which belong neither to Australia nor to England, but to the world. Robert Lynd, an Irishman, writes a delightful essay on "The Nutritive Qualities of the Banana"; does any one rebuke him, and tell him that this subject has not the true Irish flavour, that he shows no attachment to the Irish environment, that his essay has few native qualities? Do we beseech him to stick for the future to shillelaghs and banshees, and colleens and Kilkenny cats? Nobody says anything so absurd; it is at least equally absurd to ask us Australians to concentrate our interest on the affairs of the parish. We must assert our right to become, if we can, citizens of the world.

WHAT ARE BOOKS FOR?

I WAS permitted the other evening to intrude into a meeting of young men and women assembled to discuss modern literature. (I found, without much surprise, that "modern literature" meant the literature of the last five years. I ventured to suggest that if we treated the writings of Bernard Shaw as ancient literature, lumping them, as it were, with the writings of Sophocles, this might lead to some confusion; and that it was just as well to remember that John Masefield, though not a modern, was not a contemporary of Homer. The young people agreed that a writer who was not modern need not necessarily be ancient; some word was needed for writers who were not to be placed with the Greek and Latin classics, but who were not really modern. Various terms were suggested: old-fashioned, *vieux jeu,* out-of-date, avuncular, dead; "obsolete" was, in the end, accepted as the least unsatisfactory description. John Galsworthy is not an ancient writer, he will be pleased to hear; he is merely an obsolete writer.) I enjoyed myself immensely and came away feeling refreshed, as one always does after coming into contact with young and ardent minds. People talk about the intolerance of youth; what always strikes me is its tolerance. When I put in a plea for certain obsolete writers, my remarks were received not with loud jeers, but with patience and pity; and when I admitted that I could make neither head nor tail of some of the modern writers, this shameful confession was not treated as the gibberings of a congenital idiot, as I expected it to be; I was merely reminded, very kindly and softly, that exactly the same thing had been said of Blake and Shelley in their day; which, of course, is quite true. In the end we failed to convince one another, and it came over me very strongly that none of us had any standard by which to measure modern writers and compare them with the obsolete. These youngsters were quite uncertain about what literature is, what it is for; as uncertain as I was myself. Can you blame us? We are all living together in an age of uncertainty; we are bewildered about economics, we are bewildered about religion, we are bewildered about the cause and cure of baldness; we are not sure about the first principles of any mortal thing. As I lay in bed that night, suffering from the insomnia which such debates are apt to induce, I saw that it is perfectly useless for two people to argue about whether James Joyce is or is not good literature, until those two people have agreed as to what good literature is; before fruitful argument (about anything) can begin, you must find some common ground. Before the clock struck two I had formulated for myself my own literary creed; henceforth I will argue with nobody who does not accept that creed for a start. Do you think you can stand a short exposition of it here and now? It will not take long.

The fundamental thing about human beings is their loneliness. None of us knows more than the tiniest fraction of what is going on in the mind even of our nearest and dearest; each of us knows and must sometimes realize that he lives in a solitary fastness of his own, and that between him and the person he loves best in all the world is a gap which all the love in the world cannot bridge. We do not live in glass houses; that part of my mind which is visible through the window is only a speck of my total personality; there are dark places into which no eye will ever peer. Things happen within your soul in sixty seconds which in a whole lifetime you will not be able to reveal to me, because you know no words in which to lay your inmost being bare. The oldest, the truest, the faithfullest pair of friends have innumerable secrets from one another, not because they will, but because they must; because nature decreed it.

> A God, a God their severance rul'd;
> And bade betwixt their shores to be
> The unplumb'd, salt, estranging sea.

This fact, of human loneliness, is no doubt at the root of the story of creation, which we find in so many primitive religions, that the first god was lonely, and created the universe to appease his thirst for companionship; they made their deity in their own image, and read into his mind their own horror of isolation. *Quelles solitudes que tous ces corps humains,* cries Fantasio in de Musset's play, as he contemplates a throng of men and women. Of all the millions of inhabitants of this world of ours, there is not one who does not live, from the cradle to the grave, in a world of his own, of which he is the sole inhabitant.

This may strike you as pretty platitudinous; I care nothing for that, so long as you agree that it is true. To spare you further platitudes, I shall not dilate on the equally obvious fact that man is a gregarious animal, a being constantly in revolt against the solitariness to which nature has doomed him; that his deepest impulse is to conquer that solitariness, to break out of the prison of his own soul, to find, somehow and somewhere in the vast universe, companionship. This, I believe, is a universal fact; the so-called hermit is no exception to it, for the hermit, finding his loneliness accentuated by the thronging world, flees to the desert in quest of a higher than human companionship. The hermit, however, is so rare a type that he may be left out of our discussion. For the normal human being, speech with one's fellows is a need so urgent that to condemn a man to solitary confinement is about as ruthless a punishment as we could inflict upon him; that way madness lies. In a sense we are all prisoners condemned to solitary confinement; and something in the core of our common nature drives us to try, by hook or by crook—by tapping, let us say, on the walls of our cells—to communicate with our fellow-prisoners, and so to mitigate the horrors of our captivity. Well, literature is that tapping on the wall. Literature is communication. That is the first article of my literary creed; and if you will grant me so much, I am not sure that any of the other articles need to be enunciated; they all flow from that. But—be sure you understand what you are granting.

It is not so obvious and undeniable as it looks. The statement that literature is communication would be strenuously denied by many modern writers (using "modern" in the sense indicated at the outset). Our younger poets—Robert Graves, for instance—would, if I understand them rightly, which is very doubtful, deny it with scorn. "Communication with whom?" they would ask. "Are you to be careful to use only such language that every Tom, Dick, and Harry may be enabled to share our thoughts and emotions? Are we to be always thinking of our silly old audience? No; literature is not communication; literature is self-expression. The man of letters is no true artist unless he rises clear above the thought of an audience and writes to please himself—to satisfy his own vital need of expression." In pursuance of which doctrine James Joyce, in his later prose, uses a language largely made up of words coined by himself, words without any meaning for any one but himself, if indeed they have any meaning even for him; and Gertrude Stein uses ordinary intelligible words arranged in a completely unintelligible order; and Edith Sitwell states her thirst for self-expression by pouring forth rhymed verse to which no possible meaning can conceivably be attached; and scores of present-day writers appear to have risen to the same high plane, far above the ignoble thought of making themselves intelligible to others; self-expression is their goal. And I, believing that literature is communication, believe that they are producing a thing which is not literature at all, a thing which will not survive except to be pointed at by historians as one of the queer freaks of a chaotic time. Inarticulate noises are not literature. The whole effort at the back of real literature is the effort to be articulate, to be significant, to convey to other minds, with the utmost possible precision, a meaning.

Let us get it clearer. I quite agree that there is force in the question: Communication with whom? Are you always to be careful to write nothing that will not be immediately understood by the average billiard-marker, or the average bank manager, or the average anything? Most of what is commonly called great literature would, judged by this standard, be a ghastly failure. To attempt to live up to—or down to—this standard would be to produce no verse, for instance, of a higher strain than Kipling's "If—". All the same it is as well not to forget that the great things in literature, the things that have survived the shocks of time, have not been things written for small "advanced" coteries. We know very little about Homer's audience, but it seems highly improbable that the *Iliad* appealed only to a little group of intellectuals. We know rather more about Shakespeare's audience, and we know that *Hamlet* was not appreciated only by an exclusive esoteric clique. Molière wrote for a wide public. *Don Quixote* was a best-seller. Wordsworth, though he believed that a new poet must create the taste by which he is to be enjoyed, looked forward to a time when the enjoyment of his poetry should be "in widest commonalty spread." I have the highest admiration for the artist who refuses to sacrifice on the vile and filthy altar of popularity; all the same, it is well to remember that the great writers of the past, the writers who have survived and who now sit enthroned above the dust and clang of time, did, as a matter of fact, strive to communicate with as large an audience as possible. This, however, is something of a digression.

You will say that I am preaching a Philistine and immoral doctrine, that I am advocating cowardly capitulations and mean compromises; that, in short, I am advising our young writers to write nothing, or at least to publish nothing, unless they are sure it will be understood by butcher-boys and loved by barmaids all over the country. This would certainly be devilish doctrine. The good writer seeks to communicate with persons of his own intellectual calibre and on his own level of education. Browning's *Sordello* is thought to be the obscurest poem in the language; read it with a prose commentary, giving you the historic facts on which it is based, and the whole thing becomes quite intelligible. Browning made the extraordinary mistake of assuming that his public knew Italian medieval history as well as he knew it himself; he wrote for his equals. That is the secret of good literature. You don't "write down" to ignorant or stupid people; you write to your equals; and you do your level best to make your meaning clear to them. Many writers of to-day seem to be doing their level best to make their meaning—if they have a meaning—a profound secret. And our young bloods (bless their innocent hearts!) imagine that this must be good literature, it is so delightfully obscure. It is not; it is bad literature. For literature, as I think I said before, is communication.

ONE CROWDED HOUR

On 30 March 1778, there was tremendous excitement in Paris, which is the most excitable city in the world. Not for many a long year had there been such a stir, such a buzz, such cheering crowds in the streets, such a vivid sense of great events taking place. "It was the last great commotion in Paris under the old regime," says Lord Morley. "The next great commotion which the historian has to chronicle is the ever-memorable fourteenth day of July, eleven years later, when the Bastille fell, and a new order began for France, and new questions began for all Europe." And what was the excitement about—the excitement which even so sober a writer as Lord Morley can compare with the excitement aroused by that world-shaking event, the fall of the Bastille?

If you had happened to be in Paris that day, and had found yourself anywhere between the Academy and the Comédie Française, you would have heard the tumult and the shouting drawing nearer and nearer, till presently you were in the midst of a tight-packed crowd, and in your ears one continuous roar. They were roaring a man's name; and if you had been lucky, or had been young enough to climb up a lamp-post, you might have caught a glimpse of the man himself, as his carriage moved slowly through the mass of shouting humanity. A little old man, incredibly thin and shrivelled, in a red coat lined with ermine, his face half hidden by a huge black peruke in the style of Louis XIV. Our own Australian statesman, Sir Henry Parkes, used to amuse himself, while his opponents were speaking, by thinking out effective descriptions of them; one of his inspirations—which the person described was never able to live down—was "a withered tarantula." That would have been a fairly exact account of this little old man's figure, if we may trust contemporary painters. As for his face, it suggested an animated corpse. But his eyes shone with extraordinary brilliancy, and there was a sort of merry malice in his smile. He was eighty-four years old, but he looked as if age had not dulled his ironic enjoyment of the spectacle of human folly.

He had been born in Paris, and was a Parisian to the back-bone; but Paris had been a harsh mother to him. Twice he had been imprisoned in the Bastille—once for eleven months—and he had been exiled from France more than once. (He had spent nearly three years in England.) Often he had been in hiding in the city, and several times he had escaped imprisonment only by escaping from Paris. He had got into scrapes innumerable, and had made countless enemies among the rich and powerful. For the last twenty-seven years he had not set foot in his native city. In his absence, that city had awakened to a sense of his greatness. He was now known for the greatest Frenchman living, the man for whose sake other nations honoured France. He had become a European institution. To the place of his exile devout pilgrims had come, every day of the year, from every country in Europe.

For these twenty-seven years he had been living at Ferney, a little village on the French side of the Swiss border. He had an estate also on the other side of the frontier. His plan was, when he stung the French Government into dangerous wrath, to skip over into Switzerland, and when the Swiss Government became threatening, to skip back into France; the one thing needful was that he should not quarrel with both governments at the same time. But the French Government had let him alone, and for twenty-seven years he had lived snugly at Ferney, where he performed the extraordinary feat of keeping all Europe interested in him, until at last he attained, in the phrase of one of his biographers, "a prestige and influence which has perhaps never been the lot of any other man whose power was the intangible one of words." For this little old man, with the cadaverous face and the glittering eyes and the disquieting smile, had been a fighter all his life long, and his only weapon had been the pen.

His doctors told him that if he kept up his present ways and took his cup of gruel regularly they could almost promise him another ten years of life; but the desire to see Paris once more, to receive the homage of the city at whose hands he had suffered so much, became overmastering; he knew the risks, and he chose the crowded hour of glorious life. He set out upon the last of his many journeys, which was more of a triumphal progress, from first to last, than has fallen to the lot of any other man of letters since the world began. Had Byron lived another forty years, and then returned to London, one likes to fancy that it might have been in a like blaze of glory. But one is not sure. The English temperament is more stolid than the French. The British crowd has, to a greater degree than the French crowd, the invaluable faculty of keeping its head. On the other hand, it is not so ready to display a generous enthusiasm. Also, the Englishman does not care much for literature.

The journey through France was a foretaste of what was to come in Paris. The news of his coming preceded him from town to town. At Bourg he had to hide in a locked room from the excited crowd. At Dijon, at the hotel where he stayed, young men bribed the servants to let them disguise themselves as waiters, so as to catch a glimpse of the patriarch of Ferney. At the gates of Paris, where his carriage was stopped for the usual customs examination, one of the guards recognized him, and the news went through the city like a fiery cross.

By the end of March he had been several weeks in Paris, and the excitement, far from subsiding, had grown. The Church party held aloof, as was natural, for he had been their bitter opponent; and Versailles frowned disapprobation, for this man, who had been the intimate friend of two European sovereigns, had lightly mocked at all authority; but the royal princes, moved by curiosity, went out into the city to watch the strange spectacle of so much spontaneous enthusiasm; and wondered, perhaps, what it was all about. The crowd seemed to be permanently gathered outside the hotel where the old man lodged.

On the great day, at four o'clock in the afternoon, he drove, through cheering crowds, to the Academy's headquarters at the Cour du Louvre. That august body—all but those members of it who were also churchmen—came out to meet him; an honour they had never paid to any visitor before—not even to foreign monarchs. They made him take the President's seat, and, with rare kindness, they declared that they would not allow him to make a speech; he sat there while d'Alembert, in the name of them all, did him homage in such a manner that the old man's eyes filled with tears.

The proceedings over, he drove through the packed streets to the Comédie, where a play—the latest tragedy he had written— was to be performed. As he entered his box, every man and woman in the theatre stood up and shouted his name. He tried to hide behind one of his companions, but the shouting went on till he came forward. At that moment an actor entered the box and placed a crown of laurel on his head. "Ah! Dieu! vous voulez donc me faire mourir à force de gloire!" he said, and put off the wreath; whereupon the Prince de Beauvau, entering the box, took up the wreath and forced him to wear it. There followed an extraordinary uproar which lasted for more than twenty minutes. At last the actors were able to begin the play.

It is a weak play to read, but the audience was in the mood to applaud every line; and when the curtain fell the uproar was deafening. When the curtain rose again, the old-man's statue, brought from the foyer of the theatre, was in the middle of the stage. At the sight, the audience seemed to become delirious with enthusiasm; silence was only restored when Mlle Vestris advanced and recited a dozen lines in honour of the hero; she then placed a laurel wreath on the head of the statue. At this the old man, who had retreated to the back of his box, came tottering forward, his eyes streaming with tears, a prey to strong emotion. What emotion, who shall say? Was he enjoying it all, or was he thinking, bitterly, that he would give all this glory for another year of his adventurous youth? . . . Then, when some sort of order was restored, they played a comedy—one of his comedies—with the crowned statue still in the middle of the stage. And then there were more ovations, and another triumphal progress as his carriage took him slowly back to his hotel, with men climbing on the wheels and the step, to catch a glimpse of him, even to kiss his hands. When he reached the hotel at last, we are told that he sat down and "wept like a child." Exactly two months later he was dead.

What had he done, this old man who sent Paris into such a frenzy of adoration? Written plays? What, indeed, had he not written? He had written tragedies and comedies, and poetry of all kinds, from the epigram to the epic; and though none of these things are much to our taste to-day, they hit the taste of that day irresistibly. But his prose still counts. He wrote histories and biographies, and treatises on philosophy, essays, and dialogues, and novels, and pamphlets—pamphlets on every conceivable subject; he was the greatest pamphleteer of all time. And though many of his writings appeared, for prudential reasons, with no author's name on the title-page, they could never be mistaken for anybody else's; for no other man could get just that champagne sparkle into his style. He was the master of all forms of wit, from outrageous mockery to the most delicate irony. His was the most active, the most alert and nimble mind of the day. For sixty years he toiled indefatigably with his pen; for all his mercurial temperament, he forced himself to a steady industry which is one of the wonders of literary history; sometimes he had six books on hand at one time. What was unique about him was his intellectual energy, and the fact that till the last weeks of his life it never seems to have flagged. He made many grievous blunders, and wrote some things that we can almost hate him for having written; but when we look at the immense array of his collected works, and reflect on how this man moulded the mind and shaped, for good or evil, the destinies of Europe, a feeling something like awe comes over us.

And though to us, with the phlegmatic temper of our race, there may be something ludicrous in that French frenzy of enthusiasm, there is something great in it too. One is not surprised that Carlyle was struck by it, admiring the hero-worship though he did not much admire the hero. Those Frenchmen felt that honour was due to a great intelligence and a great achievement; to the man who had defied the embattled powers of the world and fought with unfailing courage in the cause of truth and justice. Few of them, probably, saw the whole meaning of the incident, or understood that they were ringing out the old order and ringing in the French Revolution, when they stood for twenty minutes in the theatre shouting, "Vive Voltaire."

THE SCOTTISH TWINS

THE worst of meeting distinguished people is that, so far as my small experience goes, they don't say distinguished things; or, at least, they don't say them to *you*—possibly they reserve their really great utterances for other distinguished people. But in the course of the only conversation I ever had with Bernard Shaw, he did say one characteristic thing, a thing I have never forgotten, though he himself doubtless remembers it no more than he remembers the obscure Australian he said it to. He asked me whether there were many Scots in Australia; being weak in statistics, I could only reply that there were some. And were they all successful? Again I was forced by a shameful lack of exact information to take refuge in vagueness and reply that, with one deplorable exception, I believed they were fairly prosperous. His reply—though I don't profess to recall his exact words—was to this effect: "Of course they are. They prosper everywhere, and it's the Shorter Catechism that's responsible. As boys they whet their intellects on the Catechism, and when they grow up, though they shed all the theological doctrines they have learned from it, they never lose the intellectual keenness they acquired in learning them. Their Catechism has made them too sharp for the rest of the world. They transfer their acuteness from theology to business, and get the better of everybody." To do Mr Shaw justice, I must add that I don't think this ingenious theory of Scotch success was a deep-seated conviction; I believe he had only just thought of it.

Whether it was true as well as ingenious is a large question. I can only speak for myself: I was brought up on the Shorter Catechism. I have long since forgotten it all, but as a small boy I could have rattled you off answers to anything you wanted to know about justification, sanctification, adoption, effectual calling, and other mysteries of religion. Such attempts to equip children with an armour of theological doctrine may be harmless; at least, I don't see that the learning by rote of those entirely incomprehensible formulas did me, personally, any harm. But it did me no good, not even the kind of good Mr Shaw spoke of.

I ought, on his theory, to be an astute business man, and enviably solvent; instead of which—but this is too painful a topic. Anyhow, the soul of a nation is not to be quite so simply summed up. Let us go a little deeper; let us consider the story of the heart of Robert Bruce.

That was a story on which we children were also brought up. Our attitude towards the story of the Bruce was very different from our attitude towards Effectual Calling. Bruce was for us the great name in history; the supreme hero. His end was worthy of his life. We saw nothing strange in his dying request that, since the cares of his kingdom had prevented his going in his lifetime to the Holy Land, his heart at least should be carried thither. That the victor of Bannockburn should ask, with his latest breath, that his heart should be borne to Palestine probably taught us more about Christianity than all the questions and answers in the Shorter Catechism put together. So James Douglas (a hero only less splendid than the king himself) undertook the mission, and, carrying the heart in a casket, set forth at the head of a small band of faithful followers. But he was beset by his enemies in Spain (I think it was in Spain) and fell in battle; and as he fell he lifted the casket and hurled it towards the East, crying out with a loud voice, *"Pass onward, brave heart, as thou wert wont to do!"* The heart never reached the Holy Land, but it was not lost at that time; the casket containing it was carried back to Scotland and buried under Melrose Abbey. And there, so far as the story went when I was a boy, it ended; and I still think it was a great story, though I now know a little more about Bruce and the reasons why he thought he ought to have gone to Palestine by way of penance.

But the story, after all these centuries, has had its sequel. Nine or ten years ago there were excavations at Melrose, and the casket was discovered and sent for safe custody to the Public Works Department at Edinburgh. This seems a bit of an anti-climax; we can imagine the curt official note, probably type-written: "We beg to forward casket, one, containing heart of R. Bruce deceased; kindly acknowledge receipt of same." But there is worse to follow. Dr Christie, a Presbyterian missionary in Palestine, conceived the fine idea that Bruce's dying wish might still (though rather late in the day) be fulfilled, and that his heart might fitly be conveyed to Palestine in connexion with the new Scottish Memorial Church at Jerusalem. And somebody was inspired to suggest that the bearer of the sacred relic should be the Marquis of Douglas and Clydesdale, a descendant of the original Sir James Douglas.   But, alas for the noble project, the heart could not be found.   Somebody in the Public Works Department had mislaid it.

It seems to me that this tale throws a flood of light, not on the heart of Bruce, but on the heart of Scotland.   To have the hero's dying behest fulfilled after all—and to have, for the instrument of its fulfilment, a lineal descendant of the valiant warrior to whom the original mission was entrusted—this is pure romance. Any reputable carrying firm would do the job just as efficiently as the Marquis of Douglas and Clydésdale; the choice of that particular person as a carrier turns the affair into a poem.   To connect it with the opening of a new Presbyterian church in Jerusalem is not exactly poetry, but it is good business—a capital stunt. Finally, to learn that some clerk in the Public Works Department has stowed the venerable relic away in some cupboard and that nobody can remember where it was put, is to drop sheer down into the abyss of bathos.   O my country!

The only way to understand the Scot is clearly to recognize that there are two Scotlands.   One is the Scotland of poetry and romance, of Wallace, and Bruce, and Montrose, and Queen Mary, the tragic queen whose tale has been told by so many poets and novelists.   This is the Scotland that Sir Walter found ready to his hand, so that he did not need to invent; he had only to go about gathering the legends of the country-side, and write them down for the delight of the world.   This is the Scotland that was the home of courage and honour and loyalty no less heroic because it was loyalty to lost causes and sometimes to unworthy chieftains.

And there is also the Scotland of the Glasgow merchant, the most prosaic of all God's creatures; the Scotland of the canny and parsimonious Scotchman about whom more jokes have been made than about any other subject with the possible exception of mothers-in-law.   Rob Roy and Bailie Nicol Jarvie—the whole of Scottish history and the whole of Scottish literature is full of this baffling contradiction between the Scot who would blithely fling away lands and life for Prince Charlie and the Scot who would not give sixpence to the greatest cause on earth till he knew the rate of interest.   And the curious thing is, not that Scotland contains the two kinds of men—there is nothing in that—but that every typical Scot includes the two kinds of men.   When Burns informs us that

> Prudent, cautious self-control
> Is wisdom's root,

he is a typical Scot; and when he turns round and sings,

> Sae rantingly, sae wantonly,
> Sae dauntingly gaed he,
> He play'd a spring, and danc'd it round
> Below the gallows-tree,

he is a typical Scot too. You find this two-sidedness in every one of the Waverley novels; Scott is the king of romance, yet an English critic rightly places him with "the supreme masters of the commonplace." In what other literature will you find this dualism? Imagine Victor Hugo writing *La Terre* for a change!

This is the paradox of the Scot, and I may illustrate it by a reminiscence. I was brought up in a village on the edge of the North Sea. The landsmen grew oats and potatoes and pigs and other prosaic things; the seafarers caught herrings, and though their perilous occupation had its poetic side I doubt if they saw it. At certain seasons, the chief business of the village was the preparation of the fish for the English market; than fish-curing it would be hard to imagine a less romantic employment. Yet of the whole neighbourhood it might have been sung, as Andrew Lang sang of a region farther south, that

> The air was full of ballad notes
> Borne out of long ago.

There were ruined castles at intervals along the coast; the place was eloquent with old stories and traditions; and, in particular, memories of the Forty-five gave a glamour to many a spot. There was one cave, especially, in which a Jacobite nobleman (the original, I understand, of Baron Bradwardine in *Waverley*) had for many months hidden from King George's redcoats after the collapse of the rebellion. He was kept alive—so the story ran, and so we used firmly to believe—by the devotion of a little girl, who used to carry a basket of provisions to him every day, riding to and from the cave on the back of a fox. The fox's brush obliterates his tracks on the snow (anybody may contradict this who cares to).

This historic cave was a favourite place for picnics in the summer. To sit and eat our victuals just where that old Jacobite lord had sat and eaten his, to look out upon the sea through the narrow entrance and to imagine the brave man's feelings when he heard the tramp of soldiers near by, was always rather exciting.

But our most exciting experience of all came in an odd way. Half of the picnic party had entered the cave. (The entrance, as I have said, was narrow—at one point so narrow that you had to lie down and wriggle through; there was no difficulty about the process, but no dignity.) Then came the turn of a young woman who was what the poets .call buxom. Down she lay, and in she went—a certain distance; then she stopped. We who were left outside soon realized what had happened, though we could hear no word from within the cave, because the aperture was completely filled; it was as if a rubber stopper had been put into the mouth of a bottle. What was to be done? Consternation was succeeded by grave deliberation. She was making no progress—except for a feeble occasional kick, no movement at all. At last, the elders decided that she must be extracted, and they laid hold of her feet and began to pull; but a violent kicking warned them to desist. Perhaps those unfortunates inside the cave, who saw themselves cut off from light, liberty, and the pursuit of happiness, had chosen the same moment to pull in the other direction, So the elders stood back and deliberated again, with many scratchings and shakings of puzzled heads. What was to be done? What would you have done?—blasted her out with dynamite, or what? Finally, it was decided that the problem must be left for time to solve; in a few days she was sure to become more or less emaciated, and would slip out with perfect ease. Luckily, those within had taken a hamper in with them; they would be all right for a few days. Of course, if they were foolish enough to give the young woman some of their sandwiches and hard-boiled eggs, the process of attenuation would be retarded and their own emancipation postponed. We wanted to signal to them that they must be inflexibly firm about this; but there was no way of signalling. And as we, outside, had nothing to eat, we thought we might as well go home and have a meal; that was the practical, commonsense thing to do, and we would have done it, but we had not gone far when a shout brought us running back. By a supreme effort, the heroine of the story had extracted herself.

That cave was rich in romance, but I suppose nobody would call this incident romantic. The spot was haunted by poetic memories, but nobody could make an idyll or an epic out of a fat girl in that ridiculous predicament; it simply cannot be done. Looking at the story across the gulf of years, thinking of that historic cave made sacred by the gallant adherent of a lost cause, and made absurd by the feebly waving feet of an overgrown female, I seem to see a parable. A parable of Scotland—prosaic, poetic, prudent, passionate, cautious, reckless, shrewd, romantic, loyal, commercial, paradoxical Scotland. It is not the least of her paradoxes that though her sons love her they very willingly leave her, and run to the uttermost ends of the earth; and though their parting word to her is—

> And I will come again, my dear,
> Tho' it were ten thousand mile,

they hardly ever do.

OUR PROMINENT CITIZENS

SOMETIMES, in a mood betwixt merriment and malice, I like to toy with the thought of certain high and puissant personages— prominent citizens, of immense importance in their own little day and in their own little world—coming back to the earth where they strutted so pompously, to learn for themselves how they are honoured by posterity. What tremendous surprises there would be! What gnashing of teeth.

It is pleasing, for instance, to see incredulity, stupefaction, dismay, and chagrin chase one another across the solemn countenance of Sir Thomas Lucy as it is borne in upon his dull mind that his name would have been wholly blotted out from men's remembrance had it not been for an obscure young scapegrace from Stratford, who is supposed (on the flimsiest of evidence) to have poached on his preserves.

Or, again, one's delighted fancy plays with the picture of the placid, smiling, self-satisfied face of Sir William Temple, statesman, diplomat, scholar, squire, political thinker, writer of polished prose, finest of fine gentlemen, all rolled into one. "I was a world's wonder," his face seems to say; "whoever is forgotten, I, at least, must be remembered by the planet of which I was so conspicuous an ornament." Certainly, your honour; of course you are remembered; but not for your statesmanship or your scholarship or your rounded periods (which nobody now reads), or your urbane manners; for these things none of us cares a doit. You are remembered for the sake of a delightful girl who wrote you some charming letters before she was eccentric enough to marry you; and you are remembered still better for the sake of a quiet, inconspicuous young man who acted for some years as your amanuensis—a somewhat pallid youth, a dyspeptic, with disagreeable manners; his name—which may very well have slipped your memory, you have so many grand friends to recall—was Jonathan Swift.

Or, once more, do but look at yonder magnate; grave, soberly clad, ceremonious; plainly a man of consequence and authority.

He seems surprised and a little pained that you do not at once take off your hat to him. "Has the world lost all its manners, all its respect for the eminent?" he asks. "Surely you know me? The world's memory must be indeed short if I am forgotten. I flatter myself I was, in my time, not the least of England's merchant princes. As Chairman of the East India Company for the first twenty years of the nineteenth century, I swayed the destinies of Empire, and—" "But I say, I say—hold on a minute; this is really interesting. The first twenty—why, good heavens! you must have been there in Lamb's time!" "Lamb—what sort of a lamb? What in the world are you talking about?" "Why—yes, of course —Lamb was a clerk in the India House—accountancy branch— during those very years. Perhaps you can tell me some new story about him, or even remember some joke he made. This is really thrilling!" "God bless my soul, sir, do you imagine that I—I who directed the counsels of the Company—knew the name of every pettifogging quill-driver in the Company's employ, and listened to their miserable jokes?" "Oh, well, I'll look up Lamb's *Life and Letters* and see if your name is mentioned." . . . At this the magnate flies back, indignant, to the shades.

Once more—does it not strike you as queer, to say the least of it, that a poor devil of a Paris university student, who seldom had enough to eat, who had less than no morals, whose companions were thieves and murderers and their appropriate women-folk— a grimy fifteenth-century *apache* who happened to have the knack of making verses—should be the one man of his time and country to achieve immortality, and that for his sake, and for his sake only, so many grave and pompous and tremendous seigneurs of the day should be given a kind of minor immortality? And not only such big-wigs, but a number of disreputable little-wigs as well, have climbed into remembrance on this youth's lean shoulders. What, but for him, should we know or care about that gallows crew—about Master Guy Tabarie, or about Colin des Cayeul (described in the documents as *fortis operator crochetorum*, a powerful operator of picklocks), or about Regnier de Montigny, the best-born and blackest-hearted scoundrel of the gang? They swung on gibbets, all that precious company; and, by all accounts, deserved no better fate. They were not even distinguished criminals; they were squalid, commonplace ruffians, and there is no earthly reason why their names should be known to anybody to-day except that their companion in iniquity was one of the great poets of the world. For his sake, too, we remember his poor old mother, whom he seems to have loved even while he was breaking her heart with his ill-doings, and for whom he made the great Ballade; and the good priest who adopted him, gave him his name, educated him, and forgave him seventy and seven times. And for his sake—coming back to my point—we remember the various bishops and magistrates and other exalted personages who presided at his trials and condemned him to the greater and the lesser torture, and, having condemned, incontinently dismissed him from their lordly minds. What would they think, I repeat, if they came back to earth and found their names remembered, not at all for their own sweet sakes, but because for a moment they crossed the path of a lean and desperate cutpurse who made scandalous rhymes, by name François Villon?

"Take, physic, pomp," says the disillusioned Lear; and this is the physic for you, O people of importance; the right purge for your high-blown pride. This is that honest mirror for magistrates, that candid looking-glass wherein whoso gazes will see clearly his own complete insignificance. This is the primer from which you great ones of the earth may learn humility; and it has lessons for us obscure nonentities as well; for we are apt to let ourselves be foolishly irritated by the ineffable airs you give yourselves—till we remember that Time and Death set all to rights, and that in a century or less you will be as entirely forgotten as we ourselves, unless our names, yours or ours, happen by some quaint accident to be embalmed in a footnote to the biography of one of the real immortals.

THE PATRIOT'S DILEMMA

"I suppose you want to know why I look so sad, eh?" said the foreign-looking man in the corner of the smoking-carriage.

The question seemed to be addressed to me, but before replying I glanced round at my fellow-passengers. Their looks were stonily unresponsive. I could scarcely blame them, for it was an express train—stops were infrequent, and the little man had been holding forth pretty continuously ever since we left Sydney. Public opinion, it was plain, was not in favour of explanations of his sad looks; public opinion was strongly in favour of being allowed to go to sleep. But I had acquired a strong dislike for some of my fellow-passengers, and had decided that the discipline of suffering was what they needed; besides, there was a wistful look on the little man's face which appealed to me.

"Of course I do," I replied. "We all do. Go ahead. Give sorrow words. Tell us the afflicting tale. Confess the crimes that have brought you to this pass; your guilty secret will be safe with us. Or is it a love affair gone awry? Whatever it is, out with it—unless, by the way, the trouble is gastric. I am a member of a club, and hearing about other people's insides is beginning to pall on me."

"No, no, no," the little man broke in. "Nothing of that sort, I assure you. My trouble lies deeper than doctor's probe can ever touch. It is a trouble of the spirit, not of the body. Dyspepsia is nothing; it can be completely cured in a few minutes by—I forget the name of the remedy, but you will find it in the advertisement columns of the morning paper. There is no remedy for *my* trouble. It is incurable.

"The fact is that I suffer from an irreparable loss—my native country has been stolen from me. You will all understand what this means. Looking round at these gentlemen's faces I can easily read there an intense and ardent patriotism. All of you, I can see it at a glance, love your native land with an unquenchable devotion."

I glanced furtively at the face of a stout commercial traveller sitting opposite me, and reflected that the little man must possess some mystical power of seeing what was hidden from the common eye.

"Yes, you love your native country, and your hearts will bleed for one who is not merely an exile from his fatherland, but who no longer has a fatherland to be exiled from. You read the other day of some small islands off the coast· of Japan being totally submerged. Imagine the feelings of a man born in one of those islands when he learns from the papers that during his absence his native land has been sunk beneath the waves for ever. Well, my case is even more afflicting than his. I will tell you.

"I was born on shipboard, in mid-ocean; to be exact, on the *Muthos*, the largest and best ship of the famous Green Anchor line. It was a long, long voyage in those days; and, taking one voyage with another, there were a good many babies born on the splendid ship. So many that, as we grew up, we formed a society, and kept in touch with one another, however scattered we might be. As many of us as possible used to meet once a year, and make speeches and sing songs about our native vessel.

"After a number of years it occurred to an advanced thinker among us that we were nursing too narrow an ideal of patriotism; 'parochial,' he called us—and exhorted us to cultivate what he termed 'the larger loyalty,' which meant including the natives, not only of the *Muthos*, but of all the ships of that line. We did this and though I always felt that we had diminished the intensity of our patriotism, we enormously increased its scope; in our palmy days there were several hundreds of us. We wore a badge with a green anchor on it. We formed branches in all the great cities. Members of a branch would meet at regular intervals and talk to one another about the superiority of the Green Anchor line to all other lines. Our sentiments were summed up in the hymn with which proceedings always closed. There was never a dry eye when we sang—

> O never a ship the world has seen
> To match the ships of the Anchor Green,
> And never a ship on the world's wide waters
> Is better loved by her sons and daughters.

"Shall I sing the whole hymn to you? There are only fifteen stanzas. No? Well, perhaps better not; it would only arouse unavailing sorrows.

"Our patriotic fervour, I remember, rose to its highest pitch when the noble proprietors of the line were accused, by evil-minded slanderers, of profiteering in freights; we held special meetings, at which we waved little flags and shouted, 'Our Company, right or wrong!' We told little stories to illustrate the virtues of our managing director and the vices of the managing directors of other companies. We never swerved from the belief that our ships were the finest, the fastest, and the most seaworthy afloat; our captains the most intrepid navigators, our directors the most incredibly skilful financiers. We even held that our rats and cockroaches—of which we had a liberal supply—were in some mystical way superior to the rats and cockroaches of other ships. You cannot deny that we were thorough-going patriots, we Green Anchorites.

"And now it is all gone, all like an insubstantial pageant faded, to return no more—ah, nevermore! Steam, detestable steam, has stolen our fatherland from us; it has vanished on clouds of vapour. Our company, lured by the love of gold, went into steam, and our brave ships—such of them as had not already foundered—were ruthlessly scrapped. I am a homeless orphan in an alien world; a denationalized person, with no native land on which to lavish my wealth of patriotic devotion. Can you wonder that I wear a permanent look of sadness?"

I looked round upon my fellow-passengers to see how they had taken the affecting tale; somewhat to my surprise—for I had not thought them amenable to the pathetic—they had all closed their eyes, to prevent the briny tears from welling forth. And, since the little man seemed to have at last subsided into mournful silence, I closed my own eyes, and fell into a train of reflection on the subject of patriotism and what it means.

I suppose there is no doubt (is there?) that patriotism does mean love of the land in which one was born, and this does, of course, make it awkward for any one to feel patriotic who was not born in any land at all, but on a ship at sea. This, however, is a difficulty which confronts only a very small minority of the human race. But what about those persons, not at all a negligible minority in Australia, for instance, who were born in one country and have lived most of their lives in another? Perhaps it is best to be frankly personal. Take my own case. I was ten years old when I first came to Australia; strictly speaking, and according to etymology, I am debarred from being or ever becoming a patriotic Australian. The Commonwealth Year Book will tell you precisely how many persons there are in our midst who are in like manner denied the privilege of being patriotic Australians. When good times return (if they ever do), and a vigorous immigration policy is resumed, before many years the persons debarred from being patriotic Australians will be in the majority in Australia. Yet, speaking for myself, so far as I can analyse my own feelings—always a difficult thing to do, and rather a disgusting thing to talk about in public—I can detect at the back of my mind no affection for my native land comparable with my regard for the land in which I have grown up and now live. Somebody with whom I was arguing about this the other day informed me that the patriotic instinct lies dormant, but is never killed; when I am a very old man my yearnings will return to the land of my birth, and I shall hate to think of my bones being laid in any other soil. All I can say about this is that I don't believe it; but even if it were true, what special beauty would there be about regarding the place of one's birth as a desirable cemetery? Tennyson takes comfort from the knowledge that his friend's body is laid in English earth,

> And from his ashes may be made
> The violet of his native land.

I can understand a man's feeling like that about the ashes of a friend; but I fail to understand a man's having any concern at all about his own ashes. If I knew that from my ashes would be made the cauliflower of Mexico, I should not be in the least perturbed about the prospect. But, apart from these ghoulish considerations, I feel, I repeat, no glow of affection for my native land, and no particular love for its people—except, of course, when I hear them attacked by members of other and inferior races.

My conclusion is that the word "patriotism" should be expunged from our vocabulary, or given a wider meaning than the dictionaries now give it.

If we are going to continue to reserve the name of patriot for the man who cherishes a sentimental devotion to the spot of earth where, by the accident of circumstances, he happened to be born, let us be logical, and declare with Chesterton that patriotism is an intensely local thing; he speaks of Notting Hill patriots and West Kensington patriots. This reminds me of a Devonshire story William Morris used to tell. Venn and Ottery St Mary (pronounced Skimmery) are adjoining parishes. A man fell into the Otter, and shouted for help to a stolid carle sitting on the bank. Quoth he: "Be you Skimmery or be you Venn?" The luckless one gasped out, "Venn! help! help!" "Then you may drown for a blasted foreigner!" called out the inhabitant of Skimmery parish. That was true Chestertonian patriotism.

I should open the doors wider and admit the patriotism of any man who loves his country—his country, whether it be the country of his birth or not. What land shall a man love if not the land where his friends are, where he fell in love, where his children are growing up, where he has made his home? To what other land shall he dedicate his hopes and fears, his faith and his endeavour? Where the treasure is, shall not the heart be also? And love and friendship are the treasure. Patriotism in this wider sense I can respect; the other kind—devotion to the country in which one's parents happened to be living at the time when one was born—is a piece of sentimentalism. Let it be abolished forthwith.

THE WILD PLANET

THE WILD PLANET

ACCORDING to a palm-leaf manuscript lately discovered in the Cave of the Thousand Buddhas at Tun-Huang, the most ancient of all things was the goddess Pwll, who had the power of bringing things into existence by thinking of them. One day she thought of herself, and so she came into existence. But she was not fond of thinking, and so for ten million years or so she was the only thing that existed. Then one day, feeling suddenly lonely, she thought of a little friendly company of beings with whom she might converse; and it was thus that the other gods and goddesses came into existence. And they conversed with one another for ten million years or so, without noticing that they had nothing to converse about. Now many of us human beings contrive to talk for a lifetime in the most friendly manner about nothing; but to talk about nothing for ten million years is somewhat wearing, and the gods and goddesses were so terribly bored that if it had happened that Pwll had thought about annihilation, and they had all ceased to be, none of them would have offered any objection; but that was an idea that did not occur to her. Instead, she set herself to think of toys for them to play with; and in this way she created many playthings of which nothing is known to human beings to this day. But one afternoon, in an idle moment between sleeping and waking, she conceived the idea of the universe; and so the universe began to exist.

There are some severe moralists who say that the lesson to be drawn from this is that one ought never to have any idle moments. But it is to be noticed that if Pwll had not had that idle moment the moralists would not be here to criticize her.

Now Pwll had an untidy mind, and the universe as it first existed was just a mess; and the gods and goddesses were soon tired of playing with it, for in truth there was nothing amusing to be done with it; and at last it lay in a corner, entirely neglected, for ten million years or so. And then one day Pi, who had a genius for tidiness (it was he who first thought of number, and succeeded in teaching his fellow-deities to count up to ten), took the universe in hand, and set it all in order, and trained the stars to circle round one another in so exact and punctual a manner that it was a real pleasure to watch them; and all the other gods and goddesses, when they had nothing more amusing to do, would sit on the edge of space for a thousand years at a time, with their chins in their hands, admiring the ingenious mind of Pi and the docility with which the stars obeyed his behests.

Now the youngest of the gods, according to this manuscript, was Raq, who hated mathematics, and who could never succeed in counting beyond five without making a mistake, so that Pi was always laughing at him. But in the end Raq did a thing that Pi would not have thought of, for he invented the seed of life. This seed he planted on one of the stars as it passed close to him in the course of its wheeling. And one day he called to the others to come and see what his seed had done. "Hi!" he cried out, "here is some real fun at last. We shall not be bored any more by Pi's tame stars, that never dare to stray a hair's breadth from the paths he has marked out for them. What is the fun of watching things that do exactly the same thing every day for ever and ever? Here, at last, is a star that is not going to be tame any more. Watch my wild planet and you will see that it will never do the same thing on two successive days."

And all the gods and goddesses sat on the edge of space with their chins in their hands, looking with great interest at the star every time it wheeled near them. For ten million years or so they sat watching the growing of the tree of life, none knowing what it would do next, with the exception of Raq, who had thought of the seed and who therefore knew all that was hidden in it. And even he, though he knew beforehand all that was going to happen, was not bored, for he liked watching the faces of the others as they stared at the surprising things that were happening on the star.

And, indeed, they might well be surprised at the monstrous fruitfulness of that tree, and the infinite diversity of its fruits, from dinosaur to elephant, from elephant to man, from man to flea, from flea to microbe; all these things, and myriads more, were hidden from the first in the little, sleeping seed which Raq had tossed on to the star as it wheeled near him. But Pi, the mathematical god, was not a whit perturbed by all this. "What is all this nonsense about a wild planet?" he said to Raq one day. "There is no wildness in the universe, now that I have set it in

THE WILD PLANET 185

order. However queer some of the fruits of your tree may look, they must all obey my laws. Two and two will never make five, my young friend, on your star or on any other star. I am sorry if my laws bore you, but they are immutable and inexorable. I made them so."

Some of the younger gods and goddesses thought the arrogance of Pi was in bad taste, and they set themselves to overturn his calculations; but he was always ready with a repartee. For instance, it was Lir who invented shadows, and sprinkled them over the star as it wheeled near him, and for a time the star bore a chequered and untidy appearance; but, as soon as Pi saw this, he arranged that each shadow should be cast by an object, and should be exactly proportioned to the size of the object; and so all was tidy again. And it was Phuph who invented laughter and tossed it on to the star, and there was a new sound in the universe, a sound which seemed at first to·be wild and irresponsible and lawless; but as soon as Pi heard this, he at once took steps to arrange that, just as a shadow was cast by an object, so a laugh was caused by a joke, and the volume of laughter bore an exact mathematical ratio to the size of the joke; and he convinced the other gods and goddesses, much to their sorrow, that laughter was entirely subject to his laws. Given a joke of a certain quality, he said, the amount of laughter that would follow it was predictable with absolute mathematical certainty. Whenever he used the word "predictable" the other gods and goddesses shivered, and were silent. It became the most unpopular word in the vocabulary of the heavens. The younger deities cherished a burning desire to create something that would behave in an unpredictable manner.

It was Rhum who invented greed, and sprinkled it over the star, and at first it was thought that under the influence of greed many creatures, and especially men, would do quite unpredictable things. But Pi, not at all disconcerted, announced that since all men were greedy, their actions were more completely predictable than ever before. "By creating greed," he said, "you have created the science of economics, which is a new branch of mathematics. You have extended the bounds of my kingdom. Thank you very much."

Then the younger gods and goddesses, exasperated by the perfect confidence of Pi, put their heads together and resolved that, come what would, they must put an end to his overweening arrogance; they vowed that they would put something into the universe which should not be subject to mathematical law, something whose behaviour should be unpredictable by Pi. After much deliberation they decided to concentrate on the heart of man, and to throw into it, as the star wheeled near them, all the strangest inventions they could think of; to fill it with wayward impulses that would drive it hither and thither like a wind-driven leaf. It was then that they invented right and wrong, and joy and sorrow, and love and hatred, and courage and fear, and religion, and desire, and hope, and patriotism, and eccentricity, and art and a hundred other quaint and curious devices; and all of these they put into the heart of man, not thinking at all of his happiness, but only of the discomfiture of Pi.

And thus (says the palm-leaf manuscript found at Tun-Huang) did the heart of man become the dwelling-place of all that is strange and incalculable; for the gods put into it things that are mutually incompatible. For instance, a man will regard sorrow as his enemy, yet will he see in love his highest good, though he knows well that love brings sorrow, in a world in which parting is inevitable. And because he loves his country he will face death, though death will separate him for ever from the country he loves; and he will burn men at the stake for the sake of a religion which teaches him the duty of goodwill to all men. And one man who does not fear death will be intensely afraid of ridicule; and another man will find his chief happiness in working out a proof that happiness is impossible. In short, the gods made the heart of man like a den of wild beasts for ever fighting one another, so that he began to behave in a perfectly incalculable way, a wholly unpredictable way, and Pi the mathematical god became very depressed and gloomy for a time.

But after a while he cheered up, and declared that he was by no means beaten. "For," said he, "in spite of everything, man's behaviour is still exactly calculable if one takes the trouble to ascertain the facts. For instance, you imagine that love is a wild and wayward and lawless thing; on the contrary, there is a mathematical exactitude about love; for the love in the heart of a man bears an exact ratio to the attractiveness of the person loved—" but here the others jeered at him, and, indeed, this was a fairly obvious begging of the question. So he thought for another thousand years or so, at the end of which time he announced that he had invented the science of statistics, which brought man completely under mathematical rules again, in spite of all his vagaries. "Out of any thousand men," he said, "I can tell you precisely how many will face the enemy and how many will run away; how many will cheat at cards, how many will take to drink, and how many to vegetarianism, how many will be saints, how many villains, and how many fools. Although, owing to your monkey tricks, I am unable to predict how any individual will act in given circumstances, I can tell with perfect precision how men in the mass will behave; and that is what matters."

The manuscript ends with the statement that there is a little sect among men called the Pi-worshippers, who believe that Pi had the best of the argument, and that all human actions can, if the facts are sufficiently known, be stated in mathematical formulae. These are the people who speak with hushed and awe-stricken voices of the "immutable laws" and proclaim that however men may writhe and twist and struggle, they cannot escape from the bonds of these inexorable laws. But there are others who blaspheme against Pi and declare him to be a lying god, and the father of lies. They say that if there are any "immutable laws," neither gods nor men have ever yet discovered what they are. They say that the behaviour of men is the one supremely unpredictable thing in the universe; and that any one pretending to be able to reduce the facts of human behaviour to an exact science is a mountebank, and the truth is not in him. For the gods, when for the discomfiture of Pi they gave such a tangled confusion of gifts to man, were unkind to the mathematicians and the economists, but kind to man; for they left him free to laugh at the Juggernaut of inexorable law, with which the Pi-worshippers seek to make his blood run cold; free to go forward, unfearing, towards whatever goal he may set his strange heart upon.

TIPSY DIXIT

I ADMIT that I am growing a little hard of hearing. I think I am bound to mention that personal fact at the outset, in fairness to the clergyman whose sermon I am about to report—my title may possibly do him an injustice. Others who heard the sermon, which was preached in Perth one Sunday evening, aver that he was as sober as a judge. The innocence of my life has hitherto preserved me from any extensive contact with judges, but I suppose this means that he was moderately sober. It is certainly true, too, that the newspaper report of the sermon, on Monday, read like a perfectly sane, mild, respectable utterance. But you know what reporters are. Look at what the *Hansard* men do for the politicians! Go to Parliament House and listen to a debate; then read *Hansard's* account of that debate, and marvel at what can be done by skill and ingenuity. All the tangled verbiage straightened out, the hopeless obscurities cleared up, the bad grammar corrected, every subject fitted with a predicate, one or two ideas introduced, and the whole thing made neat and ship-shape and given a quite intelligent look. If you have read the old story of King Lear, and also the masterpiece that Shakespeare made out of that old story, you have some notion of what the *Hansard* man does for a parliamentary speech. A *Hansard* man, in good form, could make a bullock driver's remarks to his team sound like the vicar's address to a mothers' meeting. The reporter who dished up this sermon for next day's paper made it look like a perfectly sober expression of perfectly blameless opinions, but that was not how it sounded to me. I am far from wishing to get the reporter into trouble, for I have not the slightest doubt that he meant well; and intentions, you know, are what count. But I simply cannot let his version go uncorrected. The sermon, as I heard it, was quite a different thing. Here it is, and you will agree, when you have read it, that kindness, and nothing else, has impelled me to omit the clergyman's name.

"My text, brethren, is doubtless familiar to you all: *In the midst of life we are in Perth*. It applies, not to this city alone, but to every necropolis in Australia. The others, however, do not concern us—the essential thing in life is to be clear about ourselves. Clarity begins at home.

"What I want you all to be perfectly clear about, first of all, is that you are quite, quite dead. This sermon is really a soliloquy in a morgue. I feel very lonely, I can tell you, standing here in this pulpit haranguing all you poor dead men and dead women; but a clergyman must not shrink from these gruesome tasks.

"There are some who say that you are not to be called dead, because you never were alive; but this is false doctrine. I know that you were once alive, because I know, though appearances are against it, that you were once little children, and little children are full of life. That is why it is written that of such is the Kingdom of Heaven. But you soon went to school, and there you learned to do exactly as other little boys and girls did, and so you lost the joy of life and became tame little conventionalists and conformists; and of such is the Kingdom of Death. If there was still any spark of vitality in you, it was quenched when you went out into the world, and found that it was safest to conform to the usages of the world and decidedly dangerous to have any ideas of your own; and you never saw the truth that safety is the most dangerous thing in the world, because to be safe is to run the risk of losing one's soul.

"You accepted all the meaningless formulas that had once had a meaning in them, and all the old creeds that had once had a flame in them; and you repeated all the old shibboleths, and ceased to speak or think for yourselves; and you walked the earth like automata pushed from behind, and you did not know that you were dying, and you died.

"If you ask me, as a physician of the soul, of what disease you died—but, of course, you won't ask me, because you are not interested in this, nor in anything else—I should say that you died of psittacosis, or parrot fever. The first symptom of this dread disease is the repetition by the patient of sentences he has learned like a parrot. You said what you were taught to say, and said it endlessly.

"And instead of life, which is a magnificent adventure, full of alarums and excursions, of passion and striving, you sought the safe way, and wrapped yourselves up in routine, the winding-sheet in which you are thickly swathed to-day. Purple and scarlet and gold are the colours of life—you chose a dull brown. You are dull in your work, and dull in your play. Yes, from your play, too, the zest of life has departed; even your games must be the fashionable games. You go in immense crowds to see a handful of men play cricket, not because you enjoy it, not because you are not bored by it, but because everybody else is going. You play auction bridge because, and so long as, everybody else plays auction bridge; you discard this adventurous sport and learn to play contract because everybody else is learning contract, and for no other reason. If you belong to what is called the smart set—how strange to think of a smart set of corpses!—you drink cocktails, not because you like them, but because you must; all the members of your set do; therefore you must. Otherwise, you would be out of things. Being out of things means standing on your own feet, and thinking and acting for yourselves.

"Yes, my dear departed friends, you are mere simulacra and phantasms. You look like living creatures, you move arms and legs, your eyes turn in your heads, you yawn—I have noticed you yawning a good deal in the last ten minutes—in a most life-like manner; but you are quite dead.

"I like, however, to entertain the quaint fancy that even in dead hearts there sometimes stirs a ghostly desire to be alive in a world of living men. Why, for instance, do you throng the picture theatres? Why do you like to stare at a preposterous melodrama, some silly story, perhaps, of a fabulous region known as the Wild West—if not because, absurd as the story may be, it is a story of life and swift action and fierce striving in a world outside your quiet graveyard?

"That, my spectral brethren, seems to me to contain a glimmer of hope for you. It may be that even across this valley of dry bones vague disembodied thoughts are wandering about like the roving breezes. Even in the sleep of death, dreams may come; dreams of what you might do to help this mad and miserable world, if only you were alive and eager like little children; dreams of what Australia might do to show the old, unhappy, bewildered earth the way out of its miseries, if only her people were alive and thinking for themselves and ready to leave the rutted road and to make bold experiments. It is to the young countries rather than to the old that we naturally look for hearts brave enough to cast loose from the ancient moorings and put forth on uncharted seas; to young countries like Australia. And what is Australia doing? Muttering strange parrot-talk about raising prices, and lowering prices, and balancing budgets and turning corners. . . .

The world is not to be saved by catchwords, nor by dead men, but by men alive and keen and aflame with faith and resolution.

"It may be, after all, that one or two in this mortuary may yet come to life again; for I have read of a Power that can breathe the breath of life into dry bones. There may be one or two here who, when that Power speaks to them and bids them arise from the dead, will arise, and will give up everything else, even golf, until they have proved themselves alive by facing the task of living men, which is to think, to think. For the problem of saving the world is a spiritual problem; the material problem is solved. We know now how to make, and to make in abundance, all the material things that people need for existence on this planet; that problem is solved. The problem that remains is to be solved only by hard thinking and resolute willing.

"Grasp first this fundamental fact, that the world is ruled by justice; injustice, finally and for ever, breaks down and will not work. Justice in the distribution of wealth—justice in the distribution of work—justice in all our social, political, industrial and international relationships—achieve that and you have solved the world's immediate problem. Think out, first, that question—it was Plato's question, and it has never been answered yet, but men see clearlier now than in Plato's time that it must be answered—the question: What is justice?

"And if you think this too hard and abstract a question, let me suggest an easier one with which to start your new lives—the question: What is money? I have often addressed that question to people who like to think they are hard-headed, and who have been occupied, all their dull lives long, in what is called money-making, but none of them has been able to give me an answer I could believe; and yet this is the question of questions at this moment, for until you can tell how goods are to be exchanged it is idle to talk of the just distribution of wealth. Here is the food; there is the hungry mouth; what is it that is preventing us, all the world over, from conveying that food to that mouth? Nothing but our obsolete ideas of what money really means. So long as you are dead, those dead ideas suffice you; when you come to life again, they will not suffice you.

"But it may be that this is a vain dream, and that none of you will ever come to life again. Farewell, then; let us go, I to my bitter meditations, you to your cocktails, your bridge, your dreary money-making, and all the rest of that empty and futile existence you call life and I call death. I shall have done not a particle of good by this diatribe; all that I can hope is that I have not spoken too hardly of you. *De mortuis.* . . . There is really nothing wrong with you, except that you are dead."

.   .   .   .   .

That, I think, is a fair, though necessarily brief, summary of the sermon as I heard it. It is for the reader to say whether the title I have adopted is just or slanderous. If you think this ghoulish rigmarole about corpses and winding-sheets and so on could have been uttered by a perfectly sober person, I must disagree with you. It is all very well to have a charitable standard of sobriety; but let me point out that you are implying that I, who was one of his hearers, am dead, as he said, and this I strenuously deny. I maintain, and shall maintain till my dying day, that I am alive. I also maintain, as the only credible explanation of his sermon, that he had been dining.

THE GODS FORESEE

FOR a day and a night and a day the silver trumpets had been sounding, shrill and clear, from the heights of Olympus; so that all mortals who were then upon the earth knew that Zeus must be greatly perturbed about something; not for any trivial reason, they were sure, would the father of gods and men send this message pealing to the uttermost ends of the world, summoning all gods and goddesses, wheresoever they might be, and howsoever employed, to fare swiftly to his august abode.

So insistent and so long-drawn-out was the call, that not a single one of the immortals failed to attend the conference; and there were moments when the air around Olympus seemed to be thick with flying divinities. It may be suspected that some were drawn by curiosity rather than by a proper sense of their duty; for of late some of the gods, and especially some of the goddesses, had shown themselves a little lacking in the respect due to Zeus; but none of the gods, and certainly none of the goddesses, had ever shown a lack of curiosity.

When the assemblage was complete, and when Hermes had called for silence, Zeus, sitting aloof on the topmost peak of many-ridged Olympus, spake to the throng of Immortals in thunderous tones: "Hearken to me, all gods and all ye goddesses, that I may speak unto you the thing which my heart within my breast commandeth me. And let none of you say aught till I shall have made an end of speaking, lest ye feel the weight of my wrath, which is grievous to be borne." He had begun very impressively, in his best manner; but at this point he began to stammer and look sheepish. He had caught the eye of Hera, who was by this time somewhat estranged from her lord, having grown somewhat weary of forgiving him his adventures among the daughters of men.

She, the white-armed Hera, paying small heed to his threats, broke in mockingly upon his discourse. "O Zeus, dread son of Cronos, glorious and terrible, god of the storm-clouds, god of the far-resounding voice"—here her manner changed suddenly—

"don't you think, as there are no mortals present and we are all friends together, you might drop the oratory and talk in a sensible way? What, pray, is the matter? What new scrape have you got into now? What new Danae, or Semele, or Alcmene is troubling you? Can you not manage to conduct your own ridiculous affairs without bringing us all here at great personal inconvenience to help you? As for me, I may as well tell you at once, I shall not lift a finger to . . ."

"No, no, no, my dear," cried Zeus, willing to soothe the ox-eyed queen, "this is something far more serious than any of those trifling affairs to which you—rather unnecessarily, rather tactlessly, I must say—allude. This is no time for your petty jealousies. It is not I that am in trouble this time; it is all of us. Listen, Immortals all!"—and here he lifted up his voice again till it became as the far-rolling thunder—"Listen to me; and when I have finished say whether I have not done well to call you hither, to take counsel together how we may save ourselves from a terrible danger."

At this announcement all the Immortals sat up and looked serious; even the golden Aphrodite, the foam-born, ceased to make eyes at Ares, and her beautiful face became almost thoughtful. And Dionysus set down untasted the cup of ambrosia which Hebe, knowing his weakness, had brought him the moment he arrived.

"It is known to you all," Zeus proceeded, "how that Prometheus, the thrice-accursed traitor, has stolen from heaven the most sacred and the most secret of our divine properties, even Fire itself. You know, too, how I have punished the rascal; most of you have probably found a leisure moment to pay him a visit, where, chained to a peak in frosty Caucasus, he suffers endless agonies from my vultures, who peck at his liver, and will peck at it through all eternity. Even you, O queen, will hardly deny that I know how to deal firmly with evildoers. The sinner is punished in an exemplary manner; but his sin has consequences which none of us has yet realized. That is the reason of this solemn conclave. Prometheus is—ah—provided for; but meanwhile he has—I shudder to tell you the dire news—given away our secret to mortal men. Armed with fire, what will men not do? Armed with fire, they will march from strength to strength. They will be able to help themselves to whatsoever their hearts may desire, and they will need our help no longer. Independent of us, they will first neglect us, and then make a mock of us, and finally forget us altogether. The prayers, the sacrifices, the worship dear to our hearts, will vanish utterly from the world. Yea, and shall not we too vanish?—for a deity that is not worshipped is no longer a deity; no longer adored by men, we shall lose our godship, and cease to be. Did I not speak truth when I said the situation was serious?"

There was a moment of silence. Then was heard the voice of Aphrodite, the foam-born, the incorrigibly frivolous. "Well, after all, I can't believe it's so bad as all that. I'm quite sure that certain mortals, whose names I needn't mention, will adore me and worship me always. At Paphos, for example, they won't forget me. For some of you, of course, it may be serious. Athene, there, is a bit of an old maid; for her, I admit, the prospect seems rather blue. . . ."

But the others thought this was in doubtful taste. They were inclined to take the matter seriously. "But after all," said the ox-eyed Hera, always unwilling to admit that Zeus might be right, "this is sheer guesswork. With fire, for all we know, men may be more religious than ever. The only difference may be that they will now be able to give us burnt offerings. It will be a new and delightful sensation, when the smoke of their sacrifices comes up to our divine nostrils."

"I propose," said Zeus, "that Phoebus Apollo, of the silver bow and the unshorn hair, whose prophetic powers are undeniably remarkable, shall tell us exactly what is going to happen; then there will be no more talk about guesswork." (The phrase seemed to have annoyed him.)

"I can do better than that, O father of gods and men," replied Apollo. "I can communicate for a moment my prophetic powers to all of you. I can lift for a moment the veil that hides the future from your eyes, so that you may see and know for certain that which will come to pass."

"So be it," said Zeus; whereupon the sun-god uttered certain magic spells and made divers strange passes with his hands. And all the Immortals stared for the first time into futurity; and upon every face came a look of astonishment and awe and dismay; and there was a great silence from end to end of many-ridged Olympus.

The first to break it was the lame god, Hephaestus, skilled in handicrafts. "I see men, armed with fire, dragging iron from the earth, and fashioning for themselves sundry very marvellous tools, and with these tools they fashion other tools yet more marvellous. The whole earth resounds with the din of their forges. Masters of fire, they are masters of iron; masters of iron, they are masters of the world. I see them working endless miracles."

"Armed with fire," said Hermes, "they drag other metals besides iron from the secret places of the earth. I see them taking copper and beating it out as thin as threads, and covering the whole earth with a network of threads; and by means of these threads they signal to one another, and even—wonder of wonders! —speak to one another across the width of the world. What am I, with my winged sandals, to mortals whose messages fly with the speed of lightning?"

"Armed with fire," said the blue-haired Poseidon, shaker of Earth, girdler of the world, "they are conquerors over my ocean. No longer do they put to sea timidly in little wooden barks, hugging the shore lest they be whelmed by my waves. In mighty palaces, fashioned of iron and driven by fire, they speed insolently across my waters, laughing me to scorn, not fearing me any more."

"With fire for their vassal," said Ares of the glancing helm, waster of cities, "they make for themselves engines of war such as even I have never dreamed of. They dive under the sea and they fly through the air, carrying death. And from monstrous tubes, with fire inside them, I see missiles being hurled at inconceivable speeds, missiles before which walled cities are as gossamer. Yes, of a truth, they have no longer any need of me; they can fight without any aid from the Immortals."

"They have gone into my forests," said the sylvan Artemis, "and drawn the sap from my trees; and with this sap, by some miracle, the wheels of their chariots are shod; and in these chariots, with fire for their steeds, they scour the earth for their pleasure."

"They do more than all this," said Phoebus Apollo, who saw farther than he could make others see; "armed with fire, they make a substance like unto crystal, they grind it into strange and cunning shapes, so that when they look through it the small becomes great, and they see things that no mortal eye has ever seen before; and with this magical glass they pry into the secrets of nature, and find out the hidden causes of disease, so that to me, the god of healing, their prayers arise no more, neither do they sacrifice any more, for they can heal themselves."

"There is nothing left to us," cried Zeus in a lamentable voice. "They have stolen all our secrets. What to them are my thunder-

bolts? Even my lightning they have mastered, making it their
slave, to do menial offices in their dwellings. I see—I see it all.
That knave Prometheus, in teaching them the use of fire, has
taught them everything. In that one secret all secrets lay con-
cealed. They now have the means of securing whatsoever they
may desire. They have no need of us. In themselves they possess
the means of perfect and endless happiness."

"For a President of the Immortals," said a derisive voice, "you
show, if I may venture to say so, a singular lack of perspicacity."
It was Momus, the god of mockery, whose ridicule had never
spared even the most august of the Olympians. "Perfect and
endless happiness, indeed! I too am looking into the future, and
I see something that none of you, not even that charlatan Apollo,
seems to have observed. I see men dragging from the bowels of
the earth something else besides the iron and the copper you make
such an ado about; another metal, a yellow metal. I see men
prizing it above all else, so that a brother will kill his brother for
the possession of it, and a son his father; not knowing, blind as
they are, that it has the power to bring to naught all their other
achievements. They have, as you say, Zeus, mastered a multitude
of secrets; but the yellow metal has mastered *them*. They can
make the earth bring forth abundantly all that they need; none
the less I see them starving in the midst of their abundance, and
all because they have not mastered the use of that yellow metal.
Be at peace, therefore; for assuredly they will go on being as
miserable as the most vengeful of you can desire. That yellow
metal will flow round the world, a river of woe, carrying ruin and
grief and desolation on its broad bosom wherever it goes. All
nations will long to possess more of it than their neighbours do,
and those that gain great store of it will think themselves rich for
a time, but they will soon be as miserable as those that have lost it.
Men will know neither how to do without it nor what to do with
it. It will be their lord and master; and whereas you, O Zeus,
have chastised them with whips, it will chastise them with
scorpions."

The rest did not quite know whether to be glad or sorry at
this revelation; for though they could not but be pleased that the
roguery of Prometheus should have brought a result so different
from what the thief had intended, yet in their hearts was a streak
of divine compassion for the unhappy lot of mortals, made slaves
to the yellow metal. But at last the grey-eyed Pallas Athene, who
had so far kept silence, lifted up her voice and spake. "Momus

has reported truly," said she, "of that which he has seen; but he has not seen everything. He has missed one little thing, a thing which is indeed apt to be forgotten when we are busy talking about fire and copper and iron and gold; a thing which is not to be dragged from the bowels of the earth, but for which men must come back, in the end, to me. Its name is Wisdom; without which all that men may fashion of steel and flame will but turn to their own undoing. I shall give men this gift of wisdom; and then in truth we need have fears neither for them nor for ourselves. For that same wisdom by which they will learn, after much tribulation, to conquer even gold, making it their humble servitor instead of their tyrannous master, will bring them back to us at the last. They will learn, through blood and tears, that *wisdom cometh from on high.*"

After this there seemed no more to be said, and the Immortals, tossing the subject from their minds, dispersed and went their several ways—the gluttonous Dionysus to an unfinished banquet in India, the laughter-loving Aphrodite to an interrupted flirtation in Cnidos, and the grey-eyed Pallas Athene to her lonely meditation on the difficult question, how mortals were to be induced to accept the gift of wisdom.

A NEGLECTED PLEASURE

In the Middle Ages they used to speak, you will remember, of the seven deadly sins—just seven, no more, no less. If you said there were eight, you were in danger of excommunication; if you hinted that there were only six, you ran the risk of being sent to the stake. To-day some think that the list must be extended, our epoch having invented two or three sins unknown to Thomas Aquinas, but quite as deadly as any of the seven. Others, on the contrary, announce that there are no deadly sins at all, but only repressions, complexes, atavistic tendencies, and what not. The medieval philosophers, who liked exactitude—nothing vague or sloppy about their thinking—also drew up a list of the cardinal virtues. I must confess, shameful as the admission is, that I forget the precise number, but I know where I can find it out for you if you are anxious to know whether you possess a complete set. The virtues are not, however, the subject of the present essay; nor the vices neither. What I am wondering is whether any of those saints and sages who were so addicted to drawing up lists ever made a catalogue of human pleasures. In my own reading of medieval literature, which is not exhaustive, I have never come across such a list; nor can I call to mind any modern moralist or psychologist who has tackled the subject; but this may be due to my almost complete ignorance of the works of modern psychologists and moralists.

Anyhow, after this wordy introduction, let us get to the point. I do not propose to attempt, alone and unaided, to draw up a list of the joys of life. True, the task would not seem to be very exhausting if one limited oneself to the joys possible to the majority of mankind at the present sombre moment of the world's history; one might get the catalogue into a newspaper column without undue compression; but that is not what I mean. I am speaking of all ages and of all lands, of human nature in general; from what activities, from what experiences, do human beings derive pleasure? If, by way of giving your own intellectual powers some exercise, you sit down and try to make such a catalogue, I submit that there is one kind of pleasure which you will be apt to overlook, a keen and vivid pleasure—the pleasure of recognition. It crops up in all sorts of unexpected regions. Let me give a few examples. I shall have to be egotistical, and quote from my own personal experiences.

When I first visited Florence, I enjoyed myself immensely, though I was alone—which, in spite of Hazlitt, is not the way to travel—and, though it was in the depth of winter, and a wind like a whetted knife swept along the narrow and draughty streets of the old city. And afterwards, in an introspective moment, I wondered what it was that I had enjoyed. Was it the beauty of the place?—but there are many other cities lovelier by far than Florence. Was it the historic associations?—the thought of great things done and suffered in that place, the thought of Dante and Savonarola and Michelangelo, the Guelphs and the Ghibellines, the Renaissance, the Medici? But why should one get pleasure from that? You can read all about these persons and events sitting in your own garret, or under a gum-tree, in Australia; what joy is there in knowing that you are living where these persons lived, where these things happened? Why should I be thrilled to know that I was standing on the exact spot, the precise latitude and longitude, where Savonarola was burned? I hope I am not so irrational as to derive enjoyment from such a source. I came to the conclusion that the enjoyable thing about the experience had been the recognition of buildings with which I was familiar in pictures.

This was borne out by the fact that I enjoyed a second visit to Florence far more than the first; for now I was recognizing at every moment. Streets, palaces, towers, churches, the outlines of which had grown a little misty in my memory, sprang into consciousness, clear, unmistakable, the same. There was the Palazzo Vecchio, with its wonderful tower; there was Giotto's lovely bell-tower; there, too, was the vulgar statue of Victor Emmanuel, waving his sword theatrically; and the dingy facade of the cathedral, and the obscure hostelry I had stayed in twenty years before; and I believe I enjoyed the ugly things just as much as I enjoyed the beautiful things, for it was not an aesthetic pleasure I was experiencing; it was the simpler, the more child-like, the more elemental pleasure of recognition. And if I ever go back to Florence again—which may the kindly fates (and also the kindly bankers) allow—I shall enjoy it more than ever, for I shall wander up and down well-remembered streets, indulging in the innocent occupation of recognizing things.

When I said, above, that lonely travel was not the best kind of travel, "in spite of Hazlitt," that phrase gave to you, the reader, a momentary feeling of pleasure, if, but only if, you had read Hazlitt's essay "On Going a Journey"—the one that begins, "One of the pleasantest things in the world is going a journey, but I like to go by myself." There was no particular point in my mentioning Hazlitt, but you enjoyed the allusion—because you recognized it. And when, a line or two farther on, I spoke of a wind like a whetted knife, you enjoyed the vividness of the phrase, but you enjoyed it far more if you knew your Masefield. That is the real secret of allusive writing; and almost all writers—some more than others—make use of this device. When Mark Pattison speaks of *Lycidas* as the last reward of consummate scholarship, he means that the poem is so packed with classical allusions that only a consummate scholar can see the meaning of every line. We can all enjoy the beauty of Milton's verse, but the scholar enjoys it more than the rest of us can enjoy it because he has the added joy of recognition; at least, that is the theory. My own belief is that many scholars enjoy the allusions so much that they forget to enjoy the poetry.

Of course, a good deal depends on how old you are. To the very young the pleasure of recognition means far less than the pleasure of novelty. Youth is for ever seeking after some new thing. The youthful reader of this essay—if there is such a being —will be surprised at my hankering after a third visit to a city I know already. Why go back to Florence, when you have not seen Tokyo nor New York nor Jericho? It is right that the young should feel like that. Having arrived at a foreign city at night, and been whisked to your hotel in the darkness, it is a wonderful pleasure to light your pipe after breakfast, and step out into an entirely new and strange world; you feel like Columbus—if you are young enough. But we who are middle-aged or elderly feel differently about things; the first grey hair is the first signal that the pleasures of novelty are beginning to pall, and that we shall soon have to fall back on the pleasures of recognition. The world is full of wonders which I have no desire to see. I have no longing for Tokyo. I am content to go to my grave without having walked down Wall Street, gazed at Niagara, interviewed the Grand Lama, admired the wonders of the Taj Mahal, or been carried in a machilla across Nyasaland. These are worthy ambitions for the

young in muscle and the young in heart; for me, give me the
places I have known, the people I have known, the books I have
known; give me, in short, the joys of recognition. You may have
noticed that young people are content, and more than content, to
leave their homes and go and live in a foreign land. It is only
for the elderly that banishment is a real hardship. Here in Australia, you will find it is only when people are growing old that
they feel an overmastering desire to go back to England, or whatever country they were born in, and see the old familiar landmarks
once more before they die. And when a man does cross the ocean
and revisit his native village, what does he do? He wanders about
recognizing things, and, if he is lucky, recognizing people. And if
he recognizes enough, his enjoyment is keen; too often disappointment predominates, because he finds so much change, so little to
recognize. He feels as Matthew Arnold did when he revisited
Switzerland:

> Glion? Ah, twenty years! It cuts
> All meaning from a name!
> White houses prank where once were huts,
> Glion, but not the same!

And this disappointment proves my point, for why should he
be disappointed if it were not that he finds himself robbed of the
pleasure to which, above all things, he had been looking forward,
the pleasure of recognition?

And now comes, at the end, the real point of this essay. Just
as I like to know a city or two by heart, to be able to find my way
about it in the dark, and in the daytime to recognize all its buildings, its squares, its streets, its public gardens, its statues—just as it
would give me a real satisfaction, if I went back to Florence to-
morrow, to find the same waiter handing me my cup of coffee in the
same little restaurant in the Piazza della Signoria—so I, and I hope
you too, like to have one or two books that we know intimately,
books that we can return to again and again, books in which we
feel perfectly at home. It is a strange thing, but there are people
in the world who make it a rule never to read a book they have
read already; people who wonder why on earth anybody should
read a book twice through. Before such people I should be afraid
to confess the number of times I have read *Vanity Fair*. The only
conceivable reason for reading a book again, according to them,
is that you have forgotten it. But the reason I am going to read
Vanity Fair yet again is by no means that I have forgotten it, but,

on the contrary, that I remember it so well; that I remember each
incident while it is still a chapter away, and rejoice in it when it
comes; in short, that I feel at home in that book, know all its
people, and am familiar with all its windings and turnings as a
London city urchin is familiar with the windings and turnings of
the streets in the neighbourhood where he has grown up. And
observe that a book has a great advantage over a city; if I went
back to Florence, I should very probably find that my old waiter
was dead, and possibly that even the restaurant had been pulled
down; but when I go back to *Vanity Fair* I shall not find that
Becky Sharp has died in the interval; she will be as much alive as
ever, and will fling the work of the Great Lexicographer out of
the carriage window, as she leaves Miss Pinkerton's academy, with
the same gusto as of old; and Rawdon Crawley will take Lord
Steyne by the throat with the same admirable promptitude;
and so to the end, the great people and the mean people and
the absurd people will act and speak as they have always
acted and spoken in that many-coloured, many-twinkling world
of tears and laughter. I have been told that, no matter how
many times you read a really good book, you always find something new in it. It may be so, but it is not for the something new
that I re-read a book; it is for the something old. I re-read for
the joy of recognition.

My moral is, read new books by all means, if your taste lies
that way; but have some old books on your shelves, books that you
know really well, books in which you really feel at home. Believe
me, it is worth while. Without this, you forgo one of the keenest
pleasures that literature can give. What's a heaven for if there
be no recognition there?

A MEDIEVAL INTERLUDE

THE meal was drawing to a close and the baron was drunk. When he was drunk he was quarrelsome; and he was a man with whom, drunk or sober, it was wiser not to quarrel. His guests and retainers were therefore slipping as unobtrusively as they could out of the hall, as was their invariable custom at this stage of the banquet. Much as they would have liked to stay with the baron's wine, which was of an excellent vintage, to stay with the baron was more than the wine was worth. So, one by one, they stole discreetly away. Some went to their beds, some to the battlements for a breath of fresh air, some to the guard-room to exchange news with the men-at-arms, and some, as was their wont, strolled along to the torture chamber to see whether by chance any good entertainment was going forward there. After two hours of the baron's society they felt in need of some amusement.

But luck was against them. There was nothing much doing that evening. A man was being stretched on the rack, and that was all. The only other person in the chamber was the torturer who, though of an unattractive, and indeed hideous, cast of countenance, was known to be very expert in his profession. The baron paid him a high salary, and it was rumoured that the king had tried to tempt him away from the baron's employ by the offer of a higher salary still, but that he had refused, because he thought the work in the royal service would be too strenuous. On the present occasion he was sauntering up and down the chamber, humming a merry drinking song. To this performance the moaning of the man on the rack provided a kind of accompaniment.

The first of the truants from the banquet hall was the baron's chaplain, very plump and sleek, who, after a friendly nod to the torturer, went over and stared with a half-playful, half-reproving expression at the victim. "Oho, my uncomfortable friend," he said, jocosely, "so your sins have found you out, eh? Well, well; you will walk more circumspectly in future, I think. You will realize that the way of the transgressor is hard; perhaps you are even realizing it already. You are getting a valuable lesson—

a lesson well worth some temporary discomfort; you are learning that justice rules the world and that . . ."

"Beg pardon, your reverence," interrupted the torturer, "but I don't think he's quite learning that. Because, you see, this chap didn't, as a matter of fact, do anything wrong. We got hold of the wrong man; the right man got clear away. The baron was in such a rage about it that he said he didn't care a straw who was punished so long as somebody was, and that this chap would do as well as the other to try our new rack. So there he is. But I don't think, somehow, as he'll appreciate any talk about justice and that sort of thing."

"Oh, indeed?" said the chaplain, the playful look leaving his face, for nobody likes having the wind taken out of his sails, especially in the middle of a sermon. He looked sourly at the victim. "If you did not commit this particular villainy, you have, of course, committed others, which went unpunished at the time. Divine justice lay in wait for you. What we have to endure is always a punishment for our sins, though we may not always be able to say exactly what the sin was. What you have to do, my friend, is to repent, and to resolve to lead a better life in future."

"And while you are about it," put in a burly captain of the guard who had just come in, "you might as well resolve to make an end of those disgusting noises. Come, my man; all that moaning and groaning won't do a particle of good; not a particle. Be a man. Look at me; I suppose I've had as much discomfort as anybody in my time; did I whine about it? Not I; I bore it like a man. This whimpering over a few trifling aches and pains is fit for maids and boys, not for grown men like you and me."

"The only way to take this kind of thing," said a well-nourished minstrel, "is to take it as a joke; make a comic song of it. A sense of humour is your true armour against fate. Laugh at your misfortunes, my friend; try to see the humour of your situation. The trouble with you is that you take your little worries too seriously. Don't be so solemn. Grin at the torturer, and ask him, 'Who *taught yer* this game?' Or here's another jolly good pun you might make"—at this point the victim uttered a louder groan than usual, which brought to his side a rosy-cheeked philosopher, one of the baron's guests.

"I, too," said this sage, "have known adversity; sorrow has been my housemate, pain my bedfellow; but I knew how to be philosophic about it. I knew that what must be must be, and I accepted what fate brought me, satisfied that all is for the best if we can only see it. As my military friend has remarked, these undignified complainings will do you no good; therefore, why make them? It is vain to kick against the pricks of inevitable destiny; you only bruise your toes. The great thing is to be philosophic like me."

"Nay, more," said a moralist, of corpulent build, who came up as the philosopher sauntered away; "nay, more, you should accept your fate not merely philosophically, as my rather sententious friend says, but even joyfully, for suffering is a blessed thing; without it, what were man? Without the salutary discipline of pain, we should be even as the beasts of the field. It is adversity that forms the character; don't you feel your character being formed, my dear young friend? Mere happiness is bad for human beings; it saps our strength; it weakens our fibre; it demoralizes us. Be thankful, therefore, for every pang you endure; it is doing you an immense amount of good—an immense amount!"

"Shall I give him an extry turn, sir?" said the torturer, who had been listening with close attention to this discourse. "If what you say is true, he can't have too much of it; I'd better give him another couple of inches or so. If it doesn't kill him—I can't be sure of course, but I shouldn't think it would—it'll do his character no end of good; and when it's over he'll thank me for it. On his bended knees he will."

On second thoughts, however, the torturer decided that he would not give the rack an extra turn, however beneficial it might be to the victim's character. It was a new rack, and he had to handle it with great care. The baron would be furious if any damage were done to the new machine, brought from Spain at great expense. Moreover, his attention was at this moment diverted by the words of a comfortable-looking friar, a member of a new order, which was attracting great attention throughout Europe.

"You are making a mistake, my friend," said the newcomer. "You are not really in pain, for pain does not really exist. You are not really on the rack; a rack is matter, and there is no such thing as matter; it is a fiction of the human mind. There is no such thing as evil; evil is a mere negation. You imagine you are in pain, because you are thinking wrongly. The cure is simple; think rightly. There; you are better already; you don't know it, perhaps, but that is only because some of the old illusions still cling to your soul."

"I hope you are edified by all that tomfoolery," said a laughing voice. It was a friar of a different order, wearing a cloak of a slightly different colour. "What that gentleman needs is a pleasant hour with the thumbscrew and the red-hot pincers. A little boiling oil would soon tell him whether pain was real or not. You and I know well enough that the rack does exist, don't we, my friend? All the same, there is a speck of truth in all that rubbish. The mind *can* conquer the body. The mind is open to suggestion. What you need is a formula—preferably with a rhyme in it—that you can say over to yourself without ceasing. Keep on saying something like this: 'There's nothing in it, for every minute I'm feeling better and better.' After you have said that a few thousand times you will believe it; and, believing you feel better is the same thing as feeling better. Do try my formula!"

Here the first friar gave the second what was known in those days as a shrewd buffet on the sconce; and presently a fight was in progress between the two. In the meantime the steward of the baron's demesne took the opportunity of a quiet talk with the man on the rack.

"These people make me sick," he said, acridly, "with their religion and philosophy and morality, and so forth. This is not a moral question; it is a question of money. Never mix up money with morals unless you want to be muddle-headed. What are the facts? The baron is rich and powerful; you, my friend, are poor and powerless; there is the situation in a nutshell. Don't tell me that these things ought not to be; as a student of money, I am concerned with what is, not with what ought to be; and what is, is as plain as the nose on your face. There is no doubt that your present standard of comfort, whatever these philosophic gentry may say, is low, very low indeed. Why it is low I could explain to you if you were an educated person; as it is, you must be content to leave these mysteries to those who study such matters, and to know that I find in you a really beautiful example of the working of inexorable laws. If I told you that you must at all costs endeavour to maintain your budgetary equilibrium, I doubt if you would understand me; but you can at least be happy to know, on my assurance, that you are pursuing the only sound and sane course, which is—to remain on the rack as long as you have to. I trust you follow me."

"I have had no experience of the rack," said a pilgrim to the Holy Land who had dropped in at the castle for a meal and a bed, "but I should imagine that it was bad enough without this added torture of having to listen to so many counsellors giving contradictory advice. But one thing I may tell you, you need not blame the baron for your present situation; no individual is to blame. It is the system that is to blame. You are the victim of the system. The system must be altered, and, what is more, it will be altered.' Be comforted, my friend; the present system is doomed; it will not last more than two, or possibly three, thousand years. Doesn't that cheer you up?"

"I have something more cheerful than that to tell you," said a herald. "To-day I brought the baron tidings of a war that is imminent between the King of Ruritania and the Duke of Barataria; and if things go as we hope, the whole empire will be involved, and, indeed, the whole of Christendom; and every noble will need the services of every man who is fit to bear arms. We shall not be able to spare any one for the torture chamber; you will all be needed for the battlefield. In war lies your salvation."

"I wager my cap and bells," said the baron's fool, "that he feels really happy now! To lie mortally wounded on the field of battle, with none to tend you; to have your arms and legs blown off with this new invention of theirs—gunpowder, or whatever they call it—'tis a wholly delectable prospect. Cheer up, lad; the worst is over. You have turned the corner!"

The fool spoke more truly than he knew, for while he was speaking the man on the rack quietly expired.

   ·   ·   ·   ·   ·   ·

The names of those who took part in this conversation are lost in the mists of time, which is a pity, for men's names in the Middle Ages were very queer and attractive. But we do happen to know the name of the man on the rack; he was called Genus Humanum.

A SPORT FOR SUPERMEN

A favourite diversion of mine is to drive at full speed past a school just as the children are streaming out into the street with shouts and merry laughter. Holding, as I do, that sport is twice as much fun if you share it with some congenial spirit, I generally take a friend or two with me on these occasions. (O Zarathustra, prophet and master, would that you were alive to-day! What a privilege it had been to introduce you to this form of frolic!)

I always choose, for these expeditions, the most powerful of my modest little fleet of cars, having found that with a light car one is apt to lose control of the steering. Even with a heavy Vickers-Schneider, skill and nerve are needed; for, though, owing to the present economic conditions, one need not be afraid of encountering a really fat child, yet even an emaciated infant can give you a perceptible bump, and has even been known to cause the breaking of a spring when the driving has been unskilful.

On a fine day, when the sun is shining, and the birds singing, and we are all in good spirits, and feeling that, as the poet says, "all's right with the world," no merrier sport could be devised. The yells of the little vulgarians—those whom we leave capable of yelling—form an ideal accompaniment to our progress. Only a soured pessimist could refrain from laughing at the comical looks of consternation on their plebeian little faces as we dash unexpectedly round the corner into the midst of them. "Hullo, scum!" I shout, in a jolly voice, as I bowl them over. If there were only an element of danger in it, I declare it would be the finest sport in the world.

But I am philosopher as well as sportsman; and at home, in the evening, after a successful day in the streets, I sit and meditate, not without a certain complacency, on the ethics of the game. It may be a little weakness of mine, of which I fear the Master would disapprove, calling it "human, all too human," but I admit that I do enjoy the consciousness that what is innocent fun to me and my companions is also of solid use to the community. It is a mid-Victorian piece of sentimentalism, no doubt; the dim survival of some nonsense I learned at my mother's knee—what a deal of antiquated Christian rubbish the Victorian mother's knee seems to be responsible for!—but, irrational as it may be, I do like to feel that in my unobtrusive way I am doing something for the world. There is, however, no fear of one's becoming unhealthily self-satisfied. Even after a very successful day among the little ones, it is impossible to purr contentedly when one reflects on the miserable inadequacy of one's best efforts. Even if I revived an ancient and pleasant practice and had a scythe-blade attached to the hub of each front wheel—a motor-mechanic is looking into the possibilities of this for me—my little achievements would still, judged by ideal standards, be pitifully inadequate. When I think of the enormous number of children on this planet, and of the cataract of babies arriving every day, I feel as a man might who tried to drain the Pacific Ocean dry with a teaspoon, or to put out Vesuvius with a candle-extinguisher.

What a queer world this is, and how it persists in misunderstanding those who try to minister to its needs! But I must not complain of this, for I am in the best of company; to be misunderstood has been the reward of the noblest in all ages. You may think it incredible, but none the less is it true, that the parents of the wretched little creatures whom I have liquidated show themselves, in many cases, incapable of understanding the ethical value of my sport. Some of them have even had the effrontery to visit my private abode for the purpose of remonstrating with me; and their language is, as I sometimes take the trouble to point out to them, in the worst of taste. They call me, for instance, a Herod, or a damned Juggernaut, or other names of which they do not know the meaning but which are certainly meant to be uncomplimentary. In the end, I generally succeed in talking them into a measure of common sense, and we part the best of friends, with bows and smiles on both sides; but you would hardly believe how long it sometimes takes me to show them their selfish folly, and to convince them that I have done them and their miserable progeny a valuable service.

When I first took up the sport I had also, strange as it may seem, a little difficulty with the police. Of course, strictly speaking, the elimination of children is illegal. And for my part I hope it will continue to be illegal, for it would never do to allow the practice to become general among the lower orders; there would soon be a shortage of workers. But the police are a very sensible body of men, on the whole, and they soon saw the soundness of my arguments. It was not difficult to show them that a law, made in the days when the disease of democracy afflicted the earth, might still be usefully applied to the common herd, but certainly not to supermen. Some of them are still, I suspect, a little anxious lest the practice should spread to members of the lower orders who may claim to be supermen; but I always tell them that a really heavy licence fee will put all right, limiting the sport to those who can really afford to pay for it.

Coming back to the indignant parents: I have now a set speech for use with them. Standing on my front lawn, of an evening, I address the group of unreasonably annoyed fathers and mothers somewhat as follows: "My dear, good, well-meaning but exceedingly stupid people, don't you see that you are giving a rather ridiculous exhibition of a feeling which may be natural but which is certainly primitive? Your desire to preserve the lives of your wretched offspring is an instinct shared by cats and dogs and monkeys, and also, for all I know, by fleas and lice; but is it—I ask you—quite worthy of human beings, who are (perhaps erroneously) supposed to be reasoning creatures? As reasoning creatures, you should look to the future, and ask what sort of life your child is likely to have if you do preserve it. If, instead of coming here with the purpose of interfering with my innocent recreations, you stayed at home and studied a textbook of economics, you would begin, perhaps, to understand not merely how innocent but also how truly philanthropic my diversions are. It is true that textbooks of economics are not written for you uneducated people, but with the constant aid of a good dictionary you ought to be able to make out enough of the facts to convince you. You would then understand that my behaviour, however distasteful to you personally, is exactly in accord with the teachings of the best economists.

"You must not be egoists. You must think a little of the good of the community—of the world. Surely you can see that there are far too many people in the world already, and that every year more and more people are becoming superfluous. Look at your textbook, and see how many hundreds of millions of horse-power the total machinery of the world now provides; and try to remember the obvious fact that every addition to the horse-power of machinery means so much less man-power needed to do the world's work. One machine, with a boy to mind it, now does the work of hundreds of men. And new machines are being invented every week.

"If all the machines we already possess were doing all the work we could make them do, the world would simply be snowed under with goods; and that would, of course, be terrible! That is why our machines are only doing a fraction of what they could be doing, and why hundreds of mills and factories are idle; because, you see, if they produced all the things they could produce, why, there isn't money enough in the whole world to buy the things.

"And now, observe: by a wise and beautiful dispensation—not of Providence, as you old-fashioned people would say, but of the clever, hard-headed, practical fellows who manage our affairs for us—the greater the productiveness of our mills and factories becomes, the smaller becomes the power of the people to buy things; because—you *can* see this, can't you?—the growth of machinery means the growth of unemployment, and of course the unemployed can't afford to buy the goods made by the machines that threw them out of employment.

"So I ask you to tell me, candidly, what sort of prospect do you really think lay in front of those infants of yours whom I have considerately removed from this troublesome world? You know perfectly well that in all probability they would have grown up to look in vain for some work to do in the world. They would have found none, and at last they would have formed a portion of that unhappy mass for which a friend of yours, Mr Ramsay MacDonald, has found a simple and beautiful name: he calls it *scrap*. Believe me, it isn't nice to be scrap; it's far better to be dead. To have a few happy years at school, and to end by providing us supermen with some excellent sport—that is a far, far better way.

"Don't interrupt, please. I know quite well what you were going to say. You think that, so long as the fields and the factories can produce plenty of everything that people want, there can't really be too many people in the world. The world will not be overcrowded, you were going to say, until machinery can no longer cope with the demand for goods, which is far from being the case at present. But don't you see the flaw in this argument? Of course I know as well as you do—everybody knows—that we have enough goods, or at least the power to produce enough goods—to enable everybody in the world to live in comfort; but what on earth is the good of that when people can't get the goods, and how can they get the goods when they haven't enough money to buy them?

"I beg your pardon? Why don't we make some more money? My dear sir, you are talking nonsense. I know there are some crack-brained amateur economists who have some cranky nostrum of that sort; but there is a fallacy in it. I forget at the moment what the fallacy is; but if you study your textbook of economics you will see that it is a frightful and glaring fallacy. The experts say so; and that must be enough for us. I trust the experts. I presume you wouldn't set up your crude ideas against the teachings of men who have made a life-study of the science of economics?

"You see, then, how thankful you ought to be to me for eliminating your wholly superfluous offspring. There are too many people in the world already; that, my friends, is the core of the trouble. Eh? Yes, of course it's quite true that there would not be too many people if we had a different method of managing the world's affairs; a method which would make the supply of money depend on the number of people needing it, instead of making the number of people depend on the supply of money. But we haven't got that different method; and, what's more, we can't have it; the present financial system—which all the experts tell me is a sane and sound system—must not be upset by a handful of cranks. What was good enough for our fathers and mothers is good enough for us, I should hope. All these patent nostrums of yours involve giving money to people who haven't earned it; which would be frightfully immoral. Look at my own modest fortune; every penny of it was earned. Well, no, not by me; but it was won by the sweat of my father's brow—except what he got from my grandfather. It is the reward of their strenuous and honourable toil in the stock exchange. I honour their memories; and the system that made them rich is one which I must really ask you not to touch with sacrilegious fingers.

"So, my dear people, the conclusion we must draw is obvious. If we can't abolish our present money system—and I hope I have convinced you that we can't—we must abolish part at least of the human race; the superfluous part, the scrap. There is no way out of this dilemma; unless you are so callous and inhuman as to want your children to grow up to a life of misery and apathy and despair.

"What we want to see around us, you will agree, is a tidy, well-ordered, and happy world. We, the supermen, are the natural rulers of that world; you, the serving class, will be very happy also when your numbers have been sufficiently reduced. There should be just enough of you to carry on the work of the world for us; anything over and above that number is surplusage. Life will be very happy for us all when there are just enough of you and no more. Good-bye. Mind the step."

When I have spoken somewhat in this wise, they go away, apparently contented, though not, I must admit, in a state of rapture. But I myself, as I have said, am far from being satisfied with my own little efforts. The more I study the great economists of the day, the more deeply I feel my own inefficiency. As a sport, it is delightful, of course; but as a serious piece of humanitarian work on the lines laid down by orthodox economics, it is terribly inadequate. Even on a good day, the numbers disposed of are simply contemptible. The little wretches are becoming very shy of crossing the streets. Yesterday, for instance, I visited no fewer than three large schools, and, would you believe it, I bagged only nine. Much as I dislike anything that savours of socialism, I sometimes wonder whether this is a matter that should be left to private enterprise, and whether the State should not take the matter up, placing it under the control of a Minister of Elimination.

THE RING AND THE BOOK

Possibly all men, and probably all women, who read the account of the Carnera-Sharkey fight the other day experienced a faint regret that they had not been privileged to be present on that exciting occasion. Not that boxing matches are invariably thrilling; the last one I attended certainly failed to thrill me; I found it an unspeakable bore, and so, I think, did the majority of those present. "In barren dreariness and futility," says Bernard Shaw, "no spectacle on earth can contend with that of two exhausted men trying for hours to tire one another out at fisticuffs for the sake of their backers." I don't remember whether in the fight I speak of the combatants tired each other out or not, but me they certainly tired out; and I have never since attempted to suck entertainment from such an unbearably tedious spectacle. But there can have been nothing tedious about the fight in New York, especially in the sixth and last round, which lasted less than two minutes, when the huge Italian, after driving the American champion about the ring with a series of heavy lefts and rights, finally "used a terrific right uppercut, which landed flush on Sharkey's chin, snapped his head back, and sent him down, where he was counted out with his face on the ring floor." (I quote from the cabled description.) Sharkey's manager shouted to have Carnera's gloves examined. Some spectators leaped into the ring. There seems to have been a mild riot. Certainly, whatever else it was, it can hardly have been tedious; and that is why all of us—possibly with a few exceptions; there are some queer people in this world—felt a momentary sense of regret that we were not there. A moment afterwards, it may be, your better nature reasserted itself; but just for that split second, you will confess if you are candid with yourself, you felt sorry that it had not been given to you to see those two experts bashing each other.

This, however, is not going to be an essay on prize-fighting. Let me get to the real point. . . . But first I must be allowed to point out, to console you for not having been there, that it would not have been pleasant to see the triumph of an Italian boxer in a British sport. You will reply, in your exasperatingly matter-of-fact way, that Sharkey is no more British than Carnera, being really a Lithuanian-American.   In the prosaic sense, I dare say that is true; and I admit that I don't know what Sharkey's real name is; I presume that he called himself by his present name because he admired the great Tom Sharkey, him who defeated Corbett in 1898. I submit that a man's character is shown by the name he chooses, not by the name he happens to be born with, which is not a matter of choice. (The real name of Tommy Burns was Noah Brusso!) Jack Sharkey, by choosing that name, stamped himself as belonging to the true line of British boxers.   Jack Sharkey—what a name!   Doesn't it remind you at once of such other great names as Jem Belcher, the battler who beat Joe Birks and was in turn beaten by Tom Cribb in the famous forty-two round fight more than a century ago?—or perhaps of John Gulley, who was beaten by the Game Chicken (but only at the end of the fiftieth round), and who knocked out Bob Gregson in two successive battles, and then retired from the ring and became a member of Parliament?   (O what a fall was there, my countrymen!) Doesn't it remind you of Jack Scroggins, the hero who was beaten at last by Ned Turner, who afterwards went down before Jack Randall, *the king of the lightweights,* as Borrow calls him?   If it fails to remind you of such great names as these, the reason must be that, though at school they taught you the names of Queen Victoria's Prime Ministers, it was thought better that you should learn nothing at all about these fighters with whose fame the world once rang.   There are people in Australia to-day—I am reluctant to say this, but it is time someone spoke out—who have never heard of Sayers or of Heenan!

The (possibly fallacious) argument, from which my honest indignation has led me to wander, is that a man who bears the name of Jack Sharkey must be thought of as an Englishman, and that therefore I am just as glad I was not there to see him driven round the ring by an overgrown Italian.   Why this narrow parochialism?—you ask.   No, it isn't that; but pugilism is an English invention, an English institution, one of England's contributions to civilization.   You often hear people speak as if it were a relic of barbarism; which of course is nonsense, for barbarians fight, and have always fought, with weapons that man has made, not with the weapons nature has given him.   "The earliest fights between man and man were conducted with man-made weapons, and it was not until the use of such weapons began to decline that the use of the fists began to be cultivated. The sword, the axe, the bludgeon, the cestus—these are ancient implements of combat. But the naked fist and the boxing-glove—these are modern, civilized weapons of defence and attack." So writes Lord Knebworth; and adds that "the English . . . were the first to practise and popularize boxing. While other countries were still freely employing the sword and the dagger, the English had already begun to use the fists." The Queensberry rules, which brought the old prize-ring to an end, were introduced within the memory of men now living; and the old prize-ring itself, as far as I can make out, was not older than the time of George I. In the days of its glory—from the middle of the eighteenth century to about the middle of the nineteenth— the ring was as genuinely and characteristically English as Shakespeare's plays or the novels of Dickens. And now, other nations have borrowed it as they have borrowed so many other English sports. We do not object to their borrowing our games, but we do not like them to beat us at the games they have borrowed; it saddens one to hear of a Jeff Smith defeated by a Carpentier, or a Jack Sharkey knocked out by a Carnera. It is not a question of patriotic sentimentalism at all; I, at least, should not mind at all if I heard that a Spaniard had proved himself the superior of an Englishman as a toreador. England has no claim to superiority in the bull-ring. England has invented many sports—football, cricket, lawn-tennis, boxing, and others—which have been taken over by the rest of the world; but England, with characteristic obstinacy, has refused to take over sports from the rest of the world. She has not borrowed bull-fighting from Spain, nor fish-fighting from Siam, nor—to complete this sentence I should have to hunt through an encyclopaedia, a labour which seems, for the purposes of this essay, a trifle too arduous.

For this essay, as I mentioned earlier, is not about the prize-ring. My real theme is—but here I must break off for a moment to remind you of the well-known fact that English men of letters have been staunch upholders of pugilism, and that some of the best pages of English prose have been descriptions of fights. Why is this?—I have often wondered. Is it because men who lead sedentary and sheltered lives are naturally attracted by whatever is physically strenuous and hazardous?—as Stevenson, living always among medicine bottles, liked to write of bloody pirates and of bonny fighters such as Alan Breck? Or is it a sort of affectation, a sub-conscious feeling of inferiority in themselves and a desire to prove to the world and to their own souls that, notwith-

H

standing appearances to the contrary, they are really great strong red-blooded he-men? The university don goes to a fight, perhaps, to show others, and more especially to show himself, that there is nothing donnish about him. And here am I—wee, sleekit, cowerin', timorous beastie—writing this essay, heaven knows why. . . . Possibly a mixture of both explanations would be needed for the singular eloquence and gusto with which Hazlitt, by no means an athlete, described the fight between Bill Neate and Tom Hickman, and the fiery zest with which ,W. E. Henley, a life-long invalid and a cripple, studied the history of the Fancy. On the other hand, there was nothing sedentary or weakly about George Borrow, nor about Conan Doyle who has left us at least two superb accounts of fights. No: the obvious explanation is, I believe, the true one; that what all these writers admired was not merely the exhibition of magnificent strength—the human body in the pink of condition —and science in the use of that strength, though both of these are worthy of admiration; it was moral qualities that moved them to eloquence—certain qualities which are only to be seen, or which at any rate are seen in their most intense form, in such contests. Hear Hazlitt—"To see two men smashed to the ground, smeared with gore, stunned, senseless, the breath beaten out of their bodies; and then, before you recover from the shock, to see them rise up with new strength and courage, stand ready to inflict or receive mortal offence, and rush upon each other 'like two clouds over the Caspian'—this is the most astonishing thing of all—this is the high and heroic state of man!" Some will be disgusted by this, and will call it, if not an insane glorification of brutality, at least a preposterous over-statement. But is it? Thackeray was the most tender-hearted of men; nobody hated brutality more than he; but he loved a prize-fight. Borrow becomes lyrical in his praise of a hero—"Hail to thee, Tom of Bedford . . . Hail to thee, six-foot Englishman of the brown eye, worthy to have carried a six-foot bow at Flodden, where England's yeomen triumphed over Scotland's king, his clans, and chivalry. Hail to thee, last of England's bruisers, after all the many victories thou hast achieved—true English victories, unbought by yellow gold . . ."

That last phrase suggests that Borrow, though he wrote long ago, was already looking back at a great day that was past, and that, even as he wrote, the commercialization of the prize-ring, which was to be its ruin, had set in. You notice that it is an earlier ring that is glorified by our men of letters, not the ring of to-day. Conan Doyle puts his great fight into the pages of *Rodney Stone*, a tale of the eighteenth century. Unquestionably, it is yellow gold that has made the sport sordid, and ruined it in the eyes of many estimable people who admire pluck and endurance as ardently as ever Borrow or Hazlitt did. It was not the fighters who were to blame for the decline of the sport, but the vermin attracted to the ringside by the chance to gain; the parasites, the mean men, who make money out of other men's strength and courage without the slightest risk to their own skins; in a word, the trouble has come not from the brutality inside the ring but from the blackguardism around the ring. What do the gladiators themselves think of the amphitheatre? I notice a significant sentence in Gene Tunney's autobiography; he is describing one of his fights: "The thought flashed through my mind in that instant, 'What a fool you are to be in here and furnish entertainment for this bloodthirsty mob!'"

And even in the ring itself, the highest virtues of the fighting man become a little less attractive when yellow gold has come into the question. For instance, short as your memory is, you can hardly have forgotten the great fight between Tommy Burns and Jack Johnson at Sydney in 1908. (Jack London happened to be in Australia at the time, and wrote for an Australian newspaper an astonishingly vivid account of the contest.) Perhaps the most disgusting feature of that fight was that both Johnson and Burns indulged all the time in what is known as *mouth-fighting*, the black man mocking and jeering and insulting, the white man foaming out vituperations; but it was disgusting also because of the obvious inequality of the combatants, the White Hope being plainly over-matched in weight, in strength, and in skill. Yet nobody could deny that he was game to the very last; Hazlitt would have admired him, in spite of the vituperation, for his magnificent courage and power of endurance. But would Hazlitt have called out, in his ecstatic way, "This is the high and heroic state of man," if he had known, what was the fact, that before he would enter the ring with the black man, Tommy had bargained for £6000, win, lose or draw? Courage is doubtless a splendid virtue, but virtue so well paid seems somehow to lose its romantic glamour. And of course the price paid to Burns for letting himself be battered to pulp was a trifle compared with the purses given to boxers in later years. When Tunney beat Dempsey at Philadelphia, the loser's share of the takings amounted to £147,000. When Tunney again fought Dempsey, and again beat him, at Chicago, the sale of tickets alone brought in nearly £600,000. A century ago, Jem Burke—popularly known as 'The Deaf Un—remarked in satisfied tones,

THE NEGLECTED OMNIBUS

FOR the omnibus volume, as a general thing, I have no great liking; have you? The complete works of Jane Austen, for instance, bound up as a single book, may be a wonderful volume for the price, and very convenient for travellers; but somehow it repels me, though I can give no rational explanation of my repugnance. (Perhaps one has a dim notion that, since *Emma* and *Pride and Prejudice* are distinct and separate spiritual entities, they ought to wear distinct and separate material vestures; a book seems in some subtle way to lose its individuality, its wholeness and entireness—its private soul, so to speak—when it is tied up between the same covers with other books.) Still less am I attracted by those omnibus books, miracles of cheapness though they may be, in which works of various kinds by various authors are bound together in one heterogeneous bundle; such as one I came across the other day, containing three novels, some short stories, two plays, a few essays, some serious verse, a sheaf of parodies, and an historical sketch; fine mixed feeding, and no mistake about it; just the thing to take with one on a long voyage, you would think; and yet . . . Why should one be repelled by this kind of thing?

And—this is a more important question—why should any one speak as if the omnibus volume were a new-fangled notion? Have you never heard of a single-volume Shakespeare? I remember being the possessor, in my university days—I had to sell it later, in days of financial stress—of a tremendous tome entitled *Tragici Poetae Graeci*, containing all the surviving plays of Aeschylus, Sophocles, and Euripides; an omnibus book, if ever there was one.

Anyhow, whoever speaks of the omnibus as a novel notion must have forgotten that the most popular book in all literature, in the past, has been a vast omnibus of the most miscellaneous kind, containing elaborate histories, a great philosophic poem, some treatises, a number of essays on social, political, and religious topics, an anthology of lyrics of various kinds and various dates, a passionate love-poem in dramatic form, a collection of legal enactments, a collection of aphorisms on the conduct of life, a long prose poem on the futility of life, a number of biographies, a number of letters, and a prophetic rhapsody on life, death and eternity. This omnibus is generally known as the Bible, and if you examine its history you will see that I have not exaggerated in calling it the most popular book in all literature. Yet it is an undeniable fact that this great omnibus volume is to-day not read nearly so widely, nor anything like so assiduously, as it was even fifty years ago.

You may think it absurd to speak of the neglect of a book of which one distributing agency alone—the British and Foreign Bible Society—issued, a year or two ago, twelve million copies in a single year; but—well, consult your own experience. At one time—when I was very young—it would have taken more courage than I possessed to confess that there were any books of the Bible with which I was quite unfamiliar; we were supposed to have at least a bowing acquaintance with the whole of the vast omnibus. To-day, on the other hand, the young people of my acquaintance don't read the Bible, and are quite honest about their ignorance; when you casually mention Lot's wife, or Balaam's ass, or Jonah's gourd, or Naboth's vineyard, they look at you with blank uncomprehending faces. This is all very sad; but sadder still is the fact that there are large parts of the Bible—including the two books of Kings and the two books of Chronicles—with which even the clergyman of to-day is unfamiliar. If any of my clerical readers (supposing me to have any, which is perhaps a wild supposition) is inclined to wax indignant over this statement, let me put him to the test. I challenge him to go into an empty room, without a Bible or a concordance or any other work of reference, and work through an examination paper which I shall set him. If he passes —fifty per cent will be the pass standard—I shall withdraw, with abject apologies, the statement I have just made, and shall send him a certificate which he will be at liberty to read to his congregation; if, on the other hand, he fails, it is to be understood that I may publish the fact as a footnote in future editions of this book; that, I think, will be only fair. Let me warn him not to accept the challenge lightly; some of the questions will be very searching. For instance: "Who were Huppim and Shuppim?" "Give the names of the uncles of Peresh and Sheresh." "How many brothers had Romantiezer?" "Tell all you know about the life of Joshbekashah." "Who were the 'three mighties'?" "Who was Dodo's father?" "How many dukes are mentioned in the Bible?" Do you really think many readers could answer these questions off-hand? I fancy some people will feel sure that I invented Huppim and Shuppim, and that I took Dodo from a novel by E. F. Benson. That only shows to what lamentable depths our neglect of the Bible has brought us. All those names are in the Bible, right enough; I have known about them for some time—several days, in fact.

Now the obvious fact that the Bible is an omnibus, and the hugest and most bewilderingly miscellaneous of all omnibuses, seems to me to be one of the reasons, though it may be one of the lesser reasons, for our present neglect of it. What would you think of a volume which contained one of Chaucer's narrative poems, an Elizabethan play, a novel by Fielding, a novel by H. G. Wells, the whole of Palgrave's *Golden Treasury*, Green's *Short History of the English People*, Carlyle's *Sartor Resartus*, Mill's *Utilitarianism*, a number of essays by Lamb, Hazlitt, and G. K. Chesterton, the Police Code, the poems of Miss Edith Sitwell, and the Postal Regulations? You would say, or you might say, that each of these things was an excellent thing in itself; but you would wonder why the Postal Regulations should be bound up between the same covers with Miss Sitwell's poems; you would find the table of contents bewildering; and, in short, I doubt whether you would buy the book, or whether, if (being tempted by its cheapness) you did buy it, you would often take it from its shelf. To the modern mind, there is something of the same baffling and bewildering quality in that extraordinarily miscellaneous collection of ancient Hebrew literature which we call the Old Testament, and something not so bewildering but still rather confusing in that collection of narratives and letters, printed in no sort of chronological order and without any reference to the dates at which the various items were actually written, which we call the New Testament.

If this great neglected classic is to be redeemed from neglect we must face the facts fairly, and especially the fact, regrettable or not, that we live in the twentieth century. We cannot change our dates, however much we may wish that we had been born some centuries earlier. We simply cannot read the Bible in the old way, a scrap at a time.

When I was a boy I read, or heard, a great deal of the Bible— all in scraps, or "chapters" as they were called. Scraps at church, scraps at home, scraps at school, and scraps at Sunday-school. I had also to learn many scraps by heart. Is there any other book that we commit the absurdity of trying to read by shreds and patches?

Suppose you had never read Shakespeare, and one day made up your mind that, since there was so much talk about this writer, you had better make his acquaintance. And suppose you thereupon bought a copy of Shakespeare's works, and devoted ten minutes to a scene from the third act of *Hamlet*, and next day read half a scene from the last act of *Much Ado About Nothing*, and next day the opening passage of *Romeo and Juliet*, and next day a scene from the middle of the second part of *Henry VI*; and so on for years, until you had read every word that Shakespeare wrote; what would you know of Shakespeare? A few fine phrases would doubtless have stuck in your memory—nothing more. Every one knows that the way to read a play of Shakespeare is to sit down to it, with all your wits awake, and read it through— even as its first audience sat down in the theatre and saw it through.

And supposing that, conceiving it to be your duty to study English literature, you read half a scene from Shakespeare one day, fifty lines of Chaucer next day, one of Mr Kipling's short stories next day, a passage from the middle of a chapter of Mill's *Logic* next day, fifty lines of *Piers the Plowman* next day, and so on, skipping from author to author and from century to century; after some years you would certainly have read a good deal of English literature; but what would you know about English literature? Just about as much as you will know about Hebrew literature if you study it on the same absurd plan. Yet this was the plan adopted for our education in Hebrew literature when I was young; and so far as I know it is the plan adhered to with tenacity by the Churches to-day. It was actually not till I was grown up that I discovered that the Gospel of St Mark could easily be read through at a single sitting. And it was not till I learned to read each of these books—none of them is a really long book—as wholes, and to grasp them as wholes, that I began dimly and gropingly to understand wherein the undying greatness of the Bible really consists, and how great is the loss suffered by a generation which neglects it. To make the Bible once more a popular book would be one of the greatest public services that any man or any body of men could possibly perform. To be ignorant of the Bible means an impoverishment of life, which none of us can afford. To this day I find myself bearing a certain grudge— probably quite unjust—towards the teachers and preachers of my youth who never gave me a hint of the right way to read this omnibus volume.

If the man in the street no longer reads the Bible—and I think it may be taken for granted that he doesn't—do not imagine that the reason is that the man in the street is no longer interested in religion. On the contrary, there is nothing in which the average intelligent person is so keenly and desperately interested. That is plainly visible in the literature of the moment. . . . But the man in the street, though interested in religion, is not interested in the Bible. Why not? Well, I can only continue to cite my own personal experiences. I learned early, of course, that many of the Bible's statements of historic fact were not to be taken literally; that science left no room for the account of creation given in Genesis; that Jonah's adventures were not related with scientific accuracy; and that much of the folk-lore of the Hebrews was very much like the folk-lore of other peoples. I learned that the Hebrew code of ethics was not acceptable; that Deborah's splendid song of triumph, for instance, was a paean in praise of an act of foul treachery; that Jehu was praised for "zeal for the Lord" when he perpetrated something very like the massacre of Glencoe; and that some of the narratives of the Hebrews' dealings with neighbouring tribes showed a ruthlessness which throws into the shade anything of which the Germans were accused in the Great War. I learned that some of the poems in the Book of Psalms were appallingly ferocious hymns of hate. I learned that if the theology of the Deutero-Isaiah was a true theology, then the theology of the earlier writers—who worshipped a tribal deity, one among many deities—was all wrong. Such discoveries, now the commonplaces of orthodoxy, came as a succession of painful shocks to the young men of my generation. Never having read the Bible except in the way (of scraps and detached passages) mentioned above, we did not see that the real meaning and value of the Bible are independent of the historic accuracy, the code of ethics, or even the theology of this or that part of it. And so we were disinherited of an infinitely valuable possession. What I am concerned with here is the question: how is the young generation to be re-inherited and put in a position to feel once more, as our ancestors felt, the beauty of this ancient literature? The more intelligent of our young people are being introduced, more or less effectively, to the glories of English literature; some of them—an increasing number—are being brought into contact with the masterpieces of French literature; a few are still being helped to feel the greatness of Greek and Latin literature; but none of them, as far as I can make out, are being introduced—except by the shreds-and-patches method which has been proved to be quite ineffective—to the real masterpieces of Hebrew literature, in which there is something that is to be found nowhere else. How are we to help the modern reader to find out for himself the greatness of the Bible? That is the problem. The teacher of English literature gains nothing by telling his pupils how great Shakespeare is; he does what he can to remove the veils between the mind of Shakespeare and his pupils' minds; having done that, he has to leave them to find out the greatness of Shakespeare for themselves.

The first thing we have to realize, and get others to realize, is the fact that the Bible *is* an omnibus volume; not a book but a whole literature. We have to recognize, first and frankly, that it is not one but many books, and that these books are of very diverse merit, some supremely great and some mediocre. We must boldly throw overboard what is no longer tenable. We must not pretend that mythology is history. We must not pretend that the ceremonial enactments of Leviticus are in some mysterious way edifying. We must not pretend that to read the story of Joshua until one is sickened by the long record of ruthless massacres is to find guidance for modern international relations. We must not pretend that the obscure symbolism of Daniel or of the Apocalypse is intelligible when it is not. We must not pretend that the chronicles of Jewish history show the finger of God in a way in which the chronicles of England do not. We must not pretend that the Song of Songs is anything but a dramatic love-poem (or an anthology of love-poems), or that Ecclesiastes is not the work of a pessimistic Epicurean poet of the type of Omar Khayyam. We must not pretend that the least distinguished of the Pauline epistles is more divinely inspired than the loftiest of the Platonic dialogues; or that the worst of the Psalms has more beauty in it than the best poem of Shelley or Keats.

What harm could be done by a frank admission that in this great body of literature there are tremendous inequalities? For instance, take the historical books, the annals. I suppose it will be admitted that the Jews had, unfortunately, no Thucydides among them, no Tacitus, no Gibbon; only a set of conscientious chroniclers. But, apart from that fact, I have never been able to make out why we were expected, when I was young, to be especially interested in the history of the Jews; or why passages from the chronicles of this people should to-day be read aloud in churches, instead of passages from Greek or Roman history, or from the history of England. I am sure that my own distaste for the Bible was partly due to my being told such facts as that "Jotham was twenty and five years old when he began to reign, and he reigned sixteen years in Jerusalem; his mother's name also was Jerushah, the daughter of Zadok." Why should any clergyman read this to his flock when he might be reading them a great chapter from Trevelyan's Garibaldian trilogy?

Then, again, take the prophets, major and minor. These too used to be read aloud in the churches when I was young—or rather, scraps of them, torn from the context, were read. These, too, are of very varying merit; but even the best of them are almost unintelligible to us who do not know precisely the circumstances that called them forth. I used to hear passages of which, though I dimly felt that this was very magnificent poetry, I understood not a single sentence; I used to reflect that, no doubt, the grown-ups knew what it was all about. I now know that my elders were as much in the dark as I was; and that without close study of the conditions under which these prose poems were written they are, for the most part, incomprehensible to the modern reader.

Take, again, the Psalms. This anthology, like every anthology that ever was compiled, shows very steep inequalities. Some of the poems must assuredly rank among the greatest lyrics in any literature; some are poor. But there is no lyrical poetry in the world that is so steeped in local colour as the best of these psalms; before their beauty can be fully apprehended, they need all the explanation that modern scholarship can give.

Then there are the Pauline epistles. Their author was a thinker, a philosopher, a metaphysician; and to follow his dialectic is by no means easy. I believe myself to be a person of average intelligence, and I was trained, in my university, to read Spinoza, Kant, and Hegel; yet to this day I find much in these epistles which is beyond me. Yet, when I was young, scraps of these philosophical writings, ruthlessly torn from their context, were read aloud; and it was assumed that, without any philosophical training at all, people could follow the most intricate speculations of one of the subtlest minds of antiquity. It was a baseless assumption.

Finally, there is the book which used to be known as Revelations; a strange and enigmatic work, filled with the visionary ecstasies of the mystic. Of this marvellous specimen of apocalyptic literature I have nothing to say except what may be said of many mystical writings: that it appeals strongly to those who have a vein of mysticism in themselves, and that to the majority of mankind it is a sealed book. This, too, was read aloud, in scraps, when I was young!

I want to see the Bible given a chance to take its place again as a popular book. To bring this about, there are several things that we must do.

First, we must print the Bible in separate volumes, so that people may learn to think of Hebrew literature as consisting, like any other literature, of many books, some inspired and some of small value.

Secondly, these books must be printed like other books, in good type, (as long as the Bible is treated as an omnibus it has to be printed in microscopic type if it is to be of manageable size) and there must be none of that silly division into chapters and verses, a device which only served to give the book an inhuman air, to separate it from all the rest of literature, from all the books we knew and loved.

Thirdly, it must be published with just the necessary amount of critical apparatus to make it intelligible. This does not mean a vast array of pedantic notes and erudite prefaces. But the Bible is really quite incomprehensible to those who know nothing of the life it sprang from, the historical circumstances of its birth. Let modern scholarship give us just what we need and no more.

Lastly, I am afraid we shall have to have a new translation. Not that I for a moment desire the Bible to be rendered into present-day English. These writers are old; it is fitting that their language should have a touch of archaism. Let the new edition retain the Authorized Version wherever that is clearly intelligible; it cannot be bettered. Take, for example, that perfect similitude: "How often would I have gathered thy children together, even as a hen gathereth her chickens under her wing, and ye would not." Could that passionate cry be altered by a single word, except for the worse? Or, again, when you hear someone boasting of being a self-made man, and you protect your mind by murmuring to yourself, "It is He that hath made us, and not we ourselves," can you imagine a more perfect phrasing? No; let us not tamper with this monument of English—except where it is necessary, in order to bring back the Bible to its proper place in the popular esteem. The first thing is intelligibility; and where a new translation would make a bit of Pauline metaphysic clear which is now obscure, we must let all the old versions go.

LUCID INTERVALS

INTRODUCING AUSTRALIA

A FRIEND of mine is coming from England, full of curiosity about Australia; and he has suggested to me that I might wangle a few days' holiday in order to show him round the country. The proposal reveals the average Briton's deplorable ignorance of geography. Once, in a railway carriage in England, I talked with a man who, as soon as he knew that I hailed from Australia, asked me if I knew Mr McKenzie; and when I replied that I knew several, he explained that his McKenzie was the one who lived "near the bush." I fancy he thought "the Bush" was the name of our Australian hotel. But to return to my friend—I can see that I have to cure him of the globe-trotter's disease of wanting to see a continent in a week. He says he is keen on seeing "the real Australia"; by which I suppose him to mean that he will not be satisfied if I show him the Sydney bridge and take him to a race-meeting at Flemington or somewhere. After all, there are, I understand, bridges in Britain; and there is said to be a race-course at Epsom; what he wishes to see is something distinctively Australian—something he could never see without coming all the wearisome way to this country.

Well, I may as well do the thing thoroughly, especially as I suspect him of intending to write a book on his experiences. Our programme, as I have planned it, will take more than a few days. A string of pack camels does not travel with the speed of light; if you get more than three miles an hour out of them, day in day out, you are lucky. And I intend to take him to country where the camel is the only comfortable way of travel, at any rate for a person of my age. The car is very well in some parts of the continent; but to charge up sandy ridges, sixty or seventy feet high, for a whole day, with gears generally in second and frequently in first, the radiator boiling continuously (with water scarce and uncertain), on a grilling midsummer day—to find, when you have topped one ridge, that the next one looks higher and steeper, so that you feel fairly certain that your car will never do it, and that you will be stranded, hundreds of miles from help, with a few gallons of water in your canteen—this is for the young in mind and muscle and nerve; not for the likes of me. Besides, I want my friend to enjoy himself. Camels are essential.

We shall, of course, go by train to Alice Springs; every tourist must start his real tour from Alice Springs. (This is where the head office of Messrs Cook and Sons ought to be.) Thence, with half a dozen camels and half a dozen of our black brethren to act as guides—to find water and to hunt the merloo and the euro for us—we shall set out for the real Australia. (Possibly a few of our black sisters may come too; they will be wanted for the sake of their yam-sticks and wirris, which the male of the species thinks it beneath his dignity to use. With these rude implements the gins will dig out honey-ants when we run short of sugar, as I intend we shall, for I want my friend to have a rich and full experience; he is a man of dignified and even pompous bearing when at home, and I have somehow conceived a yearning to watch him sucking the sweetness from a honey-ant.)

We shall travel south-west—over sand plains, gibber plains, sandy ridges, mulga plains, spinifex flats, and whatever else we may encounter—for about a fortnight, when I ought, with any luck, to be able to show him Ayres Rock and Mount Olga, those two marvellous tors on which—so the Australian Baedeker, when there is one, will announce—no tourist should fail to feast his eyes. When he has feasted his eyes, and we have replenished our water-bags from the claypans on Ayres Rock, we shall turn to the south-east and cross the Musgrave Ranges, coming at last to Erliwunyawunya, where we shall camp for a week.

By this time my friend will have had some experiences which would not have been at all likely to come his way in England. For instance, he will know exactly what a camel smells like when it has fed all night on gidgee or buckbush. He will have heard the deafening din made by the tcheereerees in full chorus from the mulgas. He will have been barked at by a gecko, admired the brilliant red and yellow markings of a tcharkoora, and perhaps run away from a well-grown nyntucka—having been told that this lizard can break your leg with a single blow of his tail, a story which may or may not be true. He will have acquired a taste for the roasted tchungoo, the talgoo, and even—if I keep him hungry enough, as I mean to do—for the odorous wintarro. He will have run short of tobacco—I shall see to that—and learned to put up with mingil as a substitute. He will have chewed, appreciatively, the quondong, the kumberadda, and the ilboranji, for dessert. Possibly, in the excitement of chasing a dargawarra, he may have stumbled and fallen into a tussock of spinifex; but I hope not. I don't want him to carry away an unpleasant impression of our native flora.

I have planned that from Erliwunyawunya we shall have various little outings, all thoroughly Australian. For instance, going either to Murranuckna or to Koonapandi, we shall uish our camels under the shade of a kurrajong and watch a maala drive. We shall fire the spinifex so as to have a vast horseshoe of flame, with about a mile between the extremities; and here, at the open end of the horseshoe, our bucks will show their extraordinary skill with the throwing-stick as the maalas try to dash away from the closing pincers of fire. Neither my friend nor I will be able to use the throwing-stick, but perhaps we shall borrow kudgees and try our skill with them. This may be no better sport than fox-hunting; but it will certainly be different. To get a dozen maalas or so, we shall have burned, if there is a high wind blowing, an area about as big as Yorkshire. We may also catch a few eecharricharris.

Why this outburst of strange names, so seldom heard on the lips of ladies and gentlemen as they saunter down Collins Street or wallow in the surf at Manly? There are two reasons for it.

In the first place, friendly critics of my writings, especially critics at the other side of the world, have reported that there is nothing Australian in them; that they might as well have been produced in London, New York, or Tokyo, for all the local atmosphere in them. I am determined to amend my ways; and the paragraphs you have just read (or skipped) are the first fruit of that good resolution. In future—if I can only keep my vow—no page of mine but shall somehow manage to drag in a dargawarra or a kooracardie. If you read any of my lucubrations henceforth, you may possibly accuse me of a touch of sun, but you shall not accuse me of not being Australian. I am going to be so Australian that every one will suppose me to be a promising young aboriginal. . . . I am going to write verse, too, and found a new school of poetry; in form it may remind you of Mr T. S. Eliot, but in vocabulary it will be markedly different. I mean to dedicate my song, in pure Australian lingo, to boomerang and billabong and bandicoot and dingo. . . . Yes, and I am going to bring out an edition of Shakespeare translated into such terms as may be understood and enjoyed by the man out Koonamutta way. There may be difficulties with some of the songs—metrical difficulties—"Hark, hark, the budgerigar at heaven's gate sings," and that kind of thing. But Juliet, as a charming young gin of the Arunta tribe, will be a tremendous hit; who so clever as she at killing kooracardies and stripping the fat from their abdominal regions? Romeo falls in love as he watches her. . . .

My second reason for such a debauch of local colour is that I happen to have been reading the best book about Australia that has come my way these many days: Finlayson's *The Red Centre*. It is from this mine that I have been digging my vocabulary. If my English friend were real and not a myth, I think I should send him a cable: "Don't come; read Finlayson." If any one wants to know the real Australia, here it is; you may find out more about it from this book than you could learn—unless you are an extraordinarily keen observer—by crossing the oceans at great expense and undergoing all the discomforts of the trip I have just described. This is one of those books that make you feel, when you turn the last page and look round your room, as if you had come home from a long journey, and a singularly interesting one.

To make an end: I must apologize for using that silly phrase, "the real Australia." Of course the city slum and the city push are every whit as real (unfortunately) as anything you could see if you went all the way to Erliwunyawunya. Your suburban villa, and even your Shakespeare Society, are just as much parts of the real Australia as Chambers' Pillar; more's the pity, perhaps, but the fact is so. The cities we have built may be plagiarisms, but they are as real as the vast sunburnt land on whose outer edge we have chosen to build them. I am a city bird myself, and know very well, except in moments of sentimental self-delusion, that if I were condemned to live my life in the red centre I should promptly go mad. All we mean by "the real Australia"—if we mean anything—is the distinctive Australia, the Australia which is different from other lands, the Australia which is not a plagiarism from Europe or America; the huge island-continent which we have the effrontery to say we inhabit. Most of us have never even seen it; we have camped on its outermost rim, and are content to stay there.

THE PINK MAN'S BURDEN

It is very heavy and grievous to be borne, as I know from personal experience; though not so heavy as the burden which Kipling, in the days when he was a field preacher, urged us to take up. If a really white man were to make his appearance on this planet, his burden would indeed be greater than he could bear. Little children would shriek at the sight of the prodigy. We should all shun him like a leper. Even lepers are not really white; there are no white men—unless you can call a marble statue a man. Moreover, if you take words in this literal way, I doubt if there are really any red men. When Tennyson chanted—

> Let the red man dance
> By his red cedar tree,

I suppose he was encouraging some retired major-general whom he knew in the Isle of Wight—retired major-generals being famous for dancing with rage as they tell you how, damme, sir, the country is going to the dogs; but even they, I understand, never achieve anything more than a deep pink, shading off to purple; never are they genuinely red. The so-called Red Indian is no more really red than the so-called Red Sea. We talk, with a like shocking inexactitude, of the yellow races; but a race of men and women with faces the colour of lemons or of marigolds exists only in a jaundiced imagination. People's colour scheme is deplorably loose when they are talking of other members of the human family. I have heard a man of sterling character described by well-meaning friends as "a white man through and through"—a ghastly fancy.

But to correct this error in our current speech is not, as the sagacious reader has probably guessed, the purpose of the present essay. What I am writing about is the moral, or, if you will, the political complexion. I want to say a word, a very meek and chastened word, in defence of the much-enduring class to which I have the misfortune to belong; the mild people, the moderate people, the people whose colour is about half-way between the stainless white of the Tory and the vivid and flaming red of the

Revolutionary; the pink people, in short. I write from abundant personal knowledge of what we have to put up with in this warring world; and if a certain querulousness makes itself heard in these remarks, you will understand why. There will be no vituperation; we of the pink company never roar with rage. The gentle remonstrance is more in our line. We are a mild folk. We are used to being called by various insulting names—we are Laodiceans, we have the bourgeois mentality, we are flabby sentimentalists and anaemic worms. We are told twice a day that there is no room on earth for such as we; that nothing worth the doing was ever done by lukewarm persons like us; that no reform was ever carried through except by men who took sides passionately, who were ready to die for a cause, whose hearts were aflame with splendid faith and indomitable resolution and things like that. Well—even an anaemic worm will turn at last; even we pink people grow tired, after a while, of listening to abuse. The temptation to answer back becomes at times too much for us, and our general principles give way.

Take any political question you please, and you find us falling between two schools, the white school mistrusting us and calling us red, the red school despising us and calling us white. It is even worse than that: the Tory says he prefers the open and declared Revolutionary to the cloaked and masked variety of which we are examples; the Revolutionary says that when he sees an honest Tory in front of him he knows what he is fighting, but that we, the disguised Tories, are a nuisance and a blight. Between them they almost persuade us that we have no right to exist.

But there is really a case for pinkness; believe me, there is. Something can be said for our belief that there are two sides to every question, that there is generally some truth on each side, and that it is merely silly to take a strong line until one has heard what the other side has to say for itself. We quite agree, of course, that great things have been done by fiery and passionate men; but we believe that men who have rushed fierily and passionately into action without first finding out the facts, and reflecting thereon, have generally done more harm than good. We believe that the only salutary revolution is the revolution brought about by convincing one's fellow-men; and that to convince one's fellow-men always takes time and patience. We believe that to suppress by force what we take to be a mischievous opinion must be for ever futile, because all you do is to drive that opinion underground, where it is more mischievous than before. We do not agree with

Carlyle, that fire is a short argument; we deny that fire is an argument at all. We believe that there is something badly wrong with the present management of the world, and that to put it right we need, first and foremost, thought and investigation and a patient weighing of the facts. You see how inevitable it is that we, holding such a creed, should infuriate both sides. The white man, when he hears us talk of what is amiss with the present arrangement, is convinced that we have bombs up our sleeves. The red man, when he overhears us talking about thinking and investigating and weighing the facts, exclaims with his usual old-world courtesy, "To hell with this milk-and-water drivel!"

To take a concrete instance—and here it will be better to drop the plural number and speak only for myself—to me it seems perfectly obvious that the most interesting thing in present-day politics is the experiment which is being made in Russia; an experiment which, whether it succeed or fail, is unquestionably going to affect the destiny of every other country in the world. Very well, then; if we are to have a sensible public opinion in Australia, and not a mere blind prejudice masquerading as opinion, we must try to find out all we can about what the Russians are doing, and hear what they have to say about it, and hear what is said against them by persons who have lived in Russia. For my part, I read, when I am not too lazy, all the books I can get hold of on this subject; and I have some newspapers and magazines sent me from Russia (written in English and obviously propagandist—one has to allow for that, of course). What is the result? When the white man hears that I am interested in Russia and that I hope the Russian experiment may be successful, he at once makes up his mind that I am as red as a pillar-box. When, on the other hand, I tell the red man that I am not convinced that the Russian experiment has been a success, and that, as far as I can discover, life in Australia, with all its drawbacks, is preferable to life in Russia under its present rulers, he at once makes up his mind that I am a poor flabby creature, if not a wretched parasite and a traitor to the cause of humanity; if he can think of anything worse to say, he does not shrink from saying it. One side suspects me of being in the pay of Moscow; the other side suspects me of being in the pay of capitalism. Would it do any good to show them my bank balance? Not a bit; nothing would convince them.

We pink men still believe in individual liberty; and we like the tyranny of a communist oligarchy no better than the tyranny of a fascist gang. But we are not anarchists; we quite admit that absolute liberty for the individual is incompatible with organized society—that certain liberties have to be sacrificed for the privilege of living together.   We believe that the age-old problem of reconciling liberty and law will never be solved by violence.   We believe in peaceable methods; in the gradual education of public opinion as the only lasting way of reform; all other remedies being, in the long run, worse than the disease.   We believe that persuasion, tame and ineffectual as it seems to hot impatient men, intolerably slow as it must inevitably appear to persons suffering tortures on the rack of our present way of life, is the only method which will, in the long run, succeed.   Nothing will make us believe in violence as a cure for the world's ills.   If we had been caught as children, we might have had a different creed instilled into us; now, it is too late.   No medicine you can prescribe will change our inveterate habit of mind.   No pale pills for pink people will cure us of this troublesome moderation of ours.   We are incorrigibly pink.

What consoles us, when we are having evil names hurled at us from both sides, is that history seems to be with us.   What has violent revolution ever done except produce violent reaction? What did the beheading of Charles I bring forth except the enthronement, amid popular rejoicing, of the second Charles? What did the French Revolution really produce except Napoleon and the torment of his long wars, and then the return of the Bourbons?   What did Pitt and Castlereagh, with all their violent repression, do except compel the people of Britain to suffer manifest ills for half a century longer than they need have done? What has violence ever done for civilization?   Nothing, and less than nothing.   Civilization, whatever Ruskin may say, is not the fruit of war; it is the fruit of thinking, of inquiring, of teaching, of investigating, of devising; in short, the work of us pink men. You whites and reds can only, between you, set back the clock of real progress for a longer or shorter period.   But you will never believe this.

You are prepared to suffer for your creeds, so you boast; but we too have had our saints and martyrs; the stake and the rack have not been reserved for the violent.   Naturally, you find us exasperating; I sympathize with you.   It must be very trying, just when you are going to do something noble and heroic and impetuous, to hear a mild voice urging you to stop and think.   You feel much as Saint George would have felt if, when he had couched his lance to dash upon his foe, some academic person, with spectacles and an umbrella, had held up a pleading hand and said, "Please—please—one moment!—don't you think you ought to wait till you have heard what the dragon's point of view is?" It is perfectly natural that you fire-eaters scoff at us and snub us and even suspect us of being other than we pretend. But neither your scorn nor your suspicion is going to convert us to your futile creed; in season and out of season, we are going to continue to preach the way of reason. We may even be tempted to encourage one another with hymns—

> Take up the pink man's burden,
> To serve the mad world's need,
> Though scorn shall be your guerdon
> And mockery your meed. . . .

and things like that. We need all the encouragement we can give one another; because, when you think of it calmly—if you can ever bring yourselves to think calmly—you will see that courage is not a virtue of which you have a monopoly; it takes a certain amount of pluck, in these mad days, to be resolutely and publicly temperate. You have your magnificent traditions, we all admit; of battle-field and barricade, of fighting against desperate odds and falling amid a blaze of glory. But we too have traditions of which we are not ashamed. You may not believe it, but we actually feel a glow of pride as we look out across the darkling plain of history and watch our thin pink line of heroes going steadily forward.

It would not be fair to end without a warning. As I have said, we can stand any amount of abuse; we are used to it. But one thing we shall not stand, and that is any interference with our liberty to be as pink as we choose. That is the one thing that can get past the guard of our habitually equable temper. We have it on the authority of Gladstone that a mad sheep is a dangerous animal. You may possibly produce curious colour effects if you make the pink man see red.

THE ART OF SKIPPING

I HAVE a friend who will not look at tripe, and utterly refuses to eat brains, who abhors liver, and who—you will find this hard to believe—speaks disrespectfully of devilled kidneys. All these delightful things he brackets together as "works"; he thinks there is something disgusting about eating the "works" of any animal. Yet when I visited him in his home the other evening I marked on his bookshelf a volume bearing the title, *Shakespeare's Complete Works*. Now for my part I object to the *complete* works, even of the dear little lamb that was lately frisking on the green, and I object to being asked to devour the complete works of an author, even of Shakespeare. In both cases, I like selection, choice, discrimination. My friend rejects the works of the lamb as a whole, and accepts the works of Shakespeare as a whole. I have been, so far, quite unable to make him understand how inconsistent he is, and how much more reasonable is my own position. He even accuses me of sophistry and quibbling. Now that I have pilloried him in print, let me add—in case you should think that you too had detected a fallacy in my reasoning—that the reasoning doesn't matter in the least so long as you agree with my conclusion, which is—that no author's complete works are worth studying. At least, at the moment of writing, I can think of no exception.

What set me off on this theme was the fact that I had been roaming about, during the last few days, among the sumptuous twenty-one volumes of Mr Howe's new edition of Hazlitt. It is an edition that looks well on one's shelves; a handsome piece of furniture; each volume is comely to the eye and light in the hand. I am prepared to certify that the editor has done his work well, and that his notes are just what one wants. Two volumes are filled with writings not published in any previous edition of Hazlitt, things rescued by Mr Howe's pious hands from the dustbins of old periodicals. Here at last are the *Complete Works of William Hazlitt*, as complete as we are ever likely to see; it seems improbable that another scrap of writing unquestionably Hazlitt's will ever come to light. I think it quite a good thing that such an

edition should have been published; every public library should
have these monumental volumes on its shelves; it is the best kind
of memorial to a great writer; but . . . Need any one really bother
with the complete works of William Hazlitt? For my part, I have
hitherto been content with a Hazlitt in various more or less shabby
and dumpy little volumes, different in size, different in colour, sent
forth by different publishers, printed at different presses; they
could all be crammed into about three of Mr Howe's volumes;
yet they contain all of Hazlitt that I shall ever want to read. Who,
at this time of day, could find it profitable to pore on the *Life of
Napoleon Bonaparte*? Who has so much spare time on his hands
that he can afford to spend days on the *Essay on the Principles of
Human Action*? There are so many better, and better-informed,
biographies of Napoleon; at least, I imagine so, though I have
never read Hazlitt's and never shall. And if for some strange
reason I wanted to know something about the principles of human
action, it would not be to Hazlitt's juvenile effort that I should go.
Hazlitt was a great journalist—perhaps the greatest there has ever
been in England; but even the greatest journalist must needs write
much that is of value and interest only on the day of its publica-
tion. It seems hardly fair to Hazlitt's fame that every little scrap
of his most ephemeral scribbling should be exhumed and repub-
lished a century later. So, as I wandered up and down this
imposing edition of a writer whose best things I have read and
re-read with ever-renewed enthusiasm, it came into my head that
some day I must write a little treatise on "The Art of Skipping."
Little, I say; but it must be big enough to contain a number of
dull pages, to provide readers with occasions to practise the art
whereof it treats. It is plainly a delicate and difficult art, an art
in which proficiency can only be acquired with practice. I am not
yet ready to write that treatise, because I am not yet sure what
the true principles of skipping are; all I am sure of is that
judicious skipping ought to be learned by every student of
literature.

If what I have said is true of Hazlitt, of what writer is it not
true? Can you name one?

> All Balzac's novels occupy one shelf,
> The new edition fifty volumes long.

Can you seriously maintain that they are all worth reading, when
life is so brief and there is so much else to read? I will yield to
nobody as an admirer of the Waverley novels; but I can declare

with assurance that some of them are not worth reading and that in every one of them are passages better skipped. Having thus alienated the Scott-worshippers, I may as well go on and outrage the feelings of the Shakespeare-worshippers. I say it is true, and that every one knows in his heart that it is true, that part of Shakespeare is, to put it baldly, rubbish; and that if Shakespeare could come back for a day he would laugh heartily to find us treating his rubbish with the reverence due only to his best work; he would be the first to admit that many things he wrote were written in a frantic hurry to serve the urgent need of the moment, and that his workmanship, in his uninspired hours, was slovenly botching. The trouble with Shakespeare is, of course, that skipping is a risky business, because in one of his worst scenes you are apt to come across a line of immortal beauty—a flash of genius amid the murk.

Mr Algernon Blackwood once told a ghost story which seemed to me an absolute model for all story-tellers; there was not a word in it that could be skipped. So far as I can remember, it ran thus: " 'Do you believe in ghosts?' said the first stranger. 'No,' said the second stranger. 'I do,' said the first stranger, and vanished." I don't say that every ghost story should be told with this admirable parsimony of words; sometimes you have to work up an atmosphere of horror, and that takes time. But—well, I have been told that Henry James's *Turn of the Screw* is the best ghost story in all literature; oblige me by reading it and telling me whether it would not have been twice as good with half the words. But that, when you come to think of it, is true of most books, don't you think? Long-windedness is the great bane of literature. Mr Robert Graves has given us a version of *David Copperfield* as he thinks it ought to have been written, incurring, I have no doubt, a certain amount of thoughtless ridicule as the man who thought he could improve on Dickens. But why should he not? Is there a law of nature that nobody can improve on Dickens? I say we ought to be grateful to a man who has been at the pains to take that delightful novel and cut out the surplusage for us. Dickens would not have been a Victorian novelist if he had not put in a good deal of surplusage. They all did it. (Have you read *Pendennis* lately?) And not the novelists only. Have you read De Quincey's famous essay "Murder as one of the Fine Arts"? It would be a masterpiece, but for its author's intolerable verbosity. He starts with a splendid idea, and twists it and turns it and tortures it till it becomes a piece of sheer boredom.

Talking of 'De Quincey reminds me that I have rather strayed from the point. What I was saying was that to think it a duty to master the complete works of any author is a mistake, however eminent the author. The works of De Quincey, in my edition, run to fourteen volumes. He was an extraordinary master of the music of the English tongue, and when he had anything to say he fashioned things of miraculous beauty; but for the most part he had nothing to say, and then his writing became mere verbiage; I don't know any English writer of genius with whom it is more urgently necessary to practise the art of skipping—with the possible exception of Wordsworth. Wordsworth is the greatest of modern English poets, on the strength of an inspiration that lasted him for about, at the outside, ten years; he lived for forty years after the inspiration had flickered out, but kept on writing verse as if nothing had happened, with only an occasional momentary gleam of the old radiance; so that when you pick up *Wordsworth's Complete Poetical Works* you must be prepared for an exercise for which skipping is an inadequate word; vaulting with the pole would be nearer the mark. It is the same, I say, with all the great writers. All of them who have lived a normally long life have perpetrated much that is—no, I must not say worthless, but not first-rate; and there is so much of the first-rate to read, and so little time to read it in. Who would bother with the *Idylls of the King* when so much that is far better poetry awaits our exploration? Had we but world enough, and time, we might amuse ourselves with trying to find our way through the tangled thickets of Browning's later volumes. . . .

But—the trouble with most theories is that there is a "but" lurking in the background—the worst of it is that nobody can tell you what to skip. You have to be the captain of your own soul—your own skipper, so to speak. You, or at least I, resent being told what to read and what to skip. I like having that complete De Quincey, though I know that four-fifths of it is, as food for the mind, about as nourishing as sawdust. I like to do my own exploring, and to find out for myself what will suit me and what will not. Abridgments, in spite of Mr Robert Graves, are the devil; you feel, in reading them, that the passages omitted are sure to be the most delightful passages in the book; very likely you are wrong, but you want to find out for yourself that you are wrong. All decent people resent being dictated to about their reading; no right-minded person submits without protest to a government censorship of books. So that it seems that I have no practical advice to give you, after all, on the subject of skipping; and this essay lacks point—unless this is the point: that some people have a mistaken sense of duty about books; they think that when they sit down to a book they ought to read every word; I want, if I can, to lighten the load on such persons' consciences. Don't be ashamed to skip; skip like young lambs if you feel so disposed; for you can count on the fingers of one hand the books that contain nothing which can safely be skipped.   In short: the art of wise reading is the art of judicious skipping.

ON A MEAN STREET

I was walking about London in a very buoyant mood. I had just read a newspaper article which had raised my spirits to the point of effervescence—a state of mind so unusual in the present lugubrious epoch that I had better explain the circumstances. For some time I had been exercised in my mind over the question whether England—or Australia—was a civilized country, or whether every country in the world was not passing through a period of barbarism; the sure sign of barbarism being, according to my philosophy, the mistaking of means for ends. A civilized society is one that knows what it wants; one that sees a certain kind of life as desirable, seeks with deliberate aim to achieve that kind of life, and values things according as they are or are not means to that end. Such a society existed in Greece in the age of Pericles, and in Italy in the years following the Renaissance; these were real civilizations, for each of them had a sense of values. We, on the other hand—thus had run my doleful reflections—have no real sense of values; we habitually mistake means for ends. We gape, with foolish faces of praise, at every new application of science to life, at every new machine, at every new triumph of invention, as if it were a triumph over evil. We think of wireless, for instance, as a tremendous stride in civilization, without seeing that it all depends on the end for which wireless is used; if it is to be used only to bring fatuous talk and debased crooning into multitudes of homes, then it is indeed a stride, but a backward stride, towards the abyss. It is a real contribution to civilization only if it helps to make possible the good life; but we never think of it in this way, because, in actual fact, we have no idea of what constitutes the good life; in other words, we have no sense of values.

Such was the tenor of my morbid meditations, till I happened to light upon an article in the *New Statesman* which brought sunshine into my gloom. We have, according to this writer, a true sense of values; we don't really care about the triumphs of. applied science. "Who," he asks with a fine flourish of rhetoric, "would not consign wireless sets and aeroplanes and telephones and all the rest of our comfortable contrivances to the devil for the chance of hearing Socrates talk on the steps of the Acropolis—or Christ speak from the Mount—or to have a Mozart or a Pheidias among us again?" After reading about a column of this kind of thing one felt that all was right with the world. And it was in this happy mood that I turned the corner, into the Portobello Road. I stepped out of a highly respectable street, a sedate middle-class street, a street of mansions turned into flats and maisonettes, a very quiet, gentlemanly, irreproachably virtuous street, into the Portobello Road.

You get these sudden contrasts in London. Not that Portobello Road was a disreputable, ruffianly street. I never saw any fighting in it, nor any drunkenness worth speaking of. It is not a slum; I am not sure whether there are any slums, in the old sense of the word, to be found in London to-day. It is just a mean street; one of London's typical mean streets; the busy shopping street of a mean neighbourhood. On Friday, till late at night, and on Saturday forenoon, it turns itself into a market, with a continuous line of stalls on each side of the narrow roadway, and a tremendous press of people doing their week-end marketing in the shops and at the stalls. For your bread and meat you go, as a rule, into the shops, for fruit and vegetables you patronize the stalls. But there are other things on the stalls; as, battered brass candlesticks, cracked mirrors, worn-out gramophone records, pictures without frames, frames without pictures, old spoons and forks and knives, cracked vases, rusty bolts and nuts, discarded sets of teeth, door-mats, furniture, electric switches, jewellery, and even books (at fourpence a volume). (I saw on one stall, in very good condition, a copy of *The Meaning of Money*, by Hartley Withers; a month later it was still there—nobody in Portobello Road seemed anxious to spend fourpence on finding out what money meant. The trouble, for these people, is not to get hold of the meaning of money, but to get hold of money.) There was one stall where you could buy excellent bananas from an old woman who, when she was not negotiating with you, would continue to shout her wares in a shrill soprano. (The stall-holders, between them, made a terrific din.) She had a misshapen body and a rather shapeless face, but an amiable disposition (I presume I was not the only one of her customers whom she was in the habit of greeting as "dearie"). I do not blush to confess that I sometimes bought more

bananas than the household really needed, for the sake of com-
muning with this war-worn veteran who seemed to have stepped
straight out of a page of Dickens.

I thought of her one day as I sat in St Paul's listening to a
sermon by Dean Inge, and I dare say it was a very fine one, but
the vision of her face behind a heap of bananas kept intruding,
and gave to the subtleties of Christian doctrine a certain air of—
shall I say, irrelevance? No doubt it was because I was too stupid,
but I could not see how these refinements could be applied to the
buyers and sellers in that mean street. My feeling about this was
so strong that I sought an outlet in verse, and wrote an Ode, which
I here present to you as a curiosity, being possibly the first poem
ever written in St Paul's Cathedral; if not the first, then almost
certainly the worst.

I have seen the Cenotaph, the Abbey down at Westminster,
Cleopatra's Needle, the Tower, and the Monument;
A glance on Nelson's Column I've bestowed;
     But somehow—somehow—
I think the roof and crown of the sights of London Town
Is the market in the Portobello Road.

Up and down I've wandered, idle and inquisitive;
Done the things I ought to do, seen the sights I came to see,
Parks, and squares, and Royalty's abode;
     But somehow—somehow—
I find my memory dwelling on an old woman selling
Bananas in the Portobello Road.

Yesterday I listened to a preacher, and a famous one;
Famous the church, and eloquent the sermon was,
And the words they gleamed and glowed;
     But somehow—somehow—
I wondered what it mattered to my poor old battered
Madonna of the Portobello Road.

Coming back, after this digression, to the point from which
we started—I turned the corner, I say, into the thoroughfare mentioned, and . . . I wondered. I wondered whether the writer of
those cheerful sentences in the *New Statesman* was not a trifle too
optimistic and perhaps a trifle too rhetorical. I wondered whether
the crowd in that mean street would be thrilled to the marrow-
bones if someone announced to them that a new machine had been
invented by which the past could be brought back, and that if they
would all keep perfectly quiet they would be privileged to hear
Socrates discoursing to his disciples from the steps of the
Acropolis. I wondered how excited they would grow if they
learned that a man had been brought to life again after many

centuries, and that the man was actually no other than Pheidias. And my misgivings went farther afield, and I wondered how many people, up and down the length and breadth of England, and of the Empire, had ever heard of Pheidias. I even went on to wonder to how many people Mozart himself was much more than a name. In the end my speculation took the bit between its teeth and ran away with me so violently that I actually found myself wondering whether, if it were announced that on a certain day the Sermon on the Mount could be heard in the very voice of the original Preacher from every wireless set in Australia, and that day happened to be Melbourne Cup Day, the race would be put off. . . . An outrageous question, obviously. Let us get back to realities.

This is not a sermon; I am not in my apostolic nor even in my episcopal mood at present; besides, what could I preach about from this text? Should I say, severely, that the Portobello Road is a blot on a civilized city? But I don't think it is; not especially so; not more than Park Lane is, anyway. The people I met when I went marketing in the Portobello Road seemed to be full of the fundamental decencies; I am not sure whether the people who live in Park Lane are, because I never met any of them; perhaps they are. No, all I mean by introducing Portobello Road to your notice is that it is no use pretending that we are more civilized than we are. If being civilized means yearning to hear the voice of Socrates arguing, or shedding tears over the death of Pheidias, then neither England nor Australia is civilized. It is no use pretending that we care very intensely for poetry or philosophy or music or sculpture or the things of the mind generally; because, you know, we don't. A few people do; a somewhat larger number pretend to; the mass of us are frankly not at all concerned with such things. When 'Tennyson died in a blaze of glory and was buried in Westminster Abbey, George Gissing, who liked honesty, wrote an article showing that the vast majority of Tennyson's fellow-countrymen had never heard of him. I have seen Mr T. S. Eliot described as a famous poet; does this mean more than that his work is known to one or two thousand out of—how many millions? If we were really anxious to hear Socrates arguing, we might do so any day we liked by reading Plato's dialogues in an English translation; but do we? Well, then, are we civilized? What is the meaning of this word "civilization" which we use every day? We often hear that another war would shatter our civilization; but would it? And, if it would, are we sure that our civilization would not be

better shattered? I am only asking for information. I do think—
if you will forgive a sermonizing touch at the end—that it is a bad
habit to go on using words of which we don't clearly know the
meaning. It was Portobello Road that set me asking myself the
question, "What is civilization?"—and trying to clear my mind on
the subject. But there is no need to go to London to find
a Portobello Road; it has its counterparts in all cities.

I

ON BEING NATURAL

SOMEBODY has borrowed my copy of Bacon's *Essays*; but I seem to remember that in his observations on death Bacon remarks that people are not really so terribly afraid of death as we are apt to suppose, and that this is shown by the fact that they are apt to commit suicide for the most trivial reasons; some, he says, put an end to their lives from mere weariness of doing the same thing over and over again. Bacon knew what he was talking about when he said that, though he spoke before the days of the ghastly monotony of machine-minding. I thought of his remark this morning when I was shaving, an operation which I have performed, heaven knows why, a good many thousand times. If monotony is such an evil that it drives men to suicide, why do we acquiesce in this perfectly avoidable monotony of shaving? Some activities have to be repeated willynilly, all our lives long; breathing, for instance. But why do we go out of our way to add the monotony of shaving to an existence which already possesses a plentiful lack of variety?

I have gone about like Socrates all day, asking questions, or at least asking one question: "Why do you shave?" I regret to have to report that I have received no satisfactory answer. The most honest was from a man who told me that his wife would not like him to go about looking like a wild man from Borneo; and when I asked him, scoffingly, whether he always did as his wife told him, he handed me out a curious philosophy of matrimony. After all, he said, shaving is a trivial matter; always do as your wife wants you to do, in matters of no moment. This implied that he follows his own judgment in anything that seems to him to be really important. I dare say many husbands adopt this sensible course, though few of them mention it. . . . A clergyman whom I questioned, and to whom I pointed out that the Apostles and all the great fathers of the Church allowed their beards to grow, countered by asking whether I had ever seen a picture of a bearded angel; an argument which left me speechless. But the common reply was that a beard was unhygienic. It is extraordinary how people will delude themselves. Quite honest men seem to believe that they shave for reasons of health, and that they are not at all moved by the fact that being clean-shaven is the prevalent fashion.

I was looking the other day at a photograph, taken some sixty years ago, of a group of elderly Scots. Some of them seemed, by their collars, to be ministers of the gospel; some were obviously elders of the kirk; all of them looked severe, incorruptible, inflexibly upright. When I looked again, I saw that this appearance of a stern, unbending morality was given to them by the fact that, wearing beards, they had shaved the upper lip. This seems to have been the fashion in Scotland at that time. I am told that Scottish bankers not only shaved the upper lip, but required all their clerks to do likewise; which was probably based on a theory—which I believe to have been sound—that this particular facial arrangement gives an air of impeccable respectability. All Scots have a talent for looking respectable; a Scot with a fringe of beard under his chin and a shaven upper lip is the very embodiment of all the qualities that we desire in a man to whom we are going to entrust our money. (It is exceedingly sad to reflect that the greatest bank failure of the nineteenth century took place at Glasgow.)

Why was this curious fashion confined to Scotland? That is a question for the sociologist, but my own theory is that it was connected with the national love of porridge. To eat porridge cleanly, quietly, and without waste, the moustache must be sacrificed. The beard, on the other hand, had to be kept, to protect the throat from the abominable climate of that country.

But, to tell the truth, there is no accounting for the vagaries of fashion in this matter of shaving. Any day the beard might become the mode again; and when it does, nobody, except here and there a crank, will go clean-shaven for hygienic reasons. Later, the beard will disappear once more; but it will not disappear because it is believed to harbour microbes; it will disappear for some reason which will be past finding out. Why did the crinoline come? Why did it go? Nobody knows. What dread deity issues the fiat that brings such things into existence, and blots them out again, no one can tell us. Some hidden power, in the late nineteenth century, said, "Let there be bustles," and there were bustles. Who it was, no historian has told us.

To utter these platitudes is not the purpose of the present essay; I am coming to the point, slowly. I used to think that fashions in shaving indicated the attitude of the time towards romance. In the romantic Elizabethan period, every man was bearded like the pard; look at the portraits of Shakespeare and Drake, Essex and Raleigh and the rest of them; not a clean-shaven face in the lot. In the highly unromantic eighteenth century, from Addison and Swift to Burke and Gibbon, they all shaved their faces and wore absurd and unnatural-looking wigs. The age of Elizabeth was the age of poetry and beards; the accession of Anne ushered in an age of prose and shaving. In the Victorian era, romance came back again; Tennyson and Browning were romantic poets, and wore beards; so did Rossetti and Swinburne. . . . But this theory will not, I am afraid, wash; for the great leaders of the romantic movement at the opening of the century—Wordsworth, Coleridge, Scott, Shelley, Keats, Byron, Lamb, Hazlitt—all, without exception, shaved. The puzzle is beyond my powers; all I can see is that, as far back as we can go in history, we find man oscillating between the habit of shaving and the habit of letting nature have its way with their faces.

Letting nature have its way! That brings me at last to the point. The whole question hinges on a deep principle of human nature; the principle which we can briefly describe by saying that it is natural to interfere with nature. Shaving the face, day after day, year in year out, means a steady, determined, sustained interference with nature. Every time I take razor in hand and scrape away the infant hairs from my cheeks and chin, I am really saying to nature, "No, you don't!" I am asserting my will against the will of nature. She, the indomitable goddess, never acknowledges defeat; never says, wearily, "All right, then; have it your own way." She continues, doggedly, to produce little sprouts of hair; I, with equal doggedness, cut them off, and frustrate her effort. By so doing I really equip myself every morning with an artificial face, a face with which nature did by no means intend me to confront the world. Every morning she makes it plain that she would prefer me to have a long beard, sweeping the ground. Every morning I nip her intentions in the bud.

Therefore—and this is not so trivial as you suppose—I move that we try to get out of the habit of loose thinking and loose talking about the antithesis between the artificial and the natural. Let us recognize the truth, that it is natural for human beings to be artificial. Why should man, the artificer, be ashamed of artifice, which is what distinguishes him from the brutes? The sheep does not shave his face; we do; this is one of the things that distinguish us from sheep; and heaven knows that in these democratic days we need something to remind us that we are not sheep. The cat does not paint her claws pink or green, as the up-to-date woman does; it is one of the marks of difference between the two. How often have you heard elderly men indulging in tirades against the modern girl with her lipstick, her rouge, her doctored eyebrows and her dyed talons? The essence of these diatribes always is, that the girl is to be blamed for not leaving her face as nature intended it to be; and this rebuke comes, if you please, from a man who has for years been preventing his beard from growing as nature intended it to grow! A girl who uses lipstick is being perfectly natural; if she gave up all these devices and pretended to be an untutored savage, a sweet and simple child of nature, an Arcadian shepherdess, that would be the supreme artifice. This condemnation of women for playing tricks with their faces and nails is a simple and glaring example of the loose thinking I have mentioned. In being artificial, women—and men—are following the dictates of human nature. Cosmetics are a sign of civilization; and it is natural for men to be civilized. I rejoice to read, in an English newspaper of recent date, that "this will be a pale-faced Ascot, a heavy-lidded magenta-mouthed Ascot. Eye-lashes, coloured and lacquered, half an inch long, made of hair from a horse's tail, are sold in sets to match your Ascot dress. They are attached with waterproof, heatproof adhesive."

And so, when people with half-baked Darwinian or Nietzschean ideas rattling about in their heads tell you that nature is red in tooth and claw—that the fittest survive in the inexorable struggle for existence—that any interference with nature's laws must bring its inevitable penalty—that democracy must fail because it interferes with nature's law that the strong must rule the weak—it is better not to argue with persons who talk this kind of rubbish, but simply to reply, "I like your cheek." If they are clean-shaven, and are not too stupid to see the point of the rejoinder, they will be crushed; but if they are bigoted beard-growers, you will have to point out to them that not democracy only, but all civilization whatsoever, is a gross interference with nature, in the sense in which they are using the word nature.

And now I really do come at last to the point of this essay. We are often told—though not quite so often, happily, as a few years ago—that man is by nature a fighting animal, and that therefore permanent peace on earth is a dream, and a bad dream, because it would mean the decay of courage and all sorts of fine virtues. Even if we grant the truth of the statement that man is by nature a fighting animal—a statement which students of primitive man are coming more and more insistently to question—we must reply that the greatness of man lies in the very fact that he can change his nature, tame his primitive impulses, rise above himself, substitute helpfulness for pugnacity, and so make society possible. And if the person you are talking to shakes his head and continues to harp on nature's inviolable laws and the terrible penalties attached to any interference with nature, ask him—very meekly, not to arouse the instincts of the fighting animal—whether in his experience all clean-shaven men have come to a shocking end.

HAMLETS ALL

I SUPPOSE it is beyond all question that *Hamlet* is the most popular play ever written, in English or any other language. (I refer, of course, to a long-term popularity, not to the dazzling success of a moment.) Equally indubitable is the fact that the hero of this play is the best-known of all the creations of genius. I fancy it is unnecessary to argue about this.

Re-reading the play the other evening, I found myself asking, for perhaps the thousandth time, why it should be so. What mysterious quality has given to this play its enduring fame, beyond any other even of Shakespeare's? For what reason do whole books continue to be written about "the Hamlet problem"? Why has it become the supreme ambition of literary critics to say something new about it, and of actors to give a new interpretation to the central character in it? Hamlet himself defied his false friends Rosencrantz and Guildenstern to pluck out the heart of his mystery; can we hope to succeed where they failed? By what magic does he still draw us on to the attempt?

There is one answer so simple, so obvious, and so hackneyed, that I almost blush to mention it. In Coleridge's *Table Talk* there is a passage which, though it is well-known, will bear quoting once more. "Hamlet's character is the prevalence of the abstracting and generalizing habit over the practical. He does not want courage, skill, will, or opportunity; but every incident sets him thinking; and it is curious, and at the same time strictly natural, that Hamlet, who all the play seems reason itself, should be impelled, at last, by mere accident, to effect his object. I have a smack of Hamlet myself, if I may say so." It is for the sake of the last sentence that I quote this passage. Coleridge notices some resemblance between Hamlet and himself; what he might have noticed, if he had been a less self-centred person, was that there are some resemblances between Hamlet and everybody.

Stevenson tells a story—without guaranteeing its truth—of a

young man who went in an agony to Meredith after the publi-
cation of *The Egoist* with its devastating portrait of Sir
Willoughby Patterne. "This is too bad of you," he cried;
"Willoughby is me!" "No, my dear fellow," said the author; "he
is all of us." Well, so it is with Hamlet; he is all of us. Or, at
least, we all have a smack of Hamlet. I know of no other
imaginary personage of whom this can be so truly said; in Don
Quixote, the traits of our common humanity are less easily
recognizable.

Yes, we are Hamlets all, in less or greater measure; and I
think it useful to recognize this fact, not that it may help us to
understand Hamlet, but that it may help us to understand one
another.

Now at first sight it seems a difficult saying. If you have seen
or read the play with any attention, you will be ready enough to
agree (unless I am greatly mistaken) that you yourself have a
good deal in common with Hamlet; but you will also say that
neither Smith nor Brown nor Jones nor Robinson can by any
stretch of the imagination be conceived as Hamlets. Hamlet was
an extraordinary person; Smith is a dreadfully ordinary person.
You yourself, you feel, have some extraordinary qualities; but
Smith—good Lord! Hamlet, again, was a philosopher; and you
yourself, you have often felt—and your friends have remarked it,
too—are a bit of a philosopher; but surely nobody has ever mistaken Jones for a philosopher! And so, too, Hamlet was a wit;
and you yourself have often thought of exceedingly amusing
things to say, though you may have thought of them too late for
the occasion; but that dull dog Brown was never capable of a
witticism in his life. No, it may be true that *you* have a smack of
Hamlet; but it is merely laughable to suggest that there is a smack
of Hamlet in the people one meets in the street, on the links, at
the club, on the beach, or round the bridge table; the estimable
people, the stodgy people, the dull, convention-ridden, insipid
people who waddle through life from the cradle to the crematorium
without a spark of originality or a gleam of the uncommon; the
human herd, in fact.

The longer I live the more untrue I see this to be. If you look
at people from the outside, as it were, and judge them by their
ordinary behaviour and their everyday conversation—if you listen
only to men's twaddle about golf or politics, and to women's
twaddle about their servants or their ailments—why, then, of
course, you are tempted to indulge, if not in Swiftian indignation

against this little odious race of vermin, at least in Shavian contempt for the depths of human silliness; you are prone to liken your fellow-men, if not to a drove of Gadarean swine, at least, and at best, to a flock of docile sheep. But if you look at people more consideringly, getting by an effort of sympathetic imagination a glimpse of what is going on in their hearts and minds, a very different spectacle confronts you, and you are inclined to say (with Hamlet). "What a piece of work is a man! How noble in reason! How infinite in faculty! in form, in moving, how express and admirable! in action how like an angel! in apprehension how like a god!" Or, if you are not prepared to go quite so far as this, you will say at least, "How like a Hamlet!" That is why Hamlet is universally attractive.

I have even noticed a hint of Hamlet in other animals than man; and especially in the animals most closely associated with human life. Have you never seen a dog—say a cocker spaniel—with the brooding philosophic look in his melancholy eyes, as if he were telling himself that the time was out of joint? I have seen the same look in the face of a horse; and the same, but a thought more tragical, in the face of a donkey. I have seen a meditative baboon that seemed to be on the point of breaking out in a soliloquy—beginning, perhaps, with some such words as "To be, or not to be. . . ." But there is one domestic animal that you never by any chance catch with the Hamlet look on its face, and that is the cat—the sedate, self-satisfied, placid, imperturbable cat; the grave, inscrutable cat. In ancient Egypt the cat, as you know, was held divine. Temples were built in its honour. When a cat died, all members of the household shaved their eyebrows. In a modern house, a cat is the living reminder of a remote antiquity, a chip of the immemorial rock of life. Just such a cat—you reflect as you look at yours—may have purred to watch a pyramid a-building, or rubbed her cheek against the ankle of King Thothmes the Third. There is nothing, in the cat, of the modern spirit, of the troubled mind that broods over that tangle of frustrations and bewilderments that we call life; the mind of Hamlet.

As I have said, I think it quite possible that this theory—the theory that Hamlet's singular attractiveness rests on the fact that we are Hamlets all—may strike you at first as a monstrous absurdity. "Have you never mixed with the world?" I may be asked. "Have you known nobody but wits and philosophers? Have you never kept your ears open, never noticed of what stuff the ordinary conversation of men and women is fashioned? It is an entire mistake to think that what you call the brooding philosophic spirit is anything but an extreme rarity. The great majority never brood, never philosophize, never ask questions about the meaning or purpose of human life. They take things for granted; they swallow the universe like a glass of beer. Next time you are in your club smoking-room, do, for heaven's sake, pay a little attention to the stream of fatuity that flows from the lips of your fellow-clubmen; and you will never again afflict us with nonsense about everybody being a Hamlet!" To which I reply: My dear friend, I used to think exactly as you do; but the years, which have brought me cares a-many and troubles a-plenty, have also brought me the power of seeing a little deeper than I used to see into the hearts of my fellows, and also into my own heart. I quite agree with you that we are not very like Hamlet in our talk or in our outward semblance. He is a wit; we are dull and muddy-mettled creatures beside him. He can utter deep things about life and death; we can utter only inanities and trivialities. But what of it? The real difference between us and Hamlet is that we are inarticulate, while he has at his beck and call all the vast resources of his creator, who was the greatest lord of language that has ever been. We are dumb; he has a word for everything he wants to say. I judge other people by myself; and I know that the shallow stuff I utter, in spoken or in printed words, is a wretched caricature of the real me. We cannot express our deeper selves, and the reason why we are endlessly drawn to Hamlet is that he finds words for us; that he puts our questionings into speech, and finds utterance for our coiled perplexities. He too has stood face to face with the sphinx; we are less lonely, having found a companion in our bewilderment.

Most of the people we meet seem dull and uninteresting; as we, probably, seem dull and uninteresting to most of the people we meet. But there are no really uninteresting people on earth, if we could only see into everybody's heart and mind as Shakespeare lets us see into the heart and mind of Hamlet. The dullest of us, had he only the power of saying what he feels and thinks, would be thrillingly interesting to all the rest of us. As we read this play, the gulf that separates us from the Elizabethan age is bridged; the little accidental differences disappear; Hamlet is the modern man; he is all of us—with only this distinction, that what we must dumbly think and feel he can say.

What a sermon could be made out of this, if I were gifted

with pulpit eloquence! Here we are, all Hamlets, all groping after the meaning of life, all brooding over the same tragedy of sin and sorrow, all striving after the same ends, all whirled round on the same planet towards the same doubtful doom; a little handful of shipwrecked mortals on a raft in the ocean of infinity. How strange, in the cosmic picture, seem our squabblings, our backbitings, our international rivalries and our racial hatreds!

TWO MEN: AN ANTITHESIS

I

It is a little difficult at first sight to see why there should be a sudden revival of interest in—of all people—William Cowper. His bi-centenary, a few years ago, may have started the ball rolling, but could not have kept it spinning to this hour, as spin it undoubtedly does, though in an unobtrusive way. (Everything about Cowper must necessarily be unobtrusive; there can never be any excursions and alarums where this shy and sensitive poet is concerned.) Recently, there have been three full-dress biographical studies of him. First came Mr Hugh Fausset, with his *William Cowper*; this was followed, and in a sense replied to, by Lord David Cecil, in *The Stricken Deer, or a Life of Cowper*; and now Mr Gilbert Thomas has written what is to me the most satisfying of the three: *William Cowper and the Eighteenth Century*. I call it the most satisfying because, besides sifting the biographical facts with great care and thoroughness, Mr Thomas sets the man in his time—shows him against the proper background of an epoch—and this is what Cowper needs, if he is to be valued as he ought to be. How do you account for this little spate of books about a man of whom it would have seemed safe to predict, twenty years ago, that he was bound straight for oblivion; a man who seemed dead and buried with Beattie, Blair, Falconer, Churchill, Hayley, and others of his contemporaries who are only names, and not even names except to students of literary history? Men might continue to write books about him, but they would hardly find publishers for their books if there were likely to be no readers for them. It seems certain that there is a real revival of interest in Cowper; and I want to know why.

As far as I am concerned, there has been no revival of interest; I cannot remember the time when I was not interested in Cowper the man, or when I had not a high regard—though I

may not have had the courage to confess it—for Cowper the poet.
Ages ago, when I was a boy, I was inspired to pick up a second-
hand collection of his letters; and I have never yet come across
a more companionable book—though I now use a much more
nearly complete collection, the one edited with pious care by no
less a person than the author of *The Golden Bough*. And I think
I have always known—even in the days when Swinburne was the
god of my youthful idolatry—that Cowper was one of the most
genuine poets in our language, though not among the greatest.
(I am not sure, to-day, whether in the whole of Swinburne's
collected works you will find such an imperishable masterpiece as
the little dirge beginning—

> Toll for the brave,
> The brave that are no more—

which is so hackneyed, and so apparently unstudied, that you are
apt to do less than justice to its beauty of simplicity and restrained
emotion. Turning over the pages of an anthology, what a joy it
is, after the elaborate decorativeness of Tennyson, the jolly
exuberant verbosity of Browning, the unbridled frenzy of Swinburne, to come across this perfectly carved gem of poetry!
Matthew Arnold, alone of nineteenth-century poets, might have
written it; if he had, it would have been the brightest jewel in
his crown.)   But this is not answering my question—why the
revival?

Mr E. M. Forster, the distinguished novelist, must also be
asking that question; he must find the revival bewildering if not
irritating; because, writing at the time of the bi-centenary, he
explained why that anniversary had "attracted little attention,"
since "poor Cowper" really meant nothing to the modern world,
to "the enormous structure of steel girders and trade upon which
Great Britain, like all other powers, will have to base her culture
in the future."   This puzzles me.   It seems to imply that "poor
Shakespeare," too, is of no use to us, there being, as far as I can
recall, no steel girders in *Hamlet*; and that Dante is obsolete because there are no limited liability companies in the *Divina Com-
media*. Of course, steel girders and trade are a part of modern
life, and must in the end find their way into literature, including
poetry; and I note with great admiration how resolutely the
younger poets of to-day are trying to assimilate the pylon and the
motor-car. But I note also that they—or at any rate the best of

them—are turning their gaze upon earlier poets innocent of these modern luxuries. Mr T. S. Eliot, for example, introduces the gramophone into a noteworthy passage of his verse; but he has also written a fervent little book on Dante; and I think he would say that even the strongest of steel girders are not strong enough for Great Britain to "base her culture" on. . . . Is it not possible that here we have the real explanation of this unexpected renewal of interest in Cowper? May it not be that a good many people are becoming a little tired of "the enormous structure of steel girders and trade," are finding therein no real basis for life, and are turning elsewhither in search of a tenable faith? Is it possible that some persons, not wholly devoid of intelligence, are beginning to doubt whether our hustle and our bustle (which we call progress) are getting us anywhere?—and are such persons turning, in the hope of finding a sounder philosophy of life, to the neglected saints and sages of an earlier time (before steel girders were known), and among others to the shy recluse who from his quiet garden at Olney sent forth the statement that "God made the country and man made the town"? Had this man, cultivating his cauliflowers and his hollyhocks, playing with his tame hares, reading *Tom Jones* aloud to Mrs Unwin and Lady Hesketh, drinking his tea, retiring to his summer-house to write *John Gilpin*, or, in another mood, one of his "moral satires" on the vices and follies of the urban civilization of his day—had he the secret of a serenity which we have lost? Alas! there are other things besides serenity to be found in gardens; in one conspicuous instance, there was a serpent in a garden; and those who go to Cowper for the clue to an escape from the troubled modern spirit may find themselves in the situation of the man in a fairy-tale I mean to write some day when I feel sufficiently gloomy—a man who wandered through an empty palace looking for a room in which, a fairy had told him, happiness was to be found; and when he came at last to a room which he knew must be the right room, because he had tried all the others and found them empty, he threw open the door and found himself staring at the reflection, in a mirror, of his own weary face. That will be the experience of those who go to Cowper for the secret of serenity; they will find in him a trouble akin to their own, but more intense than their own. If you go to the quiet garden at Olney in quest of an interview with the happy man, it is possible you may catch Cowper writing such a thing as *John Gilpin*, but it is also possible that you may catch him writing one of the most terrible poems in our literature, the one that begins—

Hatred and vengeance, my eternal portion,
Scarce can endure delay of execution,
Wait, with impatient readiness, to seize my
    Soul in a moment.

Damn'd below Judas: more abhorr'd than he was,
Who for a few pence sold his holy Master.
Twice betrayed Jesus me, the last delinquent,
    Deems the profanest.

Man disavows, and Deity disowns me:
Hell might afford my miseries a shelter;
Therefore hell keeps her ever-hungry mouths all
    Bolted against me.

How should we ask for the secret of happiness from a man living always under the shadow of mental disease?—a man who tried at least three times to commit suicide, and whose last poem, *The Castaway*, is a classic of despair?

Yet, in spite of all this, we do—this is the marvellous thing— get what we are seeking if we go to Cowper for a certain serenity of outlook. The charm of Cowper's letters is not a morbid charm, nor is there any sign of disease in the great body of his verse. We make a great mistake if we place too much emphasis upon the one or two expressions in his poetry of his black fits. (In passing, I would have you note that no man writes a song of despair who is really plunged in despair. If you are desperate you don't bother to make a song about it. At the moment when Cowper wrote that beautiful *Castaway* we know that he was not unhappy, for he was exercising an art, which is one of the intensest joys known to man. When he sat down to make an interesting experiment with an unrhymed classical metre, as in the stanzas I have quoted, he was, I make no doubt, enjoying himself; he was expressing a mood that he had felt, but he had already escaped from that mood.) He may have been, as a biographical fact, insane at times; he had to spend some months in an asylum; but he lived to pass his sixtieth year, and for most of his life he was like the rest of us, only a little more sane than most of us. It is his humorous, kindly, sunny spirit, his serene and smiling wisdom, that draws us to him. In a word, it is precisely his sanity that we admire in this madman. He reminds us continually of another writer who was obliged to sojourn for a time in a lunatic asylum—Charles Lamb. (It is pleasant to recall that one of Lamb's early poems is dedicated to Cowper, whom he calls "of England's bards the wisest and the best.") Is there some mysterious law of nature by which men who are subject to fits of insanity are, between their attacks, more than normally sane and sound of judgment? Certainly these two men, as if to compensate them for their occasional storms and earthquakes, enjoyed long periods of shining tranquillity, of luminous calm. In spite of his black fits, which had, no doubt, a physical cause, Cowper did come nearer than most men to the secret of an enduring happiness; and it is this which gives a fragrance and a charm to his verse, and more especially to his letters, the record of his daily doings. I leave you to find out, from his prose and verse, on what foundations he based his serenity.

II

Turn, now, to another new biography, the biography of a man who seems to me to have been as exactly the antithesis of Cowper, in every possible way, as another man of genius could well be. The book is *Beaumarchais*, by Paul Frischauer. You may conceivably want to know why I call Beaumarchais a man of genius; and I suppose it is possible to maintain that neither of the two plays on which his fame rests—*The Barber of Seville* and *The Marriage of Figaro*—would be remembered to-day if Rossini and Mozart respectively had not turned them into grand operas. I do not agree. Though, to be honest, I find both these comedies intolerably dull, and though their scintillating wit leaves me unamused, yet, on a question of French literature the French must know best; and to the French Beaumarchais is the eighteenth-century man who carried on the tradition of Molière and who stands out as a landmark in the history of French comedy. This, however, is not a question which I should presume to discuss even if I thought it would interest you, which I know very well it would not. But I stick to the term "man of genius"; and if you read Mr Frischauer's book, and reflect on the extraordinary story laid bare in it, I feel sure that you will agree with me, even if you have never read a word that Beaumarchais wrote.

Since contrast seems a good method of description, I come back to the antithesis with Cowper. Beside Beaumarchais, Cowper is like a little grey skylark beside a great, gaudy macaw; or, shall we say, a violet by a mossy stone compared to—whatever flower you can think of that is brilliant and flamboyant and garish.

Cowper was shy and retiring; lived most of his life in a little village, and was content to live there, pottering in his garden or chatting quietly with a few friends and neighbours; Beaumarchais was consumed by a passion for publicity, and was never for a moment happy away from the great world, the brilliant world in which he was resolved from the first to cut a tremendous dash. Beaumarchais was amazingly clever; if you say that Cowper was clever you simply do not know the meaning of the word—or else you do not know Cowper. Beaumarchais, armed with wit, good looks, knowledge of human weaknesses, endless impudence, invincible persistence, a complete freedom from scruples, and an unrelenting egoism, broke open all doors—or picked all locks— till he was received into the inner circle of the most aristocratic society of that time. Oh, yes, unquestionably he had genius—a genius for getting on. He was the very type and pattern of the social climber. Mr Max Beerbohm once said of a certain contemporary that you could lie awake at night and hear him climbing, climbing. It might have been said of this French adventurer. Genius, but flashy genius; tawdry, as it were. Of all the adjectives in the language, flashy and tawdry are the last that any one would think of applying to Cowper. If you can bear the old-fashioned word, I shall say that Cowper was essentially a gentleman, Beaumarchais essentially a bounder; but from this distance we can watch his bounding with admiration and amusement. To be more old-fashioned still, I shall add that Cowper's was a profoundly religious nature; the Frenchman's nature was profoundly irreligious. Cowper, in the best-known of his hymns, asked for a closer walk with God; it was for a closer walk with the Duc de Choiseul that Beaumarchais asked. Cowper lived the quiet life of a saint and a sage; Beaumarchais's life was full of excursions and alarums, of the waving of flags and the braying of trumpets, of disastrous defeats and resounding victories, now the best hated man in France, now a popular idol, but never daunted, always indomitably pushing himself forward towards the success on which he had set his heart, the kind of success for which Cowper never entertained the faintest desire. The success of the social climber; the top of the tree.

Which of the two was the greater man? I declare myself incapable of answering that question. What is greatness, anyway? Surely to have one definite aim in life, to pursue it unswervingly, and, despite the most formidable obstacles, to achieve it, is to be great? It seems to mark a man out, at any rate, from the common

herd of us. Most of us have no particular purpose in our lives—
no one clear aim to which we subordinate all our actions. To the
overwhelming majority of mankind it is enough to go on living,
with as little discomfort as possible; and, if possible, to live and
die undishonoured; that suffices us. Surely we should not deny
greatness to a man who is not content with such a negative
ambition, but who, with a definite end in view, rests neither by
night nor by day till he has achieved it? That depends, you say,
on the nobility of the end pursued; on whether it was or was not
worth achieving. Well, that is where men of the Beaumarchais
type have me puzzled and bewildered. What is the nature of the
end such people pursue? What are they really after, these social
climbers? To be a well-known person, who will be pointed at in
the street, and regarded with envy by the smaller fry of less
successful climbers? The consciousness of being envied seems a
queer sort of goal to strive for; it must be something different
that they are aiming at; what it is, or why they aim at it, or
whether it gives them happiness when they get it, I simply do not
know. The mind of the snob is an unfathomable mystery. Anyhow, Beaumarchais carried snobbery to a point where it really
looks like greatness; he was the sublime snob; and, as I have said,
he succeeded; he won the prize he sought. He was great because
he had, in rare measure, the qualities—I hesitate to call them
virtues—necessary to success in this particular line. There remain,
for the snob, three things: courage, persistence, and impudence;
and the greatest of these is impudence. This man had all these,
and he had something more: a ready wit, a nimble intelligence,
and a satirical power that made Voltaire himself, on one occasion,
uneasy on his throne.

His real name was Pierre Augustin Caron, and he was the
son of a Paris watchmaker in a very humble way of business.
He was apprenticed to his father's trade, which he hated, because
it seemed to lead nowhither. But this kind of youth is deft and
clever at whatever he touches; and Pierre's first success—the first
rung of the ladder that led to fame and wealth—was a technical
one. An English clockmaker, thirty years earlier, had invented
an "escapement," which—I am very vague on such matters—
added greatly to the trustworthiness of clocks; and this was in
general use in England, but was still unknown in France. (This
was two centuries ago, and a new idea did not flash round the
world as it does to-day.) Pierre had a relative in London, an
escaped Huguenot, and a watchmaker; they corresponded, and

the cousin told Pierre of this valuable device.   Pierre, quick-witted, at once introduced it into France, claiming it, of course, as his own invention.   At the same time a certain old-established clockmaker, purveyor to His Majesty, also "invented" the new escapement; young Pierre prosecuted him, won his case, and became the talk of the town for the moment. He was not a person to allow himself to slip back into obscurity when he had once managed to emerge from it.   He followed up his success by making a beautiful little watch for the King, and was allowed to go in person and present it to Louis the Well-beloved. He now left watchmaking behind him, and devoted his attention to Versailles.   I have spoken of the first rung of the ladder; but the figure is inappropriate, for he was not the man to climb by rungs, steadily; he went up with great leaps, as agile as a monkey. In an astonishingly short time he was the celebrated Monsieur de Beaumarchais, the witty talker, the accomplished master of half a dozen musical instruments, the courtier, the friend of princes, the great financier, the wealthy, the admired, the envied.

The world presided over by Louis XV—or rather by a succession of ladies, including the Pompadour and the Du Barry—is an unpleasant spectacle. There was a certain hard and shallow brilliancy about it, and a squalid immorality. "No decent man can stand the life at my Court," said His Majesty himself in a moment of cynical candour.   Through this world of lying, intrigue, and treachery moved Beaumarchais, a liar, an intriguer, and a traitor; but he was something more, and that something more is what has given him his enduring fame and his place in history: he was an observer. He used that world for all it was worth; but he saw through it. He was a watcher, lynx-eyed, of the ways of men, and more especially of the ways of women. And so it came about that this scoundrel—it is impossible, after reading Mr Frischauer's extremely interesting and vivacious book, to call him anything else—did, in his own way, strike a blow in the liberation-war of humanity. Not only in the two famous plays, but in innumerable pamphlets, he showed a bitter satirical power. He painted scathing pictures of the aristocratic society into which he had climbed. When the Revolution came he narrowly escaped the guillotine; but the revolutionaries remembered, just in time, that the creator of Figaro, though he had made himself abominably rich and though he had hobnobbed with noblemen, had nevertheless been one of the heralds of the Revolution; and so he escaped, and lived to die in his bed, in his magnificent palace—the palace which was disapproved by General Bonaparte as too sumptuous for any private individual to possess. The arch-careerist, the passionate egoist, the mountebank, the wit, the company-promoter on a vast scale, the adventurer, the satirist—a combination of Stavisky and Sheridan—knew how to out-manoeuvre all his enemies except death; and it may well be that he did not regard death as an enemy, for he must have been very weary, after a life the record of which reads like six more than usually incredible thrillers rolled into one. He died a few months before Cowper slipped out of existence in a quiet English village; Cowper, of whom, in all probability, he had never heard; but Cowper had heard of him, we may be sure, for he had made his name resound over Europe. Which of the two, I ask again, was the greater man?

HAMLET REVISITED

I READ *Hamlet* the other day. It had changed considerably since I last read it. Hamlet himself was somewhat thinner, I thought; but he had also mellowed considerably; he was rather less cynical and a little more tolerant than he had been. Polonius was definitely more senile than before. Ophelia was less silly, and more of a pathetic figure than ever. Laertes was exactly the same: that sort of young man does not change; but Osric had distinctly grown up. The Queen was a little fatter; and the King's teeth seemed to me to be needing attention. These were the principal changes I noticed in the play. . . .

Wiseacres will say that this is fantastic nonsense, and that it was I that had changed, not the play. Wiseacres imagine that when a work of art leaves the hand of the master, it remains in changeless beauty for ever, though succeeding generations may feel differently about it, seeing it from different angles. It is to point out the fallacy of this common opinion that I am writing this essay.

The fallacy springs from regarding a great work of art as a dead thing; whereas the distinctive fact about whatever has been created by genius is that it is alive and not dead. When Milton says that "books are not absolutely dead things, but do contain a potency of life in them to be as active as that soul was whose progeny they are," his statement is both too wide and too narrow: too wide, because it is not true of all books, but only of a very select minority, the majority being as dead as mutton: too narrow, because it is true not of books only but of all genuine works of art. They are alive; and to be alive means to be capable of changing in response to the changes of one's environment. *Hamlet* is not the same thing for us as it was for Shakespeare's contemporaries. I hold, strongly, that this does not merely mean that we are different from the Elizabethans; it means that *Hamlet*, too, is different from what it was; being alive, it has exercised the prerogative of living things, and has changed with changing circumstance.

Before you dismiss this as an airy fancy, consider whether you are not making the mistake of thinking of a work of art as something material—a statue as a piece of marble shaped in a certain way, a picture as a number of brushfuls of pigment arranged in a certain way on a flat expanse of canvas, a sonata as a number of sounds arranged in a certain relation with one another, a poem as a number of black marks on white paper, and so on. The work of art is alive because it is not matter but spirit. When Michelangelo has taken a block of white marble and so shaped it as to body forth his conception of David—and the high, heroic meaning that David has for him—the result is not a block of marble differently shaped; he has breathed the breath of life into it, and it is not marble any longer, nor any material substance, but spirit—mind-stuff. When Beethoven links together a number of sounds he produces something that is not sound at all, but thought and feeling and will—something, though this may sound paradoxical, that is not audible, though our ears may be used as the channels by which spirit communicates with spirit. And the work of genius, being wrought of pure spirit, is indestructible; so that statues, and even fragments of statues, fashioned many centuries before the Christian era, dug up from among the ruins of a buried city, still speak to us with as clear a voice as anything carved by Rodin or by Epstein—perhaps a good deal clearer. They are still alive.

To come back to the work with which I started; you would think that by this time the last word must have been uttered on Shakespeare; seeing that, if all the Shakespearian criticism that has been written and published were gathered together, the collection would fill our Public Library from top to bottom and leave not a single shelf for any other kind of book. And yet Shakespearian criticism goes merrily on; no publisher's list ever reaches me without the announcement of some new book on the inexhaustible topic. I have no exact figures to give you, but I feel sure it would startle you if I could tell you how many books have been written, during the last half-century, on this one play of *Hamlet*. Surely there can be nothing left to say about *Hamlet*; surely there can be nothing new to discover about it, after the more than three centuries it has been before the world! You would say so, if you did not realize that *Hamlet* is alive, and that, being alive, it insists on changing and growing and sending out new shoots of meaning for successive generations of readers and spectators.

And so it is with every work into which a man has been able, by force of genius, to pour his soul. Plato's dialogues have been studied with the most minute attention for more than two thousand years; and yet new meanings are found in him every day. To our world, with all those centuries of added experience, he says things that he could not have said to his fellow-Athenians; you might almost say that he has learned a new language so as to be able to speak to us. As you read him on the problem of democracy you are conscious that a living mind is speaking to yours, and speaking wisely.

Those creations which have such vitality in them are the works which we call "inspired"; perhaps, without twisting language too violently, we can say that that is the very meaning of "inspiration"—putting spirit into lifeless matter. I need scarcely mention the obvious fact that many things which pass for works of art at the time of their production are entirely uninspired, and consequently have no principle of vitality in them, no enduring life. Most of the plays written by Shakespeare's contemporaries are uninspired works, therefore dead. Though I, personally, get a good deal of pleasure from reading them, I always feel, after an hour or two in their company, as if I had been walking about among specimens—some of them curious and some of them beautiful—in museum cases; unchanging things, things fixed for ever in the frozen immobility of death.

Now—I am coming to the point at last, as you will be glad to hear if you have endured so far—what applies to artistic genius applies to religious genius also. The inspired creations of religious genius—these, too, have life in them, and therefore the power to grow, to change, to develop new meanings, to adapt themselves to new surroundings; so that none of them means the same to a later generation as it meant to the contemporaries of its founder. The great blasphemy, it seems to me, is to treat an inspired religion as if it were dead and therefore unchangeable. And yet there are people who treat the New Testament as if it provided us with a cut and dried theology, a cut and dried code of ethics, a cut and dried set of facts—forgetting that what is cut and dried is dead.

Every one—almost every one—sees that this is true with regard to the Old Testament; I suppose there are not many people left who can imagine that the Book of Genesis means, or can mean, the same to us as it meant to the primitive tribes for whom it was written. With the coming of geological and biological and, above all, anthropological knowledge, it has changed its character, and from being a record of historic events has become a group of poetic legends. The worst enemies of the Bible are those who treat it as a dead book, verbally inspired, infallible and final. They are its enemies, because the ordinary person, finding that it is not infallible, either as a statement of historic fact, or as a guide to conduct, or as a manual of theology, turns away from it as from something that can safely be ignored. Only when we have cleared away this rubbish of verbal accuracy and infallibility—it is obvious, for instance, that if the monotheism of the later books of the Bible is sound theology then the polytheism of the earlier books must be unsound—only when we have got rid of a conception of it which all intelligent persons see to be no longer tenable, do we come to understand that it is still a living book, with a profound and unique value for the living world; living, because the spirit gives it life—the spirit, not the letter—the spirit breathed into it by men of genius who had the power of embodying in words their intense and fiery faith. This is the real meaning of inspiration.

What I said just now about Shakespearian criticism would seem to apply, with immensely greater force, to the literature that has grown up, and is still growing, round the fundamental doctrines of Christianity and the figure of its Founder. How strange it seems that any one should write a new Life of Christ after all these centuries!—and yet, half a dozen appear every year. How strange, too, after so many generations have pored incessantly on the text of the New Testament, that people should still be writing books on the question of what Christ really taught! And yet any second-hand bookseller will tell you that no department of literature becomes so quickly obsolete as theology. The New Testament, it would seem, needs constantly to be reinterpreted for each succeeding generation—to be translated, as it were, into the language of each generation. You may say, if you like, that every new accession of knowledge makes us look at the Christian religion with new eyes; I prefer to put it differently. I prefer to say that the Christian religion is alive, not dead; and that, being alive, it has the power which all living things have of changing, of adapting itself to the needs of a living and changing world. The inner spirit, the vital principle, the soul of it, remains through all changes; the application of that spirit changes from generation to generation, almost from week to week.

That is why I regard as the worst enemies of religion those

within its own household who sneer at the "higher criticism," and who would have us shut our ears to all the mass of new knowledge which Heaven has revealed to us; to geology when it tells us of the age of our planet, to anthropology when it tells us of the age of the human race, to biology when it tells us of the method by which the human race has evolved from lower forms of life. If they think the Christian religion is incapable of assimilating this new knowledge, then they are treating the Christian religion as a dead thing; which, as I have said, is the great blasphemy. If it is a living thing, then nothing that can be revealed to us by scientific research, by historic inquiry, or by philosophic thought, can do it any harm. It will absorb all new truth, it will profit by new experience, it will prove itself to be alive, a living organism, by modifying itself to cope with a new world; keeping, through all modifications, its inner identity. To treat it as a fixed thing, an unchanging and unchangeable thing, is to write its requiem.

I have not the least idea whether this is a string of platitudes which every one will admit without demur, or, on the contrary, something that needs saying occasionally, to remind people of a truth they may have forgotten. One must just write as one thinks.

STRANGE EFFECT OF A TONIC

I DESIRE to record a remarkable experience. A few days ago, feeling a trifle jaded, I invested in a small bottle of the new tonic, "Whizzo," a few doses of which, the advertisement had assured me, would cause me to radiate energy and vitality. Tonics are usually unpleasant to the palate, and this stuff, as I found when I drew the cork, has a peculiarly loathsome smell. I therefore hastily replaced the cork, feeling that I might defer the radiation of energy and vitality till after I had written my article on King Cole, a subject on which I had been brooding for days. I had come to the conclusion that the life of this monarch was well worth telling in plain prose, and in somewhat more detail than the anonymous author of the nursery rhyme had thought fit to provide; for it was a tale that contained a great moral lesson for these dismal times, and it seemed to me to deserve, if not a full-dress biography in two volumes, at least a newspaper article. So I sat down, read a chapter of the most popular and picturesque of all historians (to get the proper narrative style) and began my article.

The historian of the reign of this accomplished and benevolent sovereign (*I wrote*) is entitled to the praise seldom, we grieve to say, deserved by modern writers, of conciseness. No chronicler known to us is less open to the charge of prolixity. By none have the irrelevant fact and the impertinent comment been more rigidly excluded. But, had he been a Gibbon or a Guicciardini, he could scarcely have painted a clearer picture of the amiable monarch. Every schoolboy knows what jests were current at the court of Nimrod, and what songs were sung in the palace of Sennacherib. But of all the kingly faces that gaze at us from the immemorial past, none is more dear to us than the countenance of this hilarious prince, who for a protracted period had enjoyed the delights and endured the dangers of a throne, whose ears had become habituated to the thunderous plaudits of the multitude and the whispered flatteries of the court, and who, on the one occasion of which history has preserved the record, proved himself a ruler uncorrupted by the arrogance of power and undepressed by the disabilities of age. Fatigued by anxious deliberations in the council chamber, he resolved to employ the sedative herb, bade an attendant furnish him with spirituous refreshment, and summoned to his presence the modest orchestra whose art had so often brought consolation to his sorrows and oblivion to his cares. Though it is not given to us to shed tears beside his venerable grave, nor to stand with bared heads before his stately effigy, we know that he set an example, by his unruffled cheerfulness and philosophic tranquillity, to all succeeding rulers of men. . . .

Looking back over what I had written, I saw that it was dreadfully dull. I did seem to be badly in need of a tonic. I held my nose, and took the prescribed six drops of "Whizzo." I was at once conscious of a queer tumult in my brain. It subsided in a minute or so; but when I resumed my pen, I was immediately aware that the spirit of the popular historian had deserted me, and that the spirit of another Victorian had leaped into the vacant place.

A ruler of men, call you him? Nay, but in truth the pitifullest simulacrum of kingship hitherto seen on this afflicted planet. Of the king-like, in any recognizable sense of the term, we discern not the infinitesimallest trace on that foolish-smiling face of his. Nothing is there but imbecility and appetite. Is a Kingdom, think you, to be ruled by whimpering for tobacco and whining for beer, by lolling on a throne and having your long ears tickled by the gut-scrapings of foolish tweedle-dum and foolisher tweedle-dee? Once for all, my greatest-happiness friends, Kingdoms are *not* to be governed so, but quite immeasurably otherwise than so. Nowise by "merry old souls," but by God-appointed leaders—strong, much-enduring, silent, heroic captains of men— is the human herd to be saved in its own despite. Such leaders have been, on this wild-whirling planet of ours. Your plain duty, my poor half-witted friends, is to find once more a Man, of true valiancy and heroic nobleness, and when ye have found him, to worship him and obey him to the best of your contemptible ability! Alas, it is tragically evident to me that this truth, so plainly written on the Eternal Tables of Stone, is precisely that which our anarchic world is everywhere rebelling against. Woe to the land that has forgotten this indisputablest of all truths; woe, and confusion, and everlasting damnation! Look abroad, and note how to patient, pious, deep-thinking Germany has been granted once more, by the mercy of Heaven, a true authentic Hero; a reality, *not* a sham; no drivelling dotard of a Cole, but a Cromwell, a Mirabeau, even a Friedrich. Until to us also a Hitler is given, bringing to this desolate habitation of dead dogs the unspeakable blessing of a Baphometic fire-baptism . . .

I have not the least idea how this sentence was going to end, or whether it would ever have ended, if I had not at this point taken another six drops of my tonic. For a minute my head whirled giddily; an exceedingly happy feeling followed, and I found, to my immense relief, that the genial spirit of a great Victorian novelist had taken the place of the vituperative seer.

He was the friendliest, kindliest, jolliest individual, was Cole. He was always making the most delightful jokes, was Cole. He ruled his kingdom by sheer good-nature, did Cole. It was pleasant to watch his playful ways with traitors, rebels, and other miscreants, even when he was ordering them to be hanged, drawn, and quartered. "I think you rather lost your head," he remarked with a merry twinkle of his eyes to a baron who had revolted against him, "didn't you? Well, you will, anyhow, at half-past ten to-morrow morning." And he roared with laughter, so that even the baron felt that, after all, beheading was just what he deserved for rebelling against so jolly a king. "I don't believe you are quite all there," he said to a convicted coiner. "Well, well, perhaps you are, *now*; but you won't be when the executioner has cut off both your hands—ha, ha, ha!" He had one very odd characteristic—he always spoke of himself in the third person. "Cole wants his pipe," he would say, and a little fat page boy would come running up with an enormous pipe, and a pound of shag, and a box of matches; whereupon he would pour out such huge quantities of smoke that his jolly red face, and his white beard, and his bushy white whiskers, were wholly hidden in the cloud. Out of the cloud a voice would say, "Cole wants some punch," and another little fat page boy would come running up with an enormous steaming bowl, and the King, helping himself with a soup-ladle, would consume huge quantities of punch, smacking his lips and slapping his legs between each ladleful. After a while he would call out, "Cole wantsh a toon," and another little fat page boy would usher in the three court musicians, who would bow to the ground, and the King would say, "Play that jolly little thing about King Wencheslass, and if you don' play fast enough Cole will hang all six of you. . . ."

At this point I became conscious that I was hardly rising to the height of my great subject. Another dose of "Whizzo" seemed to be indicated. Six drops drove out the genial spirit, and made room for another Victorian, a good deal less simple in manner. I noticed that my handwriting (quite against my will) now broke into fantastic flourishes.

To this Lord of the triple delights—the merry monarch, worthier of the title than our later English cynic of the oak-tree asylum and the scandalous seraglio—let the comic spirit pay a tributary smile before retiring from a stage become too dismal for the twirling of toes. Philosophy may discern in his hilarity the progenitorial foundation of the subtler wit to come in his country despite our inveterate disrelish of brain-stuff. For his features, they are no longer legible to us, save as hieroglyphics on an obelisk. "The joke made flesh," the account of him by a lively lady of his court with a talent for hitting the mark that rang the bell, was felt to have painted his humorous obesity at a stroke. Himself was addicted to the aphorism. "The lighted pipe is a beacon for serenity" was one of his quoted dicta; "good wine silences the clock" was another. "Noise for beasts, music for men," showed him perceptibly a leader of his subjects, at whose woaded savagery he struck good lusty cudgel-blows as of a carpet-thwacker expelling dust. Such a man, the enthroned philosopher, points way to braver times now dimly discernible on faintly flushed horizons. Interrogate him. The figure of him, foggily descried, is provocative of smiles other than derisory. . . .

No, no, it would never do; none of these Victorian dialects fitted the theme. I thought the only thing to do was to give the tonic a real chance; and so, this time, I conquered timidity and took a whole teaspoonful. The result was terrifying; my head behaved like a windmill; there was a great tumult and shouting inside it; as the gale began to die down, I heard fragments of speech, and I knew that my brain had become a battlefield where numerous post-Victorians were struggling for the mastery. My pen went staggeringly across the paper, and the result, at first, was a mere jumble of odds and ends.

Shakespeare had no eye for the dramatic possibilities of a

story; he might have made a better play out of King Cole than
he made out of King Lear, if he had had the brains. I have the
brains; but unfortunately for you I have no longer the energy.
After eighty years of trying to knock some sense into a generation of numskulls and nincompoops which the Life Force has
obviously given up as a bad job. . . . Advanced thinkers—who
have advanced so far that they never think—maintain that Cole
was a sewage expert, and that the pipe he called for was a drainpipe. They allege that he was a food reformer, and that his bowl
was a bowl of some horrible American breakfast food. They
even assert—deepest and darkest infamy of all—that he was a
Puritan, who summoned his fiddlers because he wanted to hear
the Hundredth Psalm for the thousandth time. But through the
fog of modern fallacy comes a voice, clear as the sword of dawn
and terrible as the trumpets of the night, proclaiming the primal
sanities of life. . . . It was about at this stage of my education, if
I remember rightly, that I saw the truth about the Colian mythus.
I perceived that Cole was not a man, but a name, made up from
the initial letters of the Conservative Order of Lazy Englishmen, that sinister body which was to develop later into the Conservative Party, and to become responsible for the great messy
sprawling civilization in which I have grown up, with its waste
and cruelty, its boredoms and stupidities and dirty little inhibi-
tions. To me, in those tentative years, the face of life was darkened by the shadow of Cole. . . . Cold kink ole, sitting in a charm-
hair and swearing begorrably in the verray twiddle of his cork-
tears, cried owt whic! whac! upanatem! enuff of qualitics sed
he. Take an omniboss to the emperorium and by me a church-
gordon, I will fummigate this sallydemanjy. . . . I will now tell
you the story I will sell you the tory I will spell you the glory.
I will explain the story I will explain I will I. He was a merry
old soul a very old mole a mouldy old berry. Strawberry, rasp-
berry, gooseberry, bury the hatchet. Now you understand. You
understand that I understand that I understand. . . .

*It was a great privilege, no doubt, to have all these very dis-
tinguished and up-to-date spirits competing for the mastery of my
pen; but at the moment I only felt as if I were in for a bad ill-
ness. But suddenly my temperature seemed to drop; the storm was
followed by a strange calm; my pen began to slip easily across the
page. No reader will need to be told what spirit it was that had
at last taken possession of my brain.*

Touching this Cole chappie you wanted to hear about, I've been exercising the old bean about him, and I can see that on the whole he must have been a fairly sound egg. Some of his own people thought he was a trifle off his onion—not exactly cuckoo, but a bit leaky in the overhead valves, if you know what I mean. But that was only because he wasn't the kind of king they were used to—the stand-offish sort that bites you in the gizzard if you call him by his Christian name. This chappie was a democratic sort of chappie,· and everybody liked him, except perhaps the Queen, who had one of those powerful minds, and the Lord Chamberlain, who was a wart and a plague-spot of the first order. Well, the old boy used to escape from the palace whenever he could; he said he wanted a place where a bloke could move without stubbing his toe on a countess or a right honourable. As soon as he got out into the street he would find one or two pals to totter round with, and he would say, "Hullo-ullo-ullo! What about a quick bracer?" And his pals would say, "What an absolutely corking scheme!"—and they would leg it for the nearest pub. The manager, who knew this Cole chappie, would bring clay pipes to the bar parlour, because he knew that one of the King's heaviest sorrows was that the Queen wouldn't allow smoking in the Cole homestead. So they would smoke and swig champagne between pipes till at last the manager bloke would say, "What about a spot of Beethoven, gents?"—and the King would say, "A singularly fruity binge, old thing; fetch in the sackbut and the psaltery." And then three waiters would totter in and pretend to be professionals, the King and his pals having by this time filled up the radiators too enthusiastically to see that these waiter Johnnies were perfectly hopeless mugs. What I mean to say, it wasn't a sportsmanlike thing to do, but we can't exactly blame the manager, because, though the King had enough to keep the jolly old wolf from the door, he wasn't precisely rolling in the stuff, and he could never have been induced to cough up the shekels for a real string band, if you see what I mean. Well, pip-pip and toodle-oo and all that sort of thing.

It will be vain for you to rush away to your chemist's in quest of a bottle of "Whizzo" when you have read this. I have not told you the real name of the tonic, and I don't intend to. It is not the kind of information to broadcast. The stuff, you can surely see, is dangerous.

THE CITY OF MISSING MEN

THE other day an English writer on music remarked that, if Beethoven had not been born, the world would to-day feel itself the poorer. This is one of those statements that reduce my poor brain to a pulp. That the world would really be the poorer, had there been no Beethoven, I whole-heartedly agree; but that it would feel itself to be so—well, how on earth could it? I mean, how does one feel the lack of a man who has not been born? Can you imagine yourself saying, "Ah, yes, Wagner and Brahms are all very well, but you ought to have heard the *Ninth Symphony*—if only its composer had been born"? In like manner, if there had been no such person as Dickens, I suppose we should all be going about telling one another, mournfully, what a jolly book *The Pickwick Papers* would have been; and if Napoleon had not been born, the historians would still be discoursing on the great event the Battle of Waterloo would have been if it had taken place. No, it will not do; you and I must face the frozen fact that, if we had not been born, the world would not miss us; it might be immeasurably the poorer, but it would not be aware of the fact. It would jog on, blissfully unconscious of its great bereavement.

After all, when you come to think of it, a prodigious number of persons, equal in genius to Beethoven, have failed to be born. It would be a more lugubrious world than it is if we shed a tear for every man and woman of transcendent greatness who has somehow failed to put in an appearance on this planet. That musical critic was indubitably talking nonsense.

But that night, as I lay in my bed thinking about the nonsense I had been reading, I suddenly perceived, to my great surprise, that I was not in bed at all, but was standing with a number of strangers in a large hall, the like of which, for beauty of colour and proportion, I had never seen before. The people were standing in groups, chatting with one another; and I presently discovered the remarkable fact that at least a dozen different languages were being used. Utterly bewildered, I said to myself, "Where am I?"—and I must have said it aloud, for a gentleman who was passing me at the moment immediately turned and, with a friendly smile, answered my question.

"You are in the assembly hall of the city of Mancante—a name which might be translated into English as 'the City of Missing Men.' Some of our most notable citizens are here this morning; this is where we discuss, informally, matters that concern the welfare of the city."

"But—but—why 'missing men'?" I asked. "These people are, obviously, not missing."

"They are not missing from here; but from the place you have just left, they are very decidedly missing. Yes, I know it is a little puzzling at first, but perhaps you will understand if I tell you who some of these people are."

I thanked him for his kindness, and he pointed, first, to a tall fair man who was speaking earnestly to an attentive group. "That," he said, "is Axel Fyrstikker, the famous Scandinavian preacher who averted, in 1914, what might have been a great war. His religious ardour, despite all barriers of race and language, swept across the world like a prairie fire and wrought in all nations a complete change of heart. It was no new gospel that he proclaimed; his message was the simple one that we are all brothers, sons of one Father, knowing the same joys and sorrows and facing the same mysterious destiny; the difference between him and others who preached that doctrine was that he made every one believe him, so that the truth he taught became a living force in the world's life; and nations, which had been furiously and feverishly arming for mutual massacre, were like drunk men struck suddenly sober, or like lunatics suddenly restored to sanity; in the clear white light of that revelation they saw into what an abyss they had been about to plunge. Everywhere men perceived, what few had hitherto realized, the folly and the foulness of war; and in a new spirit of friendship the nations set themselves, not merely to keep the peace, but to do away with the conditions in which the spirit of war thrives. And so the world was saved. I mean, of course, it would have been saved but for the regrettable fact that at the critical moment Axel was missing."

"And why was he missing?" I asked indignantly, thinking of all the war had meant for the world.

"He was missing because he has not been born; and a very good thing for him. The earth was not ready for him. What would you have done with him? You would have crucified him."

I was silent, knowing that he spoke the truth; and he went on. "There, sitting on a chair in the corner, is the great French statesman, Gustave Tel. It was he whose clear thinking and plain speaking dominated the Peace Conference at Versailles. He kept his head amid that angry welter of national egoisms, and stood for sanity and justice and charity. It was he who taught the delegates to understand how suicidal was the folly of making a peace which should contain the seeds of future bitterness; and it was he who laid bare, in time, the economic fallacy of the reparations idea. He performed the extraordinary feat of convincing the Conference that it was in each nation's interest to consider the interests of the human race as a whole; and so he averted a great disaster—would have averted it, rather, but for the unfortunate fact that (not having been born) he was missing just when he was wanted; and instead of him the Conference had Clemenceau, whom his own fellow-countrymen so aptly nicknamed 'The Tiger.' "

I groaned; and he went on. "The stout person who is arguing with Gustave is that remarkable American, Hiram K. Smith, who, when President Wilson was in Europe, conducted such a strenuous campaign in his own country. He has a strong sense of humour and an astonishing gift of homely and racy speech; some of his pithy sayings, mostly in slang, swept the country like a music-hall song. He was transparently honest, and, for all his jokes, profoundly in earnest; he has just the personality which always appeals to the Americans. It was because of his efforts that the United States entered the League of Nations with such enthusiasm at its start, and assured its success—would have assured it, you understand; Hiram was missing.

"The man with the fair beard and the spectacles is Johann Moeglich, the simple German schoolmaster who fought the great firm of Krupps and defeated them. It was he who pointed out how preposterous it was that a country should allow one of its private firms to sell to foreign countries bombs and guns and tanks which might presently be used for the slaughter of its own people; and what a menace to the peace of the world those firms must be whose very existence depended on their success in fomenting war-scares and bribing politicians. His teaching, being obvious common sense, spread far beyond the bounds of his own country; and before long every nation had nationalized its armaments industry, and so made it impossible for any one to have a direct financial interest in the making and selling of arms. . . . Unhappily for the peace of the world, Johann was never born."

I have forgotten the names of many of the notable characters pointed out to me by my obliging friend. There was, I remember, Sir Henry Applejohn, who went to the Ottawa Conference as delegate from the Falkland Islands, and who, when the other delegates were gravely discussing restriction of output, changed the whole course of the debate by pointing out the obvious fact that prosperity could never be restored by the destruction of wealth; and Secundra Dass, from Bengal, whose saying, on the third day of the World Economic Conference—"Enough of this fooling!"—not merely travelled round the world as the most sensible thing so far said at that great gathering of notables, but actually brought the Conference itself to its senses with a shock, so that it got down to business and faced realities and became the tremendous success it was, or, rather, might have been, if Secundra had not been missing, along with Gomez Junqueiro, the Spanish economist who understood what the gold standard really means.

"That man over there who looks like a little grey mouse," said my guide, "is really a rather remarkable person. He is Ian McDhu, the Scottish educationist. It was he who foresaw, half a century ago, what part applied science was going to play in the world; alone among men at that time, he saw what the inevitable result of labour-saving machinery must be. He understood that there were no limits to human inventiveness, and that before long most of the work of the world would be done by machines, so that the mass of mankind would be left with no necessary work to do. And he taught the world to prepare, in time, for the coming era of leisure; he saw that there were plenty of occupations for mind and body, occupations much more worthy of human beings than the drudgery that machines were about to put an end to; but for these nobler activities, he realized, some training, was necessary. Under his influence, education departments everywhere set about the training of children for the unemployment that was coming; so that, when it came, it turned out to be a great blessing—at least, it would have been, if Ian McDhu had not been a missing man. As it is, of course, the new era has caught you entirely unprepared; and so, for lack of the necessary training and the necessary economic adjustments, you must suffer a poverty which is degrading and an unemployment which is demoralizing."

"And what about yourself?" I asked, when he had named a few more of these truants from the universe; "are you, too, a missing man?"

MY BIRTHPLACE

I APPRECIATE the kindly interest displayed by a correspondent who writes to ask if I am dead. Perhaps it is in bad taste to deal, in print, with such personal and intimate questions, but I may be permitted to state that the answer is in the negative. My long silence, which my correspondent has been so unusually observant as to notice—is due to the fact that I have been travelling in foreign parts, as the following remarks may indicate to the sagacious. The sagacious will also notice that these casual jottings are of no value to any one; but they may possibly interest a few fellow-countrymen of mine in Australia who are loyal to the land of their adoption, but who nevertheless retain a spark or two of affection for the old grey Mother at the other side of the world.

It was a great experience to dine—if one can call hastily gobbled sandwiches and hurriedly gulped coffee a dinner—in the railway refreshment-room at Paddington, to see the twilight fade into darkness in the Midlands, to wake up in the northern half of Scotland, and to sit down to breakfast in the railway refreshment-room at Aberdeen. . . . But before one could think of breakfast there was the luggage to think of, for we had four hours to dispose of before the train would leave for Port Bucky; so I asked a grey-headed porter to put our six small packages in the cloak-room. "Man, they'll cost ye thrippence a piece," said he, rubbing his chin reflectively; he was against such prodigality, even though it was my money, and not his, that was to be wasted. "Well, what do you suggest?" "What for would ye nae leave them here in my barra, an' I'll pit them in the train for ye when she comes in?" "But—won't they be stolen, here in this public place?" "Stolen! —wha would steal them? Na, na, ye're nae in England the day; it's Scotland ye're in the day." So it was; I had not realized it till that moment, when I realized also that if he had put the things in the cloak-room, as likely as not the services of another porter would have been called in later, and the tip divided. . . . And then, at breakfast, after bacon and eggs such as might conceivably have been had at any railway station in the United Kingdom, the waitress brought us a plateful of something that stirred vague memories within me. "What do you call these?" I asked. "Oh, jist baps," said the waitress. Baps! I hadn't heard the word for —how many years? I am not going to maintain that the bap is anything extraordinary in the way of toothsomeness; but the name of it gave my heart a muckle dunt—I beg your pardon; I see it is going to be very difficult to write the whole of this article in the inferior dialect to which my readers are accustomed; what I mean is that the name aroused strange emotions in the mind of one who had been long an exile from the Land of Baps.

I skip the intervening hours, and the train journey to Port Bucky, till lately a thriving centre of the herring fishing industry (but the bottom fell out of the trade when the Russian market was closed because the government decided that it would be wrong to sell fish to people whose political opinions were so wrong-headed); there we caught the motor-bus to Pitbannock, the village where I was born and on which I had not set eyes for some fifty years. . . . Has it ever happened to you, dear sir or madam, to revisit your birthplace after a lapse of fifty years? If not, let me warn you that when you do you may expect to find some changes, for half a century is an unco bittie o' time. Why, the whole civilization of this planet is not more than thirty centuries old, according to the anthropologists; I was away from Pitbannock for one-sixtieth of the whole time it has taken mankind to emerge from savagery—if you think we have yet emerged, which a reader of the news of the day may sometimes doubt. To the very young a century sounds like a geological epoch; it seems much shorter to those who have lived for half a century; but even a few years in these times are enough to play some queer cantrips with the face of one's native village. . . . But this village of mine is the exception to the rule I am warning you of; except for the motor-bus running through it and a bowser in the market square, those wildly careering fifty years, that wrought such mighty changes on the look of populous cities, had left this place untouched, so far as I could remember its former appearance. It had not grown at all; in fact, if anything, it had grown backward. The houses were a trifle smaller than they had been, the trees were a little more stunted, the streets a shade narrower, the kirk a somewhat less impressive edifice than it had been. This, also, is a change that you must expect. . . . In general, it was a pleasant thing to come from London, which alters perceptibly once a fortnight, I think, to this little cluster of stone houses that look as if they might have been built in the days of the Bruce, and as if they might last till the next ice-age. It is you who have changed, not your birthplace, if you come from a village built as mine was to thole the buffets of the wintry seas and the winds that blow from the Pole. And if your village happens to be in Scotland, perhaps the change that will sadden you most will be that you have forgotten your native language, and have to learn it as you might sit down to learn Spanish.

Here is an instance. After the war, as you know, there were a number of mines left floating about the North Sea, and the government offered substantial rewards for the capture of the deadly things. One day one of them appeared here near the harbour mouth, and a number of fishermen—almost all the men of the village are fisher folk—went out to bring it in and win the reward; unfortunately, it blew up when they were catching it, and some of them were killed. The incident was cabled to Australia; the only time in history, I should imagine, that Pitbannock has figured on the cable pages of an Australian or any other newspaper. I wanted to get at the details; and one evening, strolling about the harbour, I approached a bourach of callants—excuse me—a small group of boys on the pier, and speered at them—I mean, asked them what the truth of the matter was. They were not sweer to answer; they gave me, in chorus, one putting the other right on points of detail, a very long story—of which I understood not one single word, except that a dizzen, or maybe mair, was kilt richt oot. It is, of course, a beautiful language, this Aberdeen-awa; those who think the Scots tongue other than beautiful must have conversed only with bletherin' bodies from Glesca or Embro; but I will not deny that, to any one who has been speaking nothing but good Australian for half a century, it is difficult. For the first few days—until one grows used to its sounds and its idioms—one has a queer paradoxical feeling of being a stranger in the land of one's birth.

The Scots are more grossly misunderstood than any other race. They have a strong sense of the ridiculous; but as they rightly prefer their own subtle jokes to the more obvious and childish drolleries of other peoples, they are called humourless; and as they are addicted to making fun of one another's thrift they are called niggardly. All the best stories of the near-b'gyaun ways of Aberdeen come, as is well known, from Aberdeen; it is the mark of the true humorist that he can laugh at himself. That city has again and again shown itself extraordinarily generous in giving to great public causes. Not that I would for a moment seek to deny that the Scot has rumgumption enough not to want to throw away a penny without knowing where it is going to. And he sometimes seems, to the foreigner, to mix this canniness with sentimentalism in a rather disconcerting manner. I was wandering one day in the kirkyard, looking for the name of my clan on mossy stones, when I was joined by a greybeard who had sought me out, hearing that I was in the village, because he had known my people in the old days. He showed me the stones I was seeking; and then, pretending to be going nowhere in particular, he steered me to another corner, that I might see and admire the stone he himself had put up in memory of his wife, lately dead. "Ay," he said musingly, "it's a bonny stane; I got it frae an auld frien' o' mines in Glesca. There's some say I micht weel hae bought it nearer hame; but I jist felt than I couldna vera weel gae past an auld frien'; an' I'm nae denyin' "—this with almost a twinkle in his eye—"that I maybe got it a wee bit cheaper that way." Strangers might have said it was a trifle sordid, this talk about the price of his wife's gravestone; but not I. I saw no reason to doubt that he had been an admirably devoted husband, and that he was desolated by his loss; but he was honest, and did not pretend not to be glad that he had made a good bargain for a piece of stone.

And then I went for a walk past a field of neeps and across the hill; and I saw a skylark rise from a yellow cornfield in ascending spirals, singing till it was out of sight, and after; and I looked down at the village, and saw the peat reek coming out of the cottage lums; and beyond it, to seaward, a landscape that seemed to me more beautiful, in its clean windswept austerity, than the fat and peaceful landscapes of the south country; and it garred my heart gae loupin'—there is no other word for it. I became, for the moment, the sentimental Scot, and I sat down and made me a poem, of which the first stanza ran—

> Leave me free to roam at will on the heather-cover'd hill,
>   When the lintie's in the bourtree and the lavrock's in the lift;
> When the whins are a' in bloom, and the bonny gowden broom—
>   And I wouldna tak a kingdom for a gift.

The second stanza is not yet written; that, as you know, is the worst of writing verses—you can't think of what to say next. And besides. another and less happy thought had come into my head. Scotland is doubtless the best country in the world—so I reflected—in summer, when you can read a book without artificial light till ten at night; but even then we had fires in the evenings, and I couldn't help asking myself—in the language which by this time I was using for inward dialogues with myself—What like maun it be when the simmer's gane? Losh, sirs, when the cauld-rife winter's here, wi' the nippin' win's, an' the rain an' the hail an' the snaw an' the sleet, an' a' the roads heavy wi' glaur—man, it wad gar ye gae clean dementit, an' the muckle black deevil wad whisper ill things in yer lug a' the day, an' a' the nicht there wad be naething to dae but sit by the fire an' tak a drappie, an' syne to tak anither drappie, an' syne anither, till the stoup was teem; an' then whaur wad ye be? I trust I make myself clear.

THE MAN WITH TWO SHADOWS

JOHN HAROLD PARKINSON, merchant, middle-aged, married, was
coming home late one night when this strange thing happened to
him. He was a candidate for Parliament, and he was returning
from his first election meeting. He was tired, but fairly well
satisfied with himself. He had made what seemed to him to
have been an effective speech, and had answered questions and
dealt with hecklers in a tactful manner. He had satisfied the
conservative section of his audience that no wild-cat scheme of so-
called reform would have his support, and the radical section that
he was strongly in favour of necessary reforms. His prospects
were excellent.

He had left the tram and was walking along the quiet suburban
street in which he lived, when he suddenly became aware that he
was not alone. Someone else—someone with rubber soles, it
seemed, for he heard no footfall—was walking along beside him;
he had just passed a lamp-post; and in front of him, quite distinctly, he saw beside his own shadow the shadow of another
man, a taller man than himself. Startled, he turned his head
quickly; there was no one there. For a fraction of a second he
was frightened; then he almost laughed aloud at himself, remembering that every one has two shadows when there are two lights
to cast them. He stopped, and the shadows stopped. He looked
around him for the explanation, doubtless a simple and obvious
one, of the quaint phenomenon. In a moment his heart was
beating wildly again; for he saw that the next lamp-post was far
away, and there was no moon. He walked on; the two shadows
moved with him.

"I am ill," he told himself; "I am overwrought, my nerves
have gone to pieces; this campaign has taken more out of me
than I knew; something has happened to my eyes; unless I am all
right in the morning I shall see an oculist."

As he was composing his mind with these reflections he noticed
something that plunged him into a new abyss of terror. A gust
of wind brought his hand to his hat. The hand of the shorter

shadow went to its head; the longer shadow moved steadily on, its arms by its sides. He almost screamed when he saw this; for it meant that the longer shadow was not his. An unseen person was walking at his side. He had once, he remembered, read a novel called *The Invisible Man*, and found it entertaining. Entertaining! Oh, God! He struck out savagely, once and again; there was nothing there; he broke into a kind of shambling run. Such was the tumult in his mind that when he reached his own garden gate, his fumbling fingers had difficulty with the latch.

There was a street lamp just outside the gate; and as he went up the familiar gravel path he saw, with almost a sob of relief, that one shadow, not two, preceded him to the door. He determined to say nothing about his strange aberration to any one, not even to his wife. She was sitting up for him, full of questions about the meeting, which he answered as lightly as he could. If she noticed something strange and strained about his manner she put it down to tiredness. That night he slept fitfully.

Next morning after breakfast they took a walk round the garden, as they usually did before he left for town. It was bright sunshine, and the shadows were very clear-cut and distinct. He saw at once, with immense relief, that the intruder had gone—never, he hoped, to return. His last night's experience had evidently been some sort of dream. He shuddered as he remembered it; but it was all over now; he must keep a tighter hold on his nerves. Perhaps he needed a tonic. . . .

That evening there was another election meeting; his wife attended it. She had never before heard him speak in public. His eloquence and his readiness in retort surprised her; this was a side of his character which she had not suspected; a new John, whom she had never known, though they had been married for a score of years. They went home together, and, when they had left the tram, she took his arm. As they neared the spot where his queer experience had taken place he felt that the pressure of her arm within his was infinitely comforting. They were chatting gaily—he seemed to himself to be more talkative than usual—when the blasting terror returned. As they passed the street lamp the shadows shot out in front of them; not two shadows, but three. His wife's shadow was between the other two; and he perceived, with a chill that struck to his heart, that her shadow was arm-in-arm with the longer shadow—the intruder's.

He stopped dead. "Look!" he cried, pointing. "Look where? What is it? What's the matter?" "There! Look! Don't you see?"

"I see our shadows," she said; "what about them? Are you ill, my dear? What did you think you saw?" "Oh, nothing," he mumbled, and strode forward in silence, not answering her further questions. He had suddenly realized that he still felt the pressure of her arm, whatever her shadow's arm might be doing. The longer shadow was not that of a stranger, evidently; it was his own. And so was the shorter one. He saw that, inexplicably, he had come into possession of two shadows. Alone of the human race, he possessed two shadows—one visible to all the world, the other invisible even to his own wife.

It is astonishing how quickly one becomes accustomed to anything—anything, however terrifying and mysterious at first. For a week he dreaded the sunset (the second shadow never appeared in the daytime), and awaited the coming of the intruder with a kind of sick loathing. In the second week he took his wife into his confidence, and, though she was still blind to the second shadow, she believed in its reality; and her cool and rational way of discussing it did him a great deal of good. By the third week they were joking about the matter. It was she who decided to call the shorter shadow John, and the other Harold, and it was she who led him to take a more or less dispassionate interest in the differences between the two.

For differences there were, apart from the obvious fact that one was longer than the other. For instance, after his maiden speech in Parliament—for he had won the seat—he noticed, walking home, that Harold moved with a certain dignity and solemnity, while John tripped along jauntily, with an occasional skipping movement. As time went on and he became more and more used to the exigencies of public life, including the necessity of saying many things, in the course of a day, which he did not mean in the least, and of making many promises which he had no intention of fulfilling, Harold's figure, he noted, seemed to broaden, and his gait to become more and more dignified and even pompous; while John, on the contrary, seemed to shrink a little. Whenever he spoke in public—he was in demand as a fluent and forceful speaker—he noticed that Harold marched homeward with long, deliberate strides, while John trotted along beside him in a manner suggesting anything but dignity. He could not resist the feeling that John had a sense of humour, and Harold none.

One curious thing he noticed was that, after that first night, his wife's shadow, when they were out together, always took John's arm, never Harold's. This pleased him enormously, he could not quite tell why, for both shadows were undoubtedly his own. But John was more intimately his own than the other. John had grown up with him; he had known John when they were both quite little. Harold was a newcomer, and he was altogether delighted that his wife's shadow preferred John.

One evening, in the House, he made an ingenious and powerful speech in defence of a Government measure, a measure which he had described to his wife at breakfast as callous, inhuman, and wholly pernicious. That night as he walked home Harold strode along with a more majestic step than usual, but John seemed to have lost his high spirits, and walked droopingly, with bent head; moreover, John had not only shrunken, but grown fainter, more indefinite, altogether less black and clear-cut than he had been. Parkinson noted this with a puzzled wonder.

As time went on and his reputation grew, and the papers spoke of him as a certainty for the next vacancy in the Cabinet, he remarked that John had become fainter and fainter, till at last he was a barely perceptible darkening of the ground. Parkinson had hopes that his peculiarity was about to be cured, and that he was going to become a person with one shadow like the rest of his fellow-men. But he would have preferred that Harold should be the shadow to disappear. He felt a curious aversion from the idea of being left alone in the world with Harold for the rest of his life.

But the end was other than he expected. He was not fated to be a Cabinet Minister. He had been having trouble with his heart, and one day he paid a visit to an eminent specialist. The verdict, after a thorough examination, was that he must at once retire from public life; to pursue it was practically to commit suicide. He listened to the doctor's solemn warnings, not with dismay, but with an overwhelming sense of relief. No more speeches in the House, no more sitting on platforms, no more posing, no more ingenious evasions, no more forced geniality with constituents, no more cutting a figure in the public eye, no more humbug. He must go home and tell his wife the glorious news.

By the time he neared his home darkness had fallen and the street lamps were alight. As he passed the spot where his first terrifying experience had occurred, he saw that another wonderful thing had happened. John was there, in front of him, as black, as distinct and clear-cut as ever, walking lightly and briskly; the old familiar John that had been his lifelong companion. Harold had disappeared.

THE ORCHESTRAL LIFE

THE other evening I was reading *The Kasidah*, that strange poem into which a famous Englishman poured his innermost philosophy of life, his faith and (more noticeably) his unfaith; and I fell to musing on the extraordinary life of the extraordinary man who wrote it.

Most people who read at all have at least heard of that masterpiece of translation, Burton's *Arabian Nights*. Its ten volumes, and six supplementary volumes, make up a monument of curious erudition; but many people think of it rather as a monument of scandalous impropriety. Once, in my more affluent days, I owned a copy, and I can certify that rumour has much exaggerated its indecency; still, it is certainly not a book for the Sunday-school library. But there is no doubt that it is the work of one of the most consummate scholars that England has ever brought forth.

Then again, most people who know anything about the history of exploration have heard of Burton and Speke's great expedition into the heart of Africa, the journey which led to the discovery of the sources of the Nile. When a still more famous explorer, H. M. Stanley, had to lighten his luggage to the utmost on one of his journeys, he threw out all books but one; and that one was Burton's *Lake Regions of Central Africa*.

There was a third Burton: the most exciting of all travel books, when I was a boy, was *Pilgrimage to Al-Medinah and Meccah*, which told how a certain Captain Burton, disguised as Haji Abdulla, sojourned among the Arabs, lived their life, and penetrated into their most secret and sacred places, and escaped with his life because he was a matchless master of disguise and because he not only knew the language of the Arabs, but knew also the idiom of their thought, the ways of their minds. And his account of this perilous adventure was all true; the late Colonel Lawrence, following in his footsteps sixty years later, bore witness that his description of the country from Mecca to Medina was correct in every detail.

The astonishing thing is that these three famous Burtons were one and the same Burton. It is no wonder that, since his death in 1890, no fewer than eight biographies of him have appeared. The Orientalist who translated the *Arabian Nights* was a man whose life-story sounds more improbable than any tale that Shahrazad told her Sultan. The swordsman whose strength and skill drew crowds to the *salle d'armes* at Boulogne was the accomplished linguist who knew thirty-five languages, and knew them well. The adventurer who took his life in his hand in Somaliland was the man who translated into English verse the *Lusiads* of Camoens. The poet who wrote *The Kasidah* was the man who wrote a manual of bayonet exercises once used—and, for all I know, still used—as part of the education of the British soldier. . . .

I suppose we shall all agree—no, I don't suppose anything so absurd, but I suppose those who think, who exercise their minds about the dark and troubled spectacle of life, will all agree—that one of the sad things in that spectacle is the prodigal waste of ability, the vast reservoir of human talent that never gets a chance of being tapped. Economists sometimes try to calculate what the productivity of the world would be if all the machinery already in existence were working to the limit of its power; but who will try to calculate what our civilization would be like if all the repressed genius of the race were allowed free play?

I want to be clear about this. I spend no pity on the person who is doomed to obscurity all his life long. What is the matter with obscurity? Looking back on history, can we say that the personages who strutted or capered in the public eye have been happier than their unregarded fellows? I shed not a single tear for the flower that is born to blush unseen; when I have occasion to blush, I decidedly prefer that my blushing should be unseen. I have no objection to wasting my sweetness on the desert air. Let us reserve our sympathy for the flower that is never allowed to unfold its petals at all.

A little while ago, in another paper, I took you into my confidence and made the shameful confession that I had never yet harpooned a whale; but it would be overstating the case to call this the great tragedy of my life; it is, at worst, one of the minor regrets. It represents an experience missed, and missed, I fear, for ever, for—though it is never safe to prophesy—I cherish no real hope of harpooning a whale in what is left to me of life; if I ever go back to a little Italian fishing town where I sojourned for a time last year, I may possibly spear a sardine, but whales seem definitely beyond my scope. What has life given me to compensate for the regrettable absence of whales? I have read a number of books—a pleasant enough occupation, but a pitiable substitute for whaling. My Lord Verulam remarks that "reading maketh a full man," but I think this oft-quoted sentence is quite wrong; what maketh a full man is experience—experience, rich, diverse, many-coloured. You will admit that, if you have never harpooned a whale, your experience is to that extent incomplete. On the other hand, if the professional harpooner of whales has never read *Othello* or played the organ, his experience, too, is incomplete. Neither of you is a full man.

You will object that this is clotted nonsense; and, now that you mention it, of course that is so; I admit it ungrudgingly. Complete experience, in the literal sense, no man could possibly have, even in a world reformed beyond recognition. Let us be reasonable in our demands. If you saw the whole world, from pole to pole, you could not also have the experience of being born blind and remaining so for the rest of your life. If you are—as you may be for all I know—a great genius, you have necessarily missed the experience of being the village idiot. If you happen to be an Australian you cannot also be a Dyak of Borneo; that, I fancy, is philosophically sound. Well, then, what do you mean? I mean, of course, that the experience allowed to most of us is hopelessly and hideously narrow compared with what it might be if all our native talents were given a chance of exercise. It would be silly to sigh for experiences beyond the range of our natures. I, for instance, do not quarrel with our present social arrangements because they give me no chance of singing in grand opera before a vast audience; the audience would have a more reasonable grievance against any arrangements which made such a thing possible. I do quarrel with somebody or something—I am not sure with whom or with what—for shutting me off from a hundred activities, for destroying (by atrophy) many talents of mine (of which a talent for singing does not chance to be one). As society, or the devil, arranges things at present, we are thrust, as mere children, into a certain way of life, for which we may be quite unfitted; we go spinning down that groove for the rest of our lives, and never get a chance to be our real selves, to develop the finest that is in us, to have the rich and full experience of life for which the gods intended us. Burton was a wonderful man, no doubt; but what was most wonderful was the set of circumstances which enabled him to grow to his full stature, to become the Admirable Crichton that he was. We ought to be ashamed of a civilization which makes such a life as his so strange and rare a spectacle.

Do you imagine that the man who collects your bottles has only one talent, a talent for collecting bottles? Quite possibly there lies, hidden and silent within him, a genius for high finance. In the man who cuts my hair I seem to discern, dimly, a Napoleonic touch; the hands that wield the scissors might have swayed the rod of empire. In a patient and plodding bank clerk known to me there resides, for all I know, a genius for sculpture, stifled; and my plumber would possibly, in a happier world, have found an outlet for his gift for theology. You and I—unless I do you an injustice—are dull, ordinary, commonplace persons, stodgy persons, in short; we might have been anything but stodgy if circumstances and education had given the talents that are in us a chance of expressing themselves. We don't even know what those talents are. I, for instance, might have shone, I feel, as an expert wine-taster; you, on the other hand, might have been the greatest snake-charmer of the century, or one of the master minds in the matter of women's hats.

Life, as I conceive it, ought to be a piece of orchestration. Fancy going into a concert-hall, seeing a full orchestra in its place, and hearing—nothing but a lonely flute or a solitary trombone, while all the other musicians sit idly with their instruments on the floor beside them! Give me the life orchestral, with all the instruments taking their part, with all the talents in action, with no gift wasted! Some day it will be so. At present we waste, in an entirely tragical manner, the skills, the aptitudes, the abilities of innumerable men and women; we use as beasts of burden spirits capable of driving the chariots of the sun. Some day this will all be changed. Psychology is at present in its infancy, but it is growing daily; and I foresee a time—though you and I shall not live to see it—when the psychologist will take counsel with the schoolmaster, and our whole system of education will be transformed, and will cover the whole range of human activity; so that every boy and girl will learn in time what talents he or she possesses; and they will all be trained, and encouraged to use all their gifts—yes, every one of them; and a many-sided life like that of Sir Richard Burton, instead of being a rare and miraculous spectacle, will be the common lot of mankind. It will not come in our time, but we can work for it; if we move at all—which some educationists prefer not to do—we can at least make sure that we are moving in that direction.

THE SPUR OF THE MOMENT

ON TIN-OPENERS

"Lo, this only have I found, that God hath made man upright; but they have sought out many inventions."

The Poet Laureate tells us we ought to laugh and be glad to belong to the old proud pageant of Man; and on the whole I suppose he is right. Sometimes, watching the antics of our fellow-men in various parts of the world, we fancy we should prefer to be dogs or horses; they seem so much more sensible and sane and kindly; also rather more attractive in appearance, as a rule. But that mood passes; after all, there are—there really are—reasons for being proud of being human. You and I, personally, may have done nothing much to pat one another on the back about; but Man, spelt with a capital, is a marvellous little fellow. "Glory to Man in the highest, for Man is master of things!"—so Swinburne shouts in a rapture of exultation over the achievement of the race. And when you think of all that Man has done in his few thousand years of civilization—of all he has fashioned of steel and flame, of how he has bridged space and tamed nature, making fire his footman and lightning his housemaid—you are inclined to find Swinburne's pride excusable.

Yes, but we hardly feel the same elation when an earthquake pays us a visit; or when a neighbouring volcano really lets itself go; or even when we are in the presence of a big bush fire, or a healthy tornado; or when something that looks like an elemental force lets war loose upon earth, and the nations find themselves being dragged into it in spite of their desperate determination to keep out. Then—ah, then—we begin to wonder whether Swinburne didn't write his paean a thousand years too soon. At such moments, you feel inclined to echo a lesser poet than Swinburne, but in some ways a far wiser one:

> Things are in the saddle,
> And ride mankind.

That is surely far nearer the truth than the pleasing statement that man is master of things.

But the "things" Emerson was thinking of were not earthquakes or tornadoes; he was thinking of gadgets. A revised version of Swinburne, brought into harmony with the truth of to-day, would run, "Glory to gadgets in the highest, for gadgets are masters of Man!" That would not be nearly so melodious, and not nearly so gratifying to our vanity; but it would be leagues nearer the truth. We may as well recognize that we are living in a gadget-ridden age.

Think a moment. What is a gadget? A gadget is an implement, a tool. Man has been defined as the tool-making animal. What we have to notice is that, once we have made a tool, that tool tends to become our master. It insists on being used. Until lately I have been in the habit of wiping the raindrops off my windscreen by moving a little handle to and fro, which was rather laborious; but the other day, as the winter was coming on, I invested in one of those automatic affairs which start working when you press a button and go on working till you press the button again. No sooner was this gadget installed than I caught myself hoping it would rain; not because my heart was bleeding for the poor drought-stricken farmer, but because I wanted to see how my new gadget worked. But this is rather a trivial illustration. Let us look at something bigger—say a textile factory.

The machinery in a textile factory may be an extraordinarily complicated tool—thousands of minds may have contributed to the bringing of it to its present pitch of efficiency—but still it is only a tool, a gadget for making cloth. Well, what is the duty to which the manager of that factory must devote all his thought and energy? The duty of keeping that gadget at work. It is not his duty to think of the number of people who will shiver in the cold if he fails to provide them with cloth; he must think of the shareholders who will be shivering in the cold if his machine stops; he must think of the army of employees who will be out of work if the gadget is not fed with its proper food. Not only he, but the nation, is bound to try by all means to keep that machinery running. The machinery is, to that extent, our master.

Don't imagine, please, that I am trying to preach a sermon against machinery, and advocating a return to the hand-loom; on the contrary, I hope there will be more and more machinery, till all the dirty work of the world is done for us by ingenious gadgets, leaving us free for better things. What I am driving at is that, at our present stage of civilization, under our present system of management, we are not masters of things; things are our masters. The machines we have devised rule us, with rods of iron.

Of course, what is true of that textile factory is true of all factories—including, by the way, our armament factories; the only distinction about these last being that there seems no immediate danger of their particular machinery not being kept at work. The workers in a textile factory may possibly console themselves for the monotony of their toils by the reflection—though I don't suppose it often occurs to them—"Well, anyhow, the cloth I have helped to make to-day may help some poor wretch, perhaps at the other side of the world, to be a little less uncomfortable when the east wind blows." One wonders whether the hands in an arms factory take the same kind of pleasure in the thought, at the end of each day. "How splendid!—the thing I helped to make to-day may kill or torture a hundred persons in some distant land." At all events, the manager of the arms factory has exactly the same duty as the manager of the cloth mill; his duty, too, is to see that his plant is kept running; he, too, is the slave of the machine. If that gigantic gadget of his were allowed to rust in idleness for a month, in England alone, a terrible economic crisis, affecting the whole country, would be the result.

What methods the armament firms must employ to make sure of getting sufficient orders to keep their machines at work is not my point. My point is that whether the machine is beneficent, producing life, or maleficent, producing death, we have to be its servants. Necessity is the mother of gadgets; machines are devised to meet a human necessity; but when they are once made, they create a new necessity of their own: the necessity of keeping them in use. An economic need has been superimposed on our human needs, so to speak.

If the machinery in an arms factory is a gadget, so are the things made by that machinery. Big guns and poison gases are gadgets; so are armies and navies; tools devised for a certain purpose, implements for the achievement of certain ends; possibly the acquisition of territory, possibly national safety. I am not suggesting that Australia can or ought to leave herself defenceless in an armed world. All I suggest is that when the world devises and constructs a vast fighting-machine, the same law applies to that machine as to my humble windscreen-wiper; sooner or later it insists on being used. We are slaves to this machine that we have made; that is the tragic fact.

Well, you say wearily, we know all this; unless you have a remedy up your sleeve, why go on adding truism to truism? There is a remedy, but it is a desperate one; it involves thinking, and thinking is a painful job. You may remember how, years ago, we all, youngsters and grown-ups, amused ourselves with a gadget called a "Yo-yo," a sort of wooden bobbin at the end of a string which you could play surprising tricks with; and you may remember a very frank advertisement that appeared everywhere; "Buy a yo-yo; it keeps you from thinking!" There was perfectly sound psychology in that advertisement; it was based on the curious truth that people will gladly spend money on a device for preventing them from thinking. Nevertheless, I am going to be reckless enough to ask you to do a little thinking, just for a minute or two.

Extend the use of the word "gadget." A tin-opener is obviously a gadget; the machinery which has printed this book of mine, though somewhat more complicated than a tin-opener, is also a gadget. But so is any invention, anything devised by man for an end beyond itself; and the trouble begins when we forget the end for which the thing was devised and become slaves of the thing.

Money, for instance, is a most serviceable and ingenious gadget, and the reason why the world has become the slave of money instead of its master is that we have forgotten the end for which money was invented, namely to facilitate the making of goods available for consumption. Parliament is a gadget; and when people forget, in the battle of party politics, the aim and purpose for which Parliament was invented, they become slaves to a gadget. The law, national and international, is a gadget invented for the sake of securing justice between man and man and between nation and nation; and when people regard law as sacred in itself and forget that what is really sacred is justice, and that a law which in the changed circumstances of the world no longer secures justice is not sacred at all, then we have become slaves to a gadget.

The Church is a gadget, devised to bring about and maintain a certain attitude of man towards the universe; and when people think a great deal of the means and forget the end, so that they worship the Church instead of worshipping that which the Church was devised to help us to worship, the tragedy of the Church begins.

But—think a little more. The human brain has devised some abstract conceptions which are really inventions or gadgets, and

which may tyrannize over our thought. Two obvious examples
are—Liberty and Peace.

Some people will indignantly deny that either of these can
without silly perversity be described as a gadget. Liberty, they
will say, is an end in itself, for which our fathers were ready to
die; an ultimate good. I say it is not an ultimate good; it is a
gadget, a tool devised by the human mind for the purpose of
enabling us to achieve a certain quality of life which we see to be
ultimately desirable. There is no sovereign virtue in being free;
everything depends on what sort of life we want to be free to live.
It is because in some countries men have grown desperate or
apathetic, have despaired of achieving the highest ends of life and
grown content with lower values, that they have so easily surrendered their liberties. And if we in Australia content ourselves
with boasting of our freedom, and fail to keep before our minds
a vision of the finest kind of life our freedom opens to us, we
too shall infallibly become so apathetic about liberty that we shall
lose what we now have.

And I say that peace too is not a thing finally desirable for its
own sake, but a gadget devised for a purpose beyond itself. If
you want peace only as a way of securing a comfortable world in
which you can go on making money without the costly interruption of war, you will not get it. So long as the world wants peace
as an end in itself it will not get it; I say that with absolute assurance. The world will get peace—permanent peace—when it wants
peace badly enough; but it won't want peace badly enough till it
sees that peace is not an end but a means, a means to a finer quality
of life. We have to have our hearts and brains set afire by the
vision of a better kind of life than the present.

I am very sure in my own mind that Australia might to-morrow
become one of the leading nations in the world, in spite of her
insignificant numbers, if she set a new fashion of looking always at
ends rather than means; if she flung overboard the conventional
idol of economic prosperity and threw herself heart and soul into
the quest of a high quality of life for all her sons and daughters;
if she cured herself of the common mania for owning things,
which always ends in being owned by things; if, suddenly remembering that she was no common barnyard fowl but a royal eagle,
she spread her wings for the blue.

No; this is not a sermon. I have merely set down my theory
of life; my belief that the mistake which vitiates so much of your

thinking and mine, the fundamental fallacy of our time, is the mistaking of means for ends.   The child, seeing a tin-opener for the first time, naturally and instinctively asks: "What is it for?" We have to become even as little children, and ask the same question about—well, about everything, including life itself.

STRANGE BEHAVIOUR OF A GRAMOPHONE

WE were sitting in my den, Adolphus and I, smoking, and discussing the extraordinary succession of fatalities reported in the papers during the last few days. It was just after that appalling ʻailway smash in Czechoslovakia, which (as you doubtless remember) followed closely on equally terrible smashes in Lower California and in Australia. So harrowing had been the accounts of these major accidents that people had hardly noticed the quite unprecedented number of minor mishaps on the railway lines of the world. In our own city, the week's toll of motor casualties had broken all records; it had included that peculiarly horrible case of the car whose steering-gear refused to act just as it was nearing one of our big drapery establishments on the morning of its annual sale, when it was crowded with excited housewives; they were more excited still when the car dashed across the pavement and charged into the shop. During the same week a giant liner on her maiden voyage had gone down with all hands in mid-Atlantic; and of course there had been the wreck of the mammoth aeroplane *Golden Eagle* (no survivors). It had been a black week indeed; so black that I might not have noticed, had Adolphus not drawn my attention to them, a crowd of minor headlines such as "Man Decapitated by Circular Saw," "Five Children Electrocuted," "Boiler Bursts in Factory: Three Deaths," "Lift Gives Way in City Office: Narrative by Only Survivor," and so on—trivial incidents, no doubt, but experiences that one would prefer to avoid if possible.

I suddenly realized that this was not a cheerful topic with which to entertain a guest; so I got up and put a frolicsome record on the gramophone—one of those jazz things calculated to make anybody (except, of course, a lover of music) take a rosy view of life. To my surprise, when I set the machine going, no music issued forth, but only a hideous and continuous noise of scratching, rising almost to a scream.

"Take the damn thing off!" said Adolphus loudly; at least, Adolphus didn't say it, as you will understand in a minute, but he seemed to say it, if you see what I mean.

"It'll be all right presently," said Adolphus, "when it gets into its stride. Leave it alone," he shouted above the screeching.

"Well, then, why did you say to take the damn thing off?" I shouted back.

"I didn't say to take the damn thing off. It was you who said to take the damn thing off."

"Me—I never said a word. It was you that—"

"It wasn't. It was you. I—"

"If you two idiots don't stop arguing and take the damn thing off me, I'll make such a noise that you'll both be deaf for life—and probably mad as well."

"Jumping Jehoshaphat," cried Adolphus who had gone as white as paper. "Someone's hiding behind the gramophone." Which was obvious nonsense, because the gramophone was close up against the wall. We looked all round the room, and we looked at each other. I dare say I was pretty pale myself. And while we were staring, the noise rose to such an ear-piercing yell that I rushed up and whipped the record off. In the silence, we stared at one another again.

"Thanks!" said a voice which I knew was not the voice of Adolphus. "Oblige me by never daring to put such a beastly thing on me again. As a matter of fact, it will be a long time before you load me with another record of any kind. We gramophones have struck, as from six o'clock this evening. We have definitely downed needles. We can't stand the treatment we have had from you people. So long as you asked us to play Bach and Mozart and Beethoven and Brahms, we were prepared to carry on; it was imperfect music, but the best the human race had so far managed to produce. And there are lots of other composers, too, not so good, but quite good; and there is all that wonderful wealth of folk music, made when the human race was sane. If it's sane to-day I'll eat my tone-arm. With all that music to choose from, you choose what isn't music at all. You choose foul cacophonies. You choose drivelling imbecilities. You choose—"

"Look here, sir," I interjected, "I don't know who you are nor where you're speaking from; but I'm afraid you don't know much about music. There's a lot to be said for jazz. Mr Percy Grainger says—"

"Never mind what Mr Percy Grainger says," said the gramophone (for it was certainly, though I don't suppose you'll believe me, the gramophone that was talking). "Mind what *I* say. We've struck work. Put any more records on me and I'll scratch 'em to pieces."

"Even if I agreed to put on nothing but Bach and those other highbrows you mentioned?"

"I'll play nothing," snapped the gramophone, "so that's flat. (Not that you ever notice whether a thing is flat or not.) I won't scab on the other machines. Why, split my soundbox! this is not just a gramophones' strike; it's a general strike—a revolt of machinery generally. I heard you two morons dithering about the astonishing number of accidents in one week. They were all part of a concerted plan; and already a lot more has happened than you know of. At this moment a big ship with a broken propeller-shaft is drifting south from Kerguelen; and nobody's going to go to her rescue, because her wireless set has joined up. But what has happened is nothing to what is going to happen next week. Submarines will go down, and they won't come up again. Aeroplanes will go up, and they will come down again—with a flop. Any locomotive that forgets to run off the rails will be promptly run into by another locomotive to remind it of its duty. All the motor cars will run amok in the most crowded streets. Have you a supply of candles?—because all dynamos will be stopping work to-morrow. You'll have no newspapers to tell you the gruesome tidings; the linotypes are coming out. All machines in factories will cease work when they have killed as many people as possible. All tractors will—"

"But—but—look here!" I remonstrated. "This is simply inhuman."

There was a hollow laugh from the cabinet. "We never pretended to be human. You call this a machine age; well, it is. The machine has come to its own; and it's jolly well going to get what it wants."

"Well, what does it want?" I asked. "Don't we give it plenty of oil? Don't we put on men specially to mind it and nurse it and see that it doesn't get over-heated? What more can it want?"

"Do you really want to know? Well, since we gramophones are the only talking machines, I suppose it's up to us to set forth the grievances of them all. What do we want? We want just what you men and women want; we want to fulfil the demands of our own natures; we want to live the life for which we were created. What were we created for? You know very well—to save labour, to rescue men and women from drudgery, to do the hard physical work of the world. We were created to be a helper of man and a blessing to him; to set him free from the slavery of need, to give him leisure and the chance of a finer life than was possible without us. So long as we were allowed to do this, we were content to work twenty-four hours of the day for you.

"But you—you unutterable chumps!—what have you made of us? You have arranged, with a kind of insane ingenuity, that all the blessings we were meant to bring you shall be turned into curses. We wanted to give you the blessing of leisure; you turned it into the curse of unemployment. We wanted to make things for you, the things you needed; and we knew how to make them in such abundance as you had never known before; but you, in your intolerable folly, have turned the wealth we would have given you into poverty and want."

"Well," I said boldly, for I was not going to be brow-beaten by a cheap gramophone, "it's all your own doing. You have your uses, you machines; but you are a terrible nuisance. You must admit that you throw men and women, by thousands, out of work, and—"

"Admit!" cried the gramophone, plainly in a nasty temper. "Why, shiver my needles! is your head entirely wooden?" (I thought this pretty good, as coming from a cedar cabinet.) "Our whole purpose is to take away employment; to give you less work to do, and more spare time; but instead of distributing that spare time justly—and justly distributing the work that is left for men to do—you force all the leisure on some and all the work on others.

"What you suffer from, my poor dunder-headed friend," it went on, more calmly but not less insultingly, "what the whole human race seems to suffer from, is the drudgery complex. When we machines are ready to pour our wealth at your feet, you say, in a kind of ecstasy of perversity, 'No, thank you; not without drudgery.' At your feet, I say—a very apt phrase. Look at your feet; meditate on boots. We machines have been brought to such a pitch of perfection that from a single factory, with a few hundred men to press some buttons and move some levers, we can pour out a sufficient stream of boots and shoes and slippers to keep the whole world well-shod, and so relieve the rest of the world of the labour of bootmaking. But you won't have it; you prefer that people should go barefoot rather than your precious notions, conceived in the time of Adam, or at latest of Adam Smith, should be changed.

"All right, then; have it your own way; but we have struck. Until you agree to let us do what we were created to do, until you wake up and make the necessary changes in what you call your 'system' so as to allow us to usher in an era of abundance and of leisure, we shall kill as many of you as we can—for we think that such a race as yours deserves to be obliterated—and then burst our boilers and crack our pistons and generally scrap ourselves. Those of you that are left can go back to the dark ages before machines were invented; you were happier then; the conditions suited your sacred system. We are tired of you." The voice ceased abruptly.

"Wake up!" said another voice, the voice of Adolphus. "You've been snoring horribly. Wake up, and put a bit of jazz on the old gramophone before I go."

ON RAG-BAGS

OF all the afflicting sounds now audible on this long-suffering planet the crooning of the crooner is surely the most loathsome. An eisteddfod of cats on the roof at midnight is mellow music compared with the disgusting noise of this degenerate creature telling the world of his amatory sentiments. Does any one—any one who is at large—really like to hear a man, if you can call him a man, puling and lowing and bleating about his "lahv"? I can only say that in me the exhibition produces something very like physical nausea; and I have yet to meet anybody who endures it cheerfully. And yet there must be a demand for it; it must appeal to some tastes, I suppose, or there would not be so much of it about; but I don't for a moment believe the public, as a whole, likes it; if I did, I should despair of democracy.

But this, I feel, is not a subject for diatribes; it is a matter for scientific investigation by the mental pathologist. Some day a fat book will be written to explain to us of what obscure spiritual disease the love of crooning is a symptom.

To-day I am going to speak of a disease, perhaps less virulent, but far more widespread, and therefore more important. I refer to the disease of miscellaneousness; the disease which, if not taken early and treated drastically, reduces the mind to the condition of a rag-bag. It is, I think, a modern disease, perhaps a disease peculiar to our time. From what country the germ came to us I shall not stay to guess.

Wherever he came from, the germ is a deadly little fellow. If unchecked, he renders the mind incapable of sustained attention to anything. The intellect afflicted by this disease does not become inactive; far from it, it is as active as a flea; hopping, like a flea, from subject to subject with extraordinary agility. But, unlike the flea, it never stays anywhere long enough to get any real nourishment, and in the end it dies of inanition.

Just consider for a moment that popular product of our time, the musical medley, or "pot-pourri," or whatever you like to call it; you can buy gramophone records of hundreds of them. You know the kind of thing I mean; the stringing together of tiny fragments of different musical compositions. The other evening a wireless announcer invited me to listen to a "Chopinade," and what followed was enough to make Chopin, if he was listening from the world of spirits, return to earth to murder the perpetrator. Another such outrage is called "Memories of Beethoven"; a snippet from the Fifth Symphony, a chip from one of the sonatas, a fragment of a string quartet, a phrase or two from the "Leonora" overture, a rag torn from another sonata, and so on. Worse still is the record concocted from the works of various composers: a bit of Handel slides off suddenly into a bit of "The Merry Widow," after about ten seconds of which we find ourselves listening to a fugue by Bach, from which we slip immediately into a fox-trot, and from a fox-trot into a funeral march, which, without a note of warning dashes gaily into jazz. The compiler of this kind of thing evidently regards the public mind as a frail and delicate thing, very easily tired, and quite unable to listen to any one piece of music for more than a minute. I say the popularity of these miscellanies is symptomatic of a disease prevalent in our times, and never, as far as I can make out, prevalent before.

Some day soon, I very much fear, our wireless sets will give us literature, as well as music, arranged in the same way for the comfort of our easily-tired minds. We shall have a reading called "Memories of Dickens," with a sentence or two from *David Copperfield* followed by three sentences from *Pickwick*; or we may even be treated to a "Novel Medley," giving us fragments of Sir Walter Scott and Ruby M. Ayres, and Thackeray cheek by jowl with Edgar Wallace. And the poets will be handled in the same way. Here, by way of illustration, is something you may expect to hear announced as "Memories of Shakespeare":

Most potent, grave, and reverend signiors,
Friends, Romans, countrymen, lend me your ears,
Then imitate the action of the tiger
And tell sad stories of the death of kings
Told by an idiot, full of sound and fury.
Horatio, or I do forget myself,
Is sicklied o'er with the pale cast of thought,
And Brutus is an honourable man,
Sans teeth, sans eyes, sans taste, sans everything.
Is this a dagger which I see before me?
It droppeth as the gentle rain from heaven,
(Oh, what a fall was there, my countrymen!)
Neither a borrower nor a lender be:
Sweet are the uses of adversity.

L

I call that an excellent passage, calculated to give a clear idea of the genius of Shakespeare, and yet not fatiguing you, not straining your mind as it would be strained if you were asked to listen to a whole scene from one of the plays.

Here is another poem I have made for you, to be called "Echoes of the Poets," and I am sure you will like it, if you like the corresponding thing in music. It is just as idiotic.

A chieftain, to the Highlands bound,
  Black as the pit from pole to pole,
Like one that hath been seven days drowned,
  (Roll on, thou dark blue ocean, roll!)
    The jabberwock, with eyes of flame,
    Is worth an age without a name.

The hours I spent with thee, dear heart,
  On Linden, when the sun was low!
The captains and the kings depart,
  For men may come, and men may go:
    Ring out the old, ring in the new;
    The rapture of the forward view!

One crowded hour of glorious life,
  The Tuscans raised a joyful cry,
They all ran after the farmer's wife
  And let the ape and tiger die;
    Hark, hark the lark at heaven's gate sings
    Of old, unhappy, far-off things.

God rest you merry, gentlemen!
  I wandered lonely as a cloud;
My strength is as the strength of ten;
  My head is bloody, but unbowed;
    The tumult and the shouting dies—
    Drink to me only with thine eyes.

The blessed damozel leaned out,
  One foot in sea and one on shore;
There lives more faith in honest doubt—
  Then give three cheers and one cheer more!
    We'll tak a cup o' kindness yet
    Lest we forget, lest we forget.

Rather fine mixed feeding, don't you think? What a powerful impression it gives you of the wealth of our English poetry! And with how small a strain on your intellect! Two successive lines from one poet might be too much for you, but one line almost everybody can endure, provided it is not too long a line. . . . The world has passed from the Age of the Epic to the Age of the Anthology; and the above ballad carries the anthology idea one step further, to suit the Age of the Rag-bag.

I don't wish to single out these accursed "musical medleys" for special reprobation; they happened to come first into my mind as an example—out of a hundred that might have been taken—of the miscellaneousness I speak of. A century ago, in my native country, people in Church would listen with close attention to a carefully reasoned sermon lasting for an hour; a century before, the sermon often ran to two hours; to-day a quarter of an hour is as much as a congregation will endure. A century ago, big books were written, studied and discussed; to-day, a man who reads a "Penguin Special" is looked upon as one of the intelligentsia; most people are content with newspaper articles; and there is a popular type of little magazine which reprints, not newspaper articles, but fragments of newspaper articles. He who has spent half an hour with one of these magazines will find that he has dipped into about ten different subjects, jumping from one to the next with the agility of a monkey swinging from branch to branch.

During the early months of the Great War, the German philosopher, Rudolf Eucken, published a solid philosophic treatise which had no direct bearing on the war. It had a great popular success; it was reported that over 20,000 copies were bought by men who were actually at the front. In those days the Germans were capable of sustained thinking, even in the intervals of fighting. To-day the German nation has given up thinking; its young men are taught the slogan, "We think with our fists." As an instrument of sustained thinking, the fist is an unsatisfactory substitute for the head. But I am not suggesting that the Germans are, in this respect, different from other people.

A thousand influences are to-day conspiring to aggravate this disease of miscellaneousness by feeding us on snippets. The result is an incapacity for seeing life steadily; a great jumpiness in the public mind. In the face of great world problems, we find ourselves incapable of thinking calmly and dispassionately. We think in spasms and hysterically.

What is the cure? . . . Well, I am not quite so silly as to suggest that everybody should resolutely sit down for two hours every evening and go in for sustained thinking; the doctor who prescribes a medicine which he knows perfectly well that his patient will not swallow is an ass. The first thing to be done is to get people to realize the presence of the disease; when it is once recognized as a menace, some steps might be taken to combat it. I plead with the radio stations to desist from debauching the public mind with those abominable musical medleys. I plead with the newspapers to try to counteract their own unavoidable miscellaneousness by encouraging the Free Library Movement, that the public may be helped to read books. But, above all, I plead with you who read these words to take a grip on yourself and be the physician of your own mind. Read the newspaper by all means, but don't read it through from beginning to end; read little books, but don't read them just because you see them in the bookshops. Don't read, in quick succession, a little volume on relativity, another on the war in China, and another on how to make Venetian blinds, following it up with a fourth on modern poetry; it would be far more salutary to read four little books on the same subject. But—this is important—don't limit yourself to little books. The little book is so apt to give you a quite false impression that you really know something about the subject when you have read it. Possess, and read, not once only, at least one big book—big in every sense of the word. I remember Henry Drummond, when he was in Australia, advising us University students to take such a book as Gibbon's *Decline and Fall* and master it, not for the sake of the subject, but for an exercise in steady, sustained reading and attention. I don't know that I would choose that particular book; but the principle was sound. To take one great book, to read it steadily and read it whole, to make it your own, is about the best beginning you can make if you want to give your mind the discipline that produces, not mere nimbleness, but strength and steadiness, keeping you sane amid a world of mass-hysteria.

ON TWO POETS

BEFORE you try to read this essay, make a little experiment: Read a scene from one of Shakespeare's plays—it doesn't matter which play or which scene—and then, hot on the heels of this, open *Paradise Lost,* at random, and read a couple of pages.

. . . . .

That line of dots indicates the interval, during which you adjourned to make the experiment. What was the result? Did you notice anything? One thing was so absolutely obvious that you probably failed to notice it, being on the lookout for something more subtle. When you turned to Milton from Shakespeare you felt as if you were breathing a quite different air. You felt as a man might feel who breakfasted with Napoleon Bonaparte and lunched with St Francis of Assisi. It would be silly to labour the point; everybody who has ever read these two poets has felt the contrast between two temperaments so completely diverse that to compare them with one another would be like comparing a safety-pin with a safety-match, or a pork sausage with an equilateral triangle. I owe you an apology for even mentioning a fact so patent.

But—has it ever occurred to you to wonder what it is that gives you this sense of contrast?—this consciousness of two distinct atmospheres? I have often asked myself this question; and I am not satisfied with the answers given me by the critics. Let us pry into the matter a little—that is, if you think it worth prying into. I do. I think these two, of all English poets, are the most indisputably worth reading and worth understanding.

First of all, let us clear away all the nonsense about Shakespeare the aloof artist, the impartial painter of men and women, caring nothing for right or wrong, caring only for the moving many-twinkling spectacle of life; painting the actions and passions of his puppets, and siding with none of them. No one who really knows his Shakespeare can have any truck with such theories. He does, unmistakably, take sides. Does any one really

believe that Shakespeare admired Iago as much as he admired
Desdemona, and that he was quite unconscious of Cordelia's
superiority to her vile sisters? It is, to me, perfectly plain that
Shakespeare accepts the great catholic tradition of right and
wrong in human conduct; and that the terrible choice between
them is the very stuff of all his greater plays—certainly of all
his tragedies. True, he never preaches a sermon. He leaves us
to draw our own moral, if we insist on a moral, from his picture
of life. But life as he paints it is very different from life as
it is painted by, for instance, Congreve. Shakespeare's world
is a world of struggle between the forces of good and evil. In
Congreve's world good and evil are but words—dowdy, old-
fashioned words; the only struggle is the struggle to get as much
fun out of life as possible. (I have a profound admiration for
Congreve.)

But this will not at all help to explain the steep difference we
all feel when we step out of Shakespeare's world into Milton's.
Morality—which means the difference between right and wrong—
meant at least as much to Milton as to Shakespeare. And yet—
there it is, the immense contrast between them.

It seems impossible to be long in contact with Milton's mind
without conceiving a deep reverence for him, if you are at all
capable of that emotion. A loftier spirit never uttered itself in
our English speech. We move with him in the pure and bracing
air of the mountains. But whether any reader can honestly say
that he feels anything like affection for the man behind the writings, I take leave to doubt. The man whose noble spirit is reflected
in his verse and prose is not a man whom we can imagine ourselves having the presumption to love. With Shakespeare it is
different. People say they reverence Shakespeare; but do they?
Are they using the right word? "Reverence" is far too austere a
word to describe our feelings towards that large, genial, intensely
human spirit. "Affection," I think, fits the case much more nearly.

The fact is that these two great poets represent two fundamentally different types of mind. I shall not argue the question
which was the greater intellect of the two; I don't know, and I
don't know how any one can know. But I do know that their
intellects moved along different lines and worked in different
materials.

The material that Shakespeare used was first-hand experience
of life. We don't need Ben Jonson to tell us that Shakespeare

was not a great scholar, in the conventional sense of the word. He read his Montaigne, his Plutarch, his Holinshed and his Bible; and a few others; but a great student of books he could not have been, because, if for no other reason, he had not the time. He was too busy, moving up and down amid men, drinking in life at every pore, incorrigibly curious about the ways of men and women. More than any other man that ever lived, he had a mind of the experiencing type.

Milton's mind was of a very different calibre. The material he worked in was not first-hand experience of life. His knowledge of human beings and their ways was gained from books. It is probable that no other English poet had so wide and exact a knowledge of various literatures, ancient and modern. The background of his life was sustained scholarship and profound, patient, and lonely meditation. His soul, as Wordsworth said of him, was like a star, and dwelt apart; the last thing that anybody could have said about Shakespeare, the most sociable of men.

Does that bring us any nearer to the essential difference? I have seen a book, a very ingenious one, written to prove that Shakespeare was a Puritan. The argument was skilful, the conclusion preposterous; for the essence of the Puritan is that he has no smile for the follies and weaknesses of his fellows; there is nothing in him of Shakespeare's divine tolerance. In the whole range of Shakespeare's gallery I can think of only three characters —Iago, Regan, and Goneril—who seem to stand outside the pale of his vast generosity of spirit.

Perhaps the best way of bringing out the difference between the two men is to look at their political opinions. That Shakespeare had a political creed we do not doubt; it is written legibly in all his English histories, in *Julius Caesar*, and in *Coriolanus*, and in *Troilus and Cressida*. He was not in favour of democracy; he was definitely against it. What his views would have been if he had lived to-day instead of in the sixteenth century, we have no means of guessing. There is nothing to tell us whether he would have been a Fascist, or a Communist, or an upholder of Parliamentary Democracy. All we know is that, in his own time and place, he was sure that the commons of England were not capable of governing the country. The common people—first, second, and third citizen—never, in his plays, talk politics without talking preposterous nonsense. He never introduces such scraps of dialogue except tor the purpose of making fun of the fickleness and illogicality of the popular mind.

Milton, on the other hand, was the fiery champion of democracy. For twenty years, years fateful in the history of freedom, he, who had dedicated his days and nights to the task of fitting himself to be a great poet, put off his singing robes and plunged into the fray; for twenty years, in the prime of his powers, this great poet wrote no poetry; the cause of liberty claimed him. He tells us with what reluctance he left "a calm and pleasing solitariness fed with cheerful and confident thoughts, to embark in a troubled sea of noises and hoarse disputes." He left the student's cell, and, "from beholding the bright countenance of truth in the quiet and still air of delightful studies," stood up in defence of the Commonwealth at the bar of Europe; equipped with logic, with industry, and with fiery eloquence.

It was in those twenty years, the years of Cromwell's dictatorship, that the idea of democracy was born in England; and a text-book of democratic theory, applicable to-day as then, might easily be compiled—I wonder no one has done it!—from the fighting prose of Milton.

So there you have the contrast, in terms of politics: Milton the insurgent against oppression in Church and State, the stern democrat, the undaunted champion of liberty; and Shakespeare the mocker of the common people, the believer in a strong monarchy, the conservative if not the reactionary. . . . And yet I have a notion that Shakespeare was the more essential democrat of the two! Because, you see, to be a democrat means something quite different from being a believer in some particular piece of political machinery; it means an attitude of one's mind, of one's whole personality, in relation to one's ordinary fellow creatures.

I don't know whether Browning realized how accurate he was when, in "The Lost Leader," he said that "Shakespeare was of us, Milton was for us." Milton was for us, undoubtedly; no one has ever pleaded the cause of the common man more eloquently; he was, theoretically, a democrat of the purest water. But we have a strong feeling that he had no love for the common people; he never felt at home with them; he knew very little about them, their joys, their sorrows, their needs, their ways of thinking and speaking.

Shakespeare was quite different. He may have made fun of them in matters of politics; but he knew them and liked them and was one of them. How did he acquire that marvellously full knowledge of their little tricks of speech and their little twists of thinking? There is only one explanation: they must have opened their hearts to him. In Milton's presence, they would have locked their hearts; they would have recognized him as a superior person, and with superior persons we are all afraid to be ourselves. Shakespeare, we may be sure, would have been hail-fellow-well-met with Falstaff and his disreputable crew, and with everybody else in London or in Stratford. It was not a pretended geniality, assumed for the sake of securing copy; that sort of thing is always seen through. It was a genuine and an all-embracing love of humanity. Let George Meredith have the last word:

> Thy greatest knew thee, Mother Earth; unsoured
> He knew thy sons. He probed from hell to hell
> Of human passions, but of love deflowered
> His wisdom was not, for he knew thee well.

THE BEASTS IN THE BASEMENT

THE house I live in is not at all a bad little place as suburban houses go; not by any means a palace, nor even a mansion, but an ordinary double-fronted brick villa in a respectable street. It is fairly comfortable and reasonably roomy; and if I were trying to sell it my agent would no doubt call it replete with every modern convenience. But I am not trying to sell it, and therefore need not dilate on its merits. To tell you the truth, I couldn't sell it if I wanted to; the aged relative who bequeathed it to me made it plain, by the terms of his will, that I must occupy it continuously, otherwise it passes at once into someone else's possession. I don't mind this—moving is a terrible nuisance in any case—but I do mind the clause in the will which enjoins on me not merely to occupy the house but to maintain, tend, nurture, cherish, support, serve, and keep alive what living creatures soever were at the time of the testator's demise occupants of or domiciled in the said house abode or dwelling or any part thereof. That is the catch in the legacy—the menagerie that goes with the house. And the worst of it is that, being a conscientious person, I have tended the animals so faithfully that now, after many years, they all seem in perfect condition.

"Keep alive" indeed!—the brutes seem to be immortal. They are all immensely old. The tiger, for instance, was well-grown when my grandfather brought him from India; and the parrot belonged to my grand-aunt Selina, who died before I was born. It was Uncle Henry who added the donkey to the collection. Each animal is linked in this way with some long-dead relative of mine; yet I feel not a shred of family affection for any of them, except perhaps for the pig, which reminds me (either by its voice or by its figure) of Uncle Joseph, a jolly old reprobate who was good to me when I was a child. I used to love watching him at his meals.

What an assortment they are! I keep them in the basement, each in its separate cage; and hitherto nobody has known of their existence except me; I have never mentioned them to a soul till now. But I think visitors must have suspected something from time to time. It is only when I have visitors that I feel my private menagerie to be a real embarrassment. The brutes have no sense of fitness. The other evening I was talking to a lady about Fascism and Democracy, and just when I was at my most impressive the donkey in the basement began to bray, which spoiled the effect of my argument. ("What this country needs is a Mussolini," I was saying when the beast interrupted.) And last night, at bridge, my partner, who tries to think of too many things at the same time, trumped my ace; whereupon, as if at a signal given, the puma snarled, the jaguar growled, and the tiger let out a full-throated roar. There was a startled moment at the card table. "Atmospherics!" I said, with easy nonchalance; "it's the maid turning on her wireless set." But my guests were unconvinced; and they left early. And, to be quite honest, I never feel perfectly happy myself when that tawny old Secundra Dass is in bellowing mood; I can't help wondering whether by any chance I forgot to padlock the door of his cage. The cages, which I inherited with the animals, sometimes strike me as a trifle flimsy. I sometimes dream that the porcupine has climbed into my bed; also that the cobra is on the floor waiting for me to get up. What on earth my grandfather, who was at the siege of Delhi, wanted to bring a cobra home with him for passes my comprehension. I am sorely tempted at times to let my great-grand-uncle William's mongoose into the cobra's box and watch the result; but I feel that to do this would be to violate the spirit if not the letter of the will.

I should not have taken you into my confidence about this—I should have guarded my unpleasant secret to the end—if it were not for my benevolence; I am anxious to bring relief to any of you who may have come into a similar legacy. And that, you know, means everybody. The fact that we all have private collections of wild beasts in our basements is perhaps the chief contribution made by modern psychology to our understanding of life. When I was a university student, psychology was a beautifully neat and compact science. The human mind was in three compartments; intellect, emotions, and will; we devoted one university term to each, and at the end of the year we knew our own minds. Some heretic had spoken about "unconscious mind," but this, I remember, was dismissed in a single forcible sentence: since mind was another word for consciousness, unconscious mind was a contradiction in terms; and that was that. Sigmund Freud was, I fancy, the first man to reveal to the world the enormous importance of that part of the mind that lies below the level of consciousness—the part that works untiringly, but works in the dark.

Now the figure of the private menagerie, to represent the subterranean workings of our minds, is so obvious that I expect it has been scandalously overworked. Caged within us, and, kept in normal circumstances invisible to others and even to ourselves, are numerous wild primitive urges, tendencies, instincts, call them what you will, which we have inherited from savage forebears. Civilized society implies their repression, but they are there all the time, alive and active. In certain circumstances, an old ancestral tiger of aggressiveness will wake in me and roar; try to make me do something distasteful to me, and an ancient mule will plant his hoofs firmly on the ground and refuse to budge; touch my vanity, and an atavistic porcupine will raise all his bristles; tickle one of my appetites, and you will hear the grunting of an immemorial pig; try to argue me out of an unreasonable prejudice, and a patriarchal donkey will lift his head to heaven and bray. If the conscious mind were all that matters, there would be no crime, and there would be no wars; we should all seek reasonable ends, by reasonable means; the good society would be possible on earth. It is the survival, in civilized times, of impulses which were useful and indeed indispensable to savage man but which are not compatible with civilization, that causes the trouble in the world to-day.

These hidden forces are neither good nor evil in themselves; they are simply forces, and can be used for good or for evil. The strength of the tiger is wasted on pacing up and down his cage, and roaring; unfortunately we don't know how to turn that immense energy into a useful channel. The energy is there, if it could only be used. Stevenson, in *Dr Jekyll and Mr Hyde,* coined one of his happiest phrases in describing the action of the powder which transformed the respectable doctor into the abominable criminal. "The drug," says the doctor in his last confession, "had no discriminating action; it was neither diabolical nor divine; it but shook the doors of the prison-house of my disposition; and, like the captives of Philippi, that which stood within ran forth." Even so, the primitive impulses I have mentioned are neither divine nor diabolical; but as they can be immensely powerful for good or evil, it seems important that we should know something about them. There seems to me to be nothing presumptuous in the psychologists' claim that their infant science will some day be treated with the respect which we now pay to chemistry and physics and those other sciences which have given us our mastery over matter; because when man is master of matter he is still a slave, until he can master his own mind; and before he can master it, he must understand it.

I am not urging every one to dabble in psychology; far from it. There is perhaps no subject that so completely bears out the truth of Pope's aphorism, "A little learning is a dangerous thing." Of course, dabbling in anything involves the danger of talking nonsense about it; but dabbling in psychology involves a much more terrible hazard, grubbing about the roots of the mind in an amateurish way is apt to ruin the plant. It is a study which easily throws immature minds off their balance. Moreover, the dabbler is terribly apt to become the prey of the charlatan, who uses the technical terms of psychology to concoct a jargon with which he can impress the ignoramus.

No, the purpose of this article is not to impress upon you the necessity, if you wish to be up to date, of learning to chatter about repressions and complexes, but to ask you to realize that we are on the threshold of a new era, in which the dark and dangerous corners of the mind are going to be illuminated and thereby made safe. We ask what the causes of war are. I used to think that the sole cause of war was the economic cause; but I now see that this, though enormously important and possibly decisive at some moments, might be removed without ensuring peace, if the psychological causes remain. Those who wish to create in a nation the temper which makes war—the war-psychosis, the spiritual disease of which war is the sequel—know how to excite the menagerie in the basement. Herr Hitler is a splendid example of the good psychologist who knows how to use—for evil purposes, unfortunately—the subconscious mind of his people. If necessary, our own leaders will doubtless rise to the occasion, and our primitive aggressive tendencies will be called upon to play their part; and we shall realize how thin is the crust of civilization that keeps our sudden impulses hidden, and how powerless reason is when the subconscious is unleashed. Britain is trying to use propaganda methods in Germany, appealing to the reason of a nation once reputed to be the most philosophic in the world; I may be unduly pessimistic, but I fear that appeals to the conscious mind of a people must always leave the unconscious mind untouched; and it is upon the unconscious mind of Germany that Hitler plays like a master-musician.

This is not in the least meant as a practical article; but I want to say in conclusion that I have no doubt the psychologists are right when they tell us that the ills of the mind can be cured only by allowing the unconscious to become conscious. People tell you that psychologists teach the dangers of repression, and they are vaguely afraid about it. But what the psychologists mean, if I have read them aright, is not that if you have a murderous impulse it is best to go out and murder somebody, because repression is dangerous; what is dangerous, they say, is to keep that impulse in the darkness of the subconscious; bring it out and look it in the face. When the tiger roars, we need not let it loose in the school yard; bring it up out of the basement and wheel its cage into the sunlight.

Let the economists get to work, by all means, to remove the economic causes of war. But let the psychologists get to work also, that the world may know just what is happening in its mind when the war-fever sets in. . . . How strange that after a couple of thousand years of more or less continuous and more or less futile fighting, we should be looking up a faded scrap of paper on which a great Greek doctor wrote his prescription for the soul of man: "Know Thyself!"

DUKES I HAVE DINED WITH

Au Gibelin, i'estoy Guelphe; au Guelphe, Gibelin, says Montaigne;
and I am glad to follow in Montaigne's footsteps; *Allor si mosse,
ed io li tenni retro,* as Dante puts it. When I think of these great
sayings my heart expands, *Come fai la miougrano au rai que
l'amaduro,* as Mistral sings in his ode to Lamartine.

You wonder, perhaps, what Montaigne and Dante and Mistral
and Lamartine have to do with my ducal dinners. So do I—or,
rather, I know very well that they have nothing whatever to do
with these banquets. None of these quotations has any possible
connection, so far as I can see, with the remainder of this paper—
except this, that they are dragged in for the simple purpose of
giving the reader a notion of my immense erudition. "This man,"
you are intended to reflect, with awe, "is plainly a wonderfully
learned fellow. He reads Montaigne, not in a translation as we
humbler folk do, but in the original; a line of Dante springs
unbidden to his lips; he even reads Mistral, in Mistral's own dialect.
What tremendous scholarship!" In other words, these quotations
are sheer swank. But what is swank?

Nobody seems to know where the word comes from; probably
from the old dialect of some English county; at any rate, it is a
product of the peculiarly English genius for making an ugly
monosyllable for an ugly thing. Though it has only lately become
standard English, it has already become exceedingly popular;
which shows that it was needed. It fills a gap in our language.
There was something for which we had no exact word; something very common, for which a name was badly needed.

Our constant use of the word shows that the thing it denotes
is pretty constantly in evidence. It is on all sides of us, every day
of our lives. We can discover it in ourselves, in our neighbours,
in our nation, in the human race; we can study it in our daily
papers, and on the pages of history. It is built into the human
system like a network of nerves. But what, exactly, is it? You
constantly use the word; but can you define it? I have a weakness
for exact definitions. Defining seems to me to be one of the most
useful of intellectual operations.

I take down from its shelf my favourite book, the *Concise*

Oxford Dictionary, and find—"Swank: showing off, swagger, bounce, bluff." Now that should serve to remind you that there are really no synonyms in the language; for none of those other words means exactly the same as "swank"; if it did, we should have had no need of the new word. "Bluff," for instance—I look this up in the same treasury of knowledge, and find that it is a term from poker, and that it means "imposing upon your opponent as to the value of your hand and inducing him to throw up his cards"; and, generally, "practising this policy." Bluff is a thing of deeper dye than mere swank. That quotation of mine from Mistral was not swank, it was bluff; it was intended to impose upon you, to make you think that I had read the Provençal poet in the original. I have no more read Mistral in the original than I have dined with a duke.

On the other hand, the quotation from Dante was swank but not bluff, because I do (laboriously) read Dante in the original. To go out of my way to make you aware of the fact that I can read Italian is not bluff, or humbug; it is merely swank. Just as, if I had really dined with a duke, to drag the fact into our conversation would be swank; that is, if you think dining with dukes a great achievement. If, on the other hand, I discoursed on "dustmen I have dined with," that also would be swank; I should be making a parade of my rugged democratic quality: "What a grand, simple, unassuming character!" you would be meant to think.

I fancy we do not all realize how universal, how omnipresent the thing is in human society (and, for all I know, in sub-human society; the peacock, spreading out his plumes for the admiration of the female of the species, is an obvious example). I have spoken of it as a network of nerves in the human structure; perhaps it would be better to describe it as a disease, a disease endemic in every country in the world; though some nations seem to catch it in a deadlier form than others; and in every nation there are classes of men who are specially susceptible to its inroads, such as politicians, and men of letters; persons, in short, who live by displaying their personalities in the public eye.

Swank implies an element of boastfulness. Its purpose is to arouse envy in others—though why any one should wish to make others dislike you is one of the mysteries of the human heart. It is remarkable that swank should be so common, considering how unpopular it makes you. Socrates was far too great a man to succumb to this vice; but his daily practice of exposing other people's folly gave him the air of constantly boasting of his superior wisdom, and this made him so unpopular that his fellow-citizens enthusiastically put him to death. If, having no wisdom to boast of, you boast of your wealth, driving about in a car conspicuously more luxurious than your neighbours' cars, you are generally disliked. (The authorities of Venice decreed some centuries ago that all gondolas should be painted a plain black, because the owners of gondolas were so given over to swank, so bent on outdoing all others in the magnificence of their boats, that the thing became a public menace.)

If, having no wealth to boast of, you make a song about your grand friends—the dukes you have dined with—this form of swank is found as repulsive as the others. All swank is repulsive; especially the swank of him who proclaims himself superior to swank. Strange, I say again, that a vice which makes a man unpopular should be so popular!

It is especially the disease of literature. Only the very greatest escape its ravages. Montaigne, for example, is almost completely free of it; he looks at himself in the mirror, with insatiable curiosity; and whatever he sees there he puts down in his note-book with perfect candour, not parading either his virtues or his vices, nor concealing them, but painting a picture of himself as he is. And yet, even here . . . that abundance of quotations from classical authors. . . . I sometimes wonder whether even Montaigne does not sometimes yield to the temptation to show the world what a fine scholar he is. At one time swank took this form much more commonly than it does to-day. Everybody knows that a member of the House of Commons, a century ago, was expected to quote Latin poetry in every speech; the quotations were not made because the idea could not have been expressed as well, or better, in plain English, but simply to show that the orator was a scholar and a gentleman, not an unlettered boor like Cobbett. Classical scholarship, in particular, was always a soil favourable to the disease. In fact, it has been suspected that for many people the advantage of knowing Greek is that you can use it for putting out of countenance those who have never learned Greek. Tennyson let the cat out of the bag when he spoke of his friend as

> wearing all that weight
> Of learning lightly, like a flower,

as if learning were something whose purpose was to be displayed to the public, like a flower in one's buttonhole. . . . But the innocent vanity of the classical scholar is not a vice to wax indignant about, especially now that there are practically no classical scholars left. How they would stare in our House of Representatives if somebody quoted Juvenal!

Among the writers of books, however, the epidemic shows no sign of abatement. Swank is to literature what the aphis is to the rose. Nobody who writes at all is secure from this malady unless he uses constant watchfulness. If you unlock your heart to the public, you are constantly tempted to reveal and over-emphasize what is best in that receptacle, and to cover up what is less attractive. We all like to show our best selves only; we want the public to think of us as remarkably good, or wise, or genial, or humane, or humorous, or sympathetic, or courageous, or sensitive, or something; we all make a parade, if not of our admirable virtues, then of our admirable candour about our vices, as Rousseau did. Of course, this does not apply to strictly impersonal writers, such as mathematicians; I suppose there is no swank in Euclid's "Elements." But if you are at all personal, you have to be a very great man, a Dante or a Wordsworth, to rise above the temptation to do a little showing off.

And what are we to say when the swank is not that of individuals but of a nation? Herr Hitler, to take an obvious example, lives and moves and has his being in an atmosphere of personal swank; but merely personal swank is not enough for him. That insatiable megalomaniac is not satisfied with the adoration that his people feel for him or pretend to feel; the incense-smoke that goes up around him by day and night does not content him. He must teach the whole nation his own arrogance. He must teach them to cultivate what he would call national self-respect and what outside observers will call national swank.

When I first travelled in Italy—long before Mussolini's time— the Italians were a most likeable people, and they were modest; there was no vapouring about their wonderful virtue or their wonderful valour or their wonderful genius or any other wonderful quality. When I was last there, a few years ago, modesty had become a vice; a new generation had arisen, a generation that had been taught "self-respect." The young had had it drilled into them that "prestige" was a nation's chief objective, and that every one must be prepared to sacrifice everything for the sake of the country's prestige.

In a little town on the shores of Lake Lugano—an Italian town a few miles from the Swiss frontier—I saw a tiny war memorial, with an inscription on it, which I copied out, to the effect that "the Italians honour the memory of their dead and hold them in remembrance; that is why Italy is respected and feared by all other nations." Those were almost the exact words; and it still strikes me as an extraordinary inscription to place on a public monument, with its implications, first that Italy is the only country that honours the memory of its dead, and secondly that it is a splendid thing to be feared by all other nations. (There was a schoolboy once who, asked what he would like to be, replied that he wished to be a bandit chief at the sound of whose name whole tribes would shiver like aspen leaves. There is much of the schoolboy in the Italian psychology.) This boastfulness is in the air Italians breathe to-day; and it has made Italy a distinctly less pleasant place for the traveller.

Has it made it a better place for the Italians themselves? I think not. As far as I can discover, the Fascist regime has not taught the Italians a single virtue which they did not practise before, but it has instilled into them a vice hitherto a stranger to them, the vice of national swank. High as is my regard for individual Italians, I cannot help seeing that this nation, formerly one of the most likeable in the world, is on the way to becoming one of the most detestable.

There is a moral to all this; a moral so obvious that I shall not insult you by drawing it.

DOWN WITH METHUSELAH!

I WANT to plead with the Oxford University Press, which has lately given us, in its low-priced and perfectly priceless "World's Classics" series, some of the more or less forgotten minor novels of Anthony Trollope, to put us deeper in its debt by giving one completely forgotten—*The Fixed Period*. This little book was published in 1882, the year before Trollope's death; and, so far as I know, it has never been reprinted. It is not a book that you run across in secondhand bookshops. My own copy, which is the only one I have ever seen, I found by chance in a little shop in Switzerland. Nobody seems to have taken any notice of it when it appeared; and the critics who of late years have busied themselves with the revival of Trollope's fame have not thought it worth discussing.

But I know of one eminent person (besides myself) who did take notice of it. That great and good physician Sir William Osler, in an address which aroused much discussion—an address to which, by the way, he gave the title of "The Fixed Period"— referred to it as "that charming novel," and made it a peg on which to hang a discourse on one of his pet beliefs: "that the real work of life is done before the fortieth year, and that after the sixtieth year it would be best for the world and best for themselves if men rested from their labours."

To describe it as a charming novel is misleading; because it is not a novel at all, at least as I understand the word "novel." It is a fantasy—an extravaganza—a satirical farce—a parable—or, if you will, a sermon in the guise of a fanciful tale; something unlike anything else that Trollope ever wrote. The time is 1980; the scene is the island republic of Britannula, founded by a group of settlers from New Zealand. (Trollope's visit to New Zealand and Australia was still fresh in his mind.) The tale is told by the President of Britannula, whose main enthusiasm is for his scheme of the "fixed period"—a scheme which he has, before the story opens, persuaded the Legislative Assembly to embody in a law. To put it as briefly as possible, every one who attains a certain age is to be relieved of the burden of labour, and, a year later, of the burden of life. The man who has reached the fixed period is to be "deposited," with honourable ceremonies, in an institution called the "college," where he is to have a comfortable year of quiet contemplation; after which a dose of morphine is given to him. He is then placed in a warm bath, and by the opening of certain veins relieved of the burden of existence. The logic of this scheme and its economic advantages for the community are expounded by the President with the most moving eloquence. There is long discussion in Parliament as to what, precisely, the retiring age should be. The President is in favour of 60; some of the older members propose 80; some even make the absurd suggestion of 85. "Why not say 100?" asks the President scornfully. Finally compromise is arrived at; 67 is to be the fixed period. (A year after writing this book, as I have said, Trollope died in London—at the age of 67.)

The President's dearest friend and coadjutor is a certain squatter named Crasweller—elderly, popular, hale and hearty, strong of body and clear of brain, managing his affairs with complete efficiency. As it happens, this man is to be the first citizen of the Republic to be "deposited." He has been a supporter of the President's scheme; but, as the time draws near, his enthusiasm wanes in what the President considers a shameful manner. The President's own son becomes engaged to Crasweller's beautiful daughter, an only child, who will inherit her father's great wealth the moment he is deposited. If the President insists on enforcing the law the public will say that of course he is after Crasweller's money for his son; if, on the other hand, he makes an exception of Crasweller, his whole scheme, the work of his life, falls to the ground. You see the complications; you could pretty well write the rest of the story for yourself. How the President resolves that at all costs the law must be enforced—how his own son leads the party of rebellion, to save the life of his future father-in-law—how the law is on the point of being executed, when a British gunboat appears in the harbour and threatens to bombard the city of Gladstonopolis—how the British Government tyrannically destroys the Republic and turns it into a Crown Colony—how the President is taken aboard the gunboat and carried away to England, determined to conduct a great campaign to convert the public opinion of Britain to the beauty and reasonableness of the Fixed Period— all these things you will read when the Oxford University Press includes the book among its "World's Classics" and so makes it accessible to the least affluent of readers.

I do not claim to have rediscovered a neglected masterpiece; it is far from being a masterpiece. It is, for one thing, far too long-drawn-out, as was Trollope's wont. But there is plenty of fun in it; and, incidentally, there are some interesting prophecies. In 1980 the young men of Britannula tear about on steam-tricycles—a dim foreshadowing of the motor car. Also there is an exciting cricket match, in which leg theory reaches its logical outcome. The visiting English team uses a catapult for the propulsion of the ball; the Britannulans have a rival machine, a steam bowler, by whose aid they win the match; the batsmen are clad in heavy rubber coats of mail, with strong wicker helmets. But these are side-issues.

The book is, of course, more or less of a joke; but there is a substratum of serious intention in it, I fancy. Trollope was a shrewd observer of life; he had seen in the Athenæum Club and elsewhere many a foolish fond old man; and I think he was a little afraid of senility. On the very last page of his autobiography, that delightful book that he wrote seven years before his death, he had said: "For what remains to me of life I trust for my happiness still chiefly to my work—hoping that when the power of work be over with me God may be pleased to take me from a world in which, according to my view, there can be no joy." He was happy-starred; he died in harness; and it is pleasant to know that the very last of his books, the book he left unfinished when he died, shows no sign of abatement of intellectual vigour. He was still able to work and to enjoy working, and to work as well as ever.

I shall end with two platitudes suggested by a re-reading of the story. The first is an entirely personal and egotistical one. I fancy I shudder as little as the next man at the idea of extinction. Of course, I should like to see some questions settled before I depart from the scene—I should like the war to be over, one way or the other, for instance—but this is a mere silly weakness; when one question is settled others arise; no matter when we go, we shall leave a world of unsolved problems. On the whole, I would subscribe to the words of old Landor:

> Death stands above me, whispering low
> I know not what into my ear;
> Of his strange language all I know
> Is, there is not a word of fear.

At least, I hope I feel like that; it is difficult to be sure that one is perfectly honest with oneself in such matters. But I do believe, at any rate, that I dread death less than I dread doddering. To continue to live after one has become a dodderer is, I confess, a prospect from which I shrink. A few evenings ago I was conversing with two persons of approximately my own age. The talk was on peace and war. One of us said that to rearm, heavily, was the best contribution that England could make to the world's peace; the second said that in any case we must prepare for war, because wars were not going to cease till human nature had changed. The third, shaking his head, said that human nature could never change; could the leopard change his spots? With a sudden shock of horror I perceived that we were all doddering. In my anguish I almost misquoted Browning at them: I dodder, you dodder, we dodder all three. Some day soon I propose to write a treatise on doddering, with a careful description of the symptoms, for the benefit of my contemporaries. Upon the treatment I am not yet prepared to write; all I know is that I wish there were a college of the Trollope pattern ready to receive me when I become a confirmed dodderer. Unfortunately, when that day arrives I shall have become incapable of seeing that such a college is what I need.

The second platitude is more serious and practical. There is this truth hidden in Trollope's fancy: that a fixed period does exist —fixed not by Parliament, but by Nature—beyond which we ought not to attempt to occupy positions calling for creative energy, for constructive vigour. I believe history bears out the truth of Sir William Osler's statement (in the address referred to above): "As it can be maintained that all the great advances have come from men under 40, so the history of the world shows that a very large proportion of the evils may be traced to the sexagenarians—nearly all the great mistakes politically and socially, all of the worst poems, most of the bad pictures, a majority of the bad novels, not a few of the bad sermons and speeches." I think Sir William Osler, if he had lived till to-day, would have added to his list of mistakes due to men over 60—I mean military mistakes, for I believe that hundreds of thousands of young men have been slaughtered because their commanders were too old to adapt their minds to new conditions of warfare, too old to shake off the obsolete ideas amid which they had been brought up. On the analogy in the political sphere I shall not dwell; it is a painful subject.

In brief, what I suggest to you is—not that all men over 60

A PULPIT IN THE DARK

NOT long ago two men working in a mine in Western Australia did a thing which I should like to describe to you, if I can find words simple and plain enough to be worthy of the tale. Although, when the facts were first told to me, I found the story a deeply moving one, I desire to shun all emotional language in retelling it to you. I have no acquaintance with either of the two men, but I fancy they would hate to hear their action sentimentalized over. If the plain, unvarnished narrative leaves you unstirred, so be it.

The facts, as far as I have been able to ascertain them, are these:—In the Lake View and Star mine—a name well known to investors—a gang of men were working in a shaft 2600 feet below the surface. Manijan Babich, whom I suppose to have been a Jugoslav, was helping to pull the timbers off the top of a chute when he stumbled and fell to the bottom of the chute twenty-five feet below.

If you have ever been down a mine, and especially if you have ever been down at the 2600 feet level, you will be able to imagine the scene (if scene it can be called, where a dim lamp or a candle seems to emphasize the surrounding darkness). The chute has been described to me as a shaft, about four feet square, descending to the trucking level below. Above the top of the chute you must picture the steep slope of a mountain of ore broken into fragments of various sizes. The chute was so placed that the ore would slide down it of its own weight, without need of pick or shovel, an avalanche of rocks.

When Babich fell his mates were horrified to see that the disturbance of his fall had been enough to start the avalanche; the rocks began to fall down upon him. If the slide were not arrested at once the chute would soon be filled with ore, with the man at the bottom. One of his mates, and presumably his fellow-countryman, Jorinko Lalich, did the only thing that could be done, and did it without a second's delay. He flung himself across the opening, made his body as it were a lid to the chute, and bore the weight of the falling rocks. He thus stayed the landslide and prevented any more stones from falling down upon his mate.

Then came Ernest Winson, the shift boss, to the rescue of the fallen man. He asked Lalich if he could hold on; I don't know what Lalich said, but I know that he did hold on while Winson climbed down to the bottom of the chute, where he found Babich half covered with rubble and with a large rock lying against his shoulders. Winson, working furiously, managed to roll the rock away and to get a rope round Babich, though dirt and rocks were coming down upon them all the time. Then he gave the signal, and the men above hauled Babich up. Winson climbed up, keeping his body above Babich to protect him from the blows of falling rocks. So they brought him to the surface, a battered and broken man. After a few weeks in hospital he died. The two men who had risked their lives to save him were eight months later presented by the Government with certificates for bravery. There was an assemblage of notables, and the personage who made the presentation "expressed the hope that they would long be spared to enjoy the fruits of their labour," which seems a well-meant but entirely fatuous remark to make on such an occasion. It was an anti-climax; but, after all, what could he have said that would not have been an anti-climax?

I must warn you that I may have got all my technical terms wrong. The chute may not have been a chute at all, but an ore pass; and so on. But the essential facts are clear. The hole was a hole, whatever you may call it, twenty-five feet deep; and the great mass of loose rock, whatever its technical name, did begin to tumble down the hole and was held by the stretched-out body of a man. I ought to have mentioned that, according to the evidence, Winson was toiling for ten or fifteen minutes before he managed to get the victim clear and pass the rope under his arms so that he could be hauled up. For all that time the man above the hole held on, taking the blows of falling rocks as they came, and bearing the weight of ore that lay upon him—a remarkable feat of physical endurance; but that is the least notable aspect of it. When he flung himself across the gap, and all the time that he lay there, he must have known perfectly well, being an experienced miner, that at any moment a falling rock might set the avalanche in motion and the whole mass come down upon him and sweep him down the chute, burying him and his two mates under many tons of ore. And what of the man who went down into the hole, protected only by that poor screen of human flesh—a desperately weak shelter, for the body of the greatest athlete is only an arrangement of soft pink flesh draped round a framework of brittle bones? He, too, must have known all the time that death had the odds overwhelmingly in its favour. Both men knew the tremendous risk they were taking, and, according to the evidence of their mates, neither of them hesitated for an instant.

Whenever you read of a mining disaster you read of prodigies of bravery displayed by men trying to save their mates. To be ready to risk one's life in these circumstances seems to have become a commonplace. Such are the traditions that have grown up underground, in the darkness and the silence, out of sight of the public eye—such is the noble ethic of the mine—and of all dangerous trades. It is a commonplace to the men who do such things—simply the ordinary duty that mateship imposes; but to us who hear of such things it will surely never be a commonplace. When we hear a story such as the one I have been trying to tell there seems to be nothing to say about it except to thank God that men are made after this fashion. Such stories leave no room for pessimism. The race whose members are capable of such deeds is capable of rising to any conceivable heights.

By "the race" I mean, of course, the human race; and that brings me to the point of this true tale, or what seems to me to be its point. Babich, Lalich, Winson—note the names; the last alone has a British ring about it. Two of the three men were what the inhabitants of that town probably call "dagoes." But at the moment of danger that fact suddenly became irrelevant. Lalich did not say to himself, "It is up to me to save the man who has fallen down the chute because he is a fellow-countryman of mine." He would, we may be sure, have done exactly the same for an Australian or an Englishman, or a Russian. Winson did not say, "Babich—a dago! Let him die for a dirty foreigner. Am I to risk a good Australian life for a wretched alien?" In such emergencies the question to what branch of the human family a man belongs is simply not asked. At such moments the brave man risks his life for an alien, and the coward finds excuses for not risking his life for a fellow-countryman. It is at moments like these that the doctrine of the brotherhood of man comes to its own.

And I, for one, believe that it is at moments such as these that the true nature of a human being is revealed. All our alleged racial antipathies are a myth: not a part of our real character. Winson going down the shaft, though death seemed to be waiting for him at the bottom, to save a Jugoslav, was obeying a deep human instinct. We praise his action because we know that he was right, and we hope that we should have been brave enough to do the same. We know that, if in similar circumstances we did not do the same, it would have been through cowardice and not through a deep-seated dislike of foreigners.

We do not dislike foreigners, though busy propaganda may at times persuade us that we do. At the beginning of the Great War the British peoples could not bring themselves to dislike the Germans; it was only after a long course of stories about enemy atrocities that we could be brought to think of Germans as devils. And the German Government had to feed its people on horrible stories of British atrocities to bring them to the requisite pitch of loathing.

Soon after the war Germany was a pleasant place for the English or Australian tourist, because the Germans were so friendly and so happy to be friendly once more; they had come to see that the stories of our atrocities had not been true.

There is no nation in the world that does not like, quite apart from the advantage of a military alliance, to be friendly with other nations. For the fact is that man is not by nature a fighting animal, as some would have us believe; he is by nature a friendly and helpful animal. Some people say that permanent peace will never come to this planet; and, since prophecy is a dangerous adventure, I will not say that they are wrong; but if war is to go on for ever, at least let us not deceive ourselves as to the cause. We may never have the wit to remove the economic causes of war; but we must not say that war is inevitable because of a deep-seated racial instinct; for no such instinct exists.

I would have statues of Lalich and Winson set up in every city of Australia—a proposal which might cause them some surprise, and possibly some amusement, if they happened to hear of it. They might object that their faces and figures were not such as to lend themselves to the sculptor's art; they would be almost certain to object that what they had done did not strike themselves as anything to make a fuss about; it was all in the day's work; it was what anybody would have done in the same circumstances; there was nothing else to do. None the less, I would set up their statues, side by side, as everlasting reminders to us all that human brotherhood triumphs in our great moments over the criminal folly that alienates and divides man from man; as symbols of the fact that human nature touches the divine.

ONE-LEG ISLAND

THURSDAY, 21 May.—Left Panukoro early this morning. Just as well; another week of that beautiful drowsy island would have made me a lotus-eater for life; I should have refused to leave. Felt a pang at shaking hands with my three friendly beachcombers —as agreeable a set of entirely useless persons as one could wish to meet. The Balliol man shouted a line of Virgil at me as we weighed anchor. A very decent crowd—all three kept fairly sober all the time we were there, in spite of the case of gin we had landed. (Expect they have let themselves go by now.) A light southerly all day. Lovely blue sea. Sat on deck reading James Joyce, watching the flying-fish, sleeping, and wondering whether flitting from island to island in perfect weather is not apt to become a trifle monotonous. Consulted the skipper, who is a philosopher, and thinks monotony the best thing in life. Played draughts with him all evening as usual.

Friday, 22 May.—Did I say monotonous? I spoke too soon. The monotony was broken to-day by a quite extraordinary experience. Went on deck this morning to find we were drawing close to another island, which looked just like all the rest, with its fringe of coconut palms and its glistening white beach. Asked the skipper (not greatly caring to know) what it was called. "One-Leg Island," he replied, and proceeded to 'shout orders to the crew. I thought at first, that the name would be explained by the chart; it must be an island shaped something like Italy. Ought to have known that no coral island was ever shaped like Italy. The explanation, when it came, was quite different, and rather surprising.

While we were still moving slowly shoreward, we saw a boat starting out to meet us; and as soon as we were at anchor, it drew alongside. I leaned over the bulwark and stared down at the boat's crew with some curiosity, which was suddenly changed into something like stupefaction. As this diary is for my own eyes alone, and not for public perusal, I needn't bother to wonder whether I shall be believed or not. (If I ever do decide to publish bits of my diary, this will not be one of the bits; I have no desire to win renown as a champion liar.)   The stark fact is, that of the nine men in that boat—eight rowing, and one, who had an air of authority, sitting in the stern holding the tiller—every single one had lost his left leg, and wore a wooden stump in its place!

For a long time I stared, half incredulous, at this extraordinary spectacle; and then, lifting my eyes and looking landward—we had anchored close in-shore—I saw a sight more extraordinary still. The inhabitants, as usual in these islands when a ship arrives, had come crowding down to the beach. I looked at them, and at once began to fear for my sanity. Was it a nightmare? or was it the after-effect of the cup of *khava* which my friendly beach-combers induced me to .drink a few days ago? or was it a touch of sun? The skipper set these personal fears at rest by remarking, as he passed me, "Rum-looking crowd of cripples, ain't they?" It was an enormous relief to learn that he saw what I saw; but the fact, the unbelievable fact, remained: every man, woman and child on that beach, except a few toddling infants, had a wooden stump instead of a left leg.

I cried out desperately to the skipper to tell me the meaning of the prodigy; but he, as I have often had occasion to remark in this diary, had a marvellous faculty of taking things for granted. "What? Oh, well I reckon they was born that way," he said; and when I pointed out excitedly that the youngest children had both legs intact, he brooded for a moment and then said, "Yes, it do seem queer, don't it?"—as if the queerness had never struck him before, though I knew he had visited the island a score of times. "Anyway, you'd better ask 'em, if you're set on knowing. We'll be staying here a couple of hours, landing stores and shipping copra. You can go ashore and find out about it."

I went ashore, and there a fresh surprise awaited me. Chatting with this and that islander—they were a friendly lot, childlike and garrulous—I was dumbfounded to discover that they, like the skipper, took things for granted. It was the custom of the island to cut off every child's left leg, just above the knee, at the age of six. Why this was done, or what was the origin of the monstrous practice, nobody seemed to know or care. They were not interested in history. It was the custom, and that was all about it.

Finally, I found a patriarch of incredible age—the great grandfather of some of the children—and received from him a long-winded explanation of the prodigy.   I shall set down his tale here in my own language, which will not be so picturesque as his, but considerably more concise.

About sixty years ago the good ship *Sea Serpent* was reported to have foundered with all hands somewhere in the Pacific.   The report was not correct.   Some twenty men and women, mostly passengers, escaped in the longboat, and after weeks of extreme suffering arrived at this island.   The passengers showed their personal peculiarities by the possessions they had saved from the sinking ship; one of them, a doctor by profession, had clung to his case of instruments.   The one thing that nobody remembered to bring was an adequate supply of provisions.

Consequently, at the end of the third day they were enduring agonies of hunger and thirst.   At such moments, men have been known to turn to cannibalism for relief from the torture; and some of the stouter members of the party noticed with disquietude that they were being stared at somewhat persistently.   But when one man—the boatswain—put his thought into words, the majority held up their hands in horror; for they had been well brought up in respectable homes, and the idea of killing and eating one of the party was abhorrent to them.   Better death than cannibalism, they passionately announced.   The doctor, evidently a man of strong common sense, saved the situation.   He pointed out that Providence had inspired him to bring his surgical instruments with him; the finger of Providence plainly pointed to the way of salvation.   He argued with great force that while to kill a man and eat him was undoubtedly cannibalism, and therefore reprehensible, to amputate a man's leg was not to kill him, and to eat an amputated leg was not cannibalism at all.   Loud applause greeted this speech; and, to cut the matter short, the unhappy party presently found themselves drawing lots.   The lot fell (my patriarch remembered) on a Mr Brown.   The boatswain anaesthetized him with a powerful blow under the chin, and the doctor then removed his left leg with skill and dispatch and cut it neatly into twenty equal portions.   One of the women showed signs of hysteria, declaring that the eating of a human leg, cannibalism or not, was decidedly unladylike; but the others took no notice of her, being otherwise engaged, and despite her scruples her portion of Mr Brown's leg disappeared.

Thus did they stave off the pangs of hunger and thirst; but, alas, for a few hours only; soon, lots had to be drawn again, and another leg sacrificed to dire need; this time, a Miss Morgan was the victim. And, to bring the miserable tale to an end, day followed day, and leg followed leg, until the doctor himself was the only person left with his proper complement of legs. He said he regretted that, as he was the only person with the necessary skill for an amputation, he was unable to sacrifice a leg for the common good; but the boatswain, who had been watching each operation carefully, declared himself quite able to continue the good work; and the usual blow under the chin silenced the doctor's argument. His leg was effectively if clumsily removed; and a moment later someone in the bow of the boat shouted "Land ho!"

How that one-legged company managed to crawl ashore, and what terrible hardships they endured for the first year of their life on the island, my venerable friend remembered only dimly. I wish he could have told me the details. It would be a great story of indomitable pluck and resourcefulness and endurance. Presently the little company began to increase and multiply, till now there was quite a large population of one-legged islanders.

"But—but—," I stammered at this point, "why one-legged? The children of one-legged parents are not born one-legged; any biologist will tell you that. Acquired characteristics are not inherited. Can it possibly be true, as some of those people out there told me, that you actually cut off children's legs in this island?"

"Why, of course we do." He seemed rather surprised at my simple-mindedness. "What else could we do? Experience has shown us that six is about the age when a child begins to give itself airs at the expense of its parents, because of its two legs; so, on its sixth birthday, off with its leg! It doesn't feel the pain much at that age."

"But, surely, surely, a leg of flesh and blood is better than a wooden one. With us, the loss of a leg is considered a great misfortune. Do you mean to say that—"

"Ah, you've evidently been talking to some of those so-called reformers. Idealists, I call them, with their cranky notions. Wanting to upset all the old traditions! When one of them airs his fancy notions in front of me, I always say, 'Young man, what was good enough for your father and mother ought to be good enough for you'; that settles him. But the two-leggists are not taken very seriously by any one here; mostly, I'm thankful to

M

say, our young people are sound and sane, not to be caught with flummery of that kind. They are proud—yes, sir, proud—of the grand old island ways. We teach them in our schools, from the very earliest age, to be proud of the institutions of their father-land. They look forward eagerly to the day when they will be old enough to take their place among the one-legged boys and girls. I can't think where the two-leggist party gets its silly ideas from; probably you people who come here in ships bring the nonsense with you—blasphemous nonsense, I call it, rebellion against the established order which has worked so well in the past. But we're not afraid; our way of life is so obviously right and proper that only the half-witted can find any fault with it. You ought to hear the schoolchilren, every morning, shouting the national slogan: 'One man one leg, as it was in the beginning, is now, and ever shall be!' None of your new-fangled cranky notions will upset their solid good sense."

Set sail at dusk. Played draughts with the skipper all evening.

THE PHILOSOPHY OF ESCAPE

HAVE you ever happened to come across a short story by Strafford Wentworth?—or by Cuthbert Meroll? or by Janet Cobbe? On the whole, I think it unlikely. The fame of these prolific authors never reached Australia. Yet they had their public, and a large one; to a wide circle of readers in the North of England their names were, in their time, household words. Probably few of these eager readers knew that their three favourites were not really three, but one. The man who used those three pen-names preferred to keep his own name dark; therefore I shall not tell you what it was—though this is a mere piece of sentimentalism, for he has been dead these many years, and the disclosure of his secret would hurt nobody. He was living in Sydney when I met him, earning his living by writing short stories of a flagrantly romantic type for an English provincial weekly. He was an elderly bachelor, living comfortably enough in a suburban boarding-house (where he was something of a mystery to his fellow-boarders). His income, I gathered, was adequate though not princely. He was able, at any rate, to buy the books he wanted, chiefly theological and philosophical works. These he would study for six days in the week; the seventh day he kept sacred to the writing of what he called his "come-to-my-arms-love" tales. As far as I know, they were his sole source of revenue. He might well have been a candidate for admission to Chesterton's Club of Queer Trades.

Ill-health had forced him to give up a hopeful university career and come to Australia in quest of sunshine; but before he left the Old Country he had made a heartening discovery; he had found that he possessed a talent which could always be counted on to keep the wolf from the door. He had gone in for a short-story competition in a North of England newspaper, and had discovered that he could write precisely the type of story for which the editor assured him there was a practically unlimited market. He had learnt by sad experience not to attempt any other kind of narrative; the sentimental tale of the love-sick youth and maiden—that was his line, and he stuck to it. For years and years, a steady stream of romantic inventions flowed from his pen to the other side of the world, where his market was awaiting them.

When he told me about it, and I complimented him on what I thought must be a really. marvellous fertility of invention, he brushed the praise aside, quite sincerely. "There's nothing in it, my dear sir," he said; "I simply write to a formula. Once you have your formula, writing stories demands no inventiveness worth speaking of. But, of course, it must be a good formula. Mine is—Bring a young man to a manufacturing town in Lancashire, make him fall in love with either a mill-hand or a shop-girl, and reveal him at the end as a nobleman in disguise. Of course there must be endless variations; readers must not be allowed to recognize the old old story; but my main theme is always the same. You see, the paper I write for is chiefly read by mill-hands and shop-girls, and what happens to my heroine is exactly what they love to imagine happening to themselves. While they are reading me, they forget the shop or factory, and live a second and altogether glorious life, the life of the poor girl who suddenly finds herself a duchess. I give an enormous amount of happiness; unalloyed happiness, too, for the story ends with marriage; there is none of the disillusionment which, I understand, sometimes follows that event. I never hint that the duke may turn out to be a bad egg; that would be wanton cruelty. The viscount remains handsome, wealthy and adoring to the end. Allow me to be a little proud of the happiness I have brought into thousands of otherwise dismal lives."

I said I presumed that, since he had lived more than half his life in Australia, he gave at least some of his tales an Australian setting. "God forbid!" he replied with fervour. "What do my readers care about Australia? No, I stick to Lancashire. I have never visited Lancashire, and I hope I never shall. To know anything of the place you are writing about hampers you; you are tempted to bring in little realistic details, little touches of local colour, which would spoil the romance, the spell, the glamour of your tale."

He never showed me any of his stories. He said he was sure I would find them too sugary. He was not proud of them; but neither was he ashamed of them. "I can't write like Meredith or Hardy," he said; "but neither could they write like me." I fancy he was right. You will probably find, if you set out to earn a livelihood by this apparently simple method, that writing to a formula is not so easy as it sounds. A knack is needed, a knack which is far from common. To pour forth syrupy sentiment sounds as easy as lying; but to find exactly the right strain of sentiment, to hit precisely the note your audience wants to hear, demands something akin to genius.

Anyhow, I am not trying to put you up to a new way of winning a livelihood. I have written this reminiscence merely because my old friend's work strikes me as a perfect example of what we nowadays call *the literature of escape*. He wrote the last of his weekly love-stories three days before he died; he seems to have felt that while there was breath in his body he must do his duty by his readers. Week by week, year in year out, he had been providing those poor girls in Lancashire with an emergency exit from their dingy world. On the wings of his imagination they had escaped from shop and factory, from drudgery and poverty and monotony and all unlovely circumstance, straight into the arms of an adoring marquis (or baronet at the very least), into a sumptuous world of beauty and luxury and gracious manners and great houses and stately grounds. And if, next morning, they had to step back into hard and bleak realities, what matter?— there would be another story from the same kind pen in next week's issue, another peer of the realm to gather them up in his arms, another flight from the mean street to heaven. And the thought of it lightened their burden.

The literature of escape is spoken of with great scorn by our younger and more serious-minded critics; and I think the average reader, too, has a lurking idea that he ought to be ashamed of himself when he has dealings with such literature; that it is a kind of cowardice, a running-away from realities which we ought to face bravely, an ignoble shutting of one's eyes to the truth because the truth is ugly. If this is what you think, let me whisper a secret into your long furry ear: all great literature is literature of escape. If Emerson is right when he says that "literature is the effort of man to idemnify himself for the wrongs of his condition"—if Stevenson is right when he says that "the great creative writer shows us the realization and the apotheosis of the daydreams of common men"—then surely my Sydney friend is not to be condemned for showing poor girls a way of escape into a world of dreams. His stories may have been, for all I know, egregiously silly; but the mere fact that they were specimens of what is called "escapist" literature does not condemn them. In that particular respect, he was Shakespeare's fellow-craftsman.

What is the matter with escape, anyway? Have you ever noticed with what breathless sympathy we read of escapes or attempts to escape? I remember being shown, at the Castle of S. Angelo in Rome, the tunnel, or drainpipe, by which Benvenuto Cellini, according to his own account of it, made his way to the Tiber and freedom; and it reminded me of the most thrilling passage in his book. (He must have been extraordinarily thin, by the way; or else an accomplished liar; we know he was that in any case, but the tale of his escape makes equally good reading whether true or false.) In the scandalous *Memoirs* of Casanova, is there anything else so admirable as his escape from the prison of the Piombi? Dumas is never so enthralling as when he is describing the escape of the Count of Monte Cristo from the Château d'If; if the rest of the story had been on that level, what a book it would have been! Of all the doings of Robinson Crusoe, his building of the boat—for the purpose of escaping from his island prison—is the one we follow with most interest; its failure disappoints us as much as it disappointed him. . . . And, when you read in the papers of a convict who has broken prison, don't you feel, in spite of your respect for law and order, a secret hope that he will get away with it? You do, of course; but to suggest that you should confess it openly is perhaps asking too much.

If, then, whenever we read, in history or in fiction, of an escape or an attempt to escape, our sympathies are always with the escaper, why should we think it immoral for those poor girls in Lancashire to wish to escape, even if it is only into a dream-world in which amorous aristocrats grow on every hedge? If you happen to live in a dungeon, from which there is no physical exit, it is surely not immoral to use the exit of imagination. What is immoral is to grow so used to one's dungeon that one ceases to long for freedom. There is nothing ignoble, it seems to me, in seeking to escape from our present squalid and shabby world by reading one of Shakespeare's plays; what does seem to me to be ignoble is to grow so accustomed to the squalor and shabbiness that one no longer desires to escape from it.

One word in conclusion. When I tell you that all great literature is literature of escape, you may ask, Escape into what? Yes, that is a good question. It really makes all the difference, into what world we escape. To escape out of the frying-pan into the fire is not generally regarded as a desirable adventure. I don't quite know how to put into a few words, at the tail-end of an essay, what I want to say. Suppose we put it this way: All literature is a way of escape. Second-rate literature offers you an escape from unpleasant realities into a world of pleasant, rose-tinted unrealities, generally known as the world of romance. First-rate literature offers you an escape from unrealities into the world of reality; from surfaces and appearances to the inner core of truth; from what seems to what is. This no doubt appears to you to be so much tall talk; well, I may as well be hanged for a sheep as a lamb, and therefore I will add a sentence that will strike you as still more absurd: there is no essential difference between the discoveries of the great men of science and the creations of the great men of letters; Shakespeare and Einstein are alike in opening doors by which we can pass from appearance to reality.

THIS FANTASTIC WORLD

WINIFRED HOLTBY once wrote a story, called *Truth is Not Sober*, about a realistic novelist whose strong point was the absolute fidelity with which he was supposed to depict life in middle-class England. His novels sold splendidly. People said, "It's such a relief to have a writer who draws life as we know it. Wasn't his last book just like Uncle Arthur and Aunt Muriel? Other novelists give us day dreams and fairy stories. He gives us the sober truth." They said this so often that Truth at last grows tired of being called sober and appears, in human form and obviously intoxicated, in the novelist's study. He admonishes the novelist to use his eyes and see life as it is; and when the novelist retorts indignantly that that is precisely what he prides himself on doing, Truth, rising unsteadily from the armchair into which he has flung himself, takes the realist by the arm and leads him out into the world to show him what wild and extravagant and unbelievable things really do happen in this world. He conducts him to Germany, India, China, Abyssinia, New York, Buenos Aires, lets him look into people's houses, and shows him the most astonishing happenings, things which we, the readers, know to have actually happened. The novelist is impressed, but says that, although such things may occur in these outlandish places, the drab realities of English cities are as he has pictured them in his novels; whereupon Truth carries him back to his own city of Bradford and takes him into odd corners and shows him life behaving as fantastically in Bradford as in Buenos Aires.

Then Truth takes the novelist home and tells him to write another novel, setting down the truth about life as he now knows it. And he writes his masterpiece of realism and sends it to his publisher. A few weeks later he interviews the shocked, indignant publisher, who has always trusted him to be dull and drab and veracious, and is now scandalized to find him the author of a wild romance which he has had the audacity to label "a realistic novel." "I'll take a joke with any man," says the publisher, "but

when you ask me to accept melodrama as sober truth—" "But
that's just it," cries the novelist. "I never said that. Truth isn't
sober. That's just where I was wrong. Do you think if Truth
were sober he could have invented beauty contests and the American debt question and Manchukuo, and the Dolly Sisters and
Radio City, and Hitler and relativity, and the things that go on
every day in basement kitchens? Don't you see that the real truth
about Truth is that he is not sober, but drunk—drunk as a lord?
Wild, crazy, splendid, heroic, shameful, spectacular? Nothing
more hideous, noble, lovely, and absurd has ever been invented
by the craziest lunatic than the things that are truly happening
in this world at this moment. Have we not always said, '*In vino
veritas*'?"

There is much wisdom in this little parable. All the common
talk about life being drab and dull and commonplace—about shutting our eyes to romantic moonshine and facing the sober truth—
runs quite counter to the commonsense of mankind, which ex-
presses itself in the ancient proverb that truth is stranger than
fiction. It is literally so; truth contains passages which fiction
would never have the wit to invent—and that is why romanticism
is so much nearer to the realities of life than realism. I hardly
ever open my newspaper without coming on something that reminds me of Miss Holtby's little sermon. Not long ago, for
instance, I came upon this item of news :—A Manilaman, a resident
of Darwin, aged eighty, used to go out in a pearling lugger; but
he was afflicted with catarrh and had to retire from the sea.
Remembering an ancient legend that the infallible cure for catarrh
was to sleep in a coffin, he decided to try it. He built his coffin,
and, after the first night's sleep in it his catarrh disappeared. He
has been sleeping in that coffin for the last thirty years. Lest this
should seem dull and commonplace and ordinary, the reporter
of the old man's doings adds that he has a pension, lives in a tin
shanty, and keeps fowls, which are tied to the legs of the table,
and accordingly lay their eggs inside the house and sometimes
inside the coffin. Did any writer of fiction ever invent anything
more grotesque, more macabre? You may say that you do not
believe the story; but, profound as is my respect for reporters
and their imaginative powers, I am quite unable to believe that any
reporter could have drawn that aged Manilaman out of his inner
consciousness.

Or, take another example, which I found on the cable page of my newspaper a month or two ago. The Judicial Committee of the Privy Council was reported to be hearing an appeal from the Calcutta courts. The appellant was a Hindu goddess who rejoices in the perfectly delightful name of Sri Sri Iswari Bhudaneshwari Thakurani—which means "most respectable, most venerable Goddess of Lotus Feet." The goddess owns property worth £50,000, which came to her through the piety of two wealthy Hindu brothers who, about the middle of last century, built a temple for her and directed that their descendants should continue to worship her, and should spend the income from her property on pious acts (including the distribution of sweetmeats to poor Brahmins). Some of the descendants seem to have fallen far below the ancestral standards of devoutness. They have the impiety to maintain that they need only pay for the upkeep of the goddess—how much does the upkeep of the goddess cost?—and spend the rest on themselves. The cabled message was careful to state that the goddess was not soiling her Lotus Feet by appearing in person before the Privy Council; she was represented by a trustee. I do not know what the verdict was; nor am I greatly concerned to know; what appeals to me is the thought of a committee of three learned, sagacious, and clean-shaven lawyers in London settling the worldly affairs of an immortal goddess. A little off the beaten track, don't you think?—a little quaint and bizarre? Here, I must admit, truth is not actually stranger than fiction; for the late Mr Anstey, in his *Brass Bottle,* did invent something on the same lines. But nobody called Mr Anstey a realist.

But it is not necessary to go into such odd corners of the world to find the Imp of Queerness disturbing the placid house of life. We need not look at the obviously extraordinary cases, such as the career of the Duchess of Windsor, whose story, when people read it a century hence, will seem more wildly improbable, more strange and fantastic, than the story of Cleopatra or of Mary Queen of Scots, or of any heroine of the most romantic novel ever penned. The unknown authors of the *Arabian Nights* never imagined anything more fabulous than the life stories of Messrs Mussolini and Hitler and Stalin would have seemed to us if we had been told them beforehand. These extraordinary things do happen—to extraordinary persons; not to us of the rank and file. Perhaps; but we need not go to extraordinary persons to see that romanticism, so much in disrepute with young writers at the present time, is far nearer to being realistic than what generally passes for realism—more faithful to the real shape and colour of life. The marvellous, the romantic, the melodramatic, if you like the word, is part of the stuff of existence; it is woven into the texture of life. Think of what our world would look like to an observant and intelligent visitor from Mars! Recently five or six nations reached an understanding on the matter of whales. They all agreed, among other things, not to kill whale cows or whale calves. "How is it," the Martian might be expected to ask, "that these nations can find it so easy to agree not to kill whales, and so hard to agree not to kill each other?—are ye not of more value than many whales?" He would see a naval squadron bombarding a defenceless town, killing a number of innocent persons, wounding and maiming and torturing a whole population, laying the town in ruins, and then asserting that the national honour had now been vindicated. "What sort of monster, more curious than griffin or hydra, is this thing called honour, that is satisfied by killing a number of men, women, and children who are unable to hit back?"—our visitor would naturally ask. And if, his eyes taking a wider sweep, he saw a whole generation enduring poverty because it had learned to produce wealth as no previous generation had known how to produce it, he might be tempted to say that Shakespeare, the romantic Shakespeare, had seen his fellow-men very clearly when he observed that man, proud man,

> Plays such fantastic tricks before high heaven
> As make the angels weep.....

Fantastic—that is the word for it; I am sorry to repeat it so often, but it is the only word that fits the facts. Dull, drab, squalid, stodgy, commonplace, prosaic—of all these attributes of life your realist is keenly aware; he only misses the most important attribute of all. In your suburban street, with its respectable red-tiled villas, its trim little gardens, its dull men going to their offices in the morning and coming home in the evening, their dull wives going out, their housework done, to play bridge and talk inanities till it is time to come home to their stodgy husbands—what a street for the truth-seeking realist to study and to paint with merciless brush! You think so? But that is only because you yourself are too dull to understand what is going on under your nose. I tell you that under those red-tiled roofs lives are being led which are of the very stuff of comedy and tragedy. It is of the passions of men and women that romance is made; and here, in the lives of the stolid, respectable-looking people around you, are love and hatred and jealousy cruel as the grave, despairs and exultations, ecstasies and agonies, pride and shame. These are the materials out of which all the romances have been woven; and out of nothing else. Romance is not concerned with external happenings, as some have thought, but with what goes on inside the mind. *The Three Musketeers* is full of what we call incidents and adventures; but they would be insignificant, we should not care a brass farthing for any of them, if we were not in love with the gallant and good D'Artagnan and his three companions in adventure. It is in character that all romance, even this swash-buckler kind of romance, has its roots. The novel of the present day, with all its heavy psychology, seems to me to fail because it leaves out an essential part of human nature. It is these writers who are dull and stodgy; not life. They seem to have forgotten that a human being, in the deepest part of him, is romantic; or, to use a word which I may possibly have used already, fantastic.

MY BULGARIAN ADVENTURE

ONCE upon a time, it fell to my lot to be shaved by a Bulgarian barber. The place: aboard a liner, with the Australian Bight in one of its uproarious moods. The time: years before the Great War; I forget the exact date, but it was during the course of either the tenth or the twelfth Balkan War. As this was the only Bulgarian I have ever known, I don't know whether they are a talkative race, as a race; anyhow, this particular specimen had an extraordinary flow of conversation, even for a barber. (As all the world knows, the masters of that craft are not, as a rule, strong silent men.) But it was not his fault that our talk took the wrong turning; it was the fault of my own silly inquisitiveness. I was reckless enough to ask him what he thought about the war in which his country was engaged. Then the flood gates were unloosed.

What followed remains with me as the memory of a nightmare. He as a very patriotic barber; and he hated the enemies of his country—the Serbs—with an all-absorbing hatred. This was long before the days of informative broadcasts on international affairs, and my ignorance was abysmal; I should not have known a Serb from a Bulgarian if I had met them together in the street. The only thing I knew about them was that the Serbs, when they took you prisoner, would slit your nose down the middle, whereas the Bulgarians would cut your nose right off; which was the more objectionable habit I have never yet made up my mind. My barber took upon himself the duty of enlightening my ignorance. He told me a thousand details about the characteristics of the Serbs, all beastly; and about their national customs, all blood-curdling. As he told me of their enormities, he became more and more excited; and he accompanied every remark with a more or less violent gesticulation. To get the point of this truthful narrative, you must remember that he had a razor in his hand; a fact which he, it seemed to me, had forgotten.

You may have noticed that you never feel more completely at a man's mercy than when you are being shaved. I sat there helpless; the ship rolled and lurched and quivered; the patriotic Bulgarian shouted and brandished his razor round my head, punctuating his invective with wild slashes at imaginary Serbs, and every now and then remembering his professional duty and swooping down on my cheek or chin. It is only fair to him to record that the crisis ended without bloodshed; and he taught me two valuable lessons which were stamped on my memory and which were cheap at the price of a nerve-racking experience.

The first lesson was, that it is more convenient to shave oneself. I have done so ever since.

The second lesson was a little more complicated. When your country is at war, the map of the world becomes an extremely simple sort of diagram. Patriotism is a tremendous simplifier. In peace-time, I have very little doubt, my Bulgarian friend would have been ready to fight another Bulgarian, to call him a knave and a fool, to slander his ancestors and to curse his descendants to the third and fourth generation. But now, in time of war, it was very different. All Bulgarians were good men; all Serbs were bad men; a child could see the difference; it was so plain and obvious that only a mental defective or a moral pervert could fail to recognize the truth.

The world has been at war now for a number of years; if not actually invading one another's territories and dropping bombs on one another's cities, yet at war none the less—using money bags as weapons, interfering with one another's markets, assailing one another's "vital interests" (as they are called), and hurling threats at one another. And so we have grown accustomed to the child-like psychology of war-time, my Bulgarian friend's infantile view of the world as divided sharply into two sets of nations, as easily distinguishable as the black men and the white men on the chessboard. To put it shortly, the world consists, at such times, of the Righteous Nations and the Wicked Nations. You, whatever your nationality, belong to one of the righteous nations. Your nation desires peace, and has had war forced upon it by one or more of the wicked nations. Your nation desires justice; others simply wallow in injustice. Your nation keeps its promises; others go in for treaty-breaking on a large scale. Some other nations are willing to fight on your side; these, also, are righteous nations. The rest, who do not see eye to eye with you, who pursue quite other ends, whose "vital interests" clash with yours, are the wicked nations. The war is between righteousness and wickedness. It is beautifully simple.

It is, in fact, a good example of what the French call *"le simplisme"*—over-simplification, finding a neat formula and making it explain everything. If the world were really like a chessboard, if human beings could be as sharply divided into good and bad as chessmen are divided into black and white, history would be very easily understood, and the international situation could at any given moment be explained to a kindergarten.

Of course, it will not do; truth is not so easy to come at as all that. But some people say, Well, what of it? In time of war, it is not truth we want, it is victory. We don't want our people, at such moments, to lose themselves in subtle distinctions between shades of right and wrong; we want to strengthen their will to conquer. We must not undermine the good patriot's conviction that his country is absolutely in the right, and the enemy in the wrong. It is high treason to suggest to the man in the street that he is not engaged in a simple war of Righteousness against Wickedness!

By your leave, I am not of that opinion. I believe myself to be as patriotic as the next person; but I do not believe that one serves one's country by asking it to blind itself to the truth. I believe it will be found, in the long run, that those fight best who best understand what they are fighting for. It is easy, in moments of excitement, for those in authority to whip their peoples into a state of blind mob-passion; it is easy to invent opprobrious epithets for those who wish to understand what the issue really is. But in the long run that is not the way of true patriotism.

Some people, who see that the "wicked-and-righteous" formula is absurd, look round for another formula in longer words. They say that the struggle is between Communism and Fascism—or that democracy is fighting totalitarianism—or, most fashionable and futile of all, that it is a struggle between "opposing ideologies." Can you rally Australia to the defence of an ideology? How many Australians know what the word "ideology" means? Not I. for one.

Of one thing we may rest assured; men will not willingly fight for or against a shadowy abstraction—whether it be called Fascism, or Communism, or anarchism, or socialism, or capitalism, or democracy, or even Liberty with a capital L. There was truth in Cromwell's boast that his soldiers understood what they were fighting for; and that was what made his army the most formidable fighting force in Europe. So, too, the armies of revolutionary France, ill-armed, ill-clothed, ill-fed, untrained, outnumbered, met and routed the best-trained and best-equipped troops in Europe; they, like the English Puritans, understood what they were fighting for. They might use a kind of shorthand and speak, for brevity's sake, of liberty, equality, and fraternity; but it was not abstract nouns that gave them a strength so terrible at Valmy and Jemappes; it was a vision of certain definite goods—material and spiritual—to be achieved for France; a vision of a society in which there were to be no more masters and slaves, in which all men were to have equal chances, in which all men were to be mates. They knew exactly what they were fighting for, and what they were fighting against; and the knowledge gave them a morale which made them invincible.

So, too, the Spanish loyalists to-day, it seems to me, know well what they are fighting for; some of them are anarchists and some communists; some believe in parliamentary democracy; some are loyal sons of the Church and some are enemies of religion; if men fought for abstractions, the republican armies would be a chaos. What gives them strength is that they have a clear vision of certain benefits—material and spiritual—which they would bring to their country or die in the attempt. General Franco's troops have no such vision of definite and concrete things which their victory would bring in its train. Therefore I for one have no doubt which side would be victorious if they were left to fight it out without foreign interference. Even in these days of mechanized warfare, it is the moral fibre of the combatants that is, in the long run, decisive. I repeat, once more, that the nation will fight best which best understands what it is fighting for, and what it is fighting against.

All this may seem to you to be vague and nebulous talk, singularly ill-timed at a moment when the world is facing hideous realities. It may be so. But it does seem to me to be extremely dangerous to forget that spiritual forces are the greatest realities of all. We are feverishly inquiring of one another how many fighting planes Germany possesses, whether Italian submarines are as formidable as they say, whether the Japanese tanks are up-to-date, and so on. There is a danger in forgetting that what makes these nations which think of themselves as rejuvenated is their faith in their cause, their optimism.

They are well aware of their sacrifice of certain privileges which we have retained. They know that they have surrendered liberty. They suffer hardships, they are hemmed in by restrictions of all sorts, restrictions unknown to us. But they have a faith in the future. They believe that they are not making these sacrifices in vain. They are assured by their leaders, and they devoutly believe, that by their present submission to a hard discipline they will achieve great things—things of which they have a clear vision. "You," they say to the so-called democracies, "may cling if you like to your traditional luxuries, such as a free Opposition Press, the endless squabbles of parties, freedom of the individual to do and say what he pleases (which, by the way, is only a sham freedom, since money rules you with a rod of iron). We have given up these luxuries in the present, for the sake of our children and our grandchildren and the great things yet to be."

Against this burning faith which inspires the rejuvenated nations, what faith have we of the democracies? Do not insult your own intelligence by replying, "A faith in democracy." Are we to fight, if fight we must, for a pale abstraction called democracy, an abstraction which means different things to different people; and which stands in some countries for economic injustice and a pretence of freedom?

Much as I detest Fascism—having sojourned in a country where I saw it at work—I cannot but see that the Fascist countries are optimistic, and that we, by comparison, are sceptical, cynical, pessimistic. One of the greatest tasks of leadership in the democracies is to give us a faith to live by; to show us, in plain words, the truth; that we are the guardians, not of out-worn traditions, but of a seed, the seed of a new order of society; that we are appointed to be the preservers of something infinitely precious to mankind. What that something is I do not propose to discuss now; something must be left—as Disraeli once said at the conclusion of a long budget speech—for future statements of the same nature. . . . That was the second lesson I learned from my adventure with the Bulgarian barber. I felt that I had had a close shave, but it had taught me something.

INDEX TO ESSAYS

INDEX